THE CONTROL AND CENSORSHIP
OF CAROLINE DRAMA

THE CONTROL AND CENSORSHIP OF CAROLINE DRAMA

The Records of Sir Henry Herbert,
Master of the Revels 1623–73

Edited, with an Introduction, by

N. W. BAWCUTT

CLARENDON PRESS · OXFORD
1996

Oxford University Press, Walton Street, Oxford OX2 6DP

Oxford New York
Athens Auckland Bangkok Bombay
Calcutta Cape Town Dar es Salaam Delhi
Florence Hong Kong Istanbul Karachi
Kuala Lumpur Madras Madrid Melbourne
Mexico City Nairobi Paris Singapore
Taipei Tokyo Toronto
and associated companies in
Berlin Ibadan

Oxford is a trade mark of Oxford University Press

Published in the United States
by Oxford University Press Inc. New York

© N. W. Bawcutt 1996

British Library Cataloguing in Publication Data
Data available

Library of Congress Cataloging in Publication Data
Herbert, Henry, Sir, 1595–1673.
The control and censorship of Caroline drama : the records of Sir Henry Herbert, Master of the
Revels 1623–73 / edited, with an introduction, N. W. Bawcutt.
Includes bibliographical references and index.
1. English drama—17th century—History and criticism—Sources.
2. English drama—Restoration, 1660–1700—History and criticism—sources.
3. Theater—Censorship—England—History—17th century—Sources.
4. Drama—Censorship—England—History—17th century—Sources.
5. Theater—England—History—17th century—Sources.
6. Great Britain. Office of the Revels. I. Bawcutt, N. W. II. Title.
PR678C4H47 1996 822'.409—dc20 95–9277
ISBN 0–19–812246–2

1 3 5 7 9 10 8 6 4 2

Typeset by Pure Tech India Ltd, Pondicherry, India
Printed in Great Britain
on acid-free paper by
Bookcraft Ltd,
Midsomer Norton, Bath

PREFACE

The strange history of Sir Henry Herbert's private collection of revels papers—its sudden emergence in 1789, its virtual disappearance thirty years later, and the use of it made by scholars of the time—is set out in full in the introduction. The first attempt to bring together the surviving materials, J. Q. Adams's *The Dramatic Records of Sir Henry Herbert*, appeared in 1917. This was a pioneering work, but it had various deficiencies. Adams failed to include four items from the office-book which Malone had published; his versions of the documents which now form BL MS Additional 19256 were taken from not entirely reliable transcripts by Malone and Halliwell-Phillipps, not from originals; and he did not even mention material available to him, such as the provincial records published by J. T. Murray in 1910. Subsequently W. J. Lawrence discovered entries from the office-book that Malone had written into his own books now in the Bodleian Library but not published, and G. E. Bentley printed more play-licences from Ord transcripts inserted into the notebooks of Halliwell-Phillipps in the Folger Shakespeare Library.

All this material is included here, together with fresh discoveries, the most important of which is the Burn transcript in Yale University Library. This has yielded forty-nine completely new entries from the office-book, including the titles of over thirty plays hitherto unknown. An examination of notebooks compiled by Chalmers and Halliwell-Phillipps and of Malone's books and papers in the Bodleian has brought to light another twenty-six new entries. As a result, this edition contains seventy-nine entries from the office-book not found in Adams or Bentley, and for a further twenty-seven it provides a more detailed or accurate text than has hitherto been available. This enlarges the number of surviving entries from the office-book by approximately a quarter.

Paradoxically, one effect of these new discoveries has been to make it even clearer than before that we possess only a selection, possibly a small fraction, of what was in the office-book, particularly for the years between late 1625 and 1637 when Malone is virtually our only witness. It cannot be emphasized too strongly that no deductions can safely be made from the absence of evidence about a particular play in the surviving records; it may simply mean that neither Malone nor Ord happened to publish or copy the evidence. (The only exception to this would be the few occasions on which Malone asserts that a play is not mentioned.) For this reason the statements about Sir Henry's customs and practices in the introduction are deliberately cautious and tentative, and will certainly need to be modified if further evidence comes to light.

Other material from the period 1622–42 has been added to the office-book entries: play-licences written at the end of manuscript versions or accidentally included when the play was published; records involving the Master of the Revels from the Lord Chamberlain's papers; lawsuits involving players where the Master was brought in to mediate; and provincial records which specifically mention Sir John Astley or Sir Henry Herbert, either by name or in their function as Master of the Revels. Most, but by no means all, of this material is already in print, though it is not always easily available, and the present edition represents the first attempt to bring it together so as to present the fullest possible conspectus of Sir Henry's varied activities. The documents have been arranged in a continuous chronological sequence; an asterisk is placed before items which appear to derive from the office-book.

The Restoration papers in Additional 19256 are here printed from originals, as are certain items hitherto available only in transcripts by Malone (R10, R16, and R38). Many other documents survive from the earlier years of the Restoration relating more or less directly to Sir Henry's activities (though Adams made no attempt to discover them). To print them all in full would not have been practicable; the principle adopted has been to select items linked to papers in Additional 19256, such as Rogers's second petition and Killigrew's response to it (R11 and R19–20; cf. R5 and 7), or which mention Sir Henry himself or the Master of the Revels. Adams printed forty-two items, whereas the present edition prints 101. Included among them are warrants from the Lord Chamberlain's office, newspaper advertisements, and selected provincial records, mainly from Norwich. Very little of this material has appeared in print before, and it shows clearly that Sir Henry continued to act as Master to the last years of his life.

I would like to thank the officials of the libraries and archive collections who willingly gave me access to the books and manuscripts in their keeping: the British Library, the Bodleian Library, Cambridge University Library, Edinburgh University Library, the National Library of Wales, Cardiff Central Library, the Public Record Office, the Guildhall Museum, Norfolk Record Office, the Folger Shakespeare Library, Washington, DC, the Huntington Library, San Marino, California, and the libraries of the Inner Temple, the Society of Antiquaries, and Worcester College, Oxford. The Beinecke Rare Book and Manuscript Library, Yale University Library, arranged for a copy to be made for me of Burn's *Collections*, and generously permitted me to publish the Herbert items from it. Mr Donald Gibson, of Kent Archive Office, most helpfully tracked down and copied for me a number of petitions to Lord Treasurer Cranfield. Copies of documents were supplied to me by the Hereford and Worcester, Devon, and Dorset Record Offices. Messrs Bernard Quaritch allowed me to examine a revels document in their possession (**R16**). I could not have finished my work without the continuously available resources of the Sydney Jones Library of the University of Liverpool.

I am grateful for financial assistance from various sources. The Huntington Library awarded me a fellowship that enabled me to spend two profitable months there in the summer of 1990. The British Academy paid my travel expenses to California, and also made me two grants from its Small Personal Research Grants Fund to visit libraries. The University of Liverpool gave me a term's study leave, and on three occasions paid for visits to libraries.

Finally, thanks are due to those who helped me in several ways. Mrs I. H. Kenrick of the Historical Manuscripts Commission drew my attention to a number of interesting documents. Dr Brian Quintrell commented on the biographical section, and identified the Recorder of London in 1635. Professor Mark Pilkinton supplied me with a transcript of a Bristol item (**308**) from his forthcoming REED edition. Professor Robert Hume made me aware of Burn's *Collections*, and examined the Restoration section of the introduction. The late George Herbert, seventh Earl of Powis, took a benevolent interest in the biography of Sir Henry Herbert; I am very sorry he did not live to see this book. Mr E. J. Winnington-Ingram showed me the Herbert papers in his possession, and allowed me to publish a revels document among them (**B3**). My wife Priscilla read the introduction and suggested numerous improvements; I dedicate this book to her with love and gratitude.

N. W. Bawcutt

February 1995.

CONTENTS

INTRODUCTION

The Life of Sir Henry Herbert

Henry Herbert was born into an influential and well-connected family. His immediate ancestry was not noble (his father, Richard Herbert, never had a title), but the Herberts were an aristocratic Anglo-Welsh family, connected with the Herbert earls of Pembroke. His mother, Magdalen Herbert, was a woman of distinguished character and a friend of Donne, who addressed at least one poem to her, and preached her funeral sermon in 1627. Out of her ten children, seven sons and three daughters, two of Henry's brothers became famous. The eldest child Edward (1582–1648), knighted in 1603 and created Lord Herbert of Cherbury in 1629, was a diplomat, poet, philosopher, and historian, and wrote an autobiography which was first published by Horace Walpole in 1764. George Herbert (1593–1633) was a clergyman and author of *The Temple*, the finest collection of devotional verse in the seventeenth century.

Henry's temperament was a mixture characteristic of the milieu in which he grew up. He could be passionately angry and quarrelsome; as his brother Edward put it, these were 'infirmities to which all our Race is subject'.[1] He fought several duels of his own, and seconded Edward in the latter's challenge to Sir John Vaughan in 1619.[2] Henry's life was punctuated with quarrels, even at times with his brother Edward, and he had a long-running battle over tithes with John Borraston, the rector of Ribbesford. He was involved in innumerable lawsuits, as both plaintiff and defendant. At the same time he was worldly-wise and 'dexterous in the Ways of the Court':[3] he could make friends and keep them, and knew how to manage his own interests. He became a royalist, but viewed public affairs with a shrewd scepticism which may help to explain his rather lukewarm behaviour in the civil war. As befits the brother of George Herbert, there was also in him a strain of genuine and rather melancholy piety, and he composed two quite substantial devotional treatises.[4]

He was born in 1594, and was baptized at the church of St Nicholas, Montgomery, on 7 July.[5] A little over two years later his father died and was buried in the church of St Nicholas on 15 October 1596. In 1599 the family moved to Oxford so that Mrs Herbert could supervise Edward's education, and then in 1601 to London, to a house near Charing Cross in the parish of St Martin-in-the-Fields. Mrs Herbert remarried in 1609; her new husband, Sir John Danvers, was an affectionate and conscientious stepfather to the Herbert children. No evidence has been discovered of a formal education for Henry, either at school or university, but he had a competent command of Latin, and was probably educated by a private tutor.

Henry was sent to live in France, and became fluent in French, but precisely when he first went is not clear. The earliest reference to him as a resident in France is in a letter from Sir John Danvers to Sir Edward Herbert, dated 24 June 1615, which mentions 'the abbay of St Martin in Paris where your brother is'.[6] Henry was now twenty-one, and later in the same year acted as a diplomatic courier in the service of King James, so it is probable that he had already been living in France for at least a year or two. In August 1615 Henry landed at Boulogne carrying letters from the King to Sir Thomas Edmondes, English ambassador in Paris, and the Duke of Longueville, and was arrested by the lieutenant-governor of the city. As Sir Ralph Winwood put it, 'though hee hath been ill treated, and searched from topp to toe, yet the letters wch hee caryed to the Duke of Longueuille haue not been discouered.'[7] King James indignantly protested, first to the governor of Boulogne and then to King Louis XIII in Paris, but Henry remained under arrest for some weeks before he was finally released.

Nothing is known of Henry's activities for the next three years.[8] Early in 1619 Sir Edward Herbert was appointed English ambassador to France, and in April Henry, who must then have been living in England, was sent to Paris ahead of his brother to prepare for Sir Edward's arrival in May.[9] Henry lived with his brother, and in September of the same year was involved in two highly confidential diplomatic affairs. The first of these concerned Pierre Hugon, a Frenchman who had been a servant to Queen Anne. After her death in March 1619 it was discovered that a large quantity of money and jewels formerly belonging to her was missing, and suspicion fell on Hugon. Eventually he was arrested and accused of having appropriated the money and jewels and sent them to France in two chests or coffers. Henry and two servants of Edward were sent to various parts of

France to track down the chests and recover them or at least make an inventory of the contents. The chests were traced, with some of the stolen property inside, and Hugon confessed to his thefts, but because of French diplomatic pressure he was eventually released.[10]

The second matter was more important. In a letter dated 2 October 1619 the Venetian ambassador to France, Anzolo Contarini, reported back to Venice that the French court was anxious to arrange a marriage between the King's sister, Princess Henriette, and Prince Charles of England.

> They began operations in the following manner. A leading cavalier of the court received orders to invite to this city the brother of the English ambassador resident here and tell him, as if on his own responsibility without engaging the word of the king or council, that if the King of England cared to give Madame as a wife to his son, he would find the king here well disposed to agree. Accordingly the ambassador's brother came and the cavalier made this proposal. The brother reported the matter to the ambassador, who is staying at a place fourteen leagues from here and five from Paris. I hear that the ambassador at once sent off a courier to England to inform the king, and in short they consider it certain here that such a marriage will be effected. . . .
>
> I am also informed that M. de Luynes entertained and feasted the ambassador's brother right royally, showing him extraordinary favour and honour.[11]

These negotiations, like earlier ones of the same kind, proved abortive, and a binding marriage agreement was not made until the end of 1624. Henry travelled to London and back more than once in late 1619 and early 1620, and came into contact with some of the most influential men in the kingdom. On 7 October 1619 Sir Robert Naunton, one of the secretaries of state, wrote to the Duke of Buckingham introducing Henry to him and urging him to let Henry have direct access to the King.

> In Secretary Calverts absence, I am bould to address this gentleman Sr Edwrd Herberts brother to yor Lp wth the enclosed, wch I r^d by him from his brother. By wch yor Lp will perceive how Pierre Hugon hath purveyed for himself. . . . W^{ch} his Matie will more particularly vnd^{r}stand, if yor Lp shall be pleased to grace this Gentleman wth accesse to his Matie, he having had speech wth them all, & bene personally imployed in all the busines.[12]

This was the kind of opportunity that any ambitious young man of the time would naturally do his best to exploit.

Sir Edward Herbert was recalled to England in August 1621, and Henry presumably returned with him. Although Sir Edward seems to have been disillusioned with his diplomatic work, and told the Venetian ambassador in France that he would prefer a military career,[13] he went back to France for a second period as ambassador in January 1623. This time, however, he went alone, and Henry must have decided by the beginning of 1622 that he would try to make an independent career for himself in England. On 19 March 1622 a warrant was issued 'to sweare *Mr Henry Herbert* a gent of the Privie chamber in ordinarie in the place of S[r] *William Herbert* knight',[14] and he was duly sworn in the following day. This was not in itself an office: Gentlemen of the Privy Chamber received no fees, and their duties were mainly ceremonial; but the appointment gave them status and indicated that they had some access to the King.[15]

After Sir Edward's return to Paris, Henry still acted to a limited extent as his agent, forwarding and receiving letters and instructions. In February 1623 Prince Charles and Buckingham suddenly set off on their trip to Spain to speed up negotiations for Charles's marriage to the Infanta, and in a letter of 11 April Henry informed Sir Edward that the King wished to know of the French reaction to this escapade.

My Lord,
The kinge entreates your Lordpe to acquainte him wth the priuate discourse & generall reports of his Highnes iornye into spaine, vpon promise to take itt well att your hands, and to cause your bill of transportation to bee allowed. Ther is a request likewyse from my Lady of Montgomery, that if att any time you haue leisure to thinke of your freinds by reason of state busines you would remember her silkes; And the last is to beleiue mee
My lord
April. 11   Your Very Louing brother
1623   HHerbert[16]

(Despite the King's promise to 'take it well', Edward thought it prudent to delay his reply until 30 October, after Charles and Buckingham had returned to England.[17]) Simultaneously Henry was furthering his own career: on 24 July he made an agreement with Sir John Astley, the Master of the Revels, by which he became nominally Astley's deputy in return for paying him an annuity of £150, though in practice it was a straightforward sale of the office.[18] On 7 August the King knighted him at Wilton, the home of William Herbert, Earl of Pembroke and Lord Chamberlain.

It pleased the King att my lord Chamberlanes motion to send for mee unto his bedchamber by James Palmer and to Knighte mee with my lord Marquis Hamiltons sworde. He was pleased likewise to bestowe many good words upon mee & to receive mee as M.[r] of his Revells att Wilton this 7.th of Aug[t]—1623.[19]

He was now established as Master of the Revels, not an office of major significance, but reasonably remunerative to someone who exploited it carefully.

In the early months of 1624 Sir Edward's position as ambassador became increasingly precarious, though there was much manœuvring at court, and contradictory hints and signals, before he received a definite and permanent recall at the end of April.[20] Some of those who wrote to him at this time were vague and evasive, though they probably knew well enough what was going on, and suggested that Sir Henry, as we must now call him, would let Sir Edward know the full truth. Sir Edward Conway wrote on 14 April:

I must plead the hast I write in to be truely, for want of time, w[ch] cutts mee of from much more that I would say. Other Lres are coming to yo[u] from his Ma[tie]: upon second Counsells, whereof S.[r] Henry Herbert will give yo[u] a more p⟨ar⟩ticular relacon, who is indeed a better relato[r] then I am, and att this time att more leasure: And amongst many other vertues, w[ch] he is garnished w[th], he is a noble friend and a loving brother. Of w[ch], my Witnessing contentment is soe full, as I could not forbeare the declaration of it.[21]

And Sir George Calvert on 9 May:

Speaking of late wth yr brother S[r] Henry Herbert I vnderstand from him that there is order for calling you home to a nearer attendance vpon his Ma[ts] person: whereof I confesse I heard a kynd of rumor before but no certainty, till he told it me; so great a stranger am I to all those busynesses; and therefore yo[r] Lopp: I hope will not wonder that I hold not a quicker correspondency wth yo[u], not knowing what to write, unlesse it be the gazettes of the Towne.[22]

If Sir Henry did write letters, they do not appear to have survived. Possibly Sir Henry himself was reluctant to be outspoken to his brother, and there was nothing he could do to alter the situation. Sir Edward came home from Paris in July, in what he regarded as an ignominious dismissal.

Sir Henry was now an established courtier,[23] and at the same time had contacts in the City of London. In an annexe to his will, dated 30 March 1625, Richard Fishbourne, a wealthy citizen and mercer, left money to various friends and acquaintances to buy mourning for him. Among them were Sir Henry, who received £10 for five yards of black cloth and £4 for 'Clokes for his two men', and 'M[ris] Susan Plumer, a

widow', who received £8.[24] Possibly Sir Henry met Mrs Plumer, or
Plomer, through his friendship with Fishbourne; at any rate, the
couple were married in the summer of 1625, probably in July.[25] It was
the classic situation, so often ridiculed by Jacobean dramatists, of the
knight who bettered himself by marrying a rich city widow.

In the will of her late husband, Edmond, a merchant taylor who died
in August 1624, Susan was bequeathed houses and land at Woodford,
Essex, outright, lands and tenements at Kilburne, Middlesex, for life,
and a lump sum of £5,000.[26] Payment should have been made by
February 1625, but the trustees were reluctant to do so, and Sir Henry
and Lady Susan took out a Chancery suit to enforce payment.[27] The
Lord Keeper gave judgment in their favour in November 1626,[28]
and early in 1627 Sir Henry began negotiations to buy Ribbesford,
a country manor-house near Bewdley in Worcestershire. (Warner,
15–17, prints a letter to Sir Henry from Sir Ralph Clare, dated 2
March, in which he gave his assessment of the property.) An indenture
dated 3 August 1627 gave possession of Ribbesford to Sir Henry, and
on 14 July 1628 he settled the Ribbesford estate on his wife if he
should predecease her.[29] Out of Lady Susan's money £1,500 was
entrusted to Sir John Danvers, to be used eventually as dowries for
any daughters of the marriage,[30] and the rest was presumably used to
purchase Ribbesford.

In the early years of their marriage, however, the couple made their
home at Woodford, and their three children were born and christened
there: William was born on 1 May 1626, Vere (a daughter) on 29
August 1627, and Frances on 29 December 1628.[31] The year 1626 was
a particularly busy one for Sir Henry. Theatrical activities started up
again after the plague closure of 1625, and the Worth–Baskerville suit
was referred to Sir Henry for arbitration.[32] On 26 January he was
returned as MP for Montgomery borough, in succession to his brother
George, for the parliament of 1626. (This was a short parliament,
sitting only from February to June, but an important one, in which an
unsuccessful attempt was made to impeach Buckingham.) He was
impeded in carrying out his duties by a serious illness which lasted for
several weeks; on 23 May he wrote to Scudamore, 'This day makes up
the 7 weekes of sicknes, and yett I am not quitt of my fits, but they
lessen I thanke God.'[33] At about the same time George Herbert, then
at Cambridge, was afflicted with what Walton describes as 'a sharp
Quotidian Ague',[34] and went to live with Sir Henry at Woodford for
a year, in the hope that change of air and diet would improve his

health. The evidence suggests that relations between the two brothers were amicable, but George's presence in the household must have added some complications to the domestic arrangements.

From the late 1620s to the late 1630s Sir Henry's life followed a fairly uneventful routine. His duties as Master of the Revels took up a good deal of his time, especially in the months leading up to Christmas.[35] At other times he could take up residence at Woodford or Ribbesford, particularly during the summer. He was part of an extended social network of relations, friends, and patrons, and some of his letters from this period show him performing services for his superiors or keeping in touch with people who could be useful to him. It appears, for example, that in late April or early May 1630 Philip, Earl of Pembroke and Lord Chamberlain, had drunk some particularly good French wine at Endymion Porter's house, and on 5 May Sir Henry wrote to Porter on behalf of the Earl, asking him for the name and address of his wine merchant.[36] On 12 December 1634 he wrote to Sir Robert Pye, who as Remembrancer of the Exchequer could help to ensure the prompt payment of money warrants issued to Sir Henry. The letter tells us nothing, but does show Sir Henry skilfully maintaining good relations with a business contact.

Sir.

You loue not Importunity & haue reason, because you are a louer of goodnes & enioye a heart disposed naturally to Curtesies
The Knowledge of this giues you ease & mee too & I could wishe that other men for their owne good, knew you as well as I doe, who haue receiud much Kindnes without the least meritt & make use of this occasion only to putt you In minde of me, towards the ende of this oulde yeare that with the new I may receiue new fauours & remember by my receits aswell as disbursments whom I haue the honour to serue, ther being no seruice to the Kings, nor comfort œquiualent to the comforts of a frend, espetially of such a frend as you are who haue power to commande the vttermost strengthe

of,

Your weake yett willing frend
this. 12. of Decemb.   to serue you. Henry Herbert
1634   Court.[37]

He wrote a series of newsletters to John Scudamore (1601–71; created first Viscount Scudamore in 1628), of which forty-two survive, the earliest dating from 1624, the last from 1671.[38]

The network of patronage extended downwards as well as upwards. In a letter of 12 June 1634 to an unidentified correspondent, he made arrangements (with perhaps a touch of self-righteousness) for the care of his old nurse, who had apparently been harshly treated by the steward of his elder brother, now Lord Herbert of Cherbury.

I haue preuayld wth my vnkle to allow her means to mayntaine her cheerfully, & thanke my good God for enablinge mee to bee ye Elder brother In charity at this time. Giue her comforts & see that she bee plact In a good house & amongst honest people for her contents.[39]

A few months earlier, at the end of 1633, the young Richard Baxter, later to become a distinguished preacher and theologian, went to stay with Sir Henry in London.

About the Eighteenth year of my Age Mr. *Wickstead*, with whom I had lived at *Ludlow*, had almost perswaded me to lay by all my Preparations for the Ministry, and go to *London*, and get acquaintance at Court, and get some Office, as being the only rising way. I had no mind of his Counsel who had helped me no better before; yet because that they knew that he loved me, and they had no great inclination to my being a Minister, my Parents accepted of his Motion: He told them that if I would go up and live a while with Sir *Henry Herbert*, then Master of the Revels, he would quickly set me in a rising way.

I would not be disobedient, but went up, and stayed at *Whitehall* with Sir *H.H.* about a month: But I had quickly enough of the Court; when I saw a Stage-Play instead of a Sermon on the Lord's-days in the Afternoon, and saw what Course was there in fashion, and heard little Preaching, but what was as to one part against the Puritans, I was glad to be gone: And at the same time it pleased God that my Mother fell sick, and desired my return; and so I resolved to bid farewel to those kind of Employments and Expectations.[40]

This episode did not, however, bring about a permanent rift between the two men. Early in 1672 Baxter dedicated his book *More Reasons for the Christian Religion* to Sir Henry; he referred to 'my personal ancient obligations to you', and praised Sir Henry's 'approved wisdom and moderation, and taking part with the waies of Charity and Peace, in your most public capacity in these trying times'. He thanked Sir Henry for having given him, long ago, a copy of Lord Herbert of Cherbury's book *De Veritate* (though his own book is a severe attack on Lord Herbert's theological position).[41]

Sir Henry shared his brother George's concern for restoring and beautifying English churches which had become dilapidated since the Reformation. Between 1633 and 1639 he made a number of gifts to Ribbesford Church, including a large communion cup of silver and a silver flagon.[42] He assisted George's restoration projects. In March

1632 Sir Henry visited Cambridge, where the King and court were entertained with two university plays.[43] Soon afterwards he wrote to George, though the letter has not survived, passing on some Cambridge gossip and reporting that he, in conjunction with Arthur Woodnoth, had recently waited on the Duchess of Lennox and secured from her £100 for the repair of Leighton Church and the promise of more which she would procure from her son. He also offered to appeal to the earls of Manchester and Bolingbroke for further subscriptions.[44]

By 1639 the political situation in Britain was becoming dangerously unstable, and in April the so-called First Bishops' War began. Charles raised an army against the Scots, who had taken to arms in protest against his decision in 1637 to impose a new Book of Common Prayer on the Presbyterian Kirk of Scotland, and summoned his nobles to attend him at York. On 2 April Sir Henry set off from London, calling in at Ribbesford on the way, and arrived at York on the 12th.[45] On 27 May the royal party arrived at Berwick, and stayed there for a month. Sir Henry was a member of the King's entourage.

On Sunday the 16th June, the Kinge's tent had near been blowne downe, whilst he was att super. It gave me a blowe on my heade with a pole, interposinge betwixt the wynde and the Kinge.[46]

In a long newsletter to an unnamed correspondent, from which this quotation is taken, Sir Henry was scathing about the incompetence and over-confidence of the royalist party, but was impressed by the Scots and in particular by the ferocity of Scotswomen. He also recorded a number of the King's sayings and opinions. In another series of memoranda he noted:

That the busines passethe throughe two or three men's hands.
    That the Lords who are come to attende the Kinge have no respect shewed them, nor is their advise demanded.
    That the Lords refuse to parte with their horses and men.[47]

The campaign ended indecisively, without serious fighting. On 22 June the King discharged his army, and Sir Henry made his way home.

In 1640 Sir Henry became an MP once more, and was returned for Bewdley borough both for the Short Parliament, which sat only from 13 April to 5 May, and for the Long Parliament, which began on 3 November. He spoke on several occasions, and was appointed to chair the committee which investigated the conduct of Sir Lewis Dives, the unsuccessful royalist candidate for a by-election in Bedfordshire.[48] Some other contested elections were subsequently referred to this committee. Sir Henry also had a spectacular quarrel on 4 January 1641 with John Wilde, a future parliamentarian and professional lawyer (he was a serjeant-at-law and was often described as Serjeant Wilde).[49] The two men exchanged abuse, and according to Wilde, Sir Henry struck him, a gross breach of parliamentary privilege; in Sir Henry's version, Wilde threatened to kick him, and he was forced to thrust Wilde away in self-defence. On 6 January the matter was brought up in the house, which decided to mount a full investigation.[50]

Political differences, of course, lay behind the quarrel. A petition was read out in parliament on 14 December 1640 against Sir William Russell, a deputy-lieutenant of Worcestershire, for corruption and extortion. Wilde made a rather long-winded speech in defence of Russell, but Sir Henry immediately rose to demolish Wilde's arguments and continue the attack on Russell.[51] Wilde's own election for Worcestershire had been contested by Sir Thomas Littleton, the royalist candidate, and Sir Henry had supported Littleton's petition to the house.[52] The matter was referred to the Dives committee, and Wilde, not surprisingly, asked that Sir Henry should not sit in the chair while it was being considered. On 27 February Sir Henry himself volunteered to surrender the chairmanship on this issue.[53] In a speech of self-defence on 9 March Sir Henry gave his own account of events.

Sir Henry Harbert . . . shewed that Serjeant Wilde bare him a long grudge about Sir William Russell etc. and then in promoting Sir Thomas Littletons petition about his election for knight of the shire of Worstershire.

That comming into the Court of Wards about the service of the Howse ther Serjeant Wilde falling in communication gave him ill words tolde him hee spake falselie etc. hee telling him hee durst not say soe Serjeant Wilde came upp in an assaulting manner upon him offered to kicke him which made him thrust him away.[54]

The Wilde–Herbert business was brought up again in the House on 23 August 1641 and 5 March 1641/2,[55] but no decision was taken, and the affair seems to have petered out indecisively.

Sir Henry held his seat in the Long Parliament for less than two years. On 5 August 1642 a group of royalists, including Lord Coventry, Sir Henry, and two more MPs, Sir John Packington and Samuel Sandys, had served the King's commission of array, a demand for military service, on Serjeant Wilde. But Parliament had declared commissions of array to be illegal, and the matter was reported to the

House of Commons, presumably by the indignant Wilde. On 20 August the Commons voted to disable (i.e. debar) the three MPs from further attendance and to issue writs for the election of new members.[56] Sir Henry's other office, as Master of the Revels, also came to an end in this month: he recognized that theatrical activities were no longer possible, and closed down his office-book, anticipating by a few days the formal parliamentary order abolishing the stage on 2 September.[57]

In 1643 Sir Henry went to sit in the royalist parliament at Oxford, but the manner in which he went is debatable. Early in 1646, when he was negotiating to compound with the Westminster parliament, a certain Clement Brampton, presumably one of his servants, testified that Sir Henry was forcibly carried to Oxford by unruly royalist troops.

this Depon^t. was present when as Sr Edward Walgraue wth his regim^t forcibly wth Gunpowder and other Engines broke open the Gates and dores of the said Sr Henry his howse att Ribsford in Worstershire and wth their pistolls, swordes and other Armes in hostile manner in the night did breake into the said howse and arrested the said Sr Henry as a Trayto^r calling him base fellow and Trayto^r and saying that they would carry him to the king as a Trayto^r and that he deserved to be pistolld for that he had assisted the parliament and was a Trayto^r to the king and a freind to Sr William Waller, whereby the Lady her selfe and her children were putt into such a great feare & terro^r that some of them had like to have dyed vpon the fright wch they apprehended and were put vnto.[58]

This is a picturesque story, but it appears to be a fiction designed to lessen Sir Henry's guilt in the eyes of parliament. His brother, Lord Herbert, referred in a letter of 14 June 1643 to 'the best of those to whom you go',[59] which suggests that he already knew of Sir Henry's intentions (and at a time earlier than the King's proclamation from Oxford of 20 June 1643 inviting MPs to join him).[60] Lord Herbert's next letter, of 24 June, was to Sir Henry 'at Oxford'; from this and a third letter of 25 August it is clear that Sir Henry had taken bitter offence because his brother would not allow him to send his horses to Montgomery Castle for safe keeping (Lord Herbert had horses of his own to care for, and his grazing land was in poor condition).[61] The evidence of these letters indicates that Sir Henry decided for himself to go to Oxford, and was trying to make long-term arrangements for his horses because he expected to be away from Ribbesford for some time.

The records of the Oxford Parliament have not survived, but we know that Sir Henry was among the signatories of a document subsequently printed as *A Copy of a Letter, from the Members of Both Houses Assembled at Oxford, To the Earle of Essex: Dated the 27 of January, 1643* (Oxford, 1643[/4]), which urged the Earl to help in establishing negotiations for peace. His movements in 1644–5 cannot be established precisely; at some stage he returned to Ribbesford, and did his best to protect the estate against depredations from both sides in the civil war.[62] (Assertions that he served as a royalist soldier are based on misunderstandings.[63]) By the end of 1645 he must have decided that the royalist cause was hopeless and that he would submit to parliament and begin arrangements to compound—in other words, to pay a fine on his estate for having been a royalist supporter. (He was issued a pass to travel to London for this purpose on 24 November 1645.[64]) On 7 February 1645/6 the House of Commons resolved 'That Sir *Henry Herbert* be sent for, and apprehended as a Delinquent, by the Serjeant at Arms attending in this House',[65] and on 9 March 'That Sir *Henry Herbert* be brought to the Bar To-morrow Morning'.[66] Sir Henry offered no resistance. He took the National Covenant 'freely and fully' on 7 February[67] and the Negative Oath on 22 August.[68] It was not until 28 March 1648, however, that the House of Commons resolved to accept from him the sum of £1,330.10s., a third of his estate, and to pardon his delinquency and remove the sequestration of his estate, actions approved by the House of Lords on 7 October of the same year.[69]

In the late 1640s Sir Henry suffered painful losses in his private life. By June 1648 his son William was dead (he was married but without children), and his daughter Vere had left home to marry Sir Henry Every, baronet, of Egginton in Derbyshire.[70] Later that year his other daughter, Frances, died, and was buried at St Mary Bothaw, London, on 8 November.[71] A little over a year later his wife, Lady Susan, died, and was buried at St Mary Bothaw on 5 January 1649/50.[72] He was now alone, and relations with Vere were soured by a Chancery suit she and her husband took out against her father to recover the money her mother had entrusted to Sir John Danvers.[73] But Sir Henry was indomitable. Some time in late 1650 or early 1651 he married Elizabeth Offley, a daughter of Sir Robert Offley of London and Dalby, Leicestershire. Her sister Mary was married to George Evelyn, elder brother of John Evelyn the diarist, who has a few references in the *Diary* to meetings with Sir Henry.[74] Lady Elizabeth, who died in

1698, must have been very much younger than her husband, but the marriage seems to have been a happy one, and Sir Henry spoke of her with great affection in his will.[75] They had seven children, of whom only three survived the father.[76]

At the restoration of King Charles II, Sir Henry, who had spent the interregnum living quietly in London or on his estates, resumed some of his former offices. He was sworn in as a Gentleman of the Privy Chamber on 31 May 1660[77] and as Master of the Revels on 20 June.[78] He was returned as MP for Bewdley on 15 April 1661, and sat for the rest of his life in the Long, or Pensionary, Parliament which began in May.[79] The election was contested by his unsuccessful opponent, Sir Ralph Clare, but on 28 April 1662 the House of Commons declared Sir Henry duly elected.[80] Politics may now have become his main interest; in 1663 one of his subordinates in the revels office had difficulty in contacting him because of his 'much attendance at the parliament house'.[81] He never succeeded in re-establishing his earlier authority as Master of the Revels, and in 1663 appointed Edward Hayward to deputize for him. But it would be wrong to assume, as some scholars have done, that he virtually retired as Master. The arrangement did not work out, and early in 1665 Sir Henry dismissed Hayward as his deputy, and resumed his powers as Master, which he continued to exercise to the end of his life. He was active into his last years, writing long and complicated business letters a month or two before his death.[82] He died on 27 April 1673, and was buried in St Paul's, Covent Garden, on 6 May.[83]

The Ribbesford Manuscripts

The history of Sir Henry Herbert's official papers as Master of the Revels is extremely complicated, but can be summarized fairly briefly. For most of the eighteenth century Sir Henry's personal collection of revels papers, which he had carefully preserved, was mislaid and forgotten, until in 1789 it came to light and was seen by Malone and other scholars and antiquarians of the late eighteenth and early nineteenth centuries. Extracts and selections were printed, but no attempt was made to publish all the papers or even to prepare a handlist of them.[1] After about 1818 all the revels papers, apart from a group of documents dating mainly from the early Restoration, vanished from sight, and have never been recovered. For some readers this brief statement may be all they need, but others may find it helpful to read the more detailed account that follows, containing fresh evidence which helps to explain why some material in this edition has been printed in a new and unfamiliar version. In particular, it stresses the importance of Craven Ord as a transcriber, and discusses the newly discovered Burn transcript which derives from Ord.

At the death of Sir Henry in 1673 Ribbesford contained a large quantity of manuscripts. Sir Henry had preserved many of the documents connected with his work as Master of the Revels, including the office-book in which he entered a record of the licences he had issued and the legal papers relating to his unsuccessful struggle with Thomas Killigrew and Sir William Davenant to recover his full powers as Master in the early years of the Restoration. There were numerous family letters, including some to Sir Henry from his brothers George and Edward, and copies of a number of works by Edward in prose and verse. During the next fifty or so years the collection continued to expand, with more family letters and a substantial body of correspondence relating to the minor poet and diplomat George Stepney (1663–1707), though it is not clear precisely why his papers ended up at Ribbesford.

The line of direct male descent from Sir Henry ended in 1738, when his grandson Henry, sixth Lord Herbert of Cherbury, died without issue. The Ribbesford estate was bequeathed to Henry's cousin Charles Morley, Sir Henry's grandson by his daughter Magdalen, and then to Charles's son, Henry Morley, who later adopted the surname of Herbert. But it seems from subsequent developments that the family archive, with an important exception to be discussed later, went to another relative, Francis Walker.[2] At Walker's death in 1781 the papers were bequeathed to Frederick Cornewall, son of Captain Frederick Cornewall, of Diddlebury or Delbury Hall in Shropshire, whose wife Mary was the daughter of Francis Herbert of Ludlow.[3] Captain Cornewall, who outlived his son, gave a substantial group of papers, including much of the Stepney correspondence, to Jonathan Scott of Shrewsbury, Francis Walker's nephew by marriage. Scott bequeathed them to his son, also Jonathan, a distinguished orientalist (1754–1829; *DNB*), who wrote a brief account of the papers (BL MS Additional 9387) in which he noted that he had given a few items, including a manuscript pedigree of the Herberts, to Lady Powis at Powis Castle. The remaining part of the collection was donated to the British Museum in 1829 by Scott's son-in-law, W. R. Stokes.[4]

The other papers from Ribbesford were handed down in the Cornewall family until they came into the possession of Miss Ada M. C. Cornewall, who married Andrew South in 1896.[5] In 1905 Mrs South sold four collections of manuscripts to the British Museum (MSS Additional 37155–8); the first two of these are Stepney Papers, and the third contains the largest surviving collection of poems by Lord Herbert of Cherbury, as well as papers relating to Sir Henry, including one revels document (**R12**). Another substantial collection of papers by the two brothers was sold by Mrs South in 1916 to Messrs Bernard Quaritch,[6] and was acquired by the National Library of Wales, where it is catalogued as MSS 5295–5313. In 1919 Andrew South discovered a fresh batch of miscellaneous Herbert papers, and on 7 November he wrote to the Earl of Powis offering to send them to him. The offer was accepted, and the papers were sent off on 20 November.[7] These were the last items of real significance from the Ribbesford collection to pass through the hands of the Cornewalls.[8]

Unknown to any of Sir Henry's descendants, however, there remained at Ribbesford an old wooden chest which contained what modern scholars would regard as the most important of his papers. The chest must have been stored in some obscure place where its existence would easily be forgotten, and it was penetrated by water which caused severe damage to a number of items. Among the contents were Sir Henry's office-book, his personal set of revels accounts for 1635–8, signed by the auditors, letters to him from his brothers George and Edward, and revels documents from the Restoration period. There was also a manuscript of Lord Herbert of Cherbury's *Autobiography*; it has repeatedly been assumed that this was the copy used by Walpole for his 1764 edition, but there are good reasons why this could not possibly have been the case.[9] Henry Morley Herbert died in 1781, leaving Ribbesford to his sister Magdalene. She died a year later, and the estate went to her kinsman George Paulet, afterwards Marquess of Winchester, who in 1787 sold Ribbesford to Francis Ingram of Tickenhill (1724–97).[10] Two years later Ingram discovered the old chest, and its contents came to light.

At Ingram's death the estate went to his brother, Thomas Ingram, and at Thomas's death in 1817 to his nephew, Edward Winnington, who as a condition of the bequest took the name Winnington-Ingram. These three men allowed a number of scholars and antiquarians of the late eighteenth and early nineteenth centuries to see the Ribbesford manuscripts and make transcriptions from them. The first and

most important was Edmond Malone, who described the finding of
the office-book in a letter to Thomas Warton dated 17 August
1789:

I have lately been equally fortunate in a discovery that w^d have warmed the
inmost core of Tom Hearn's heart; no less than a MS which has lain for above
130 years in an old chest, and contains many curious particulars relative to
the stage a short account of which I have just sent to the press. The MS is
the office book of Sr Henry Herbert, Master of the Revels to King James and
King Charles the First. It has suffered greatly by damp, but nothing very
material has perished, though my eyes have nearly been destroyed by
deciphering some parts of it, where either the ink has faded or part of the
paper mouldered away.[11]

Malone published selections from the office-book in the *Historical
Account of the Rise and Progress of the English Stage* which forms part
of Volume 1 of *The Plays and Poems of William Shakespeare* (1790). He
acknowledged his indebtedness to Ingram, and described the contents
and condition of the manuscript as follows:

The office-book of Sir Henry Herbert contains an account of almost every
piece exhibited at any of the theatres from August 1623, to the commencement of the rebellion in 1641, and many curious anecdotes relative to them,
some of which I shall presently have occasion to quote. This valuable
manuscript having lain for a considerable time in a damp place, is unfortunately damaged, and in a very mouldering condition: however, no material
part of it appears to have perished.[12]

Malone's extracts are by far the largest surviving collection of material
from the office-book, but it must be emphasized that he published only
a fraction, possibly quite a small fraction, of the total contents. He also
noted a few licences into his own books, often his own copy of the play
concerned, which he did not publish; in one of these, dated 22 June
1789, he claimed to have made a transcript of the office-book.[13]
Unfortunately this has not been traced, and there is no way of knowing
whether it was a full transcript of all that was decipherable in the
office-book, but there was certainly material in it which he did not
publish. He entered a few items from the office-book, printed here for
the first time, into interleaved copies of his 1790 edition of Shakespeare which are now in the Bodleian Library.[14]

   Malone also published, in full or in part, a number of documents
relating to Sir Henry's activities in the early years of the Restoration.
Although Malone clearly returned the office-book to its current owner,

he did not return this group of Restoration papers. After his death in 1812 his sisters sent a boxful of his manuscripts, including those from Ribbesford, to his friend and collaborator James Boswell the younger. When Boswell died in 1822, his estate proved to be heavily in debt, and the papers he had received from Malone were sent to London to be auctioned by Sotheby in 1825.[15] The Ribbesford papers were bought by the dealer Thomas Thorpe and then sold to Joseph Haslewood, who had them bound up in a single volume.[16] At his death in 1833 they once again came on the market, and passed through various hands until they were purchased by the British Museum in 1852, where they are catalogued as MS Additional 19256.[17] Malone printed four Restoration papers which are not in Additional 19256 (R3, R10, R16, and R38), and which must have become detached from the collection before 1825. Three of them have been traced (all except the first), and can now be transcribed directly from the original, and not from Malone's version.

The next scholar to print fresh material from the office-book was George Chalmers. In his *An Apology for the Believers in the Shakspeare-Papers* (1797), pages 495–526, and his *Supplemental Apology* (1799), pages 207–13, Chalmers discussed Sir Henry's activities as Master of the Revels. Some of his evidence derived from Malone's *Historical Account*, though he made pioneering investigations into the records of the Lord Chamberlain. The new office-book material was of three kinds. In an appendix to the *Apology* he published some autobiographical notes by Sir Henry which had been entered by him in the office-book. Chalmers introduced them as follows: 'The subjoined extracts from Sir Henry Herbert's office-book, which was found in *the old chest*, at Ribbesford, came to hand after the foregoing sheets were printed; and are now added as useful notices, in respect to his life.'[18] He printed a few dramatic entries from the office-book at various points in the *Supplemental Apology*, and in two substantial footnotes, pages 208–10 and 213–20, he published firstly some licences for travelling shows and entertainments, none of which are in Malone,[19] and secondly a sequence of forty-seven play-licences, from 1622 to 1625, of which only eight had been provided by Malone. There is, however, evidence strongly suggesting that all these office-book entries were supplied to Chalmers by a scholar named Craven Ord, and were not the result of his own investigations. The arguments to justify this assertion will be set out more clearly later on, after Ord himself has been discussed.

In 1818 Rebecca Warner published her *Epistolary Curiosities, Series the First*. The bulk of the collection consisted of Herbert family letters of the seventeenth century, including a few to Sir Henry from his brothers George and Edward. There were also some miscellaneous revels documents and a few autobiographical entries from the office-book (she provided another transcript of the material in the appendix to Chalmers's *Apology*, apparently unaware that he had already printed it). There can be no doubt that everything in her book came from the old chest at Ribbesford; in her short prefatory note 'To the Reader' she did not reveal where she had obtained the papers, though she claimed that they were all 'given verbally and literally from the *originals*, which are now in the hands of the editor'.

It looks as though she was helped in her work by her brother, the Revd Richard Warner, himself a miscellaneous writer. J. Q. Adams noticed an item in the 'Minor Correspondence' of the *Gentleman's Magazine* for January 1818:

An old and respectable Correspondent (who has in his possession the original *Account-book* of Sir Henry Herbert, grandson of Lord H. of Cherbury, Master of the Revels to James I. Charles I. and Charles II., together with a large correspondence of that family) wishes to be informed where to look for an account of the office of *Master of the Revels*, its origin, and dissolution, and where to find any thing relating to the family of Herbert, whose seat was at Ribbesford, Salop, and some of whose branches represented Bewdley for many years. Mr. Malone had the Account-book of the Master of the Revels in his hands but what use he made of it our Correspondent knows not.[20]

Adams plausibly suggested that the 'old and respectable Correspondent' was the Revd Richard Warner, and this is confirmed by another piece of evidence. In 1824 Warner published three volumes of *Illustrations, Critical, Historical, Biographical, and Miscellaneous, of Novels by the Author of Waverley*. The work is a fourth-rate compilation, deservedly forgotten, but it does contain a reference to the office-book.

A very interesting document is still extant, which may be regarded as a register of the English popular amusements, for more than half a century, 'The Account Book of Sir Henry Herbert, knight, master of the revels,' an office which had existed ever since the reign of Henry VIII.[21]

A footnote reads: 'It is in possession of Rev.—Ingram, Shropshire, who obligingly indulged us with a loan of it, a few years since.' This is followed (pages 61–3) by a list of licences for miscellaneous entertainments, taken almost verbatim from Chalmers's *Supplemental Apology*, pages 208–10. Clearly Warner and his sister borrowed the office-book, and then returned it without doing more than copying from it a few entries relating to Sir Henry himself and his family.

Other scholars were given access to the Ribbesford manuscripts, and made copies or notes of documents, but did not themselves publish any of their material. The most important of these was Craven Ord (1756–1832; *DNB*). Ord saw the office-book, and copied from it a substantial number of licences, both of plays and of miscellaneous travelling entertainments. Shortly after his death his library was sold, and the sale catalogue includes an item as follows: 'Theatrical Exhibitions, 1623–1641. Extracts from an old Manuscript, containing an account of almost every Piece exhibited at any of the Theatres, from Aug. 1623 to the commencement of the Rebellion in 1641.'[22] (The phraseology is obviously borrowed from Malone's account quoted above.) The transcript was bought first by Thomas Thorpe and then by Jacob Henry Burn. Burn was interested in the history of the revels office, and compiled a notebook of manuscript and printed material, which he entitled *Collections towards Forming a History of the Now Obsolete Office of the Master of the Revels*.[23] (On the spine of the binding the title is given as *Historical Collections Relative to the Office of the Master of the Revels*.) Burn did not insert the Ord transcript in this notebook, but very fortunately he copied Ord's play-licences into it, rearranged into alphabetical order of play-titles. (Included in this list are five cuttings taken from Ord and glued on the page.) Burn also acquired a few original revels documents, which he inserted in his notebook, but unfortunately gave no hint of where or how he had obtained them.[24] After Burn's death his papers were dispersed, the Ord transcript in 1870 and the *Collections* in 1874.[25]

In 1880 J. O. Halliwell-Phillipps announced that he possessed a 'partial transcript' of the office-book,[26] but he never showed it to anyone or made any attempt to publish it. After his death his notebooks were dispersed to various libraries in the British Isles and North America, but attempts to find the transcript in them, as a separate document, were unavailing. In 1937 R. C. Bald noticed a number of cuttings relating to seventeenth-century drama, usually headed 'Herbert MS.' in Halliwell-Phillipps's own handwriting, gummed into the Shakespeare notebooks which had gone to the Folger Shakespeare Library in Washington. These were examined by Adams, who with the help of G. E. Bentley identified them as fragments of

the Ord transcript.[27] Later research brought to light two more cuttings
in a notebook in Edinburgh University Library.[28] It appears that
Halliwell-Phillipps went through the transcript, cutting out a selection
of items that interested him and gumming them into his notebooks.
The rest, apparently, he discarded. The cuttings vary in size: some are
thin slips of paper containing only one item; others are larger, with as
many as ten items in the largest. In addition, he cut a number of strips
vertically as well as horizontally, and had to write in the omitted words,
either between the lines of Ord or in the left- or right-hand margin.
Why he did this is inexplicable, since his folio-size notebooks could
easily cope with Ord's paper at its maximum width. All that can be
said in defence of Halliwell-Phillipps's apparently barbarous behaviour
is that Burn had already taken cuttings from the transcript, so it may have
been in a somewhat fragmentary condition when it fell into his hands.

   The strong probability that George Chalmers derived his office-
book material from Ord can be supported by a variety of arguments.
Chalmers openly acknowledged that Ord had supplied him with copies
of three documents unrelated to the office-book.[29] Chalmers had the
habit of compiling folio notebooks in which he assembled material for
his books, and in one of them is the copy of the first of these
documents, in Ord's handwriting, consisting of two anonymous manuscript notes concerning the Earl of Southampton which had been
written into Ord's personal copy of Wood's *Athenae Oxonienses*.[30] In a
second notebook of Chalmers is a sheet of paper, clearly in Ord's
handwriting, which contains two items: the autobiographical extracts
from the office-book which Chalmers published as Appendix II of his
Apology and some dramatic entries from the chamber accounts of
Henry VII which Chalmers published as Appendix III.[31] There can be
no doubt that Appendix II derived from Ord: Chalmers rearranged the
material, omitting two sentences and putting the rest in chronological
order, and on the Ord paper the omitted sentences are lightly deleted
with pencil crosses, and in the margin the numbers 2, 3, and 1 have
been pencilled in to indicate the order Chalmers wanted. When
Rebecca Warner published in 1818 her independent version, taken
directly from the office-book, of the material in Ord's first two
paragraphs, she included the sentence omitted by Chalmers, and
arranged the sentences in the same way as Ord, although she read 'Sir
George Reeve' as 'Sir George Keene'.[32]

   Similar correlations can be made for the office-book licences published by Chalmers. In one of his notebooks now in the Bodleian is a

folded sheet of paper on the first page of which are five items from the office-book in Ord's hand and two in what appears to be Chalmers's hand, one of which merely repeats an entry higher up.[33] (The remaining three pages are blank.) Four of these six items were published in the *Supplemental Apology*. Out of the list of miscellaneous entertainments published in the same book, six occur in the Ord cuttings in Edinburgh University Library, and of the forty-seven play-licences printed as a long footnote, only two cannot be paralleled in surviving Ord fragments or in Burn's alphabetical list. It is perhaps significant that Chalmers never claimed to have seen or handled the office-book, whereas Malone referred to it as 'a manuscript now before me', and described its physical condition.[34]

When Ord's various transcripts and the material derived from them are assembled, it becomes clear that he was a major witness to the contents of the office-book, second in importance only to Malone. He provided virtually all our information about licences for miscellaneous travelling entertainments, as Malone showed little interest in these.[35] He copied at least 103 play-licences, of which forty-nine, all in Burn, are completely new, and are here included with the rest of the surviving material for the first time. Two are undatable; from the remaining 101, all but two come from two periods, 1622–early 1625 and 1638–1642, though some of the miscellaneous licences date from the intervening years. Why he concentrated on the early and late years of the office-book can only be guessed at. Malone printed no more than seventeen of Ord's 103 licences, which is approximately one-sixth. If we may extrapolate from this, it would appear that for the sections of the office-book where Malone is virtually the sole witness (i.e. late 1625–1637) we may have only a sixth or less of the full contents. In addition, Ord seems to have taken pains to reproduce the spelling and layout of what was in front of him, in a way which is not so true of Malone and much less so for Chalmers, who simplified, abbreviated, and sometimes misread what Ord had given him. It is a great pity that Ord did not prepare and publish a complete transcript of the office-book.

The Ribbesford manuscripts were also seen by the Bewdley antiquarian Peter Prattinton (1776–1840), who worked indefatigably on his collection of materials relating to the history of Worcestershire.[36] Prattinton was purely a collector who never published anything, and in 1841 his papers entered the library of the Society of Antiquaries under the terms of his will. Scattered through the volume relating to

Ribbesford are brief extracts and summaries of Herbert family letters of the late seventeenth and early eighteenth centuries, none of which were printed by Rebecca Warner, including some by Sir Henry's second wife, Lady Elizabeth, and his daughters Vere and Magdalen.[37] Prattinton also transcribed an academic oration in Latin by Henry Herbert, Sir Henry's son, while an undergraduate at Trinity College, Oxford, in 1670, with a heading indicating its origin: 'The following Extracts are taken from a Ms in the Possession of Thom^s. Ingram Esq. Nov: 5th 1810. On the Cover is written. Henry Herbert his Booke. 1667.—It seems a Common Place Book of.'[38] Unfortunately Prattinton's extracts from the letters are so scrappy that they contain very little biographical information, but they do indicate that Rebecca Warner published only a selection of what was in the old chest.

Prattinton also copied or possessed documents relating to Sir Henry's activities as Master of the Revels, as was discovered by another antiquarian, the Revd Joseph Hunter (1783–1861; *DNB*). The British Library has a large collection of Hunter's notebooks, and in one of them, MS Additional 24497, f. 63, under the heading 'Master of the Revels', Hunter wrote:

There is bound up in Dr Prattinton's Collections for the History of Worcestershire in the volumes which relate to Bewdley (vol. IV*) his transcript of an Account from an original in the hands of Thomas Ingram Esq.

It is the account of Sir John Ashley 'Master of the Revels and Masques' for 3 whole years beginning Nov. 1. 1635 and ending Oct. 31. 1638.

Hunter then started to make notes on Prattinton's transcript, but a comment at the foot of the page ('In fact it yields nothing worth regarding J.H.') indicates that he soon came to feel that he was wasting his time. On the next page he mentioned another item in the Prattinton Collection:

There is also a Leiger Book of the Office of the Revels 1 Nov. 1637 to 31 Oct. 1638. The Original was found at Tickenhill June 6. 1817, probably one of the Herbert Papers left at Ribbesford-House.

The Account is singularly devoid of interest: but the following License is worth transcribing:—It is from a parchment cover of a book of accounts belonging to Sir H. Herbert.

This was followed by a transcript of a licence by Sir Henry, dating from 1 August 1662 (Appendix **B6**). Hunter then made notes on the manuscripts which now constitute BL MS Additional 19256; he apparently took his information from the very detailed list in Thorpe's *Catalogue of Manuscripts* (1834), not from the originals.[39] Finally came a very neat copy of a licence by Sir George Buc, 16 July 1619.[40] Hunter even described the fragments of a seal attached to the document, and was presumably working from the original.

Hunter, therefore, had access to four documents; the first two are transcripts in the Prattinton Collection, but there is no hint of where Hunter came across the remaining two.

1. Revels accounts for 1635–8;
2. A ledger-book of Sir Henry Herbert containing accounts for 1637–8;
3. An account book of Sir Henry (undated, but presumably post-Restoration);
4. A licence issued by Sir George Buc, 16 July 1619.

A careful investigation of the Prattinton Collection, which consists of nearly seventy large volumes, as well as much other material, yielded very disappointing results. The revels accounts for 1635–8 are indeed present in one of the Bewdley volumes.[41] Volume xxiv of the miscellaneous papers has a list of contents in Prattinton's own hand, and the second item is given thus: '2 Leiger Book of the Office of the Revels. 1638—from Ribbesford', but there is no trace of the transcript in the book and no sign that it has been cut or torn out. Hunter's account suggests that he saw the collection after it had been bound, and it is hard to account for his having seen a document which has now vanished. (It may have been bound in the wrong volume by mistake, but Barnard does not mention it.) If the original remained at Tickenhill, it is not among the papers of the Parker family of Tickenhill on deposit at Worcester Record Office.[42] Items 3 and 4 remain completely untraced, and we are therefore dependent on Hunter's transcripts for the licences of 1619 and 1662.

After about 1818 the office-book and the papers seen by the Warners and Peter Prattinton vanished from sight, and have never been recovered. What the Revd Edward Winnington-Ingram did with them cannot be established; he did not give them to his old college, Christ Church, Oxford, or to the libraries of any of the cathedrals with which he was associated. The present head of the family, Mr E. J. Winnington-Ingram, has a small number of papers clearly deriving from Ribbesford. The house was sold by the family in 1904, and these were preserved separately because they related to the legal ownership of Ribbesford, though among them, apparently by mistake, is one revels document (Appendix **B**3).

Several Victorian scholars showed an interest in the fate of Sir Henry's papers. In 1849 Edward F. Rimbault tried to find out where the office-book had got to, and urged that it be published in its entirety. He also copied out a list of the earlier Masters of the Revels that he claimed to have taken from a document relating to Sir Henry Herbert.

I have now before me a list of the "Masters of the Revells", with the dates of their patents, which I beg to transcribe. It is of more than ordinary value, being in the handwriting of Sir Henry Herbert himself, and copied at the back of the worthy knight's "Petition to Charles the Second against the Grant to Killegrew and Davenant to form Two Companies of Players:"—

"*Masters of ye Revells.*

"Sir Richard Guilford   — not on record.
Sir Thomas Cawerden   — [1544] 36 Henry VIII.
Sir Thomas Beneger   — not on record.
Sir John Fortescue   — not on record.
Edmund Tilney, Esq.   — July 24 [1578] 21 Eliz.
Sir George Buck   —   — June 23 [1603] 1 Jac.
Sir John Astley   —   — [1612] 10 Jac. I.
Benjamin Johnson   — [1617] 15 Jac. I.
Sir Henry Herbert, and ⎫
Simon Thelwall, Esq.[43] ⎬   Aug. 21 [1629] 5 Car. I"

As the notes to **R**4 make clear, there are two copies of Sir Henry's petition in BL Additional 19256, the first apparently the original and the second a scribal copy. Neither contains a list of the Masters of the Revels, but there is a similar list on the back of a 'Breviat' relating to Sir Henry's action against Thomas Betterton (**R**33). This list, however, does not contain the heading 'Masters of ye Revells' as given in Rimbault, so it is quite possible that Rimbault was quoting from a third copy of Sir Henry's petition.

Rimbault also claimed that he owned another revels paper: 'I am in possession of a curious list of MS. instructions, "the heads of what I gave to Mr. Tho. Killegrew the 29th of March, 1664," in the hand-writing of Sir Henry Herbert.'[44] Rebecca Warner printed a document with this title in her *Epistolary Curiosities* (**R**53). If the manuscript mentioned by Rimbault was the one used by Warner, it would follow that at least one of the items published by Warner survived and got into circulation among collectors. This is not necessarily the case, however, as Sir Henry was evidently in the habit of making multiple copies of some of his legal records. Rimbault was a distinguished musicologist with a special interest in the Renaissance, and his splendid library, containing early quartos of many Jacobean and Caroline plays, was sold at Sotheby's on 31 July 1877; unfortunately, the manuscript section of the sale catalogue makes no mention of anything specifically relating to Sir Henry Herbert.

A brief account of the family letters printed by Rebecca Warner appeared in *Notes and Queries* in 1859:

The principal portions of these letters were among the muniments at Ribbesford House, Worcestershire, formerly the residence of Lord Herbert of Cherbury. These documents passed by purchase, at the close of the last century, from the Marquis of Winchester, descendant of the Herbert family, to Francis Ingram of Bewdley; from whom they passed by will to his kinsman, the late Rev. E. Winnington Ingram, Canon of Worcester; and while in his possession were published by Mrs. Rebecca Warner of Bath. The MS. letters are most of them in the Earl of Powis's possession, but some remain in the library at Stanford Court.

Thomas E. Winnington.

Stanford Court, Worcester.[45]

Sir Thomas Winnington was an antiquarian and a nephew of the Revd Edward Winnington-Ingram, so he should have known what he was talking about; but when Sir Sidney Lee sent an enquiry to Powis Castle in 1891, he was curtly informed that the Earl knew nothing of Sir Henry Herbert's Ribbesford papers.[46] If any documents went to Stanford Court in Worcestershire, they were presumably lost in a disastrous fire that gutted the house and destroyed the library on 5 December 1882. Sir Thomas's note, however, was not the only suggestion that Ribbesford papers went to Powis Castle. In 1880 Halliwell-Phillipps confidently asserted, in the note already mentioned, that the office-book was in the library of the Earl of Powis. This claim was repeated by later scholars,[47] although whenever enquiries were made, the Earl of Powis denied that he possessed, or ever had possessed, the office-book. Certainly there does not appear to be a trace of either the office-book or the papers printed by Rebecca Warner in the Powis Castle papers now deposited in the Public Record Office and the National Library of Wales.

There is some evidence to suggest that during the nineteenth century scholars other than those listed above had access to the

office-book or to transcripts of it. J. Q. Adams drew attention to entries
in a notebook of Richard Fenton.

Bound in a collected volume of miscellaneous papers once in the possession
of Richard Fenton (1747–1821), and now housed in the city library of Cardiff,
Wales, are three short entries transcribed from the Herbert Office Book. The
handwriting, though strikingly like Malone's, is not his, nor Chalmers'.[48]

A thorough search of the Fenton Collection in Cardiff City Library
has failed to locate these entries. In 1805, in his first collected edition
of Massinger's plays, William Gifford quoted the office-book entry of
7 July 1624 relating to *The Virgin Martyr* (110), which is found in
Malone and the Burn transcript. In his second edition of 1813 Gifford
added a fresh footnote beginning. 'Since this note first appeared, an
additional proof has been discovered both of the popularity of this
play, and of the practice here mentioned'.[49] He then quoted Buc's
licence of 6 October 1620 (4), which does not occur anywhere else.
Gifford does not make it clear how and by whom the discovery was
made, but it must have occurred between 1805 and 1813. The most
puzzling item of all is the licence for Arthur Wilson's *The Corporal*,
14 January 1632/3 (247). This was first published by Fleay in 1891
and then by W. C. Hazlitt in 1892, but in strikingly different versions
and with no source given. Bentley (v. 1270–1) discussed the problems
involved but was unable to reach a definite conclusion.

   Further information about the office-book may yet come to light.
Even if the original is irretrievably lost, Malone's copy might eventually surface. Ord made more than one copy of some entries, and
further transcripts by him may survive, possibly inserted in a Chalmers notebook which has not yet been examined.

The Master of the Revels

The Office of Master

A full history of the revels office would take a disproportionate space
in a book intending to concentrate on Sir Henry Herbert.[1] The term
'Master of the Revels' was never used exclusively in connection with
the royal household. It was current at the Inns of Court: Lincoln's Inn
appointed an official with this title annually from 1455 until the earlier
seventeenth century (John Donne was chosen in 1593).[2] The earliest

surviving record of the title at the Middle Temple dates from 1501, and at the Inner Temple from 1505.[3] In 1512 Henry Percy, fifth Earl of Northumberland, had an official with this title in his private household at York.[4] When the members of the Middle Temple put on Davenant's masque, *The Triumphs of the Prince D'Amour*, early in 1636, they appointed one of their number, Thomas Maunsell, to be 'Master of the Revels', and perhaps somewhat impertinently he licensed the masque for publication, a licence entered in the Stationers' Register on 19 February 1635/6 and printed facing the title-page of the 1636 edition.[5] Sir Henry, however, seems not to have minded. Later in the seventeenth century the title could be used abusively: Milton sneeringly referred to 'that *Petronius* whom *Nero* call'd his *Arbiter*, the Master of his revels',[6] and Marvell concluded his satire on Thomas May, the historian of parliament, by terming him the 'only Master of these Revels past' (*Tom May's Death*, l. 98).

The earliest use of the title in a royal connection goes back to 1510,[7] and there were various Masters in the earlier sixteenth century; but it was undoubtedly Edmond Tyllney, who officiated between about 1578 and 1610, who did most to establish and consolidate the Master's powers and responsibilities. He was succeeded by Sir George Buc, who was obliged to relinquish power early in 1622 because he had become insane, though he lingered on for a few more months until his death on 31 October 1622. Sir John Astley took over in March 1622, but leased (and in effect sold) the office to Sir Henry Herbert in July 1623. By Herbert's time the duties of the Master were well established. Despite what his title might suggest, he was not in complete control of court entertainments. He did not commission masques, and only a small proportion of the expenses involved in producing a masque passed through his hands. His main responsibility at court, in the words of the revels accounts, was for 'Rehersalls and makinge choice of playes and comedies and reforminge them';[8] in other words, the Master chose the plays to be performed at court, checked the text to make sure that it contained nothing unsuitable, and supervised the rehearsals prior to performance. No doubt the actual selection of plays was a matter for negotiation: on 30 October 1623 the actor Edward Shakerley on behalf of the Lady Elizabeth's company brought Sir Henry 'a list of plays for Christmas', prudently adding a 'gratuity' of £2 to put the Master in a good humour (**65**).

Revels officers were required to attend at court, especially during the Christmas season, which was the high point of court entertainments.

At first Sir Henry attended every day between 31 October of one year and Ash Wednesday of the year following. From 1628 onwards he was required to start his attendance a month earlier, beginning on 30 September. He also spent a smaller number of nights at court, varying from twenty-four nights in the early years to about forty in the 1630s. There were four days at Easter and four at Whit, and twenty during the summer spent in 'airing the stuff', which must have been intended to preserve the costumes and fabrics stored at the revels office.[9] For each attendance, day or night, the Master received a fee of four shillings. He and the other officers went not only to Whitehall but to other royal palaces such as Hampton Court, Greenwich, and Windsor, regularly charging boat hire for getting to them. Occasionally they went further afield: George Wilson, Groom of the Revels, was paid £5 for going to Oxford in 1636, presumably in August when three college plays were performed before the King.[10] Sir Henry himself went to Cambridge in March 1632, when the King saw two plays; but it is not clear whether he went in his official capacity as Master of the Revels.[11]

The main practical responsibility of the revels office was to provide illumination for court entertainments, and the accounts are full of references to 'branches' (various forms of chandelier or candelabra) as well as the hooks, pulleys, and ropes by which they were kept in place. They were made from twisted wire, and the wire-drawers who constructed them were the most important of the workmen employed at the revels office. Occasionally the wire-drawers proved troublesome to the Master. Robert Wright was mentioned by name in the accounts only once, in those for 1611–12, but in late 1621, as we shall see in a moment, he came into conflict with Sir George Buc. William Hurt was named several times in the accounts between 1626 and 1633, but he was clearly not entirely reliable, and on 26 September 1629 the Lord Chamberlain ordered him to be arrested 'if hee bring not wth him to Hampton Court 8 Branches of wyre to bee imployed in A Comedy to bee acted before his Ma^{ty} on Michmas Day 1629'.[12] He also ran into debt, and on 10 January 1630/1 Sir Henry was requested by the Lord Chamberlain to repay the debt out of the moneys owing to Hurt (208).

The powers of the Master were set out in a warrant issued to Tyllney on 23 December 1581. The first part gave the Master the right of purveyance, or the power to compel workmen to work for the revels office 'at competent wages' and merchants to supply raw materials at a 'reasonable' price. Workmen who disobeyed or withdrew from the work could be imprisoned entirely at the Master's discretion. The second part, perhaps more important to modern scholars, gave the Master sweeping powers of control over plays, players, and playhouses (the precise terms are set out in Appendix A3). Here again the Master could imprison anyone who refused to accept his orders. The document was reissued to Buc and Astley but not to Sir Henry, though as Astley's 'sufficient deputy' he was fully entitled to exercise its provisions, and in the preambles to the first three licences printed in Appendix B he was clearly using its phraseology. It is this side of Sir Henry's activities that will be examined in most detail in this introduction, and the assertions made in this and the next three sections will apply only to the period 1623–1642.

Sir Henry's power was not, of course, absolute. The revels office came within that part of the royal household that was controlled by the Lord Chamberlain, and had to carry out any orders he gave it. Other bodies or individuals—the Privy Council, the Bishop of London, the Archbishop of Canterbury—could intervene in theatrical matters over the head of Sir Henry if they chose to. In 1625 the Privy Council suppressed a play dealing with the massacre of Amboyna; the letter-writer John Chamberlain described the play as 'redy to be acted', which suggests that Herbert had licensed it, though no evidence on this point survives from the office-book.[13] If he had done so, the incident may help to explain his subsequent eagerness to delete references to Amboyna from Mountfort's *The Launching of the Mary*.

The lines of demarcation between these superior powers, who seem to have felt under no obligation to consult Sir Henry before issuing their orders, were not clearly drawn. Garrard recorded a striking dissension early in 1637 between William Laud, Archbishop of Canterbury, and Philip, Earl of Pembroke, the Lord Chamberlain, over which of them should control the players.

Upon a little Abatement of the Plague, even in the first weeke of *Lent*, the Players set up their Bills, and began to play in the *Black-Fryers* and other Houses. But my Lord of *Canterbury* quickly reduced them to a better order, for, at the next Meeting at Council his Grace complained of it to the King, declared the Solemnity of *Lent*, the Unfitness of that Liberty to be given, both in respect of the Time and the Sickness, which was not extinguished in the City, concluding that if his Majesty did not command him to the contrary, he would lay them by the Heels, if they played again. My Lord Chamberlain stood up and said, that my Lord's Grace and he served one God and one King; that he hoped his Grace would not meddle in his Place no more than he did in his; that Players were under his Command. My Lord's Grace replied, that what he had spoken no ways touched upon his Place, &c. still concluding as he had done before, which he did with some Vehemency reiterate once or twice. So the King put an End to the Business by commanding my Lord Chamberlain that they should play no more.[14]

As this shows, the ultimate authority was the King, and actors or dramatists who had a powerful patron might try to get him to go over Herbert's head to the King. When Sir William Davenant, for example, was dissatisfied with Sir Henry's censorship of his play *The Wits*, he got Endymion Porter, a royal favourite, to show the play to the King (see 281). Until the breakdown of royal authority in 1642, parliament had no powers over the theatre, and needed to petition the Lord Chamberlain if it wanted playing restricted (156–7).

A complicated series of events preceded Sir Henry's assumption of power in July 1623. The financial position of the revels office was extremely precarious in the last years of Buc's mastership, because of the difficulty experienced in extracting money from the royal treasury. Accounts were filed for the two years 1615–16 and 1616–17, but were not declared until 6 April 1620, and no accounts were submitted for the years 1617–21. On 9 June 1620 a warrant was issued for £701, of which £601 was intended to pay the fees and wages for 1615–17, and another £100 was an imprest, or advance payment, to help pay for current expenses.[15] The issue of a money warrant did not, however, guarantee immediate payment. Sir George obtained £200 in March 1621, but the months went by with no sign that more would be forthcoming, and after Lionel Cranfield became Lord Treasurer in September 1621, he received a series of petitions begging him to pay the warrant in full. One of these, from the workmen of the revels, reminded Cranfield that only £200 had been paid,

wch being devided amongst soe many did but little pleasure in regard noe other mony hath beene paid for any of the six yeres past, And now the time comeing on for more service, in respect the Branches & wire rodds are much decayed, they ⟨the workmen⟩ are not able to p⟨er⟩forme the same.[16]

Early in December a further £200 became available, but after Sir George had collected the money, it was in effect stolen from him by Robert Wright the wire-drawer in collusion with other revels officers, and Sir George wrote a long letter, received by Cranfield on 12 December, furiously denouncing this 'Rare kind of offense'.[17] Wright himself did not see things in the same light, and continued to petition Cranfield on his own behalf.[18]

Problems of this kind did not deter other people from trying to succeed Sir George as Master, and the early 1620s were a strikingly busy time for transactions relating to the mastership, though there appear to be no connections linking the various individuals concerned. First in line to succeed was Sir John Astley, or Ashley, ?1571–1640, by virtue of a reversion granted on 3 April 1612.[19] Next came Ben Jonson, who was granted a reversion on 5 October 1621.[20] John Chamberlain, writing to Sir Dudley Carleton on 27 October, asserted that Jonson received the grant for 'good service' (the King had taken great pleasure in Jonson's most recent masque, *The Gypsies Metamorphosed*, performed on three separate occasions in August and September).[21] But Chamberlain also claimed that Jonson's pension was increased from 100 marks to £100, which was not true, so it is hard to know how much real knowledge he had. The Revd Joseph Mead, writing to Sir Martin Stuteville on 15 September, had asserted that Jonson narrowly escaped being knighted by the King,[22] and modern scholars have tended to accept Eccles's conjecture that there was a relationship between the two events: possibly Jonson managed to persuade the enthusiastic King to grant him the reversion rather than a knighthood.[23]

Sir John Astley took over from the ailing Sir George Buc early in 1622, but discussion of Astley's short tenure of the office and his transference of power to Sir Henry Herbert may be briefly postponed in order to take account of one more candidate for the mastership, whose efforts eventually proved unsuccessful. William Painter, about whom little appears to be known, was the grandson of a much more famous William Painter, the author/compiler of a collection of stories familiar to Elizabethan dramatists, *The Palace of Pleasure* (1566–7). The grandfather was also a government official, clerk of the ordnance; but his career collapsed in disgrace when he was accused of appropriating public money, and his estates were confiscated so that the rents would pay off the money he owed. But in May 1622 King James annulled the condemnation of William Painter Senior and completely restored his estates to his grandson.[24] The official documents do not spell out why James made this decision, and it is not clear whether it was an act of generosity or the righting of a long-standing injustice. Painter evidently regarded himself as an innocent victim, and petitioned the King to grant him the reversion as a slight compensation for his sufferings. The King agreed, and the elaborate process of granting a warrant began to operate.

What happened next can be reconstructed from correspondence among the State Papers Domestic and a pathetic appeal, not known to earlier scholars, from Painter to Cranfield in February 1622/3.[25] King James had authorized the grant to Painter without consulting his Lord Chamberlain, William, Earl of Pembroke; but Painter, considering that the grant 'had relation' to the Lord Chamberlain, thought it prudent to confirm that Pembroke had no objection. He went to Pembroke, accompanied by the Master of Requests, Sir Edward Powell, and was no doubt relieved when Pembroke accepted what had happened with a good grace. Painter started to register his grant, but matters came to a stop when the King ordered a stay on all reversions. Painter assumed that this was a temporary measure, which would not prove disastrous in his own case, but came gradually to realize that Pembroke had changed his mind and was now working against him. It would appear that Pembroke's secretary, John Thoroughgood, came to know of the matter and was resentful because the grant was going to an outsider who was not part of the Earl's patronage system. Thoroughgood therefore got to work on the Earl to arrange a rapid grant to him which would take precedence over Painter's grant.

Early in 1623 Pembroke petitioned for a reversion to be granted to Thoroughgood. On 28 February 1622/3 Sir Edward Conway, one of the secretaries of state, wrote to Pembroke; the letter must have indicated that the request had been refused, though unfortunately all that survives is a very brief summary in Conway's letter-book (Appendix A10). On 2 March Pembroke wrote back again to Conway, making a second attempt to secure the grant (A11). Pembroke rather petulantly complained that the King's refusal would cause him to lose face, and asserted that the right to appoint the Master belonged to him personally as Lord Chamberlain. But his repetitions of the idea and the general tone of his letter suggest that he was trying to get the right established rather than stating it confidently as a self-evident truth. The King's reply was blunt; Conway's next letter, on 21 March, recorded that Pembroke's application had been 'refused by the Kinge' (A13). His request was rejected not once but twice: King James clearly did not believe that the Lord Chamberlain had an unchallengeable monopoly of the right to grant reversions to the mastership.

No further documents have been discovered relating to the case, and the King's attitude has to be inferred from what evidence there is. The plan to defraud Painter of his grant was a shabby trick, and it may be that James's sense of justice stopped him from allowing Pembroke to appropriate a grant that the King had given to someone else. But perhaps the King did not want to offend Pembroke too much, and tried to placate him by withdrawing Painter's grant, which never reached the final stages that would have made it effective, so that both Painter and Thoroughgood came away empty-handed. Pembroke does not emerge from the incident very creditably; his behaviour to Painter was inconsistent, to put it mildly, and his letter to Conway was decidedly disingenuous. (It might be objected that Painter's version of events is not necessarily trustworthy, but if he seriously expected Cranfield to help him, it would have been very foolish to lie.) Painter was badly treated, and had some justification for nursing a sense of grievance.

We may now revert to the unfortunate end of Sir George Buc's mastership. The letter of December 1621 to Cranfield seems entirely sane, even if highly emotional, and Buc's printing licence for Gervase Markham's *Herod and Antipater* was entered in the Stationers' Register on 22 February 1621/2;[26] but in the next month Buc must have slid rapidly into insanity. On 30 March 1622 Chamberlain wrote to Carleton, 'Poore Sir George Buck master of the Revells is in his old age faln starke madd, and his place executed by Sir John Ashley that had the reversion.'[27] The evidence of the early months of 1622 indicates clearly that Astley had every intention of carrying out his duties. He began attendance at court as Master on 16 March, and was present every day until 6 May.[28] On 29 March a warrant was issued to swear him in as Master of the Revels (A2), and on 2 May another warrant gave Astley the powers as Master that had earlier been granted to Tyllney and Buc (A3). On 16 May Pembroke or someone in the Lord Chamberlain's office ordered one of Buc's relatives to deliver the revels archive to Astley (A4). On 20 May Buc's old warrant of 9 June 1620, on which £301 was still owing, was cancelled and reissued to Astley, though a year later he had obtained only £100 in cash, if the petition of the workmen of the revels to Cranfield of 9 May 1623 is to be trusted (A5, A15).

Astley acted as Master for sixteen months, from March 1622 to the end of July 1623. During this period he licensed at least thirteen plays, one travelling show, and a 'prize' (i.e. fencing match) at the Red Bull Theatre.[29] He also licensed for publication Massinger's *The Duke of Milan* and 'A Booke of Iiggs' (Appendix C1–2). He attended at court for 119 days and twenty-six nights from 31 October to 26 February 1622/3. There were also four days of attendance at Easter 1623, four at Whitsun, and ten during the summer of 1623 for 'the ayringe of the Roabes garments and other stuffes'.[30] He supervised the Christmas season of entertainments at court which began on 21 December 1622 but ended earlier than normal, there being no entertainment at Shrovetide 1623 because the King was at Newmarket and Prince Charles had set out on his journey to Spain on 18 February. As late as 9 July 1623 Astley licensed Middleton and Rowley's *The Spanish Gipsy*, but a little over two weeks later, 24 July, he entered into an agreement whereby Herbert was appointed his deputy in return for an annuity of £150 to be paid by Herbert to Astley. Nominally Astley was still the Master, but in reality he had made a complete transference of his powers.

This striking and unexpected event calls for explanation, but no evidence has been discovered which provides a definite solution. Chalmers made the unsupported assertion that 'Sir Henry Herbert owed his preferment to the patronage of the Earl of Pembroke, the Lord Chamberlain',[31] and this has been repeated by later scholars; but there is nothing to prove that Pembroke engineered the transference. (This is putting it mildly; Astley had every legal right to his position, and Pembroke would have needed to threaten, bully, or cajole him into surrendering it.) Dutton makes much of Pembroke's intervention on 6 September 1622 to allow the performance of *Osmond the Great Turk*, which Astley had refused to allow, but this does not necessarily indicate that Astley's position was precarious or that there was bad feeling between Pembroke and Astley.[32] If this was the case, it is surely strange that on 20 November 1622 Pembroke issued a new and elaborate warrant reinforcing Astley's authority to license and control travelling players and showmen (A8). As late as 3 March 1622/3, only four months before Astley gave up office, a letter from Pembroke was read out in the court of the Stationers' Company 'concerning the lycensing of Playes &c by Sʳ. John Ashley' (A12). This must in some way have supported Astley's authority, but very regrettably the letter has not survived, and we do not know its precise contents.

There may have been some complex political manœuvring by which Astley was eased out in favour of Herbert, but other explanations are possible. Perhaps Astley found the office more burdensome and time-consuming than he had expected and the rewards less certain. There are some hints in this direction: early in 1623 Astley used Sir Francis Markham as his deputy (34), and the licence for *Love's Royal Reward* of 3 October 1622 is oddly phrased (see the commentary on

16). He was not strikingly successful at extracting money from the treasury, and may have suffered like his predecessor from insubordination by his officers and workmen, who sent a desperate petition to Cranfield in May 1623, asserting that their wives and children were 'readie to sterve for wante of foode' (A15). If this was so (and it is no more than speculation), Astley may have welcomed the opportunity to transform his post into a sinecure with an assured income of £150 per annum.

A further, and very tentative, possibility is that Astley found himself physically unable to cope with the demands of the job. In his last years he was clearly suffering from serious illness of some kind: in 1634 he was summoned before the Court of High Commission on what seems to be a trumped-up charge of sexual misconduct, but his counsel 'alleadged that he was at this p^rsent vnfitt and vnable to travell to London wthout daunger of his Life and therefore desired a Comission to take his Aunsweares in the Country'.[33] The court considered this a reasonable request and granted it. In 1638 the King granted him a special dispensation from the proclamation ordering the nobility and gentry to live on their estates in the country because of 'ye debility of body, which through Age Hee & his wife are fallen into',[34] and he was permitted to live with his wife and family wherever he liked for as long as he liked (presumably he needed to stay in London for medical treatment). It is just possible that he suffered from an intermittent or debilitating illness which began to show itself in the 1620s and forced him to retire from court employment to his home at Maidstone in Kent.

A surviving document which has never been fully explored is the actual agreement between Astley and Herbert, dated 24 July 1623.[35] Unfortunately, like so many documents of its kind, it gives some of the basic facts but does not explain the full circumstances or motives behind them. The longer version, which is extremely repetitive, does not deserve to be reprinted in full, and will be summarized with occasional quotation.

It begins by rehearsing Sir John's right to the office, confirmed by letters patents and a commission, both under the great seal of England. He can exercise his powers 'by himselfe or his sufficient Deputie or deputies', and he goes on to appoint Herbert 'his lawfull and sufficient Deputie' during Astley's 'natural life', with all the powers and privileges belonging to the office of Master. This includes the fees and profits, which Herbert can receive 'without any Accompts thereof to

be given, or without being anye way answerable to the said Sr John
Ashley'. Astley promises that he will not revoke the grant, except
under conditions to be stated later, and Herbert will enjoy the office
undisturbed. Astley swears that he has done nothing to prejudice
Herbert from getting the full benefit of his office, though he has
already lawfully issued a number of licences and warrants (many of
which would of course still be valid when Herbert took over).

Then follows the main provision of the agreement, that Herbert
shall pay Astley £150 per annum, though if Herbert prefers he can
instead make over to Astley

lands of a good Title of the cleere yearely value of twoe hundred pounds over
and above all Chardges and Reprises with such reasonable and Collatterall
assurances for the sure and certaine payement of one hundred and fiftie
pounds yearely . . . as the said Sr John Ashley . . . shall well like and accept of.

Next come the attached conditions; if they are not observed, the grant
will lapse, and Sir John will be entitled to revoke it. They are: (1) if
the annuity of £150 is not paid at the due time; (2) if any commission
or warrant is made out by the office 'other than in the name of him
the said Sr John Ashley'; (3) if Sir Henry does anything by which the
interest of the revels office is 'hindred preiudiced impeached or in
anywise ympaired'. In conclusion, Sir Henry makes two promises: the
first is not to issue any licence or grant for more than a year 'or for
such tyme as hath beene accustomably vsed', the document being
sealed 'with the seale of the office now ingraved with the name of the
said Sr John Ashley'; the second is that if the deputation should be
revoked, he will hand back all the seals, books, and documents
connected with the office within a month.

The document does not tell us very much, but it at least makes clear
that Astley retained some residual powers and had the legal right to
dismiss Sir Henry if certain conditions were not met. In a very limited
sense Astley was still the Master, and a warrant was issued granting
him a lodgings allowance of £50 per annum as Master of the Revels
on 30 June 1624.[36] But in practice Herbert was the Master, and was
recognized as such: the requirement that documents be issued in
Astley's name was ignored from the beginning. The annuity of £150
does not appear to be a very large sum, though of course Astley's office
was now a complete sinecure. Possibly Herbert also paid a lump sum
which is not mentioned in the agreement; later he claimed to have
spent £3,000 to purchase the office, though he does not specify when
and to whom the money was paid.[37]

Astley's grant to Herbert was valid only during his own life; if Jonson was still alive when Astley died, the mastership would automatically go to him. (In fact, Jonson predeceased Astley.) Herbert made some attempt to counter this by arranging for a joint reversion to be made out in August 1629 for himself and Simon Thelwall.[38] No scholar has asked who Thelwall was and how he came to be included. There was more than one person with this name in the early seventeenth century; a possible candidate was a man considerably older than Herbert, born around 1561. He was one of the ten sons of John Wyn Thelwall, of Bathafarn Park, Llanrhudd, Denbighshire, and there were links between the Herberts and Thelwalls: Simon's brother Edward acted as tutor in Welsh to Henry's brother Edward in 1591.[39] Simon studied at Oxford and then at Lincoln's Inn, and was a reasonably successful professional lawyer.[40] The connection between him and Sir Henry Herbert was personal: both men married rich women with property at Woodford, Essex, and during the 1620s they were living as neighbours at Woodford, where Herbert's three children by his first wife were born and christened between 1626 and 1628. The only problem with this identification is that Simon Thelwall was named as co-plaintiff in Herbert's Restoration lawsuits,[41] and the man just described would surely have died by then. Possibly Herbert's neighbour interceded with him on behalf of a younger member of the Thelwall family.

The agreement between Astley and Herbert was made on 24 July 1623, and two days later Herbert took up his duties (36). On 7 August the King knighted him, and accepted him as Master of the Revels while both men were staying at Wilton, the home of the Earl of Pembroke.[42] Herbert was immediately plunged into a full-time occupation which must have kept him very busy: in the second half of 1623 he licensed or re-licensed at least twenty-one plays and nine miscellaneous shows, and there was a full season of entertainments at court, in which six or more plays were performed.[43] To summarize Herbert's activities year by year would be tedious, as all the evidence that is known to survive is set out in this edition, but a few general conclusions can be drawn. He was an energetic and competent administrator, anxious to maintain and if possible enlarge his income. He kept on good terms with his superiors, and seems to have had fewer financial problems than his predecessors. (In February 1633 he even managed to persuade the Queen to pay £50 from her private household funds towards the expenses of an earlier masque which were still owing to the revels workmen (**251**).) There is no evidence to suggest that he suffered from insubordination by his officers, who were compelled by him to enter into a written agreement to contribute proportionally to the fees that had to be paid to treasury officials (**A16**). He also got King Charles to promise in 1636 that Herbert would be consulted over the appointment of a new Yeoman of the Revels (**343**).

Sir Henry's income came from two main sources. One was the royal treasury, which paid him a variety of fees and expenses. To claim these sums, he needed to submit accounts, either annually or triennially, which were then audited. The revels accounts for 1603–42 have been edited by W. R. Streitberger as Volume xiii of *Malone Society Collections*, and there is no point in duplicating the material here. It might be pointed out, however, that there are in the Public Record Office many financial warrants and receipts relating to Sir Henry Herbert, usually for fairly small sums, which Streitberger does not mention. No full list of these has ever been compiled, and only a very few have been published.[44] Material of this kind has largely been ignored in this edition, except for one or two items which throw some light on Sir Henry's behaviour.[45] His other source of income was the fees and gratuities paid him by the actors whom he supervised. These were a perquisite of his office which he did not need to account for, and he recorded them in his office-book solely for his own benefit. They were probably especially welcome because they were paid immediately and in cash (though sometimes he was given books as a present), whereas a treasury warrant might take several years before it was finally paid out.

It is impossible to make an accurate assessment of Sir Henry's annual income because a great deal of the necessary evidence is missing. For example, twenty-four new and old plays are known to have been licensed in 1623, and thirty-two in 1624. But from 1625 onwards the number of surviving licences does not rise above single figures until 1633, when the number was eleven, and in four of these years there are only three. In 1639 there are thirteen, but ten of these survive only in Burn's copy of Ord's transcript. External factors— plague years such as 1625, 1630, and 1636–7—undoubtedly reduced the demand for new plays, but this cannot be the whole story: clearly dozens of licences were issued of which we have no record whatever. Herbert calculated the profit from licensing shows between 26 July 1623 and 12 January 1627/8 at £103. 6s. (**176**). This period of approximately four and a half years included the plague year of 1625, when playing was forbidden throughout England from July to the end of November (156–7). Whether or not allowance is made for this, Herbert's annual income for shows should have averaged more than £20, but in 1623, the year for which the largest amount of detailed evidence survives, the total does not rise much above £7.

Simply as an experiment, however, it might be worth calculating Herbert's income during the revels accounting year of 31 October 1623 to 30 October 1624, as this coincides with the period in which office-book entries are most plentiful. The revels accounts show that he attended at court for 103 days and twenty-four nights from 31 October 1623 to 11 February 1624, and a further fourteen days at Easter and Whitsun. Another twenty days were claimed 'for the ayringe of the roabes garments and other stuffe belonginge to the sayd Office'.[46] This gives a total of 161 days or nights, for each of which he received an allowance of four shillings, totalling £32. 4s. He also received £50 as an allowance for rent and lodging, though some of this must have been used for renting the accommodation used by the revels office.[47]

The office-book shows a number of sources of income. He licensed thirty-four plays, and if we assume a fee of £1 for plays where no fee is recorded, his income would have been £37. He charged ten shillings for allowing a new scene in a play. If his standard rate at this time for licensing plays for publication was ten shillings, he received £1. 10s. for three plays. His licences to companies of players brought in £15. The players also gave him £4 in New Year's gifts and the same amount for dispensations allowing them to play in Lent. Only two travelling shows are listed in this period, totalling £3. 10s. The amounts in this and the previous paragraph total £147. 14s., not all of which was clear profit. But there must have been other income which is not mentioned in the surviving records for the period covered by this survey—fees for licences to musicians, for example, and gratuities from the companies putting on plays at court (see 65). Herbert had to pay Sir John Astley an annuity of £150, and he was a shrewd businessman who would not have taken over a loss-making office. His real income can only be guessed at, but it would be surprising if it was less than £300.

In later years his income expanded. From 1628 onwards the revels officers were ordered to begin their attendance at court on 30 September instead of 31 October, for which Sir Henry would have received an extra allowance of £6. From 1622 to 1625 the standard fee for a play-licence was £1 (out of forty-four plays from this period whose fee is known, thirty-nine were charged £1). From 1626 to 1631 inclusive, no fees are available, but from 1632 onwards the standard rate doubled to £2. In May 1628 the King's company granted him two benefit days, one in summer and one in winter, based on the second day of a revived play (178). These benefit days brought in a variety of sums until October 1633, when it was agreed that two fixed payments of £10 should be made instead (268). There were also windfalls due to special circumstances: £5 in 1627 from the King's company for forbidding the Red Bull company to perform Shakespeare's plays (171); £2 in 1629 from the same company because of the extraordinary popularity of Brome's *The Lovesick Maid*, an incident which Malone explicitly says was unique (184); and £30 in 1635 from John Momford, dancer on the ropes, who was made the King's servant through Sir Henry's agency (318).

One other source of income needs to be mentioned. Sir Henry was a shareholder in several pre-Restoration theatres, though it is hard to work out the precise details. He had a share in the Salisbury Court Theatre in 1631 (see 225), and from an entry in the office-book which has only recently come to light it appears that the average annual income from that share in the three years ending September 1640 was nearly £100 (415). Apparently he was given a share in the Phoenix or Cockpit Theatre, but it is not clear when he received it or how long he held it before selling it for £100 to his deputy William Blagrave (458). In Restoration documents he claimed to have had shares in four theatres which produced, on average, £400 per annum;[48] this might seem to be an exaggerated amount, but if the figures for the Salisbury Court are accurate, the total may be perfectly truthful.

Sir Henry was evidently a wealthy man, and there are long lists of properties owned by him among the composition papers now in the Public Record Office, in one of which he estimated the annual profit from his office at £500.[49] The loss of income from his office in 1642 was not disastrous: in 1645 he acquired the manor of Great or Much Fordham in Essex, though it was subsequently sequestrated from him,[50] and a few years later Stokes Manor at Hanslope in Buckinghamshire, which remained in his family until sold by his grandson in 1713.[51] His private financial dealings were extensive and complicated, and many documents relating to financial transactions—bonds, leases, and lawsuits—survive in the Public Record Office, the National Library of Wales, and elsewhere. His main London residence was in

James Street, Covent Garden, at the time a new development which was extremely fashionable.[52] He also leased a house near Millbridge, Westminster, and Lincoln House in Tothill Street, which he used as the headquarters of the revels office (see **R60**). His brother Edward described Sir Henry as 'being no less dexterous in the Ways of the Court as having gotten much by it',[53] an entirely appropriate account.

Licensing

The licensing of plays was obviously one of the Master's main functions, and Herbert carried out this duty as vigorously as possible, though probably more from a wish to maximize his income than from a desire to assert an ideological hegemony over the drama. It has sometimes been claimed that certain categories of play or production did not require licensing—courtier plays, for example, or amateur productions. But licences are now known to have been issued for such plays as Sir John Suckling's *Aglaura*, Thomas Killigrew's *Claracilla*, William Habington's *The Queen of Aragon*, and Sir John Denham's *The Sophy*; and Herbert received twelve shillings for allowing a one-night amateur production under the auspices of Sir Robert Cotton.[1] It could be the case, however, that amateur productions at some distance from London would not bother to secure the consent of the Master, who might not even be aware that a performance was taking place. Apparently college productions at Oxford and Cambridge did not need licences. In August 1636 the King and Queen visited Oxford and saw three plays: Strode's *The Floating Island*, Wilde's *Love's Hospital*, and Cartwright's *The Royal Slave*. But no licences survive for the plays, and there is no mention of Sir Henry in contemporary allusions to the event. The visit was arranged by Archbishop Laud, then Chancellor of Oxford, who took a personal interest in the plays and had a much greater authority than Herbert's. Even though the costumes from *The Royal Slave* were given to the Queen so that the King's company could perform it at Hampton Court early in 1637, Laud stipulated that neither the play nor the costumes should appear on the public stage.[2]

A play would normally be brought to Sir Henry for licensing by the company that owned it rather than by the dramatist. Sir Henry's letter to Knight, the bookkeeper of the King's company (**265e**), as well as his licence for *The Launching of the Mary* (**258**), show that he held the bookkeeper, who had charge of the company's play-texts and also acted as prompter, responsible for the state of the text as it reached him, though this does not necessarily mean that it was the bookkeeper himself who brought the play to be licensed. Sir Henry received his fee from Knight on 12 October 1632 (**240**), but on several other occasions the fee was paid by one of the actors (e.g. **326a**, **349**, and **385**). When there were problems that required to be negotiated, Sir Henry usually dealt with one of the senior members of the company, actor-managers like John Heminges or Christopher Beeston, though on occasion he came into contact with the author of the play, as in the case of Davenant's *The Wits*.

Plays were in manuscript, and must often have been untidy and hard to read. Sir Henry seems to have been fairly tolerant, but there were occasional rumbles of discontent. He 'founde fault with the length' of a tragedy on the plantation of Virginia (**40**), and 'commanded a reformation in all their other playes'—in other words, ordered them to write shorter plays in future. He grumbled that an old play, *The Four Sons of Amon*, was not 'of a legible hand' (**81**), and the condition of Mountfort's *The Launching of the Mary* made him command the bookkeeper 'to present mee with a fairer Copy hereafter', which appears to mean that he wanted tidier texts in future, rather than that the bookkeeper was to send him a fair copy of the play he had just licensed (see commentary on **258**). It is doubtful, however, whether his complaints and orders had any lasting effect. After Herbert had suppressed the revival of *The Tamer Tamed* on 18 October 1633, he laid it down that 'the Master ought to have copies of their new playes left with him, that he may be able to shew what he hath allowed or disallowed' (**265c**). This is obviously a sensible idea, but it is probable that neither the actors nor the Master wished to pay for an extra scribal copy, and the proposal seems to have remained a counsel of perfection which was never carried out in practice.

Sir Henry read through the play carefully, noting anything that he found unsatisfactory. (More will be said of this later, in the section on censorship.) If it was basically acceptable, he added his licence, signed and dated, at the end of the play. A well-known example which still survives is Massinger's autograph manuscript of *Believe As You List*, which has Herbert's licence immediately under the last lines of the play (**215**; cf. **132** n. and **258**). A licensed manuscript of Thomas Jordan's play *The Walks of Islington and Hogsdon* (1641) was sent to the printer, who faithfully copied the licence into the printed text (**425**). It was essential for the players that their plays should contain a licence of this kind: when the King's company was asked by what authority they had performed *A Game at Chess* in 1624, 'they produced a booke being an orriginall and perfect Coppie thereof (as they affirmed) seene and allowed by S* Henry Herbert knight M* of the Reuells*, vnder his owne hand, and subscribed in the last Page of the said booke' (**115**). When the same company put on an unlicensed play a few months later, they got into serious trouble, and had to make a humble apology to Sir Henry (see the letter of 20 December 1624, **265d**).

There are, however, oddities in Herbert's practice. On 18 September 1623 he recorded a licence for John Day's lost play *Come See a Wonder* 'for a company of strangers', adding the comment, 'It was acted at the Red Bull & licensed without my hande to itt because they were none of the foure companies' (**56b**). Two months later, on 28 November, he noted the licence of another lost play, *The Fayre Fowle One*, by an otherwise unknown dramatist named Smith, again 'for a company of strangers' at the Red Bull; this, he added, was 'licensed without my name to a strange company' (**69**). What precisely does this mean? Did he allow the plays to be licensed but not add his signature? The manuscript of *The Honest Man's Fortune* contains a licence in Herbert's handwriting, but there is no signature, and there does not appear to be room for one (**148b**). This play, however, was for the King's company, the most important company in London, and definitely not 'a company of strangers'. More evidence is needed to settle this problem.

The Master needed to keep a record of the licences he had issued and other transactions relating to his office, and for this purpose used what must have been a substantial bound volume of blank paper, which Malone consistently referred to as his 'office-book'. The Revd Richard Warner, who had certainly seen the original, described it as 'The Account Book of Sir Henry Herbert, knight, master of the revels' (see above, 18–19), which may be the actual title written into the book. The Master and his clerk also made office copies of letters and other documents. It was the custom for office-books to be handed on from one Master to another; when Astley became Master, the Lord Chamberlain's office arranged for him to be sent Buc's revels papers (Appendix A4). Herbert took over Astley's book, and, as we have seen, one condition of the agreement between them was that if Herbert ceased to be Astley's deputy, he would return the complete archive of the revels office within a month. Herbert's references to licences by

Buc and Tyllney, both in his own office-book and in Restoration
documents, suggest that he owned a complete set of office-books going
back to Tyllney, though it appears that the earlier ones were discarded
by Herbert or his family before the end of the seventeenth century.

We might expect the office-book to be a highly confidential document to which only the Master or his deputy would have access, but
the evidence on this point is somewhat confusing. To some extent Sir
Henry treated it as though it were a family bible, entering in it
autobiographical material and a detailed record of the births of his
three children by his first wife.[3] But when he noted, on 3 July 1633,
his approval of James Shirley's *The Young Admiral* as exactly the kind
of play he most admired, he added, 'When Mr. Sherley hath read this
approbation, I know it will encourage him to pursue this beneficial and
cleanly way of poetry' (**259**). Were Shirley and his fellow-dramatists
allowed to read the office-book, or was the first paragraph of the entry
a copy of what he had written at the end of Shirley's play? When King
Charles himself censored an impertinent passage in Massinger's lost
play *The King and the Subject*, Herbert felt obliged to record it 'here
for ever to bee remembered by my son and those that cast their eyes
on it, in honour of King Charles, my master' (**386**). Here he seemed
to assume that the office-book would be handed down in his family,
as in fact it was, though by all existing precedents it would have gone
to his successor.

When Herbert took over Astley's office-book, it must have contained
Astley's entries for the sixteen months he acted as Master, from March
1622 to July 1623. It appears, however, that Herbert did not record
the licences he had issued in exactly the same way as Astley. If we can
judge fairly from such entries as **12** and **14**, Astley's began with the
date, a statement that it was a new play, the title and length in sheets
(or the other way round), the company and theatre involved, and the
fee. Herbert, to judge from an entry like **37**, began with the company,
followed by the title of the play, the length in sheets, the author, the
theatre, the date, and the fee. But we must not be dogmatic: Malone
and Chalmers frequently abbreviated the entries they printed, sometimes drastically. They never included the length of the play, and
usually omitted the fee. When Burn's copies are compared to their
originals in Ord, it is often clear that he transposed the different
sections of the licence so as to bring the title of the play to the front
of the entry, thus making it easier to arrange them in alphabetical
order. There are no indications of play-length in surviving licences

after 27 May 1624, even in transcripts by Ord that appear to give the complete entry. It is possible, therefore, that Sir Henry decided at this point that information about a play's length was not sufficiently useful to justify the labour of collecting it.

Sir Henry had to deal not only with new plays but also with old plays and revivals. Here we can judge of his practices only from the evidence that happens to survive, and if new material emerges, we may have to modify our conclusions. (His problems with Henry Shirley's *The Martyred Soldier*, for example, came to light through the discovery of the Burn transcript.) The players may have felt that once a play had been formally licensed by the Master, and a fee paid, it would never need re-licensing if it remained unaltered; but it is clear that from the earliest days of his mastership Sir Henry did not take this attitude. On 19 August 1623, less than a month after he had taken over from Astley, he re-licensed two plays previously licensed by Sir George Buc, Shakespeare's *The Winter's Tale* and a lost anonymous play, *The Peaceable King or the Lord Mendall* (42–3). Herbert noted that *The Peaceable King* was free from alteration (though he may not necessarily have examined it minutely himself), and he took Heminges's word that the same was true for *The Winter's Tale*. Because of this he charged no fee. On 21 August he reallowed Dekker's *Match Me in London* free of charge (47).

Two days later, 23 August, there was a minor crisis. He had already 'called in' Henry Shirley's play *The Martyred Soldier*; the phrase suggests that Herbert had taken the initiative in summoning the play-text from the players, and perhaps there had been complaints about it. He called it an 'old play', but if it was licensed by Astley, the licence on it cannot have been much more than a year old. It was 'reallowed with reformations', indicating that certain words or passages were marked for omission or revision. The players, perhaps annoyed that a play so recently licensed should have to be re-licensed, totally ignored Herbert's deletion-marks. The angry Herbert confiscated the book, and charged a fee; perhaps he had not charged a fee before, and did so now as a kind of punishment (49). But this was not the end of the story. The most plausible interpretation of the entry for 28 August (53) is that Richard Gunnell somehow learned that Sir Henry now had custody of the play. Gunnell's company was desperate for new plays, as their stock of play-texts had been lost in the fire which destroyed the Fortune theatre in December 1621.[4] Gunnell persuaded Sir Henry to let him have the play, but it still belonged to the Cockpit company, and the consent of Christopher Beeston had to be secured. Herbert re-licensed the play to Gunnell, thereby securing an extra fee.

Sir Henry continued to re-license old plays, sometimes free of charge (**99**) or in return for the gift of a book (**148a**). If the play had been revised or enlarged, he normally charged a fee. The only other striking incident concerning an old play for which evidence survives relates to the performance of Fletcher's *The Woman's Prize, or the Tamer Tamed* intended by the King's company in October 1633 (**265**). On Friday 18 October the company was all prepared to perform the play in the afternoon. But Herbert had already received 'complaints of foule and offensive matters conteyned therein', and in the morning he sent a messenger with a warrant peremptorily ordering the company to cancel its performance. (With commendable versatility they put on *The Scornful Lady* instead.) Herbert was sent the prompt-copy of the play on Saturday morning, and returned it on Monday, 'purgd of oaths, prophaness, and ribaldry'. The fact that it was an old play which had already been licensed provoked 'some discourse in the players, thogh no disobedience', and Herbert felt obliged to make the fullest statement on record of his attitude to revivals:

All ould plays ought to bee brought to the Master of the Revells, and have his allowance to them for wich he should have his fee, since they may be full of offensive things against church and state; ye rather that in former time the poetts tooke greater liberty than is allowed them by mee.

On Thursday, 24 October, two of the leading actors of the company, Lowin and Swanston, asked Sir Henry's pardon for their 'ill manners'; no doubt they had expressed rather too freely their resentment at having a performance suppressed at such short notice. On the same day the company had acknowledged at the Court of High Commission that Sir Henry was not responsible for their troubles with Jonson's *The Magnetic Lady* (**266**), and the players may have felt that for a variety of reasons their relationship with Sir Henry had become dangerously confrontational and needed to be improved.

It may not be a coincidence, therefore, that on 30 October the King's company arranged to commute their summer and winter benefits to Sir Henry into two fixed payments of ten pounds, which they paid regularly until the closure of the theatres (**268**). On 27 November they sent him 'an ould booke of Fletchers called the Loyal Subject', already licensed by Buc, which they asked him to inspect with a promise of his fee (**273**). His marginal note, 'the first ould play sent mee to be perused by the K. players', is puzzling. The company had had dealings with Sir Henry over old plays in the first years of his mastership; in two cases this was partly because the copy with Buc's licence on it was lost or missing (**43** and **148a**), but the same is not said of Middleton's *More Dissemblers Besides Women* (**61**). Possibly the company's behaviour over *The Loyal Subject* marks the first occasion on which they voluntarily submitted an old licensed play which had not been altered, of a kind which until then they would have expected to perform without needing to consult Sir Henry. There is perhaps a note of satisfaction about the entry, as though Sir Henry was pleased that the players now accepted his procedures.

The various Masters of the Revels and their deputies also issued another form of licence; between 1607 and 1640 they licensed a large number of plays for publication. At no time, however, did they have formal authority to do so, for the commission of 1581 issued to Tyllney and reissued to his successors gave the Masters full authority to license and censor plays that were to be acted, but said nothing about publication. Licensing in 1607 may have begun by accident: it has been suggested that Buc, who was waiting to succeed the elderly Tyllney, began licensing plays partly as a source of income and partly because Tyllney would not allow him to do anything else.[5] Herbert started licensing plays for printing early in 1624, and continued, together with his deputies William Blagrave and Thomas Herbert, until 1638. He stopped at that point, with one exception in 1640, not because he had lost interest, but because the Star Chamber decree about printing in 1637 did not appoint the Master of the Revels as a recognized licenser, and thereby made it clear that he had no real authority to do so.[6]

Sir Henry entered his printing licences neatly and methodically at the end of the manuscript, in much the same way as he entered his acting licences, as is evident from the printing licences which accidentally survived by being included in the printed text, as in Shirley's *The Witty Fair One* (Appendix **C62**). After 1632 printers were supposed to include an imprimatur in the published book, but in practice they did so only in a small minority of cases, particularly where plays were concerned.[7] At times Herbert's licences must have indicated that he had censored the text and was anxious that his deletions be respected. The most striking example is the Stationers' Register entry for Shakerly Marmion's *Holland's Leaguer*, 26 January 1631/2 (**C41**). The Stationers' clerk was clearly impressed by the vehemence of Sir

Henry's restrictions, and did his best to copy the actual words, though this licence cannot have been very tidily written, and he had difficulty in doing so. Sir Walter Greg believed that this was an acting licence which had been altered by Sir Henry to serve as a printing licence.[8] This may be so, but there is no reason why Sir Henry should not have entered conditions and reservations in his printing licences. He had had trouble with his censorship of Davenant's *The Wits* early in 1634 (281), and when he licensed the play for publication two years later, he insisted that it should appear 'as it was Acted without offence . . . not otherwise' (C79).

For about eight months, from June 1632 to January 1633, Sir Henry also tried his hand at licensing the printing of non-dramatic verse and prose. Complications arose in three particular cases. Herbert licensed the collected edition of Donne's poems which is dated 1633, but in the first licence entered in the register on 13 September 1632 (C48) he withheld approval for the complete set of five satires and five of the thirteen elegies in the manuscript before him. The latter group consisted of 'The Bracelet', 'Going to Bed', 'Love's War', 'On His Mistress', and 'Love's Progress'.[9] These are among the most sexually explicit of Donne's poems, and the simplest assumption is that Herbert found them morally offensive: they did not appear in 1633. On 31 October Herbert gave approval for the satires (C55), and they were rather hurriedly added to the end of the printed volume. A week earlier, 24 October, he had licensed Donne's *Paradoxes and Problems*, and the two licences, one to each section, are prominently displayed in the printed text of the first edition of 1633 (C54).[10] But on 14 November 1632 Herbert was summoned before the Court of Star Chamber to explain why he had licensed them (244). No evidence has been discovered to account for the summons: possibly something in Donne's book had been regarded as questionable, or perhaps Donne's son, John Donne junior, had begun his campaign to secure control of the publication of his father's writings.[11] The *Paradoxes and Problems* were reprinted later in 1633, but this time Herbert's licences were omitted.

The third item to cause difficulty was the collection of poems and plays by Fulke Greville, Lord Brooke, published as *Certain Elegant and Learned Works* in 1633. Herbert licensed the two plays, *Alaham* and *Mustapha*, on 23 June 1632, and the licences were printed with the text of the plays (C58). On 17 October 1632 he recorded in the office-book that he had licensed a group of poems by Greville including one on religion (241a). But when the full group of writings published in the volume was entered in the register on 10 November (C58) the treatise on religion was omitted. More strikingly, the text of the published book begins on gathering 'd'; it looks as though three gatherings were deleted containing the poem, which was not published until 1670. Malone suggested that the deletion had taken place by order of Archbishop Laud, and Wilkes agreed, noting the anti-prelatical tone of some of Greville's observations.[12] Apparently Sir Henry suffered no severe embarrassment from his troubles with Donne and Greville, but he may have felt it safer to confine his press-licensing to drama.

The warrant issued to Tyllney and succeeding Masters gave them power to supervise and control not only plays but 'players, and playmakers, together wth their playing places' (A3). At the Restoration Herbert tried to reassert all these powers as comprehensively as possible, though even at the height of his authority there were limits to what he could do. For example, he copied an entry from Sir George Buc's office-book in which Buc gave permission for the erection of a new playhouse in Whitefriars (1). In R38 Herbert quoted this licence, and claimed that he himself had 'Allowed the Play House for the K^s Company'. But Buc's licence seems to have had no effect, and there is no evidence to suggest that Sir Henry ever had the authority to permit the construction of a new theatre.

Neither could he license the creation of a new company of actors; this was part of the royal prerogative. Companies resident in London did not need a licence to act from Sir Henry (they did after all pay him numerous fees of various kinds), but travelling companies in the provinces did need an additional licence from him which had to be renewed annually. This is sometimes described in the records as a 'confirmation' of a royal patent (see e.g. 84, 86, and 150). The King's company received on 24 June 1625 a new patent from King Charles entitling it to perform not just in London but anywhere in the country.[13] It looks as though they intended to use this as a warrant to travel, which would have enabled them to escape the closure due to plague which was being enforced in London. They were now technically a travelling company, and therefore needed Sir Henry's confirmation, which he issued on 1 July (155). This was immediately nullified, however, by the total ban on playing brought about by a petition to the Lord Chamberlain from the House of Commons (156–7). Sir Henry also issued renewable licences to travelling entertainers and showmen, which are discussed below in the penultimate section of this introduction.

Herbert could nevertheless intervene in the running of companies, as when he assigned a group of actors to a new Queen Henrietta's company set up in late 1637 (367), and Richard Heton, the manager of the theatre where they performed, Salisbury Court, took it for granted that he must consult Herbert over the hiring and firing of actors (460). Herbert was regularly called in to arbitrate when legal disputes arose concerning actors (162a–b, 243, 324, 459). This could become a tedious chore. In the first of these cases, which occurred when Herbert was seriously ill, the defendant, Mrs Baskerville, proved so awkward and slippery that Herbert eventually told one of the witnesses that 'he woulde rather gyve 20^{li} then be troubled anie further in yt' (162b).

Censorship

One of the Master's most important duties was to censor plays. Herbert's own term for this activity was 'reformation', but he used the word to cover a range of revisions and additions. *The Variety* (420) contained 'several reformations made by Shirley'; this must refer simply to modifications made to an amateur play by an experienced professional dramatist, and Herbert clearly found nothing offensive in the play, since it was 'allowed upon review without exception'. The anonymous *The Peaceable King or the Lord Mendall* (42) was reallowed without a fee 'because itt was free from adition or reformation'. Here again the last word must refer to revision rather than to censorship. There is thus a certain ambiguity about the term which obliges us to examine it carefully. *The Maid in the Mill* was licensed on 29 August 1623 (54), and performed at court a month later, 29 September (58). There was a second court performance on 1 November, but this time 'with reformations' (66), and yet a third court performance on 26 December (73). It is highly unlikely that a play licensed in the normal way and then put on at court would need to be censored a short while later, and Bentley plausibly speculates that elements in the play which pleased the audience of the first court production were expanded for the second.[1]

It may be helpful to provide lists of plays for which there is evidence of censorship in Herbert's records. Included are a few plays, such as Shirley's *The Ball*, which appear to have been licensed but on production gave rise to the sort of public scandal that censorship was supposed to guard against. The lists are in chronological order; the first is of plays which do not survive.

Undated, probably 1623–4
436. William Rowley, *Fool without Book*; 'full of faults, and must be Corrected, if allowed'

27 July 1623
37. Samuel Rowley, *Richard the Third or the English Prophet*; 'with the reformation'

August 1623
40. Anon., *The Plantation of Virginia*; 'the prophaness left out . . . may be acted els not'

25 January 1625
145. William Sampson, *The Widow's Prize*; 'contayning much abusive matter was allowed by mee on condition my reformations were observed'

October 1633
264. Anon., *The City Shuffler, Part II*; 'Exception was taken by Mr. Sewster' (presumably to personal satire on him; Herbert stayed the play until Sewster was satisfied by the company)

2–5 June 1638
385–6. Massinger, *The King and the Subject*; 'The name . . . is altered, and I allowed the play to bee acted, the reformations most strictly observed, and not otherwise'. (King Charles ordered that an insolent passage be deleted)

3–7 May 1640
412–13. Herbert confiscated an unnamed play performed without licence, forbidding the playing of it 'because it had relation to the passages of the K.s journey into the Northe'

1641
421. Thomas Jordan, *Youth's Figaries*; 'all^d upon several reformations and not otherwise'

June 1642
433. Herbert burned an unnamed new play 'for the ribaldry and offense that was in it'

The second list is of plays which survive either in print or in manuscript.

23 August 1623
49. Henry Shirley, *The Martyred Soldier*; an old play 'formerlye allowed by Sir John Ashlye but called in & reallowed with reforma-

tions: which were not observed, for to every cross they added a stet of their owne'

2 January 1624

78. Thomas Drue, *The Duchess of Suffolk*; 'being full of dangerous matter was much reformed'

12 June 1624

105. Middleton, *A Game at Chess*; discussed in detail below

11 January 1630/1

209. Massinger, *Believe As You List*; first version not allowed 'because itt did contain dangerous matter, as the deposing of Sebastian king of Portugal, by Philip the Second, and ther being a peace sworen twixte the kings of England and Spayne'

26 January 1631/2

C41. Shakerly Marmion, *Holland's Leaguer*; 'the reformacons to be strictly obserued may be printed not otherwise'

12 October 1632

240. Jonson, *The Magnetic Lady*; according to John Pory, players summoned before the Court of High Commission 'for uttering some prophane speaches in abuse of Scripture and wholly thinges. which they found penned, for them to act and play'. Cf. 24 October 1633 **(266)** when the players 'did mee right in my care to purge their plays of all offense'

18 November 1632

246. Shirley, *The Ball*; 'ther were divers personated so naturally, both of lords and others of the court, that I took it ill, and would have forbidden the play, but that Biston promiste many things which I found faulte withall should be left out, and that he would not suffer it to be done by the poett any more, who deserves to be punisht; and the first that offends in this kind, of poets or players, shall be sure of publique punishment'

7 May 1633

254. Jonson, *A Tale of a Tub*; licensed, but 'Vitru Hoop's parte wholly strucke out, and the motion of the tubb, by commande from my lorde chamberlin; exceptions being taken against it by Inigo Jones, surveyor of the kings workes, as a personal injury unto him'

27 June 1633

258. William Mountfort, *The Launching of the Mary*; 'all ye Oaths left out In ye action as they are crost In ye booke & all other Reformations strictly obserud, may bee acted not otherwyse'

18 October 1633
265. John Fletcher, *The Tamer Tamed*; intended performance suppressed 'upon complaints of foule and offensive matters conteyned therein'; prompt-copy censored by Knight and Herbert and returned to the players 'purgd of oaths, prophaness, and ribaldrye'

23 November 1633
273. Fletcher, *The Loyal Subject*; 'formerly allowed by Sir George Bucke . . . with some reformations allowed of'

9 January 1633/4
281. Davenant, *The Wits*; Herbert discussed 'all that I had croste in Davenant's play-booke' with King Charles, who took a more lenient view of oaths than Herbert. Printing licence in some copies of 1636 edition, 'as it was Acted without offence, may bee Printed, not otherwise' (**C79**)

24 February 1633/4
C70. John Ford, *Perkin Warbeck*; allowed to be printed 'observing the Caution in the License'

15 October 1635
330. Glapthorne, *The Lady Mother*; licensed by Blagrave, Herbert's deputy, with the proviso, 'the Reformacons obseru'd'

The only play-manuscript earlier than 1642 which gives full and detailed evidence of Sir Henry's practices as a censor is Walter Mountfort's *The Launching of the Mary, or the Seaman's Honest Wife*, licensed on 27 June 1633, which now survives as part of BL MS Egerton 1994. Mountfort was not a professional dramatist, but an employee of the East India Company, and he wrote the play during a long voyage home from the East in 1632. The play is hopelessly undramatic, and its editor suspects 'that the most it achieved was one or two subsidized performances instigated by, or offered to, the East India Company and their friends'.[2] But the thoroughness of Herbert's censorship and the peremptory tone of his licence show that he took the play seriously and expected it to be performed, though no evidence has come to light of an actual performance.[3]

There are three strands or sections in the play (they can hardly be dignified with the name of plots). One concerns a group of shipwrights, who are preparing the launching of an East India merchant ship named after Queen Henrietta Maria, an event which took place on 26 October 1626. In the second the Governor, or Director, of the

East India Company, in conversation with an elderly Lord Admiral named Hobab, defends the company against a series of accusations. In the third Dorotea Constance, the honest wife of a seaman away on a trip to India, successfully resists a variety of would-be seducers. Herbert went thoroughly through the play, indicating in various ways material he found offensive. Some words, phrases, or lines are deleted with thick horizontal pen-strokes. Some are marked for omission by being enclosed in a box or rectangle of horizontal and vertical lines. Others are marked by underlining, vertical lines or brackets in the margin, diagonal hatching, or large diagonal crosses through the text. These can sometimes be combined, and are often accompanied by diagonal crosses in the margin. The play was subsequently revised by Mountfort to take account of Sir Henry's objections, and there were some more deletions which appear to be the work of a bookkeeper adapting the play for the stage.

Herbert responded to the different sections of the play in various ways, but in one respect he was consistent. Throughout the play several oaths were systematically deleted—'fayth' or 'yfaith', which were used frequently, and 'troth', 's'life', and 'by the Lord', each of which was used once. A line explicitly referring to Christ ('next to the sole redeemer of my soule', line 657) was enclosed with lines by Herbert and marked with a cross, and was then deleted during the revision. Rather surprisingly, Herbert ignored 'by gisse' (line 1073—he must surely have known it was an abbreviation of 'Jesus') and several examples of 'in god's name' or 'a gods name'. He also left unchanged a dozen references to the name of God in such forms as 'God bless', 'God shield', and 'God preserve'. (These occur in two passages at the beginning and end of the play, lines 35–138 and 2745–2813.) 'Heaven' and 'Heavens' were also ignored.

During their discussions the shipwrights talk at some length of the massacre of Amboyna. This incident took place in February 1622/3, when ten Englishmen, employees of the East India Company, were seized by the Dutch at Amboyna, an island in the Moluccas, now part of Indonesia, and after being tortured were executed on trumped-up charges. When the news reached England, more than a year later, there was immense public indignation, and in February 1624/5 the East India Company commissioned a play and a large painting depicting the event. The Dutch ministers in London feared that these might provoke a riot directed against them, and notified the Privy Council, which promptly suppressed both play and painting.[4] If the play was, in Chamberlain's words, 'redy to be acted', it may be that Herbert had licensed it, though there is no evidence in the surviving records to prove this. The English government did nothing to avenge the massacre, and it was still a live issue in the 1630s. It is hardly surprising that Herbert decisively eliminated all references to the event in Mountfort's play (though in the revised version Mountfort included in a speech by the Lord Admiral what is clearly a very oblique and guarded reference to the massacre).

Mountfort used much of the play to defend, at tedious length, the policies of the East India Company. Some of the arguments offended Herbert. For example, Mountfort dealt with the company's shipbuilding policy, and this was clearly a delicate subject, even though the problems associated with the levying of ship-money did not arise until later. It had been objected to the company that it had exhausted raw materials for shipbuilding produced in England, and that the ships themselves went off for long voyages to the East and were not available for military service in home waters. Among Mountfort's counter-arguments were assertions that splendid ships had been built by the late King James to strengthen the Royal Navy (lines 1425–31), that the company would supply provisions and raw materials even if it could not supply ships (lines 1441–1452), and that the company would immediately alter its policy if the King wished it to (lines 1477–9). All these were felt to be tactless or over-explicit, and were heavily marked for omission.

Two other items relating to the East India Company were deleted. Mountfort had praised the charitable activities of the company, including

> repayre of Churches, mayntenance of schollers
> reliefe of [needie] preachers, of the sacred word,
> & diuers other actes of Charitie

> (lines 1740–2)

This seems harmless enough, but sometimes rich patrons or companies who subsidised preachers tended to support those who had Puritan sympathies, and a factor of this kind may be at work here. The second item concerned the relation between the company and the Mint. Near the beginning of the play the Admiral mentioned charges that the company's activities impoverished the state in various ways, the last of which was 'the small or no imployment | the mint hath had since this East Indian trade' (lines 206–7). It seems that Mountfort answered this point at some length, but Herbert objected to it so strongly that the original leaf or leaves were torn out, and new ones (ff. 342–5) substituted. In this revised version the Governor raised the point about the Mint again (lines 2280–4), but the Admiral cut him off curtly:

> The mint's an edge toole, meddle not wth that,
> for what's the mint to you, or you to yt,
> or yt to your obiectors: a response
> to that obiection weare as friuolous
> as the obiection is wthin yt selfe:
> for as your importation doth small good
> so doth your exportation little harme
> for ought I euer heard: matter of state
> Canne brooke no dalliance. then no more of that
>
> (lines 2285–93)

The topic is abruptly dropped, and the company's representatives move on to a generalized attack on detraction, personified as a woman willing to slander everyone indiscriminately.[5]

The ship which gave the play its title was named in honour of Queen Henrietta Maria. Mountfort's first reference to the Queen, at lines 1165–85, was innocuous, but later allusions gave offence to Herbert, presumably because they were combined with virulent anti-Catholicism. At the beginning of Act 5, scene 2, the Admiral's opening line, 'A royall shippe and beares a royall name' (line 2757) provoked a violent response from the Governor:

> And blest be shee whose royall name she beares
> nor ys there any but blood-thirstinge monkes
> or hell-bred Iesuites will wish otherwyse.
> but as they swimme in synne, so lett them sinke
> vnto perdition.
>
> (lines 2758–62)

The last four lines were heavily marked for omission by Herbert, with underlining and a marginal cross and rule. In the next scene a long genealogy of the Queen was marked for omission, probably because it mentioned at some length the assassination of the French king Henry III in 1589 'by a damnd nurslinge of sanguineous Monkes' (line 2837). Herbert also deleted some lines spoken by the captain of the ship in which he promised to pray for the Queen's well-being:

This stameringe tonge shall send her orysons
to the supernall throne for the encrease
of ioyes internall, & eternall peace
vnto her sacred person

(lines 2864–7)

The last three lines are heavily marked for omission, but in this case it is harder to see what precisely Herbert objected to.

The last major omission concerns Dorotea, the seaman's honest wife who gives the play its subtitle. At the beginning of Act 4 she undergoes a series of attempts at seduction from a courtier and a clergyman, who send letters to her, and a soldier and a sea captain, who appear in person. Even though Dorotea resists them all, and converts to virtuous ways the two who speak to her, Herbert was offended, particularly by the portrayal of a lustful and hypocritical clergyman, and marked the passages concerning the clergyman and soldier for deletion. After the final temptation Dorotea meditated on her predicament thus:

Good heauns, what honest woman would suspect
this sober-seeming man? nor sea, nor shoare
free from these temptinge monsters, men with soules
as blacke as pitch.? nor Court, *nor Church*, nor sea,
nor land, nor rich, nor poore, but all alike,
brethren in euill? Heauns refine them all,
& purge them from the drosse of luxurie.

(lines 2209–15)

Herbert enclosed the italicized words in box-rules, and placed crosses in the margin. Mountfort must have felt that there was no point in trying to salvage the scene, and during his revision marked the whole of it for deletion.

A licence by Sir Henry can also be found at the end of the manuscript version of *The Honest Man's Fortune*, MS Dyce 9 in the Victoria and Albert Museum; the licence is undoubtedly in Herbert's hand, though he did not include his signature (148b; see above, 43). The play, by Fletcher, Field, and Massinger, probably dates from 1613, and had obviously been licensed by Sir George Buc before it came into Herbert's hands early in 1625. It seems that 'the Originall', the copy bearing Buc's licence, was lost, and at the entreaty of Joseph Taylor, a leading member of the King's company, Herbert reallowed it. In the manuscript several passages, mostly short, have been so heavily deleted as to be almost illegible, and a larger number of passages have been marked for deletion by enclosure in lines or loops. But none of these markings can be definitely attributed to Herbert (there are no marginal crosses by him), and it is unlikely that he minutely inspected the play, since it contains numerous oaths that he would have deleted. On 19 August 1623 Herbert reallowed *The Winter's Tale* 'on Mr. Hemmings his word that there was nothing profane added or reformed, thogh the allowed booke was missing' (**43**). Possibly something similar happened with *The Honest Man's Fortune*: Herbert may have reallowed it without reading it on Taylor's reassurances that the grosser passages had been or would be deleted.

If this hypothesis is correct, the markings were made before the manuscript was sent to Herbert, and reflect the actors' understanding of what he would be likely to find offensive. (The manuscript is in the hand of Edward Knight, bookkeeper of the King's company, who was later thanked by Herbert for his help in censoring *The Tamer Tamed*, **265e**.) Eight passages were totally deleted, though only one of these was of any length, a discussion between two unemployed soldiers who consider the possibility of setting up a male brothel (2. 1. 15–27).[6] Three short jeers at lords and courtiers were removed (2. 2. 52–3; 3. 2. 56–7; and 5. 4. 220). A reference to 'ffrench lords' in a context of fashionable homosexuality was deleted and replaced by 'gallants' (3. 3. 225); clearly the point at issue was the nationality, not the sexual practices. Three mildly blasphemous phrases were removed: 'now for a psalme of mercy' (5. 4. 63), 'pray god' (5. 4. 94, for which 'I wish' was substituted), and 'troth' (5. 4. 149).

Seventeen further passages, ranging in length from two lines to twenty-eight, were marked for deletion. Not all these markings were necessarily made in anticipation of censorship. The deletion of a stage direction for 'A Songe' and seven lines leading up to it was clearly a theatrical cut. The last eleven lines of the play were marked for omission, but this was then cancelled by the word 'stet' inserted three times in the margin. There is nothing strikingly offensive in the lines, and it is hard to see this as comparable to the players' treatment of the censored text of *The Martyred Soldier* (**49**), which so angered Sir Henry. Some marked passages contain social criticism, such as 3. 1. 81–90 (an attack on upstarts who never shake off their base origins), 3. 3. 9–38 (on the corruption needed to acquire wealth), and 4. 1. 8–16 (on greatness without virtue as like a burning palace that crumbles to ashes). Other passages are sexually explicit in a rather anti-feminist way, such as 3. 3. 158–60 (on wealthy women who take their horsekeepers or footmen as lovers), 4. 1. 102–5 (on a 'ravening woeman' who devours men's flesh), and 4. 1. 266–8 (on the smell of a woman's chamber). Some at least of these cuts may be examples of self-censorship, though the play contains unmarked passages of social criticism quite as pungent as those listed.

Comparison of the manuscript (referred to as D) with the printed text in the Beaumont and Fletcher Folio of 1647 (F) produces oddly contradictory conclusions. Of the passages deleted or marked for deletion in D all but one were inserted in F, though in the passage about the male brothel the phrase 'male stewes' (2. 1. 17) was removed. The passage cancelled in both was 3. 2. 56–7: 'pretious, tis allmost as comon as to haue a lord arrested, & lye by it.' As we have already seen, several tactless phrases were revised in D itself—'ffrench lords' to 'gallants' (3. 3. 225), 'pray god' to 'I wish' (5. 4. 94), and 'god wot' to 'good sooth' (5. 4. 227)—but in each case F used the original version. Sometimes F printed oaths in a stronger form: 'spretious' (2. 4. 135) became 'Udsprecious', and 'light' (3. 2. 63) became 'slight', and at eleven points F has 'God' in such phrases as 'for Gods sake' or 'God blesse you' where D has 'heauen' or no equivalent at all. At 1. 3. 306–7 D has 'you shall merit by it' where F has 'you shall be saved'. F has a complete scene, Act 5, scene 3, not in D but presumably in the manuscript from which D was copied, in which four servants have a bawdy discussion about their mistress's forthcoming marriage. F also has a totally new conclusion to the play, but in its way it seems to be quite as salacious as the old one in D.

At the same time there is abundant evidence that words and phrases which were allowed to remain in D were censored in F. At twenty-one points F has 'By ——', or simply a long dash, where D uses a wide variety of phrases: 'by my troth', 'pox on him', 'death', 'by my blood', 'by my life', 'the devil on me', 'hart', 'a plague of', 'by god', and 'by my faith'. Dashes replace an apparently innocuous phrase, 'never stirre', and two uses of 'humh' or 'hum'. Two of the oaths replaced by dashes, in Act 4, scene 2, are more elaborate: 'by that foule life of w^{c}h | thou art no longer m^{r}' (lines 124–5), and 'by my soule, | & what it hopes for' (lines 135–6). Two repulsive phrases were omitted: 'bitch wolfe' (applied to a woman, 4. 2. 83) and 'to kill the noysomnesse of ich' (5. 4. 84). But the expurgation was not systematically carried out in either D or F; the two texts have in common a number of relatively minor oaths, including ten cases of 'faith' or 'yfaith'.

One other manuscript play bearing a licence and indications of censorship is Glapthorne's *The Lady Mother*, part of BL MS Egerton 1994, though in this case the licenser was Herbert's deputy, William Blagrave (**330**). It seems that the play had a complicated textual history: copied by a scribe, it underwent a round of revisions by the author and the scribe. It was then submitted to the censor, after which the author and scribe made a second set of revisions.[7] In the earliest revisions words were deleted which Glapthorne or the scribe knew would be disliked: two instances of 'faith' and one each of 'yfaith', ''sdeath', and 'heaven'. In the early part of the play there were several jeers at French manners and fashions; the earliest use of 'French', at line 31, was deleted but not the others. Blagrave himself made only two changes in the text: 'buttock' in line 793 became 'bacside', and in the trial scene at the end of the play all references to the presiding magistrate as a 'recorder' were eliminated (why Blagrave found the term offensive is not clear).[8] In the second round of revisions two uses of 'death' as an oath were deleted, but several examples of the various words deleted still remained in the play.

In 1633 Herbert called in and censored *The Tamer Tamed*, a play by Fletcher better known by its main title *The Woman's Prize*. Two versions of the play survive: a manuscript forming part of the Lambarde Collection now in the Folger Shakespeare Library (press-mark J.b.3) and a printed text in the Folio of 1647 (henceforward abbreviated as L and F). The manuscript is probably earlier than 1633, and a comparison of the two versions gives an indication of what Herbert is likely to have considered objectionable, though we must not take it for granted that he was personally responsible for the differences between the two texts.[9] It is improbable that F is simply a censored version of L, since F contains two scenes (Act 2, scene 1, and Act 4, scene 1, in modern editions) not found in L, and both texts appear to derive independently from earlier versions.

It is not, however, a simple case of a one-way operation, with oaths and obscenities present in L which are omitted or altered in F. Sometimes F has stronger forms: in the opening line of the play F reads 'God give 'em joy' where L reads 'Heaven', and at six other points F uses 'God' where L does not. At 1. 2. 41 F has 'Yfaith' where L has 'Indeed'; we should expect it to be the other way round. In the opening scenes set on the wedding night of Petruchio and Maria F uses phrases like 'Tis bed time' (1. 2. 92) or 'Will you to bed sonne' (1. 3. 13). L omits the first phrase and alters the second to 'well son, well'. There are also places where both texts present bland vocabulary which suggests that both have been expurgated independently, such as 4. 4. 7 (L: 'I protest', F: 'on my word') and 4. 5. 64 (L: 'I sweare' and F: 'Beleeve me'). At eight points F has 'By——' or simply a long dash, where L has 'I sweare' or in one case 'I vow'.

There is, however, a much larger number of places where expurgation has clearly taken place in the later text. Oaths such as 'faith', 'troth', 'death', and 'Birlady' are for the most part (though not with complete consistency) deleted or bowdlerized in F, as are vulgarisms like 'pisse' (1. 1. 46) and 'pispots' (4. 2. 2)—though not 'pist' at 5. 1. 68—and 'pox' (3. 1. 47) and 'rots' (3. 3. 143). Flippant use of religious vocabulary is toned down: 'a Christian feare' (2. 2. 51) becomes 'a certaine feare', and at 4. 5. 166–7:

> PETRUCHIO. What would this woman do if she were suffer'd,
>   Upon a new religion?
>   SOPHOCLES.   Make us pagans.

'religion' becomes 'adventure' and 'pagans' becomes 'nothing'. At 2. 4. 61–77 the local women are described as staunch, not to say violent, defenders of popular entertainments such as maypoles and morris dances against Puritan opposition. Most of the passage is allowed to remain, but at lines 68–70:

> There's one brought in the Beares against the Canons
> Of two church-wardens, made it good, and fought 'em,
> And in the churchyard after even song.

'two church-wardens' becomes 'the Town', and the last line is omitted.

The play's explicit sexuality would undoubtedly have offended Herbert. *The Woman's Prize* contains so many double meanings that to remove them all would destroy the play. No attempt was made to do so, but a number of the grosser obscenities were removed. At 1. 2. 51 Livia says to Rowland, after promising to marry him and let him make love to her, 'You shall heare what I do'. In L but not in F he replies 'I had rather feele it'. In Act 1, scene 3, the other men present mockingly anticipate the bridegroom's condition the morning after his wedding-night:

> To morrow morning we shall have you looke,
> For all your great words, like Saint George at Kingston,
> Running a foot-back from the furious Dragon,
> That with her angry tayle belabours him
> For being lazie.

SOPHOCLES.   *His warlike launce*
    Bent like a crosse bow lath, alas the while.
TRANIO. His courage quench'd, and so far quench'd—
PETRUCHIO.   Tis well sir
TRANIO. *That anie privie Saint even small Saint Davy*
May lash him with a leeke.

                                              (lines 18–26)

The italicized lines are omitted in F, as is a later passage about the
sexual capacity of a tanner's wife:

                              her plackett
          Lookes like the straights of Gibralter, still wider
          Downe to the gulphe, all sun-burnt Barbary
          Lyes in her breech.

                              (2. 4. 45–8)

In Act 3, Scene 1, Rowland has an outburst against the obsequious
behaviour of men in love, part of which is omitted in F:

          TRANIO. Of what religion are they?
          ROWLAND.   Good old Catholikes,
            They deale by intercession all, they keepe
            A kind of household Gods, call'd chamber-maides,
            Which being pray'd to, and their offerings brought,
            (Which are in gold, yet some observe the old law
            And give 'em flesh) probatum est, you shall have
            As good love for your monie, and as tydie
            As ere you turn'd your legge ore, and that ended—

                              (3. 1. 50–7)

Herbert had not tolerated anti-Catholicism in *The Launching of the
Mary*, and would probably have found the passage both blasphemous
and obscene.

    Other plays by Fletcher, or by Fletcher and his various collabora-
tors, exist in two versions which contain evidence of possible censorship. It is difficult, however, to determine when and by whom the
changes were made, and to what extent Sir Henry himself was
responsible. Rather like *The Honest Man's Fortune*, *Bonduca* survives
in a manuscript copy by Edward Knight deriving from Fletcher's foul
papers and a printed text in the 1647 Folio based on prompt-copy. At
twenty-four places the Folio has 'By ——' or simply a dash, where the
manuscript has a different reading, sometimes but by no means always

an oath. As Sir Walter Greg puts it, 'in some cases the manuscript supplies what is presumably the original reading, but in others the mildness of the manuscript expression or a difference of construction suggests that the scribe undertook some purging of his own'.[10] At seven points corresponding to dashes in the Folio the manuscript reads 'I sweare' (and once 'I vowe'); 'By the gods' and constructions involving 'pox' occur three times each, and 'By the lord' twice. Other readings of this type in the manuscript include 'the rott consume you' (803; cf. 2. 2. 65), and 'the devill take this ffortune' (1575; cf. 3. 5. 87), but also such apparently harmless phrases as 'by all thats honorable' (2571; cf. 5. 3. 172) and even 'good cozen' (1558; cf. 3. 5. 70). In the opening scene the manuscript has 'the lees of *Caesars* pleasures' (45) where the Folio has 'tainted pleasures' (1. 1. 37), and 'the high sett ravisher' (99) where the Folio reads 'hated ravisher' (1. 1. 87), but Greg thinks that these changes may be due to the original licenser, Sir George Buc or his deputy.

Another Fletcher play survives in a transcript by Ralph Crane, where it is entitled *Demetrius and Enanthe*, and in the 1647 Folio, entitled *The Humorous Lieutenant*. Crane's transcript was prepared for Sir Kenelm Digby, and is dated 27 November 1625.[11] Crane removed, though not entirely consistently, many words used as oaths: 'death', 'lord', 'pox', 'life', 'plague', 'god', and 'god-a-mercy'. He also cut out a song for fairies at 4. 3. 12–43, perhaps because it was explicitly a charm designed to conjure up lustful desires in a young woman. Crane probably made these omissions on his own initiative; as R. C. Bald puts it, 'one must suppose that Crane had acquired the theatrical transcriber's habit of altering oaths and that he was as careful to tone them down for so polite a patron as Sir Kenelm Digby as Herbert was for a popular audience.'[12] At the same time both versions contain certain oaths in common, most notably five uses of 'faith'. Occasionally the manuscript has stronger language than the Folio, and it includes a salacious passage not in the Folio (578–602; 2. 1. 5–24), spoken by Timon, one of the courtiers who acts as a pander for King Antigonus.

The fourth of the quarto editions of *Philaster* appeared in 1634, a year after Sir Henry's troubles with *The Woman's Prize, or the Tamer Tamed*. It may be due to Sir Henry's influence, direct or indirect, that in more than twenty places the 1634 reprint of *Philaster* had its oaths toned down or omitted. 'Faith' was virtually eliminated, with words like 'marry', 'troth', or 'indeed' substituted. Elsewhere the treatment was half-hearted and contradictory. The play is full of references to 'the gods', but only a small fraction of the total was altered: 'by the gods' became, for example, 'by my sword' or 'by my life', and 'by all the gods' turned into 'by all thats good' or 'And I vow'. 'God' was altered three times to 'heaven' and once to 'Jove', but 'by heaven' was altered to 'by these hilts' or 'by Fate' or omitted. 'For Gods love' became 'For love of truth'. At the same time no attempt was made to alter any discussions of political issues.

One last example of revisions possibly due to censorship is Arthur Wilson's *The Inconstant Lady*. No licence for the play survives, but we know that it was performed by the King's company at court in 1630 and in public, presumably at the Blackfriars theatre, in March 1634/5.[13] Two autograph manuscripts exist, the earlier forming part of the Lambarde Collection (Folger MS J.b.1), the later in the Rawlinson Collection in the Bodleian (MS Rawlinson Poet. 9) (abbreviated as L and R). R contains numerous revisions by Wilson; many of these are for stylistic or artistic reasons, but others, as R. C. Bald suggested,[14] may indicate that Wilson had become aware of what Sir Henry found offensive, and had censored his own play. (Alternatively, R may be a fair copy of a text which has already undergone censorship.)

Wilson's play contains some scathing attacks on great men and courtiers (see, for example, Aramant's speeches in the second half of Act 2, Scene 1),[15] but very little of this was deleted. Perhaps prudentially, Wilson omitted a couple of jeers at members of the legal profession (sergeants at 2. 3. 12, constables at 3. 3. 7). The portrayal of the Duke of Burgundy, the ruling figure in the play, was made slightly less harsh and autocratic in the second version, and hints that he might be assassinated were toned down and made less explicit (4. 2. 247-9). But far more often the changes related to sexuality and religious vocabulary. Oaths like 'faith' and 'pox' vanished, and 'steept in a boule of pisse' (2. 2. 110) became 'a little Lantified'.[16] Sexual allusions were toned down or omitted; where L had

> instruct thy hart to Loue that I may find
> a hope for to enioy thee

> (3. 2. 36-7)

R substituted a new second line: 'There's something in thee Mortall'. 'Such a sweetness | the Gods themselues do couett' (3. 4. 26-7) became 'such a sweetness | The worlds impouerisht in'. Several longer passages of bawdy were omitted.[17]

Some of the most striking changes relate to religion and the supernatural. What might seem to be a fairly explicit allusion to God in L:

> ther's a Power
> that orders all things, and that great Disposer
> raises my thoughts now to a higher pitch
> then humaine loue to you

(4. 2. 193–4)

was drastically abbreviated in R:

> ther's a higher Power
> that doth dispose my Loue now.

Appeals by characters in the play to Heaven and the gods were repeatedly altered, though not with complete consistency. To quote some of the more bizarre examples, 'You Gods, you Gods' became 'Reason thou Queene of ffrailty' (1. 2. 233); 'You Powers aboue' became 'yee Guids of Reason' (3. 1. 39); and 'You heauenly powers' became 'Misguided Reason' (5. 3. 54). Towards the end of the play the Duke allows his newly discovered daughter Bellaura to marry her lover, and in L the assembled company cries out 'Heauen blesse yoʳ Grace'. This seems inoffensive, but Wilson altered it to 'And sweet peace Crowne your vertues' (5. 3. 286). Apparently Wilson was prepared to go to extreme lengths to avoid offending Herbert's susceptibilities.

A study of Sir Henry as censor must take into account his connection with a major theatrical scandal. In the summer of 1624 Middleton's political satire *A Game at Chess* was performed before packed audiences, causing a sensation by its portrayal of living figures such as the King of Spain; the former Spanish ambassador, Diego Sarmiento, Count of Gondomar; and the Archbishop of Spalatro, Marco Antonio de Dominis, who converted to Protestantism and came to England in 1616, but reverted to Catholicism and returned to Italy six years later. Sir Henry licensed the play; but modern scholars are reluctant to believe that he would have done so without powerful backing, and have tried to identify a patron on whose behalf he was acting, though no clear evidence exists to point to anyone in particular. Indeed, it has to be said that although *A Game at Chess* is the best-documented play of the early seventeenth century, we know very little of how it originated, and to what extent it was purely theatrical and to what extent part of a political campaign.

Two versions of Sir Henry's licence survive. Malone's copy gives the precise date, 12 June; Ord's, as recorded in Burn, does not, but adds the fee of £1 (105). Both versions treat the licence as a straightforward transaction at a normal fee, with no mention of 'dangerous matter' or 'reformations'. Though licensed in June, the play was not performed until early in August, and it is usually assumed that the players were waiting for the King to leave London on the progress he normally made in the later part of the summer.[18] The Folger manuscript of the play (V.a.231) shows that Middleton made revisions to his original version, the most important of which was to insert the figure of the Fat Bishop (that is, de Dominis). It is tempting to assume that some of the more daring political satire was added at the last moment, after Herbert had written the licence; but when the actors were summoned before the Privy Council, they produced the prompt-copy bearing the licence, and swore that 'they added or varied from the same nothing at all' (115).[19] The Council did not want the bother or responsibility of examining the text of the play in detail, and sent it to the King so that he could appoint someone to do the job. Sir Henry was waiting at court in case he was summoned to appear and justify himself, but no evidence has been discovered to show whether or not he actually had to do so.

Very little in the way of punishment, as far as we can tell, was meted out to those involved in the affair. Middleton himself was apparently imprisoned but eventually released, possibly because of a witty petition in verse he sent to the King.[20] The players were forbidden to act, but also sent a petition to the King; the contents of the petition are not known, but it probably emphasized their poverty caused by enforced idleness. The King was sufficiently moved to allow them to act 'any Common play lycenced by authority',[21] so that before the end of August they were back in business. So little were they chastened by the experience that four months later they presumed to act a completely unlicensed play, *The Spanish Viceroy*, which has not survived. Once again, they do not seem to have been punished, but Sir Henry was clearly infuriated, and the company had to send him an abject letter of apology, submitting to his authority and promising never to act unlicensed plays again (265d). Sir Henry continued his functions as Master of the Revels, apparently without interruption.

Our assessment of the play's daring or impertinence will depend on our interpretation of it, both historical and critical. Margot Heinemann has argued that Middleton was supported by a 'Parliamentary-Puritan opposition' led by the Earl of Pembroke;[22] but this has been convincingly challenged by Thomas Cogswell, who argues that the play needs to be considered in terms of the unusual political situation in England in late 1623 and early 1624.[23] Prince Charles had returned from his trip to Spain in October 1623, without a Spanish bride and anxious for a war against Spain. The English people as a whole were so delighted at the outcome that public rejoicing went on for days. In February 1624 the Duke of Buckingham, who had accompanied Charles to Spain, defended their behaviour to a parliamentary committee. Rather speciously he presented their main motive as a desire to expose Spanish duplicity, with no mention of the awkward fact that Charles had originally gone to Spain to speed up the negotiations for his marriage to the Infanta. For a brief while Buckingham enjoyed great popularity, even among Puritan pamphleteers. The play adopted a similar interpretation: the Infanta was not mentioned, and the Prince and the Duke (the White Knight and the White Duke) were presented as heroes whose clever manœuvring had tricked the Spaniards into revealing their own hypocrisy. The play could have been written only at this particular juncture; as a contemporary put it, 'Such a thing, was neuer before invented, and assuredly had so much ben donne the last yeare they had euery man ben hanged for it.'[24]

It is still possible, however, that Middleton insinuated into the play satire on leading members of the court. In the final scene Charles and Buckingham accuse themselves of various vices in order to lure the Spaniards into betraying their own hypocrisy. Buckingham is shown as frightened of becoming fat because of his love of food:

> for I feare Fatnes
> The Fogg of Fatnes, as I feare a Dragon,
> The Comlines I wish for thats as glorious

(5. 3. 63–5)

and also lecherous. Heinemann argues that these vices were real, not merely pretended for the occasion, and that the audience would enjoy the covert satire.[25] This may be so, but if Middleton was supported in writing the play by city patrons, merchants with Puritan sympathies,[26] as Heinemann goes on to argue, they would surely have been offended by Gondomar's scathing references to rich citizens who are not merely afraid of fatness but are grossly and revoltingly fat:

> Some of your whitehouse Gurmundizers, spetiallie
> Youre wealthie plumpe plebeians, like the Hogs
> Wch Scalliger cites, that could not moue for fat.

(5. 3. 42–4)

Although Middleton was careful to keep the White King (James I) and the Black Knight (Gondomar) entirely separate (they never converse together in the play), it could be argued that Gondomar's boasting of his successes in England for the Catholic cause reflects on the gullibility of James. As a contemporary observer said of the treatment of Gondomar, 'In going about to discouer his tricks, methinkes they make him a man of understanding with a great reflection upon them that he daylie treated wth.'[27] Jane Sherman has argued that the attempt by the Black Bishop's Pawn to seduce the White Queen's Pawn comments harshly, by a kind of role reversal, on Charles's attempt to woo the Infanta, though no contemporary commentator takes this line, and this part of the play has been interpreted in very different ways.[28]

It is hard to make a final judgement. There may have been undercurrents of criticism in the play, but it does not have to be seen as violently opposed to royal policy. John Woolley, writing to Sir William Trumbull, reported rumours that the Prince and the Duke, if not the King, had 'laught hartely' at the play (114), and more surprisingly, that there had even been a court performance: 'Some say (how true it is I know not) that the Players are gone to the Courte to Act the game at Chesse before the King, wch doth much truble the Spanish Amb^{r}.'[29] All this may merely have been unsubstantiated gossip, but Woolley clearly assumed that the leading figures at court would not be bitterly offended. Sir Henry may have licensed the play partly because he agreed with the line taken by Middleton: in a newsletter of 1639 he argued that the King's journey to the North had forced the Scots to reveal their intention of invading England just as his earlier journey to Spain had forced the Spaniards to reveal themselves: 'The Curtayne of Inuasion Is fully Drawne, thats Due to this Iorney as the truthe of the Spanishe matche was to the K. Iorney for Spayne.'[30] But the political circumstances changed rapidly; a year later the Duke of Buckingham was again deeply unpopular, and the production of *A Game at Chess* remained a unique event.

To draw conclusions from this very miscellaneous evidence is not easy. For a number of plays acted in the second quarter of the seventeenth century there are variant readings suggesting that censorship took place, but Sir Henry himself was not necessarily responsible for this. Plays written before 1623 may have been censored by his predecessors, Tyllney, Buc, and Astley. Occasionally higher authority intervened: the King looked through the manuscript of Massinger's *The King and the Subject* at Newmarket in 1638, and ordered that an insolent passage be revised; Sir Henry fortunately preserved this, though the play is otherwise lost (386b). It seems that dramatists and bookkeepers sometimes censored plays before submitting them for licensing; Sir Henry's licence for *The Launching of the Mary* shows that he expected the bookkeeper to get rid of 'Oathes, prophaness, & publick Ribaldry' (258) before sending plays to him. But there was no rigorous consistency in these matters: Knight was thanked by Sir Henry for his help over *The Tamer Tamed* (265d), but his transcripts of *The Honest Man's Fortune* and *Bonduca* were not systematically purged of oaths.

Sir Henry carried out his duties conscientiously, but his techniques of censorship were not strikingly sophisticated, and did not ensure that censored material vanished irrecoverably. It looks as though the players prepared a transcript from authorial foul papers to serve as a prompt-book, which was submitted to the Master for his inspection, but the uncensored foul papers remained with the players. Later on another transcript could be prepared directly from the foul papers, which might in its turn be censored (this seems to be the only way of accounting for the fact that some plays seem to have been censored twice but in different fashions). The Master or his deputy went through the text marking words and passages he found offensive, but only rarely deleted material himself. Sometimes the marking might be only a cross in the margin. Where cuts were indicated, they might make nonsense of the text, and the Master presumably expected the dramatist to make local revisions to cope with his instructions, as Mountfort did with *The Launching of the Mary*; but the Master's frequent warnings that the licence would not be valid if his instructions were disobeyed suggest that he did not ask for a second look at the manuscript to check what had been done. It was possible, though dangerous, to ignore his markings, as happened, to Sir Henry's great indignation, in the case of Henry Shirley's *The Martyred Soldier* (49).

Politics was of course one of the most important areas in which censorship operated, though it would obviously be wrong to portray Sir Henry as single-mindedly obsessed with politics.[31] The surviving evidence indicates that playwrights were expected to avoid any discussion of detailed and specific issues, whether domestic or international. Because nothing had been done to avenge the deaths or punish those responsible for them, the massacre of Amboyna was still a sensitive issue in 1633, ten years after it had taken place. Treatment of it could provoke anger in a domestic audience which might lead to riots, and friction in diplomatic relations between England and Holland. Not surprisingly, Mountfort was obliged to omit it from *The Launching of the Mary*. It is understandable that Mountfort wanted to defend the shipbuilding policy of the East India Company, but to make detailed proposals of what the company was prepared to do to help national defence might have seemed an attempt to dictate to the government. His original discussion of the Mint has vanished, but it must have been fairly substantial, and Herbert might simply have found it too elaborate and specific. Topics of this kind, to use Mountfort's own metaphor (line 2285), were an edged tool that could cut the user of it, a 'matter of state' that was not supposed to be treated in the relatively frivolous medium of drama.

Early in 1640 William Beeston's company of boy actors at the Cockpit or Phoenix theatre put on an unlicensed play which 'had relation to the passages of the Kings journey into the North' (413). The King came to know of it, and complained to Herbert, who got the Lord Chamberlain on 3 May to issue warrants closing down the theatre and imprisoning Beeston and two other leading members of the company in the Marshalsea.[32] The Lord Chamberlain interceded for the players, who wrote a petition submitting themselves to Herbert, and after three days' idleness were allowed to recommence acting. Beeston was not so fortunate. We do not know how long he spent in prison, but a few weeks later, on 27 June, the Lord Chamberlain issued a further warrant appointing William Davenant as manager of the company, obviously in Beeston's place, though Beeston was not mentioned.[33] But for the next year Davenant was preoccupied with war and politics, and probably took little or no interest in the company.[34] It looks as though Beeston resumed control, probably in the second half of 1641.

The records give no title for the play, but Martin Butler takes for granted that it was Brome's *The Court Beggar*, almost certainly put on by the company near this time.[35] At the beginning of Act 3 there is a passage of about thirty lines in which a character who is pretending to be mad imagines that the doctor treating him is a Scottish Presbyterian who has captured him during the First Bishops' War of 1639:

Am I then taken prisoner in the North?
Wounded, disarm'd and bound? I shall be ransom'd.
To which of your rebelliously usurp'd
Castles ha' you brought me? you sir *Presbiter*
That better can *pugnare* then *orare*,
And so abjure all duty and allegiance[36]

This undoubtedly refers to the Scottish usurpation of the royal castles in Scotland, which the King might well have regarded as tactless; but the tone is that of a loyal subject outraged by Scottish rebellion and hypocrisy, and it is hard to accept that this brief comic incident would have been deeply offensive to the King. We now know from the Burn transcript that in 1640 Beeston put on an unlicensed play named *The Challenge* (404); this might perhaps have been the play that caused all the trouble, though it is impossible to be sure, as only the title survives.

This leads to an important point. If the unnamed play, which Herbert confiscated, was *The Court Beggar*, it must have survived in some form, as it was published in 1653 as one of *Five New Playes* by Brome.[37] If it was *The Challenge*, Herbert subsequently licensed it. Very few plays were completely suppressed. King Charles himself objected to some lines in Massinger's lost play *The King and the Subject* (386) as 'too insolent', but Massinger was not haled into the Court of High Commission or Star Chamber to be punished. The passage had to be revised, but the King subsequently authorized Herbert to license it. The first version of Massinger's *Believe As You List*, set in Spain and Portugal, was not acceptable (209), but four months later the revised version was licensed with only one objection.[38] Another play containing 'dangerous matter', Thomas Drue's *The Duchess of Suffolk*, needed to be 'much reformed'; but even so, it was licensed for acting on 2 January 1623/4 and for publication on 2 July 1624, though for some reason it was not published until 1631 (78 and 109). The play has been interpreted as an allegory alluding to the troubles of Elizabeth, Queen of Bohemia; but the allegory is perfectly visible in the censored version, and it is possible that the original version contained passages of violent anti-Catholicism which Sir Henry would not tolerate. Other plays which have been seen as political allegories were licensed without apparent difficulty: Massinger's *The Bondman*, for example, was licensed for acting on 3 December 1623, for publication on 12 March 1623/4, and was shown at court on 27 December 1623 (70, 74, and 88).

Another ground on which a play might be found objectionable was personal satire on people of reasonably high social status (or with a patron who could intervene on their behalf). Inigo Jones learned that Jonson had satirized him in *A Tale of a Tub* under the name of Vitruvius Hoop; on the instructions of the Lord Chamberlain, Jonson was forced to delete the character from the play before it could be licensed, though some of his satire was transferred to another character, In-and-In Medlay (254). 'Mr Sewster', probably a goldsmith named Edward Sewster, took exception to Part II of *The City Shuffler* (264). As the play is lost, we do not know what precisely he objected to, but it is clear that Herbert forbade the play to be performed until Sewster had received satisfaction from the players. In a late case, not mentioned in Herbert's records, the Red Bull company put on a scandalous play called *The Whore New Vamped*, which jeered at an alderman, William Abell, as a drunkard 'and defamed the whole profession of Proctors belonging to the Courte of the Ciuill Lawe, and reflected vpon the present Governmᵗ'.[39] The Privy Council ordered the Attorney-General to investigate the matter and punish those responsible, including the person who licensed the play, but what happened subsequently is not known.

Some representations of living persons were even more daring. On 18 November 1632 Herbert recorded that in Shirley's *The Ball* certain 'lords and others of the courte' had been impersonated in such a lifelike way that he was tempted to suppress the play, though Beeston managed to pacify him (246). The odd thing is that Herbert had licensed the play only two days earlier (245). Either he failed to read it closely enough, or else, more probably, the characters were not identifiable until the actors had embodied them in speech, gesture, and dress. The most notorious example of all was obviously *A Game at Chess*, where the players, according to John Chamberlain, went to some trouble to make sure that Gondomar could be identified: 'they counterfeited his person to the life, wᵗʰ all his graces and faces, and had gotten (they say) a cast sute of his apparell for the purpose, wᵗʰ his Lytter.'[40] It is striking that Sir Edward Conway's letter to the Privy Council of 12 August 1624, conveying the King's reaction to the Spanish ambassador's protest, singles out the stage representation 'in a rude and dishonourable fashion' of the King of Spain, Gondomar, and de Dominis as the chief offence committed by the players.[41] (It is not clear just how fully the King was aware that he himself, Prince Charles, and Buckingham, were also presented.) Figures lower down the social scale could not expect much protection: only a month later, in September 1624, Anne Ellesden pathetically failed in her attempt to suppress the play in which she was ridiculed, *Keep the Widow Waking* (117c).

The surviving records show Sir Henry acting more often as a censor of morality than of politics. In his letter to Edward Knight of October 1633 (265e) he asserted that the 'quality' (in *OED*'s sense 5b, the acting profession) 'hath no greater enemies than oaths, prophaness, and publique ribaldry'. A few months earlier he had praised Shirley's *The Young Admiral*, 'being free from oaths, prophaness, or obsceanes', as exactly the 'beneficial and cleanly way of poetry' that he wanted other dramatists to follow (259). This preoccupation can be found throughout his career as Master; as early as August 1623 he reallowed *The Winter's Tale* because Heminges assured him 'that there was nothing profane added or reformed' (43), and in June 1642 he burned a play without recording its title or author 'for the ribaldry and offense that was in it', the only recorded example of such destruction, though he still took his fee for having read it (433).

Occasionally Herbert's distaste for oaths led him into difficulties. In the process of licensing Davenant's *The Wits* late in 1633, Herbert marked the oaths for deletion with a cross, together with other 'reformations'. Davenant clearly resented the extent of the changes, and complained to the King via one of his favourites, the courtier Endymion Porter. The King went through the manuscript of the play with Herbert (281), and allowed several of the words marked with a cross to stand, on the assumption that 'faith', 'death', and 'slight' were 'asseverations and no oaths'. As E. K. Chambers commented,

If the king had been a better etymologist, he would have realized that, while 'Faith' was an asseveration, 'Death' and 'Slight' were, at least in origin, oaths. 'By God's death' is said to have been the favourite oath of Elizabeth.[42]

Herbert's reaction, as recorded in the office-book, was somewhat contradictory: he felt obliged to submit to his master's judgement, but retained a strong private conviction that the words were oaths. When licensing the play for publication on 19 January 1635/6, Herbert insisted that it should be printed 'as it was Acted without offence' (C79). But Davenant had won a partial victory: the 1636 text of *The Wits* contains seven examples each of 'faith' and 'good faith', three of 'slight', and a couple each of 'death' and 'pox', together with a few other similar words and phrases.

Herbert believed that religion, like politics, was a subject that dramatists should not investigate in any detail. Mountfort was not allowed to refer to Christ openly as the Redeemer, and it was not even acceptable for him to make one of his characters pray for Queen Henrietta's happiness and eventual salvation. Sir Henry was a staunch Protestant, but he would not tolerate the expression of virulent anti-Catholicism, though there may have been in this a mixture of religious and political motives which are not easily disentangled or defined. The clergyman who tries by letter to seduce Dorotea in *The Launching of the Mary* was presumably an Anglican, and Herbert's deletion of the episode may seem unduly protective. Although Dorotea does not read out the letter, it clearly 'wrestes a sacred text' (line 2132)—in other words, uses a biblical text to justify seduction and adultery, and Dorotea pours abuse on him:

> Base pseudo-teacher, Nullifidian,
> thou diuelish doctour in an Angells shape
> . . . vicious vicar. painted priest,
> adulterate kindler of lascivious fire.

(lines 2138–9, 2144–5)

It is perhaps not surprising that for Herbert this went beyond permissible bounds.

In the theatre meaning is communicated visually as well as through the verbal text; costume and gesture may modify or subvert the spoken word. In February 1635 Herbert committed Cromes, 'a Broker in long lane', to the Marshalsea prison 'for lending a church Robe with the name of Jesus upon it to ye players in Salisbury Court to present a Flamen a priest of the Heathens' (313). Bentley feels that such a use 'cannot have been innocent in intent';[43] there must, in other words, have been an intention to mock Anglican ritual. He links it with an episode in 1639, apparently not recorded in Herbert (or perhaps not published by Malone), in which on 2 May

the Players of the fortune were find a 1000./ for setting vpp an Altar, a bason, and twoe Candlesticks, and bowing downe before it vpon the stage, And although they alledge it was an old playe revivd, and an Alter to the heathen Gods, yet it was apparent, that this playe was revivd of purpose in contempt of the ceremonies of the Church.[44]

There are differences between the two episodes: Cromes was released after only a day of imprisonment and a letter submitting himself to Sir

Henry's authority, and no record survives of a punishment for the Salisbury Court players. The Fortune company, on the other hand, was fined £1,000 (presumably by the Court of High Commission), a sum so huge by contemporary standards that it is hard to imagine any company of players being able to produce it. This difference in punishment might be explained by the fact that the bishops were a more sensitive issue in 1639 than in 1635; even so, it is possible that the episode in which Herbert was involved was no more than a straightforward case of sacrilege, the use of a Christian garment in a pagan setting.

Whether Herbert was a more severe and repressive Master than his predecessors is hard to decide. Scholars often quote a remark he made in 1633, after the affair of *The Tamer Tamed*, asserting that all old plays should be re-licensed by him, 'since they may be full of offensive things against church and state; ye rather that in former time the poetts tooke greater liberty than is allowed them by mee' (265c). By now Sir Henry had ten years' experience, and had called in and reviewed many old plays, so he knew more about his predecessors than any modern scholar can hope to know. At the same time, what we know of the licensing practices of Tyllney and Buc does not suggest that they were strikingly more liberal or permissive than Herbert. The ultimate effect of Herbert's censorship on Caroline drama is a very large issue, and most of the evidence has disappeared; we can only speculate on what the drama might have been like if no form of censorship had existed. Recent suggestions that various Caroline plays offer radical criticisms of Charles I and his policies may be exaggerated; at any rate, if they are even partially true, they make it impossible to assert that a ruthless censorship stifled any trace of opposition to the King.

In his praise of Shirley's *The Young Admiral* as a model for other dramatists, Sir Henry noted that the acting profession had received 'some brushings of late' (259). *OED* does not quote this particular usage, but it must mean something like 'dressing-down', 'severe rebuke', and the most plausible explanation is that Herbert had in mind Prynne's monumental *Histriomastix*, dated 1633 on the title-page but published late in 1632. It can hardly be a coincidence that several major examples of dramatic censorship date from 1633 and 1634, and are more concerned with blasphemy and indecency than with political issues. (The censorship of *Philaster* in 1634 was concerned exclusively with oaths; passages that have been regarded as politically subversive, such as the dialogue between Dion and the King in Act 4, scene 4, were completely untouched.) It was in Herbert's financial interest to have the theatre in a vigorous and flourishing condition, and part of his activity as a censor was designed not to enfeeble the drama but to protect it and make it less vulnerable to Puritan objection.[45] Obviously his efforts were not enough to prevent the closing of the theatres in 1642.

Sights and Shows

We may perhaps think of Sir Henry Herbert chiefly in connection with court performances of plays and the supervision of major theatrical companies like the King's company. Much of his time, however, was spent in licensing and controlling all kinds of little-known troupes of travelling players and showmen who occasionally performed in London but normally toured the provincial towns and cities. This side of his work must have involved a good deal of effort; the companies wandered about the greater part of England, apparently with no fixed itinerary, and there was often friction between them and the local authorities, sometimes requiring the intervention of the Master of the Revels or even his superiors, the Lord Chamberlain or the Privy Council.

The evidence for Sir Henry's involvement is of two kinds. The first, and most important, consists of licences recorded in his office-book; but unfortunately we possess only a small fraction of the total number issued. Malone showed very little interest in publishing this material, and it is to Ord that we owe most of the thirty or so surviving examples, though there might have been more if Halliwell-Phillipps had preserved the Ord transcript intact. (Burn copied out the Ord play-licences but ignored those for miscellaneous shows.) The second source of evidence is the civic records of the towns and cities where the showmen appeared and were required to produce their licences. Some of these records, most notably at Norwich, are remarkably detailed, giving full information about the performers and their entertainment, while others are tantalizingly brief. The principle adopted in this book is to reprint only those provincial records which mention Sir Henry or his immediate predecessor, Sir John Astley, either by name or in their capacity as Master of the Revels, though they were almost certainly involved at other times when their names are not mentioned. The items printed are therefore an incomplete record of Sir Henry's activities, and fresh material will come to light when the REED project finally accomplishes its goal of publishing all the provincial drama records to 1642. The evidence given here is taken mostly from printed sources, though in a few cases (e.g. Norwich) the originals have been examined.

There must, however, have been many travelling showmen of whom no detailed record survives. At Oxford, for example, players and showmen were permitted only during the week in July when the 'Act' took place, an academic ceremony involving public disputations. Thomas Crosfield, fellow of Queen's College, sometimes listed these shows in his diary, usually without naming the performers involved, as in the entry for 11 July 1631:

Things to be seene for money in ye City. 1. Playes. 2. dancing upon ye Rope & vaulting upon ye sadle. 3. virginalls & organs playing by themselves. 4. a dutch-wench all hairy & rough upon her body. 5. The history of some parts of ye bible, as of ye creation of ye world, Abrahams sacrificing his sonne, Nineveh beseiged & taken, Dives & Lazarus. 6. The Dancing of ye horse at ye Starre.[1]

A similar list was included in William Cartwright's poem addressed to Brian Duppa, '*immediately after the Publick Act at* Oxon. *1634*':

> For had you not among our Gowns been seen
> Enlivening all, *Oxford* had only been
> A Peopled Village, and our *Act* at best
> A Learned *Wake*, or Glorious shepheards feast:
> Where (in my Judgement) the best thing to see
> Had been *Jerusalem* or *Nineveh*,
> Where, for true Exercise, none could surpass
> The Puppets, and *Great Britaines Looking Glass*.
> Nor are those names unusuall; *July* here
> Doth put forth all th' Inventions of the year:
> Rare Works, and rarer Beasts do meet; we see
> In the same street *Africk* and *Germany*.
> Trumpets 'gainst Trumpets blow, the Faction's much,
> These cry the Monster-Masters, Those the *Dutch*:
> All Arts find welcome, all men come to do
> Their Trickes and slights; Juglers, and *Curats* too.[2]

(The italicized words in the sixth and eighth lines are the titles of puppet-shows.)

Contemporary writers refer to the activities of showmen in terms which suggest that their readers would automatically be familiar with them (much as most people, until fairly recently, would have known what a Punch and Judy show was like). Bentley quotes from a complaint by Henry Farley, published in 1621, against the frivolity of Londoners:

> To see a strange out-landish Fowle,
> A quaint Baboon, an Ape, an Owle,
> A dancing Beare, a Gyants bone,
> A foolish Ingin moue alone,
> A Morris-dance, a Puppit play,
> Mad *Tom* to sing a Roundelay,
> A Woman dancing on a Rope,
> Bull-baiting also at the *Hope*;
> A Rimers Iests, a Iuglers cheats,
> A Tumbler shewing cunning feats,
> Or Players acting on the Stage,
> There goes the bounty of our Age:
>   But vnto any pious motion,
>   There's little coine, and lesse deuotion.[3]

This could be linked to Sir William Davenant's burlesque poem *The Long Vacation in London*, probably written in the middle 1630s:

> Now Vaulter good, and dancing Lass
> On Rope, and Man that cryes hey pass,
> And Tumbler young that needs but stoop,
> Lay head to heel to creep through Hoope;
> And Man in Chimney hid to dress,
> Puppit that acts our old Queen *Bess*,
> And man that whilst the Puppits play,
> Through Nose expoundeth what they say:
> And Man that does in Chest include
> Old *Sodom* and *Gomorrah* lewd:
> And white Oate-eater that does dwell
> In Stable small at Sign of *Bell*,
> That lifts up hoofe to show the prancks,
> Taught by Magitian, stiled *Banks*;
> And Ape, led Captive still in Chaine,
> Till he renounce the Pope and *Spaine*.
> All these on hoof now trudge from Town,
> To cheat poor Turnep-eating Clown.[4]

The last couplet indicates that entertainers would leave London during the long vacation in order to tour the countryside.

   Some performers, on the other hand, became so notorious that it is perhaps a little surprising not to encounter them among Sir Henry's records. One example is the celebrated juggler and conjuror who went by the stage-name of Hocus-Pocus.[5] Thomas Ady praised his skill as a juggler:

I will speak of one man more excelling in that craft than others, that went about in King *James* his time, and long since, who called himself, *The Kings Majesties most excellent Hocus Pocus*, and so was he called, because that at the playing of every Trick, he used to say *Hocus pocus, tontus talontus, vade celeriter jubeo*, a dark composure of words, to blinde the eyes of the beholders, to make his Trick pass the more currantly without discovery.[6]

He performed at Oxford in 1634 and 1635,[7] and at Coventry in 1638.[8] He may have died by 1650, as a jocular epitaph on him appeared in the edition of *Wit's Recreations* published in that year.[9] Jonson alluded to him or his catch-phrase three times,[10] and poems by or attributed to John Cleveland testify to his popularity and indicate the kind of trick he performed. According to 'The Rebel Scot',

> Before a *Scot* can properly be curst,
> I must (like *Hocus*) swallow daggers first.[11]

The satirical poem 'On an Alderman who married a very young wife' describes the spittle that hangs from his mouth,

> Like *Hocus* Pocus when hee draws
> Some yards of riband through his throat.[12]

His name even figures in political controversy: Archbishop Laud was infuriated when an opponent jeeringly called him 'the little meddling hocus-pocus', and insisted that he be severely punished.[13]

As these quotations reveal, the showmen's activities were extremely varied. One large group carried out what were termed 'feats of activity'—rope-dancing, vaulting, tumbling, and juggling. Frequently one man combined several of these activities. William Vincent obtained in December 1627

A license vnder the Signett . . . wth the rest of his Company to exercise and practize the Arte of Legerdemain w[th] all his other feates of activitie, As Vaulting, danceing on the ropes for his best Comoditie in any Convenient place W[th]in any his Ma[tes]. Dominions, Any provinciall Lawe or any other lawe or Restraint whatsoeuer to the contrary notw[th]standing.[14]

He appeared in a variety of towns between 1622 and 1642—Leicester, Coventry, Norwich, and Gloucester—and is probably the 'Vincent' who danced on the ropes at the Fortune Theatre in March 1635 (315).

The Peadle family of rope-dancers included at least two generations of performers whose careers extended between 1609 or earlier and 1639.[15]

Another common form of 'activity' was fencing; usually two fencers would arrange to 'play a prize'—in other words, carry out a fencing match with a variety of weapons. This does not figure among the surviving records of Sir Henry as often as we might expect, though we do know from the Coventry records that fencers appeared there in 1616, 1623, and 1628.[16] Astley and Herbert, however, licensed fencers to appear at several of the London theatres (24, 26, 33, and 233), and it was normal for rope-dancers, vaulters, and fencers to appear on the London stage, particularly during Lent.[17] With the performers already mentioned we might include such showmen as Thomas Barrell, who was licensed to 'toss a pike' (45), and Peter Wise, a German who showed 'certaine feates of charging and discharging a gun' (249).

Another large group of showmen performed 'motions' or puppet-plays. It looks as though the best puppets were imported from Italy, so most of the puppeteers claimed to be operating an 'Italian motion' (e.g. 48, 278, and 336); in 1639 one unfortunate showman was refused permission to perform in Norwich when he admitted that his motion was not genuinely Italian (400). These shows could be surprisingly elaborate; if 'the Caos of the world' licensed to William Sands and others by Sir Henry in 1623 (25) corresponds to 'yᵉ sight call'd Chaos' presented at Oxford in 1628 and described in detail by Crosfield,[18] it consisted of several Old and New Testament scenes, almost like a miniature mystery cycle. Old Testament scenes, particularly more spectacular events like the destruction of Sodom and Gomorrah, were extremely popular, but more recent history was not ignored: Leather-head, the puppeteer in Jonson's *Bartholomew Fair*, regarded *The Gunpowder Plot* as the best 'get-penny' in his repertoire.[19]

There were also numerous 'sights' and 'shows', presumably exhibited inside a booth or tent and visible only on payment of an entrance fee (though a crude picture of the show might be hung up outside in order to tempt the audience). There were, for example, waxworks of contemporary celebrities—'pictures in wax of the King of Sweden and others' (263) and probably 'the portraiture of the King of Bohemia, his queene and Children' shown at Coventry in 1630.[20] (This last item may help to explain Crosfield's brief reference to 'The Palsgrave's family' as one of the sights available in Oxford in 1634.[21]) The 'sight of the portraiture of *Antwerpe*', shown at Coventry in 1633, may simply have been a scale model of a famous foreign city, intended to give an idea of what it looked like to those who were unlikely to visit it.[22] But 'the portraiture of the City of Ierusalem' (**317** and **352**) is more uncertain: both items clearly refer to the spectacle described by Crosfield as having been shown at Oxford in July 1634: 'Hierusalem in it's glory, destruction—The Story devided into 5 or 6 parts, invented by Mr Gosling, sometimes schollar to Mr Camden, Enginer'.[23] This may have been, as Boas thought,[24] some kind of puppet-show, or possibly a working model exhibiting the siege and capture of Jerusalem by the Romans in AD 70.

Frequently the sights were of 'monsters', human beings with some genetic defect or deformity, a display which would now seem intolerably insensitive. Humfry Bromley showed 'A strange Child with two heads' at Norwich in 1616,[25] and was licensed 'to show a childe with 3 heads' in 1627 (**175**). Balthazar Ursty was licensed in 1633 to show a woman 'overgrown with Heare from the face to the foote' (**250**), who may possibly have been the 'dutch-wench all hairy & rough upon her body' who appeared at Oxford two years earlier.[26] The 'child borne without Armes' shown at Coventry in 1637 was merely pathetic,[27] but Mrs Adrian Provoe, 'a woman without hands' who visited Norwich in July 1633, was able to perform 'diverse workes &c done wth her feete' (**261**). The most striking exhibit was a pair of Siamese twins from Genoa, Lazarus and Baptista Colloretti or Colloredo (**369**). Lazarus, who was perfectly formed, was attached by the navel to his smaller brother Baptista, who was not fully developed physically or mentally. They visited Aberdeen in April 1642, and a contemporary observer gave a vivid account of them:

When he cam to the toune he had tuo seruandis avaiting vpone him, who with him self were weill clad. He had his portraiture with the monster drawin, and hung out at his lodging, to the view of the people. The one seruand had ane trumpettour who soundit at suche tyme as the people sould cum and sie this monster, who flocked aboundantlie into his lodging. The vther seruand receaved the moneyis fra ilk persone for his sight, sum less sum mair. And efter there wes so muche collectit as culd be gottin, he, with his seruandis, schortlie left the toun, and went southuard agane.[28]

The twins could be described as international celebrities: poems were written about them, and they feature in medical treatises of the time.

There were plenty of animals on show, usually of a rare or exotic nature—an elephant (**44**), a camel (**234**), two dromedaries (**300**), and 'an outlandish creature, called a Possum' (**387**). Fish were exhibited, usually designated 'strange fish' (**236** and **345**); Malone printed the first of these licences in his commentary to *The Tempest* because of its obvious relevance to Trinculo's speech at 2. 2. 24–35. Other animals would have come into the category of 'monsters': 'a Ramme with 4 horns' (46), and 'a Sow with 6 Leggs' shown at Coventry in 1639.[29] Some animals, especially horses, were trained to perform, like the 'bay nagge wch can shewe strange feats' that came to Norwich in 1624 (124).[30] We are inevitably reminded of the celebrated William Banks and his performing horse Morocco, though by 1623 Banks had retired as a showman, and from 1637 onwards was landlord of a tavern in Cheapside.[31]

Other miscellaneous shows and devices were recorded from time to time. The waterworks shown at Norwich in September and October 1635 (327) may have been some kind of ornamental fountain, though it is just possible that they were hydraulically operated puppets ('a shewe of puppets by water-workes' was allowed at Norwich on 6 January 1670/1[32]). Bartholomew Cloyse (see 51 n.) played an organ embellished with mechanical puppets, and appears several times in the records between 1623 and 1634. Cloyse may have exhibited other devices as well; when he visited Norwich in May 1634, he had six assistants to help him operate 'diverse rare engins' (296). For one other category of showman, the mountebank, the evidence is scantier than might be expected; Chalmers preserved the names of two, Francis Nicolini and John Puncteus (440r, s). Their companies could be quite large (Puncteus had ten assistants), and it is clear from later evidence that they put on spectacular shows to draw in a large audience before attempting to sell their drugs.

Many of the activities listed above were in existence long before the seventeenth century, and wandering entertainers of various kinds were very common in the later Middle Ages. The evidence is too plentiful to be given in full; if we look only at London in the second half of the sixteenth century we find, for example, the Court of Aldermen on 16 November 1568 forbidding 'Iohn Rose of brydwell' to show his puppets.[33] On 14 July 1573 the Privy Council ordered the Lord Mayor 'to permitte libertie to certein Italian plaiers to make shewe of an instrument of strainge motiones within the Citie'; but the Lord Mayor failed to do so, and the Council had to write again on 19 July, 'merveling that he did it not at their first request'.[34] A year or so later Thomas Norton drew up regulations for dealing with the plague in London, which included the banning of sights and shows which would draw people together. Norton mentioned with particular horror 'the unchaste, shamelesse and unnaturall tomblinge of the Italion Weo-men'.[35] On 17 October 1588, at the request of Sir Thomas Heneage, the Court of Aldermen permitted 'Henricke Iohnson of Vtright' to 'make shewe of an artificiall motion of his owne devise'.[36] It is possible, however, that the number of miscellaneous entertainers expanded in the early seventeenth century. In his transcript of the Coventry records Murray noted that 'from 1615–16 on, the number of puppet-shows, art and skill men, wonder exhibitors, etc., increases'.[37] The editor of the Norwich records from 1540 to 1642, David Galloway, points out that references to travelling entertainers are very few in the first half of the period covered, but increase strikingly in the second half.[38]

It would certainly be a mistake, however, to assume that Sir Henry was the first Master of the Revels to license miscellaneous shows, as Bentley seems to imply when he claims that Sir Henry 'extended his function as Master of the Revels to the licensing of odd variety shows as well as of plays'.[39] In 1600 John Wheately produced at Norwich a licence issued by Tyllney 'for the shewinge of a beast called A Basehooke'.[40] Copies of two licences issued by the scholarly Sir George Buc still survive, one dated 1610 for showing 'a strange lion, brought to doo strange things, as turning an oxe to be rosted &c.', and another dated 1619 for 'certayne rare motions, viz. the *Creation of the World*, the *Conspiracy of Gunpowder Treason under the Parliament House*, the *Destruction of Sodome and Gomorha*, and the *Storie of Dives & Lazarus*'.[41] Other licences by Buc were produced at Norwich, one dated 1614 permitting 'Ciprian de Roson with his wife & two assistantes . . . to shewe feates of actiuity together with A beast Called an Elke' and another dated 26 June 1618 'for the shewynge of one Peter williams a man monstrously deformed'.[42] During his brief tenure of the mastership Sir John Astley issued at least one licence of this kind, 'to shewe a monster haveinge six toes on a foote & six fingers on his hand' (**17**).

Travelling players needed two licensing documents: a royal warrant authorizing them to exist as a company of actors and a confirmation of this warrant from the revels office, which had to be renewed annually. Travelling showmen seem to have required only a licence from Sir Henry, renewable at yearly or six-monthly intervals, though some of them also had a royal warrant (e.g. **331** and **369**). The performers needed to show these documents to the authorities of the towns they visited, and should theoretically have had no difficulty in receiving permission to perform, but in practice all sorts of complications arose. Perhaps the major problem was that the local authorities were often deeply reluctant to allow players and showmen into their towns, for a variety of reasons. They feared that the shows would generate unruly behaviour, and also saw them as potential disturbers of the usual rhythms of commercial activity, by distracting the members of the audience from their normal work. (There were arguments, which occasionally seem hypocritical, that men would waste on entertainments money that should have gone to support their families.) In times of plague the coming together of a local audience and strangers from outside might aid the spread of the disease. There was also among many of the senior townsmen a puritanical dislike of diversions and amusements, though this rarely becomes explicit.

The result was a battle of wits in which the local authorities did their best to refuse permission; sometimes they succeeded, and the performers were sent away empty-handed, but at other times the performers proved so obstinate that the authorities eventually gave way. On 22 October 1634 a group showing feats of activity was refused permission to perform at Norwich because of an outbreak of smallpox, but at the last moment, for reasons unknown, the authorities relented and allowed a strictly limited number of performances, which the group promised to respect (304). One way of preventing shows and plays, which became increasingly prevalent in the 1630s, was to offer the players what was called a 'gratuity', with sums ranging from ten shillings to £3, on the explicit understanding that they were being paid not to perform. Usually the players were willing to accept an assured gain which required no effort, though sometimes they pocketed the money and then gave a performance notwithstanding.[43]

It has to be said that the arrival of as many as a dozen or more showmen in a relatively small community could cause considerable disturbance. At a quarter sessions court held in Bridport, Dorset, in October 1630, complaint was reported 'that William Sands the elder Iohn Sands and William Sands the younger doe wander vp and downe the Countrey and about nine others of their Company w:th certaine blasphemous shewes and sights wch they exercise by way of poppett playinge'.[44] (The 'blasphemous shewes' were presumably the biblical scenes which Crosfield saw two years earlier.) They were currently at Beaminster, and the constable of the town and other inhabitants complained that they performed

not only in the day tyme but alsoe late in the night to the great disturbance
of the Townsmen there, and the greivance of diu⟨er⟩s of the In⟨ha⟩bitants who
cannot keepe their children and servants in their houses by reason that they
frequent the said shewes and sights late in the night in a disorderly manner.

John Sands was particularly troublesome. It appears that the local
preacher inveighed against the puppeteers in his Sunday sermon, and
John Sands and two other members of the company pursued him
'from the Church to his house and entred the said house and there
Challenged him for his sermon and gave him Threateninge speeches'.
Two days later, on Tuesday evening, there was a brawl between John
Sands and 'a disorderly inhabitant', 'the said Iohn runninge in a
forcible manner into a Townsmans house there to the frightinge of
the people of the same house'. Not surprisingly, the court ordered the
whole company to leave the county, threatening them with arrest and
trial if they returned and put on their shows.

A problem that affected both the local authorities and the Master of
the Revels was the use of spurious or invalid licences—in some cases,
expired licences whose date had been fraudulently altered. The
showmen resented being obliged to pay what they regarded as
extortionate fees to the revels office. When Henry Miller and his four
assistants produced their revels patent at Norwich in 1632, one of
them commented sourly that 'they payd dere for their patent' (239).
Presumably two fees had to be paid, one to Sir Henry himself and
another to his secretary for writing out and sealing the document. In
1639 a certain John Rawlyns or Rawlings paid an innkeeper named
Long one shilling to forge new dates on his patent because he could
not have it renewed officially for less than thirty shillings, though the
alterations must have been clumsily done and were easily detected
(401).

There were other ways in which warrants and licences, which may
have been perfectly genuine to begin with, were used fraudulently. If
a large company which had been granted a licence subsequently split
up, the individual members might arrange for copies of the licence to
be made so that they could function independently. (These were
termed 'exemplifications', in *OED*'s sense 3, 'an attested copy of or
transcript of a record, deed, etc.') But the authorities in London
strongly disliked this multiplication of copies, for which no official
approval had been granted and no fee had been paid. A particularly
striking series of abuses came to light early in 1616, and on 16 July
1616 the Lord Chamberlain wrote a circular letter to the local

authorities ordering them to confiscate these 'exemplifications or duplicates', sending them to him, and to ensure that the actors named in his letter appeared before him in London. Pembroke's letter survives only because it was copied into the Norwich records.[45] It was handed to the mayor by a certain Henry Sebeck on 4 June 1617, and three days later Sebeck was given permission for his own company to act by virtue of a licence granted to John Townsend and Joseph Moore. It is ironical that Bentley is suspicious about this transaction, since Sebeck is not otherwise known in dramatic records, and suggests that 'possibly he had obtained the company's licence illegitimately'.[46] Perhaps Sebeck reckoned that if he had the impudence to produce the Lord Chamberlain's letter, no one would suspect him of fraudulent behaviour.

Licences were regarded by showmen, though not by the licensing authorities, as valuable documents which could be hired or sold. A striking example occurred at Banbury in May 1633, when a group of showmen arrived at the town with a puppet-show, a patent under the Privy Seal, and a commission from the Master of the Revels. Banbury was notorious for its Puritan sympathies, and the local authorities, who seem to have been suspicious from the beginning, discovered that the date on the commission had been altered (253a). They imprisoned and interrogated the players, who revealed that the leader of the troupe, Richard Bradshaw, who was not present, had obtained both the show and the licence from a certain Edward Whiting. Accounts of the transaction varied from witness to witness; the most complicated, and in Bentley's view probably the most trustworthy,[47] version came from Richard Houghton, who said

that he hath heard that Edward Whitinge lett the Comission nowe in question vnto one Wm Cooke and ffluellen Morgan, and they twoe went with it wth a puppett play vntell they had spent all, then they pawned the said Comission for fowre shillings, Mr Bradshawe hearinge of it redeemed it and afterwards bought it of Edward Whitinge.[48]

A member of the company described himself as Richard Whiting, son of Edward, but on re-examination it became clear that his name was Richard Johnson. The mayor and justices of Banbury complained, not to the Master of the Revels, but to the Privy Council, which ordered the players to be sent to London, but did not apparently subject them to any very severe punishment.[49]

The fraudulent use of licences may have increased in the later years of King James's reign; Pembroke's letter of 1616 was followed by a more comprehensive circular, issued on behalf of Sir John Astley on 20 November 1622 (Appendix A8). This ordered local authorities to scrutinize all licences, sending any which appeared dubious to Sir John, and to suppress all shows not properly licensed by the Master. Like the previous document, it survives only in a transcript made at Norwich, but Sir Henry must have had a copy, since he arranged for it to be reissued on his own behalf on 31 July 1661 (R28). It looks as though the 1622 circular was widely distributed, since Sir Henry invoked its authority in the licences he issued (Appendix B1–3) ordering local authorities to confiscate and send him any dubious licences, a feature not to be found on the two surviving licences issued by Sir George Buc.

In these matters Sir Henry Herbert had to maintain a delicate balance. His main concern, it would appear, was to ensure that his fees were paid: one of the witnesses at Banbury, who admitted that the date on the revels office commission had been erased and a new one inserted, claimed that 'the m^r of the Reuells will giue allowance to the said Raysinge yf he may be paied for it' (253b). He was willing to confirm an exemplification of a company patent in March 1624 on the understanding that 'Mr. Biston' (Christopher Beeston) guaranteed eventual payment of the fee (86). He could not allow local officials to defy his authority, and on 18 October 1631 the Lord Chamberlain issued a warrant for the arrest of '*Iohn Platt* a Cunstable in *Ware*' for forbidding players to perform in the town despite their possession of a valid revels licence (223). But Sir Henry could not afford to be too high-handed; on 15 March 1641 he wrote to the mayor of Norwich authorizing a complete ban on players in the city, though what precisely lay behind this action cannot now be determined (422).

The activities of travelling entertainers declined abruptly after Sir Henry closed his office-book in 1642 (there appear to be no entries relating to them in the Norwich records during the interregnum, but plenty after the Restoration). Lacking the support of the Master of the Revels, the showmen could easily be suppressed in the provinces, though it seems that to some extent they managed to keep going in London. Puppet-plays continued to be performed at Bartholomew Fair,[50] and John Evelyn saw a variety of spectacles in London after his return from France to England in 1652: a group of strange and deformed animals on 13 February 1654 and a rope-dancer called the Turk and a strikingly hairy woman on 15–16 September 1657. Sir Henry, of course, received no fees for any of this.

The Restoration

At the restoration of King Charles II Herbert moved rapidly to resume his former powers as Master of the Revels. The King returned to England on 25 May 1660; Herbert was sworn in as a Gentleman of the Privy Chamber on 31 May, and as Master of the Revels on 20 June.[1] He assumed, no doubt, that theatrical affairs would be run as they had been before 1642; but it was soon clear that this was not going to be the case, and he never recovered more than a fraction of the control he had exercised earlier. What exactly went on in the theatrical world of the early 1660s, particularly in 1660 itself, is open to debate, because the evidence is limited and can be variously interpreted. The account that follows is in line with the views of most modern scholars, and it necessarily concentrates on events directly involving Sir Henry himself.

In the early summer of 1660 three theatres survived from those that had been closed down in 1642, and were naturally the focus for attempts to revive the drama. At the Red Bull, a large public theatre, a company of older actors was led by Michael Mohun. The other two were private theatres. At the Cockpit, or Phoenix, in Drury Lane, John Rhodes brought together a company of young actors; though inexperienced, several of them, particularly Thomas Betterton, eventually became famous for their skill. The third theatre, the Salisbury Court, was in poor condition, because the interior had been wrecked by parliamentary soldiers in 1649, and William Beeston needed to arrange for extensive repairs, which were supposed to be finished by 24 June 1660.[2] Herbert's warrant to Beeston (**R1**) authorizing him to use the building as a playhouse was probably issued near this time. By 20 August Beeston had established a company of players at his theatre, though their identities have not been definitely established.[3]

Herbert treated the three companies as he had done those existing before 1642, ordering them to pay him fees and a weekly allowance. On 14 August Mohun's company at the Red Bull submitted to Herbert's authority (**R6**). They agreed to pay him £10, presumably to cover the acting they had already done, and from then on to make payment of £2 for a new play and £1 for a revived one, as well as a regular fee of £4 per week. Hotson notes the significant phrase at the end of the agreement, 'dureing the time of acting vnder the said master of the Revells', with its implication that the actors were not sure how much longer the Master would retain his authority.[4] Two later documents by Herbert (**R35** and **R38**) refer back to this agreement, though dating it at 11 August, perhaps by a slip of memory. The second of these papers also claims that Herbert had made similar agreements with Rhodes and Beeston.

At the same time, however, transactions were taking place which would undermine Herbert's authority. At some point in the early summer of 1660, Sir William Davenant and Thomas Killigrew came to an understanding that they would try to persuade the King to grant them a total monopoly of theatrical activities in London. Davenant had experience as a dramatist going back to 1626 or early 1627, as a theatre-manager for a short while in 1640–1, and as a producer of operas, with singing, dancing, and expensive scenery, in the last years of the interregnum. He had also been issued, by Charles I on 26 March 1639, a patent to erect his own theatre, which would offer not only plays, but 'Musick, musical Presentments, Scenes, Dancing or other the like'.[5] But there was strong opposition to the grant, and Davenant was forced to sign what virtually amounted to a renunciation of it,[6] although, as we shall see, the original grant was still considered valid in 1660. Killigrew was a dramatist, though he had no managerial experience, and, perhaps more important, a friend of the King, who found him an amusing companion and was indulgent to his wishes. Davenant and Killigrew were not close friends. When Killigrew came to an agreement with Herbert on 4 June 1662 (**R35**), he promised to do nothing to help Davenant, who was still at odds with Herbert; but in 1660 they were prepared to collaborate with ruthless self-interest.

On 9 July 1660 a royal warrant was sent to the Attorney-General, Sir Geoffrey Palmer, authorizing him to prepare a licence for Killigrew to set up a company of players, over whom he would have absolute control.[7] The grant also referred to a second company that Davenant was entitled to establish by virtue of his patent of 1639, and laid down that all companies other than these two would be 'sylenced and surprest'. Davenant prepared a draft for another version of the warrant addressed to Palmer, dated 19 July, in which he gave equal weight to himself and Killigrew.[8] Palmer seems to have been reluctant to issue the grant, but when challenged, he explained, in a letter to the King of 12 August, that he thought 'the matter was more proper for A tolleration; then A Grant under the greate Seale of England',[9] but otherwise had no particular objection. On 21 August the grant was issued (**R8**), much of it in the words drafted by Davenant. All three papers, of 9 and 19 July and 21 August, had argued with gross hypocrisy that the grant of a monopoly was needed because of the prevailing licentiousness and profanity of the stage, and in the third paper a provision was added instructing Davenant and Killigrew not to perform anything offensive, and to examine and censor all existing plays.

Sir Henry must have found out about the documents prepared in July, and on or before 14 August petitioned the King to revoke the grant or at least refer it to arbitration by the Attorney-General (**R4**). Davenant and Killigrew had apparently given the King the impression that Herbert had consented to the grant, but Herbert indignantly repudiated this bit of sharp practice, and complained that the grant would destroy the traditional powers given to him as Master of the Revels under the Great Seal of England. Somewhat maliciously he pointed out that Davenant had obtained permission from Oliver and Richard Cromwell to produce his operas in the 1650s. Palmer was instructed to arbitrate, and saw the parties to the case separately; but when he arranged a time for them all to meet, Davenant and Killigrew did not bother to attend. Palmer also noted that Davenant had written a letter informing him that he need take no further action in the matter. Why Davenant did so is not clear: the most likely explanation is that the letter was written after 21 August, and that with the King's authority behind him Davenant felt that he could safely treat Herbert's objections with contemptuous indifference.

Davenant and Killigrew lost no time in trying to coerce the existing companies of players into submission. A draft exists dated 20 August for a royal warrant ordering the complete suppression of all theatrical activity. It is in Davenant's own hand, and Hotson argues that it was merely a project by him which never took effect.[10] But the grant made on the following day (**R8**) concludes with reference to 'any former order or direction by vs Giuen, for the suppressing of Playhouses and playes or any other entertainments of the Stage', and in Davenant and Killigrew's petition of 16 January 1661/2 (**R31**) there is a specific reference to the suppression order of 20 August 1660 which suggests that it was formally issued, though it does not in fact appear to have put an end to playing. Apparently Herbert had got the players to agree to pay him fees on the grounds that he would protect them against Killigrew (**R17**), but the two courtiers had more recent and more powerful documents of authority which the players were not able to resist. It is hard not to feel some sympathy for the acting companies, anxious to remain as independent as possible, but placed between, on the one side, Herbert, determined to extort his customary fees, and on the other, Davenant and Killigrew, poised to take over and dominate them.

Herbert's own resentment is easy to understand. Nothing was said about him in the royal documents of July and August, but their provisions effectively wiped out his *raison d'être* as Master of the Revels. With only two companies, under the full control of Davenant and Killigrew, who also had powers to censor plays, there was nothing left for Herbert to do as far as the London stage was concerned. Even the failure to mention him might have been construed as a snub, since in company licences in the early seventeenth century it was normal to include a paragraph explicitly reserving and protecting the powers of the Master (see Appendix A17 and Herbert's reference to the practice in R29). Davenant and Killigrew, of course, did not want an outsider taking a share in their profits, and would have been glad to squeeze Herbert out. But he was nothing if not tenacious, and a battle ensued which was not fully resolved until two years later.

It looks as though the agreement between Herbert and Mohun's company at the Red Bull lasted for less than a month: by 10 September the company had stopped paying his fees, and regarded themselves as no longer under his control, though they continued to perform.[11] What else happened in September 1660 cannot be fully reconstructed for lack of evidence,[12] but by early October Davenant and Killigrew had put together a new company of actors selected from all three earlier companies, which began playing at the Cockpit on 8 October. Herbert responded rapidly. On the same day he peremptorily ordered Rhodes, the lessee of the Cockpit, to produce his authority for using the building as a theatre (R13). Two days later Rhodes replied 'That the Kinge did authorise Him'. On 13 October Herbert fired off a letter to Mohun, as the leading actor of the Cockpit company, ordering him not to charge exorbitant prices (R16). Herbert's main motive was to outflank Davenant and Killigrew, who had used overcharging as an excuse to discipline the actors. (The use of terms like 'Restrainte' and 'Liberty' suggests that Davenant and Killigrew went so far as to imprison the actors.[13]) As an afterthought he added in his own hand a demand that the actors should submit to him for censorship all old plays they intended to revive.

The players were tired of being at the centre of a tug of war, and desperately petitioned the King for relief, apparently on the same day as Herbert's letter to Mohun (R17). This is an important document, but unfortunately survives only in a copy prepared for Herbert which has suffered water damage. Some words are missing, and others barely legible, and the transcripts of Malone and Halliwell-Phillipps are not entirely reliable. The petition seems to refer to two separate periods during which the company had been suppressed, though neither is precisely dated. The first, instigated by Killigrew, was presumably when Mohun's independent company was performing at the Red Bull, and led to the agreement of 14 August by which Herbert promised to protect them against Killigrew in return for the payment of fees. The second was later, and Killigrew kept them closed down so long that they were forced to give in and agree, though apparently with great reluctance, 'to Act with Woemen a new Theatre and Habitts according to our Scaenes' (R17). The second half of the paper is obscurely worded, but the actors seem to be asking the King to note that the date of the second warrant suppressing them is after the date of the contract with Herbert, so that in effect he has broken the contract by failing to protect them. But Herbert still wants his fees, and is trying to have the actors arrested.

What response the King made, if any, is not recorded, but Herbert persisted in his campaign. On 16 October he obtained writs against Mohun and against Davenant and Killigrew in the Court of Common Pleas, thereby beginning a series of lawsuits, the details of which were discovered by Hotson.[14] They dragged on over the next two years, and more will be said of them in a moment. Davenant and Killigrew continued to extend their hold over the actors. The united company lasted for only a month or less; by early November they had been divided up, Killigrew taking over Mohun's company, now named the King's company, and Davenant taking over Rhodes's company of younger actors, now named the Duke of York's or simply Duke's company. Killigrew had already coerced his players into accepting his management, and on 8 November moved them into a newly installed theatre in Gibbons's Tennis Court, Vere Street, Clare Market. Herbert's records indicate that they opened with a performance of *Henry IV* (R40).

Davenant took longer to make his arrangements. On 5 November he drew up articles of agreement with Betterton and the other actors (R18); included as a third party was Henry Harris, here described as a 'painter' (presumably of stage scenery), though he was later more famous as an actor. (He was also appointed Yeoman of the Revels on 6 August 1663.[15]) For the time being the actors would continue to perform at the Salisbury Court theatre, apparently as an all-male company. When Davenant's theatre was ready, they would join with additional actors and (more important) actresses provided by Davenant, to form a new company under Davenant's control. The financial arrangements of the company were worked out in considerable detail. Davenant's new theatre was installed in Lisle's Tennis Court, Lincoln's Inn Fields, opening on 28 June 1661.

Herbert's multiple lawsuits had varied fortunes.[16] The action against Mohun and his company was tried in December 1661; Herbert received a cash award of £48 for fees owing to him, but no decision was made on larger issues of principle. The action against Davenant and Killigrew was tried before a jury on 3 February 1661/2; Davenant and Killigrew were acquitted, and on 26 May 1662 were awarded £25 and costs. Herbert had issued a writ against Davenant alone on 23 October 1661; and when the action was tried on 20 June 1662, Herbert won the case, and was awarded damages of £25. Perhaps emboldened by this, on 4 July he sent one of his messengers, Edward Thomas, with a writ to suppress Betterton and his company, but the infuriated players violently assaulted Thomas, and held him prisoner for two hours.[17]

It was obvious that affairs had reached a stalemate in which neither side could decisively defeat the other. Of the two theatre-managers Killigrew was the first to decide that it was best to buy off Sir Henry, who drafted an agreement to be made by the two of them on 4 June 1662 (R35). Herbert's right to licence-fees for plays was acknowledged, and Killigrew agreed to pay the costs of Herbert's lawsuits against the King's company (see also R39); but in exchange Herbert had to renounce any pretentions to control over the players. Davenant held out longer. Angry that judgment in the one lawsuit had gone for him and in the other against, he petitioned the King on or before 30 June to appoint arbitrators (R37). The Lord High Chancellor and the Lord Chamberlain met Herbert and Davenant on 9 July, and ordered Herbert to prepare a statement of his fees, which he submitted on 11 July (R38). No evidence has been discovered to show what happened next, but Herbert must have come to an agreement with Davenant similar to the one he had earlier made with Killigrew.

Letters patent under the Great Seal of England were issued to Killigrew on 25 April 1662 and to Davenant on 15 January 1662/3, authorizing them to organize two companies which would monopolize theatrical activities in London.[18] Both men were entitled to carry out their work 'without impeachment or impediment of any person or persons whatsoever'.[19] It was thus unmistakably clear that Herbert no longer had any power to intervene. There had, of course, been earlier signs that he was losing his old authority. On 20 August 1660 he drafted a warrant granting the petition of John Rogers (**R5**, 7), but the players refused to obey it, and Rogers was forced to petition the King a second time (**R11**). On 6 October 1660 Herbert wrote to the mayor of Maidstone, ordering him to respect the licence issued to a showman named Jacob Brewer, but the mayor and recorder insolently wrote back suggesting that the Master's power extended only to the verge of the court, prompting a furious reply from Herbert (**R12**, 14, 15). On 4 May 1661 he tried to arrest John Tradescant for showing 'strainge Cretures' without a licence, but Tradescant complained to the King, who decisively supported him (**R25–6**). (Nothing in the available evidence suggests any friendship between Charles II and his Master of the Revels, perhaps now regarded as an elderly relic of his father's court.)

It would seem that from 1660 onwards Herbert was less conscientious than before in keeping records. For example, he apparently abandoned the systematic use of an office-book, and relied on loose documents. (In the absence of the office-book this cannot be proved, but Malone never presented any Restoration evidence as coming from the office-book.) Play-lists such as **R40** are neither fully comprehensive nor reliable. Several times Pepys recorded other performances during the period covered of the plays mentioned, which Herbert ignored, or performances of plays not mentioned, and in the final section 1 June and 6 July 1662 are both Sundays, when no performance would have been given. The list seems to be an attempt at reconstruction rather than a careful record made at the time of performance.[20] It is hardly surprising that in the summer of 1663 Herbert arranged the appointment of Edward Hayward as his deputy, rather in the way that he himself had deputized for Astley. Hayward was not sworn in as Herbert's deputy until 23 December 1663,[21] but it looks as though he began work in July. There is a flurry of letters and papers from that month (**R45–9**), and in his letter to Killigrew of 29 March 1664 (**R53**) Hayward said that he had 'not enjoyed the employment above nine months'. There must have been a financial agreement between Hayward and Herbert, but the details have not come to light.

Nothing appears to be known of Edward Hayward apart from the documents preserved by Herbert. He emerges as earnest and conscientious, but also insecure, anxious to be introduced to an important

figure like the Lord Chamberlain, but worried that he might antag-
onize him by repeated pleas for help. A sentence in his memoranda
for a meeting with Sir Henry (**R47**) gives a revealing indication of his
approach: 'I intend to make a Diligent enquiry after the rights of the
office, & to contend soberly and cautiously for them.' At times he
appears to be racking his brains for any kind of activity, entertainment,
or relaxation which might be considered liable to pay fees to the revels
office, an extension of authority which would be beneficial not just to
himself but also to Sir Henry 'if hee survive mee' (**R47**). The Master
had traditionally licensed various kinds of travelling showmen, but
Hayward wanted to include billiards and ninepins, rural wakes or
feasts, and dancing schools, to avoid the evil of mixed dancing (**R53**).
It was pointless, however, to devise new sources of income when
mountebanks and lottery-men, who normally paid, refused to 'come
in', as Hayward put it, in other words appear at the revels office and
pay for a licence. The anticipated profits did not materialize, and
Hayward's tone became increasingly doleful, until in the final letter to
Johnson of 11 June 1664 (**R57**) Hayward asserted that it would be 'the
happiest dayes work that euer I made in this world to bee quitt of S^r
Harry and the office'.

In one area Herbert and Hayward collaborated to a small extent, that
of licensing plays for the press. On 17 September 1660 Herbert wrote
to the Stationers' Company imperiously asserting his right to license
plays for publication (Appendix **C84**). There was an element of bluff
in this; the official press-licenser from October 1660 to October 1663
was Sir John Berkenhead.[22] Plays which had been licensed for the press
by Berkenhead were entered in the Stationers' Register on 2 March
1662/3, 14 April 1663, and 24 October 1663. He was succeeded by Sir
Roger L'Estrange, under whose name John Wilson's *The Cheats* was
entered in the register on 9 November 1663. The Printing Act of 1662,
virtually a reissue of the Star Chamber decree of 1637, made no
mention of the Master of the Revels as an authorized licenser. On 25
July 1663 Hayward assembled a series of arguments designed to prove
that the Master ought to control the printing of plays (**R46**), but as
Greg pointed out,[23] the very form of his argument conceded that in
fact he had no power to do so. Despite his warrant to the Stationers
of September 1660, Herbert licensed no play for the press until 15
June 1663 (**C85**), and on 4 February 1663/4 he and Hayward jointly
licensed four more (**C86–9**). Whether or not this provoked a response,
from L'Estrange or anyone else, is not known; but it can hardly be

accidental that Hayward and Herbert were not named again in the Stationers' Register.

Another figure involved in revels affairs at this time was John Poyntz, but he was very different from Hayward. (We cannot imagine Hayward making a flamboyant gesture such as the conclusion of Poyntz's letter to Herbert of 15 August 1663, **R49**, promising fidelity 'till death seperates'.) He was several times described as 'Captain Poyntz', and was the naval captain who wrote to Pepys on 14 November 1664 describing his problems in pressing men for a ship called the *Maryland*.[24] In his *Diary* for 20 September, a couple of months earlier, Pepys recorded a meeting with Poyntz 'who hath some place, or title to a place, belonging to gaming; and so I discoursed with him about our business of improving of the Lotteries, for the King's benefit, and that of the Fishery, and had some light from him in the business'.[25] Poyntz's connection with the revels was, like Hayward's, by deputation. On 8 October 1642 a certain John Lloyd had been granted by the King a reversion to the office of Clerk-Comptroller of the Revels after Alexander Stafford, who served until the closing of the theatres.[26] When Stafford died is not known, but the reversion was obviously of no use to Lloyd during the interregnum. By the time of the Restoration, Lloyd must have decided not to exercise the office in person, and deputed it to Poyntz, as is made clear by Poyntz's licence for a shovelboard (**R50**).

Poyntz used his position much more aggressively than Hayward. He signed the licence prepared for George Bayley on 14 April 1662 (Appendix **B5**). On 26 April the Lord Chamberlain ordered him to be arrested for issuing warrants without authority (**R32**), but he continued to do so, and a second warrant was issued for his arrest on 18 June (**R36**). In one of the breviats prepared for use against Davenant (**R30**), Herbert complained that Davenant prohibited (presumably by means of threats and bluff) a certain 'Doctor Lambert', probably a mountebank, from taking out a revels licence; Lambert thereupon 'trauelled into the Countrey by Comission from John Pointz'. Herbert probably loathed Poyntz, and initiated at least one lawsuit against him (see **R47**, item 4). Poyntz's one letter to Herbert (**R49**) asks for forgiveness and reconciliation, but the tone of the letter is simultaneously arrogant and ingratiating, and Herbert cannot be blamed for mistrusting him. That there was some kind of collaboration between Hayward and Poyntz is indicated by their joint instructions to Edward Thomas of 23 July 1663 (**R45**), but Hayward's letter to Herbert a few days later (**R48**) shows that Hayward had not made a formal agreement with Poyntz, and was reluctant to do so until he had fully sorted out their respective powers and privileges. In December 1663 Hayward complained about Poyntz's 'Domineering carriage . . . in the office' (**R52**), and the two men quarrelled.

It looks as though Hayward and Poyntz, far from making a profit from their offices, were not even able to raise the sums they had agreed to pay Sir Henry. Early in 1665 announcements were published that both men had been dismissed from their offices, and that licences signed by them were no longer valid, which seems a little hard on the showmen who might recently have bought them in good faith (**R60** and **62**). Sir Henry was once again Master, though of course he could not recover the powers surrendered to Davenant and Killigrew in 1662. One remaining area was control over travelling players and showmen. (Davenant's behaviour over Doctor Lambert was probably harassment rather than a serious challenge to his authority.) As early as October 1660 Herbert claimed that he had already made 'several grants' of licences to showmen (**R15**), and he continued to do so into his last years, probably with the exception of the year and a half during which Hayward and Poyntz were his deputies. A main source of evidence for his activities is the splendid and detailed record kept in the Mayor's Court Books at Norwich, though he certainly did a great deal more which we know nothing about because of the failure of other towns and cities to keep similar records.

Travelling shows and entertainments sprang into life with the restoration of Charles II; so too did the old problems of keeping them under control. The main issue for Sir Henry was that showmen should obtain his licence and pay for it, and he was less inhibited than Hayward in getting warrants from the Lord Chamberlain to arrest showmen who failed to do so. Sometimes these methods worked. Thomas Cosby was ordered to be arrested on 29 August 1670 (**R84**), and a few weeks later, 2 October, he produced a licence from the revels at Norwich (**R89**). Thomas Russell, a mountebank, possessed a royal warrant under the signet, which he produced at Norwich on 17 October 1668 (**R79** n.), but he had no revels licence, and was ordered to be arrested by the same warrant on which Cosby was named (**R84**). Russell showed his royal warrant a second time at Norwich on 11 December 1672, and was permitted to perform, though there is no mention of a revels licence; perhaps he had managed to defy Sir Henry and get away with it (**R79** n.).

Many of the civic authorities were deeply reluctant to allow the showmen back again. As had happened in the past, the mayor and recorder of Maidstone used the 1598 version of the Elizabethan statute against rogues and vagabonds to justify themselves (**R14**), and may even have punished some of the showmen despite their possession of a revels licence (**R27 n.**). The authorities at Norwich were more circumspect; when a company of actors including Thomas Knowles performed 'twice or thrice' at the end of December 1660 'without allowance' (in other words, without obtaining permission from the corporation), they indignantly threatened to punish the actors if they played any more, and ordered them to leave the city (**R22**). But a week later the actors humbly apologized, and produced a commission from Sir Henry (**R23**), and the authorities were virtually powerless. In February 1661 Gabriel Shad was allowed to perform, but had to pay £5 for the poor of the city (**R24**), and this kind of payment became a regular condition of performance, either in a lump sum or as a certain amount for each day.

The complex negotiations that could take place between the authorities and a visiting showman are illustrated by a case in Norwich in November 1660. Some time before 1642 Herbert had licensed John Puncteus, a French mountebank with ten assistants (**440s**). The figure who appears at Norwich in 1660 is called Mr or Dr 'ponteers', but it is tempting to believe that the same person is involved, perhaps making a return journey to England after twenty or more years. On 14 November the mayor's court decided to send an order to 'ponteers' that 'neyther himselfe or servants doe shew them selfes vpon the stage or doe any feates or vaultinge vpon the rope'. This was because

they drawe together great multitudes of poore people who neglect ther worke & loose ther times wherby ther wifes & children doe suffer much & make great compleynt therof & other mens servants Iornymen & apprentices doe neglect ther worke And that yf he will continue any longer in the City that he onely practize [& sell] in his chamber.[27]

The doctor argued against this arrangement, and rather reluctantly he was allowed to use the stage 'vpon Satterday & monday next & no more & he is to give xl[s] for the poore'. Three days later, on 17 November, the doctor made a new proposal that the court could not resist:

This daye it was moved on the Behalfe of Doctor ponteers that he maye have liberty to staye in this City till the third daye of Dec next & that he or his servants maye Shew vpon the stage twice a week till that time that is to saye vpon the mondayes & Saterdayes & that for every of those dayes he will give to the Maior for the poore of the City twenty shillings wch request is condiscended vnto by the Court & liberty is given vnto him accordingly any form⟨er⟩ order to the contrary notwthstandinge.[28]

Four years later, on 17 September 1664, 'John Puntoeus Medicus' was allowed to set up his stage for six weeks, 'he payeinge 10^s. accordinge to his voluntarie promise'.[29] Ten shillings seems a small amount in return for six weeks; perhaps his business was not doing so well as before.

The Norwich authorities could not ban a performer with a royal warrant confirmed by the Master of the Revels, but they could perhaps reasonably expect to control the length of his stay. In 1663 they petitioned the King for powers of this kind, using arguments similar to those just quoted in the case of 'ponteers', and the King granted the petition on 11 July (**R44**). Charles's letter seems explicit enough, but cannot have had the desired effect, because late in 1669 the Norwich authorities mounted a fresh campaign, using Lord Arlington as an intermediary, to secure from the King what appears to be exactly the same grant.[30] The King responded favourably on 17 February 1669/70, and the reaction at Norwich is shown by an entry in the court book for 2 March:

This day his Maties. Gratious Letters directed to M^r Ma^{ior} ye S^herr: & Ald of y^s City authorizinge them & their successors to limitt ye stay of Players &^c in y^s City, wer produced by Mr Townclarke & read, and it is ordered that the s^d Letters be fayrely transcribed in a book & ye Original layd into ye Treasury. And that a lre of Thankes be sent to ye Ld Arlington for his Lo^p great fauor in obtayning the s^d Letters.[31]

Perhaps this grant was more successful than the previous one: subsequent permissions usually contain a firm and precise indication of how long the showman is allowed to perform.

The shows seem much as before—rope-dancers, puppeteers, displays of rare or performing animals, and so on. There were numerous other shows at Norwich between 1660 and 1673 which are not printed among the Restoration documents because they do not mention Sir Henry; these include 'a Dutch man of an extraordinary stature' and 'a Monstrous Woman Seaven foote & a halfe in Stature', a man showing 'feats of activity by dauncing vpon Crutches', and 'a Motion of Whittington & his Catt'.[32] One fresh activity, seemingly not mentioned in the records before 1642, is a form of lottery or raffle described in William Lyde's licence of 1 August 1662 as a 'Blank book containing Twelve Blanks to a Prize' (**B6**; cf. **R65** and **R67**). Presumably the book contained twelve tickets, one of which entitled the purchaser to a prize, described in one licence as 'plate plush ware & other ware' (**R69**).

One particular lottery, the Royal Oak lottery (mentioned in Hayward's letter of 21 December 1663, **R52**) had a charitable purpose, to provide relief for 'loyall and Indigent officers'[33]—in other words, royalist officers from the civil war who had fallen on hard times. But the men carrying round the lotteries, who sometimes bore military titles and may themselves have been 'Indigent officers', did not always behave soberly; on 11 March 1670/1 the Mayor's Court resolved 'That Mr Townclarke doe write to Mr Jay this post about the disorders & irregular howres that are Kept by ye persons that are employed by the Trustees for Lotteries towards the releife of Indigent Officers, that he may obteyne order to restraine them'.[34] What they had in mind is perhaps shown by an entry a few weeks earlier, 25 February, when Captain Thomas Walter was 'sent for and admonished not to suffer a Trumpet to be sounded after 8 of ye clock at night to call people to ye Lottery'.[35]

One other area in which Sir Henry retained some of his former powers was that of licensing and censoring plays. The latter may seem slightly surprising, in view of the fact that the warrants to Killigrew and Davenant of 25 April 1662 and 15 January 1662/3 both contain passages which suggest that the two men as governors of the companies would have the rights and duties of censorship:

Wee doe hereby strictly Comaund and Enioyne that from henceforth noe new Play shalbee acted by either of the said Companyes conteyning any passages offensiue to Pietye and good manners nor any old or revived Play conteyning any such offensive passage as aforesaid vntill the same shalbee corrected and purged by the said Masters or Governors of the said respectiue Companyes from all such offensive and scandalous passages as aforesaid.[36]

In addition, Herbert's draft agreement with Killigrew (**R35**) says nothing explicit about censorship. But it looks as though both Davenant and Killigrew were willing to leave the matter to Herbert. Though we have no evidence on the point, they may have felt that acting as censor was a tedious chore, and that if a censored play subsequently caused a scandal, it would be convenient to put the blame on Herbert. It would in any case seem rather pointless for Herbert to have power of licensing but not of censorship.

Five plays bearing Herbert's licence are known to survive from the Restoration, three of them bearing clear signs of his censorship. The first three are manuscripts, and the last two are printed texts which have been used as prompt-copies for a revival.

1. John Wilson, *The Cheats*, 6 March 1662/3, King's company (**R41**)
2. Edward Howard, *The Change of Crowns*, 13 April 1667, King's company (**R64**)
3. Elizabeth Polwhele, *The Faithful Virgins*, ?1670, Duke's company (**R100**)
4. William Cartwright, *The Ordinary*, 15 January 1671[?/2], Duke's company (**R93**)
5. William Cartwright, *The Lady Errant*, 9 March 1671[?/2], Duke's company (**R94**)

The first two gave rise to exactly the kind of problem that censorship was supposed to prevent.

The manuscript of Wilson's *The Cheats* was submitted to Herbert in March or April 1663, and he went through it making deletions in much the same way as he had earlier done with *The Launching of the Mary*. Words and short phrases were crossed out with a single pen-stroke; longer passages were underlined or marked with brackets or with small crosses in the margin and larger diagonal crosses in the text itself. Numerous oaths of the type of 'faith' (also 'I faith' and 'good faith'), 'troth', 'pox', and 'plague' were crossed out. So too were vulgarisms like 'fart' (1. 1. 20, altered possibly by Herbert himself to 'figg'), 'arse' (4. 1. 136), and 'plaquett' (2. 4. 99).[37] The last of these was an important rhyme-word in a song, and Wilson would have had to rewrite the whole stanza. Longer oaths were also cancelled, though it is hard to see anything strikingly offensive in such phrases as 'by this hand' (2. 4. 64), 'by the faith of A Souldier and a man of Armes' (4. 4. 94), or 'as Ime an Alderman' (5. 5. 120). At two places there were jeers at Welsh customs or the Welsh language (3. 3. 142–99 and 5. 1. 58–9); these perhaps offended Herbert because of his family background, and he crossed them out.

The major deletions were connected with a character named Scruple, a cunning and hypocritical Nonconformist minister whose speeches were deeply offensive to Herbert. Passages were deleted containing casuistry and obscenity at 2. 3. 80–110, obscenity at 4. 3. 18–22, and casuistry and simony through much of Act 5, scene 4. (In the last example Scruple debated whether to conform in order to obtain a church living of £300 a year.) But Herbert's main objection was to an earlier scene, Act 3, scene 5, in which Scruple was roused to preach an extemporary sermon to a few of his flock in which he urged them to remain faithful to the principles of the Solemn League and Covenant of 1643, and passionately ordered them to defend 'this good old Cause, wch yo^w haue Contended for wth soe much Treasure and blood' (3. 5. 75–7). At one point a reference to the sword being 'yet out of our hands' (lines 84–5) gave a sinister hint that they might take to arms if the opportunity arose. Herbert underlined much of the scene, and filled the margin with no fewer than nine fairly large crosses.

Herbert licensed the play on 6 March, and it was performed soon afterwards; but even if the deletions were scrupulously observed, that was not enough to prevent controversy. Wilson had satirized members of various callings and professions, attacking them as hypocrites, but the attacks were seen as directed at the professions themselves. The King was shown a short extract from the play, and responded that if there were nothing worse in it, the play could be acted, and it presumably continued to be performed. (There are no detailed records of performance earlier than the eighteenth century.) But the controversy continued, and on 22 March a letter was sent from the King to Killigrew 'Signifying ye K^s Pleasure that ye New Play called ye Cheates be no more represented till it be reueiwed by S^r Jo. Denham & Mr Waller'.[38] Identical letters were sent to Waller and Denham; the one to Waller is as follows:

S^r. His Ma^ty. being informed, that there ware in a new Comedy latly acted at ye Theater many things of a Scandalous & offensiue nature hath Comanded mee to signifie his Pleasure to you y^t you and S^r. John Denham immediatly send for ye saide new play and reading it over together, give jointly to his Ma^ty. yor. Opinions of it, that if there bee cause for it, it may be [suspended] suppressed y^e pretended approbation it is said to haue had from his Ma^ty, hauing I can assure you noe further ground thence That a matter of twenty or thirty \lines/ of it being showed him wch. had been excepted against his ma^ty. was pleased to say, if there bee nothing worse it may bee actted, adding further to the players; that their Company should take heed aswell in this as in all their other Playes to expose upon y^e Stage any thing y^t was either prophane, Scandalous or Scurrilous observing which they should be protected & no longer.[39]

How Waller and Denham responded to the play we do not know, but they seem to have censored it, especially the part of Scruple, sufficiently for performance to resume.[40]

Late in 1663 Wilson decided to publish the play, and it appeared bearing the date of 1664. Once again it had been censored, this time by Roger L'Estrange, whose imprimatur, dated 5 November 1663, is printed on the title-page. The text supplied by Wilson had been revised from the Worcester College manuscript at several points, which removed a few of the shorter phrases objected to by Herbert, but for the most part Wilson's revised text ignored the deletion-marks inserted by Herbert. The striking feature of L'Estrange's censorship is that he ordered no deletions at these points: all but a few of the words and passages found offensive by Herbert are in the 1664 Quarto, including the most inflammatory of Scruple's utterances. To Boas this proved that L'Estrange's principles of censorship were very different from those of Herbert;[41] Nahm preferred to argue that Wilson's reputation and status gave him immunity.[42] The former explanation seems more likely. Herbert's act of censorship was only the first of a series of three, and it had little permanent influence.

Edward Howard's *The Change of Crowns* had a strange fate, both in its stage history and in the survival of its text. Herbert licensed the play on 13 April 1667, and two days later Pepys reported on the first performance, a social event which attracted a crowded audience including the King, the Duke of York, and other members of the court. The main plot, a romantic story of love, intrigue, and disguise set in the court of Naples, delighted Pepys, but he was surprised by a kind of comic sub-plot concerning a character named Asinello, a naïve country gentleman, who has sold part of his estate in the country, and takes it for granted that he will be able to buy himself a position at court with the money, though he fails disastrously. The role was played by John Lacy, who had performed Scruple in Wilson's *The Cheats*; as Pepys put it: 'Lacy did act the country-gentleman come up to Court, who do abuse the Court with all the imaginable wit and plainness about selling of places, and doing everything for money.'[43] It looks as though Lacy expanded the part: a contemporary newsletter claimed that he added several indiscreet expressions on his own initiative.[44] The King was so furious 'at the liberty taken by Lacy's part to abuse him to his face'[45] that Lacy was arrested and the company closed down, though on the intervention of Mohun the company was allowed to play again, 'but not this play'.[46] Lacy's subsequent quarrel with Howard over who was responsible for the disaster need not concern us here.

The play was long thought to be lost, but a manuscript came to light which F. S. Boas transcribed and edited in 1949. Subsequently the manuscript temporarily disappeared, but photographs of it survived, and were reproduced by Langhans. (It recently reappeared, and is now in the Folger Shakespeare Library, Washington, where it is catalogued as MS V. b. 329). Herbert's licence occurs on the last page (**R64**), but it is not indisputably in Herbert's own hand,[47] and none of the revisions and other markings in the text can be attributed with certainty to Herbert. (There are, for example, no marginal crosses.) As it stands in the manuscript, the part of Asinello seems to contain nothing that the King would have found deeply insulting. Most of the scenes in which he appears are enclosed in rectangular marginal rules, as though for omission or revision, but they are of a type not used elsewhere by Herbert. Apparently folios 8–10 of the manuscript were substituted for two earlier folios, and this may represent the beginning of an attempt to revise the play after its first performance.[48] It does seem, however, that it was Lacy's impromptu remarks that caused the trouble, and no amount of censorship could have prevented this.

Relatively little is known about the background of *The Faithful Virgins*. The play is anonymous, and its probable authorship was not established until recently (see **R100** n.). It survives only as a manuscript in a uniform hand, possibly autograph, which derives from a lost copy bearing Sir Henry's licence and signs of censorship. The licence has been copied at the beginning of the play, but unfortunately the date has been omitted. This is immediately followed by a note, again in the scribal hand:

> the Chaster witts, say; that
> (luxury), must be pronounc'ed
> for letchery in the masque throughout.
> acording to the judgement off
>
>   Docter, A: C:[49]

This must refer to the masque in Act 3, in which Lechery is a character. Doctor 'A: C:' has not been identified.

At two points the scribe has reproduced censorship markings by Sir Henry. The first is in Act 1, scene 3. Cleophon loves Isabella and was betrothed to her, but she has left him and is about to marry the lecherous Duke of Tuscany. Cleophon rebukes her, and forecasts that her husband will not prove faithful:

> but 'twas vaine in mee
> + to thinck that ought but falshood dwelt in thee
> go shackle with the duke and be Admir'd
> till he is with som new sprung beauty fyr'd
> w^{ch}: will be swiftly Isabella hee;
> should haue been woman for vnconstancy
> × he must haue mistreses and often change
> And when a does, you must not thing [sic] it strange
> such shall the soule of Tuscany Comand
> Whilst a Scorn'd Wife Must as a Cypher stand.

(ff. 52^v–53)

The words 'S;^r Henry, Herbert' are written in the left margin between the two crosses. The same thing occurs at the end of the play, where most of the characters die on the stage and Cleophon mourns their deaths:

> Each of these famous lovers I avow
> diserue more tear's, then Cleophon knowe's how
> to pay their Losses,
> to the other two; there is from me som little
>   sorrow due.
> not for the're fate's but crimes————
> × for it is fit————————————
> + all that so sinn, should punisht be for itt.

(f. 76)

(The 'other two' are the evil characters Trasilius and the Duke.) 'S:^r H: Herbert' is written in the margin by the crosses. Presumably Sir Henry considered that the first passage might be taken as an allusion to Charles II, and that the second passage went too far in asserting that death was the appropriate punishment for that kind of behaviour.

In 1672, the year before his death, Sir Henry licensed revivals of two plays by William Cartwright, *The Ordinary* and *The Lady Errant*. The plays were treated in different ways. *The Lady Errant*, basically a romantic tragi-comedy with a few mildly satirical touches, underwent a number of small-scale revisions; but these seem to have been done by someone in the theatre who felt that the language was clumsy or obsolete, and there is little or nothing in the way of deletions or alterations that can be confidently attributed to censorship by Herbert. *The Ordinary* is a much more realistic city comedy, full of intrigue and trickery, with a fair amount of bawdy language and oaths. The text of this play was not rewritten, however, but there were extensive deletions of words, phrases, longer passages, and even of complete scenes. Various methods of deletion were used: thick horizontal pen-strokes through single words or complete lines, rather wavering lines enclosing longer passages, crosses in the margin, and larger diagonal crosses written over the text itself. It is not always easy to distinguish between cuts made for theatrical purposes and those resulting from censorship.

One series of deletions is definitely by Herbert. An attempt was made, though not with complete success, to eliminate such words as 'faith', 'pox', 'God' (and 'for Gods sake'), 'heaven', 'Slid', and 'troth', by means of a thick pen-stroke, sometimes so heavy as to obliterate the word completely. One mild oath used several times, 'Snigs' (once in the form 'Godsnigs') was left untouched.[50] Two longer oaths were deleted: 'By this good blessed Light' at 1. 2. 196 and 'As God shall mend me' at 2. 5. 57, though in both cases 'stet' has been written in the margin by someone other than Herbert.[51] At 3. 3. 25–6 Jane, the heroine of the play, is addressed as 'faire Virgin, | (And yet lesse faire 'cause Virgin)'; the phrase in parentheses was crossed out.

Some longer deletions probably made by Herbert occur in Act 1, scene 2, a scene dealing with the amorous widow Mrs Joan Pot-lucke, who is anxious to remarry. When a character named Hearsay confesses, probably untruthfully, that he has been castrated, Mrs Pot-lucke is shocked, and determines to reject him:

> The holy blessing of all wedlock was
> T'encrease and multiply, as Mr *Christopher*
> Did well observe last Sabbath. Ile not do
> Anything 'gainst Gods word.

> (1. 2. 42–5)

Everything after 'multiply' is underlined, and there is a small cross in the right margin opposite line 44. The original reference to Genesis was not offensive, but Herbert presumably did not like the casuistical use made of it. Shortly afterwards Mrs Pot-lucke questions another potential husband, a soldier named Lieutenant Slicer:

> Art thou intire and sound in all thy limbs?
> SLIC. To tell the very truth, ere now I've had
> A spice o'th' Pox, or so; but now I am sound
> As any Bell (Hem) wast not shrill my Girle, ha?

POT. I do not aske thee about these diseases;
My question is whether thou'st all thy parts.

(1. 2. 60–5)

The last five lines were eliminated in stages: first of all 'o'th' Pox' was
heavily cancelled, then a wavering line drawn through the whole of
line 62. Finally lines 61–5 were enclosed in a clumsily drawn box.
Another substantial deletion, made with two large diagonal crosses,
occurs at the end of Act 3, scene 3, a song by Jane's maid Priscilla.
She is desperate to find herself a husband, and Herbert probably
regarded the song as too explicit an 'invitation to love'.

The major cancellations came near the end of the play. Act 4, scene
4, has two small diagonal crosses on either side of the scene heading,
and someone other than Herbert has written 'leaue out this scene'. In
the scene a cheater named Shape brings a mercer to whom he owes
money to a 'chirurgion'. The mercer is led to believe that the surgeon
will pay him his money, while the surgeon is given to understand that
the mercer needs treatment for venereal disease, which he is reluctant
to discuss openly. By the time the surgeon and mercer have cleared
up their mutual misunderstanding, the cheater has vanished. Possibly
Herbert disliked the references to venereal disease, though it is equally
possible that the actors decided to remove a scene not essential to the
plot and containing two characters who do not appear elsewhere.

The last two cancellations, in Act 5, scenes 1 and 3, concern Jane's
father, Sir Thomas Bitefig, an avaricious usurer, and the deletions are
made by large diagonal crosses similar to those used on Priscilla's song
at the end of Act 3, scene 3. In Act 5, scene 1, Sir Thomas urges Jane
to give money priority over all else ('First then | I charge thee lend
no money; next serve God', lines 5–6), and then commands that his
burial, when the time comes, shall be done as cheaply as possible. To
begin with, Herbert obliterated 'next serve God', but then decided that
the whole scene should be removed. Most of Act 5, scene 3, is taken
up with the re-enactment by the cheater, Shape, of the confession of
his sins of ludicrously monstrous avarice by Sir Thomas that Shape
obtained from him by a trick. It looks as though Sir Henry at first
deleted virtually all of the scene by placing marginal crosses opposite
lines 5–6 and 92–3; later he slightly reduced the amount to be omitted
by making large diagonal pen-crosses through lines 17–79. But this
passage was essential to the plot, and someone from the theatre put
'stet' in the margin five times to indicate that it must remain.

Precisely how far Sir Henry's instructions were respected in acting the play cannot be established. As we have just seen, the deletion of Act 5, scene 3, was cancelled by the use of 'stet', which is also found at four other points in the text against comparatively minor cancellations. Someone—it can hardly have been Sir Henry—had the impudence to delete the second line of his licence ('the Reformations obserued'), as if to imply that the whole process of censorship undergone by the play could be safely ignored. Although he was now an old man of 77, Herbert had examined the play with considerable care, doing his best to eliminate the grosser examples of obscenity and blasphemy (there is little in the play of political interest). But the conditions in which he worked had changed. The Master of the Revels was behaving as he had done forty years earlier, but the old respect for his authority had vanished.

NOTES TO INTRODUCTION

The Life of Sir Henry Herbert

1. Shuttleworth, 9.
2. Ibid. 9, 90.
3. Ibid. 9.
4. *The Broken Heart* (Bodleian MS Don. f. 26), written late 1620 or early 1621, and *Herberts Golden Harpe* (Bodleian MS Don. f. 27), dated 20 Jan. 1623 (i.e. 1623/4). A second copy of the latter is in the Huntington Library (MS HM 85). See Charles for a discussion of these and other writings by Sir Henry.
5. Charles, *Life*, 26.
6. NLW, Powis Castle Correspondence, 314A.
7. Letter to Sir Thomas Edmondes at Paris, 8 Sept. 1615, BL MS Stowe 175, ff. 343–4. See also PRO SP78/63, f. 276 (letter from King James to the Duke of Longueville, 9 Aug., endorsed 'By M^r: H: Herbert'), f. 264 (letter from the Duke to the King, 11 Aug., endorsed 'by Mr Herbert'), and f. 303 (protest by James I to Louis XIII, 25 Aug.); and *CSP Venetian 1615–17*, 6, 10–11. Fees to Henry for carrying letters are listed in *MSC* vi. 133.
8. Two letters from George Herbert, to Henry and Sir John Danvers, nos. IV and V in Hutchinson, 365–7, are editorially dated 1618, but the first reads like advice to someone who has only recently gone abroad, and must date from 1615 or even earlier (see Charles, *Life*, 75 and 77–8, who dates letter IV as 1614 and letter V as 1616–17).
9. See letter from Sir Gerard Herbert to Sir Dudley Carleton, ambassador at the Hague, 19 Mar. 1619, PRO SP14/107/42, partly printed in *CSPD 1619–23*, 25.

10. For a detailed account see Rossi, ii. 53–7. There are numerous references to Henry, as 'my brother' or 'your brother', in Edward's diplomatic correspondence during his period as ambassador.
11. *CSP Venetian 1619–21*, 21.
12. BL MS Harley 1581, f. 107.
13. *CSP Venetian 1621–3*, 89–90.
14. Inner Temple MS 515, vol. 7, f. 30. This appears to be a copy of a docquet and letter-book from the Lord Chamberlain's office, the original of which no longer survives.
15. See Neil Cuddy, 'The Renewal of the Entourage: The Bedchamber of James I, 1603–1625', in David Starkey, ed., *The English Court* (1987), 183–4.
16. PRO 30/53/5, no. 51, f. 94.
17. BL MS Harley 1581, f. 21, printed in full in Sir Sidney Lee's edition of Herbert of Cherbury's *Autobiography* (2nd edn., 1906), 202–3.
18. The circumstances surrounding this transaction are discussed more fully below, 34–7.
19. Apparently from the office-book; Ord transcript in Folger MS S.b.32, 59, used in Chalmers, *Apology*, 615; independent transcript in Warner, 3. A second paragraph reads: 'I sente the certificate of my Knitehood under my Lord Chamberlines hande to the Earl Marshall & herupon he certified to the Office of the Harolds & twas entered in their booke the 14th Augt 1623. The Harolds had no fee but the Lord Marshalls secretary 10^{s}—Sir Thos Morgan my Lord Chamberlines steward was knighted within an hour after mee att the same House of Wilton & payde the same fee. I was sworn King James his servant by Sr George Reeve in ordinary gentleman of his Privy chamber 20th March 1621 at Whitehall.' In Ord only this is followed by an item relating to Anthony Turner (**221**).
20. For a fuller account see Rossi, ii. 371–5.
21. PRO 30/53/6, no. 38, ff. 74$^{r–v}$.
22. Ibid., no. 48, ff. 94$^{r–v}$.
23. He carried a bannerol, or genealogical banner, in the funeral procession of King James I (John Nichols, ed., *The Progresses of King James the First* (1828), iv. 1046–7).
24. PRO PROB 11/145, ff. 464$^{r–v}$.
25. The precise details of Sir Henry's marriage have not been discovered, but he gave this date in a later Chancery suit (PRO C10 13/42).
26. PRO PROB 11/144/67.
27. PRO C2 CHAS I H84/41. The executor, Thomas Plumer, counter-claimed that Sir Henry and Lady Susan had unlawfully retained valuable jewellery (PRO C2 CHAS I P54/14, 23 Jan. 1625/6). Their answer, dated 12 Feb. 1625/6, was witnessed by George Herbert, and bears his signature.
28. NLW MS 5299E.
29. Both the documents are in the possession of Mr E. J. Winnington-Ingram. See Bawcutt, 'New Documents', 321.
30. Sir John's own account of the transaction is in PRO SP19/114/85.
31. Warner, 3–4. The Woodford parish registers for this period do not survive.
32. See **162a–b**.
33. PRO C115/N3/8537.

34. Walton, *Lives* (World's Classics, 1927), 284. Walton gives the year as 1629, but this appears to be an error for 1626 (Hutchinson, p. xxxiii).
35. For a fuller account see below, 27–8.
36. *CSPD 1629–31*, 251; PRO SP16/166/23.
37. Edinburgh University Library, Laing MS II 637/12. For Pye see M. F. Keeler, *The Long Parliament, 1640–1641* (Philadelphia, 1954), 317.
38. Thirty-nine of these are in the PRO (C115/N3/8536–74). Three more letters are found in a volume of the Scudamore Papers in the BL, MS Add. 11043, though the BL MS catalogue does not identify them as by Herbert. On f. 80 is a letter of 1 Sept. 1627 from Woodford, and on ff. 93–4^v and 95–6^v are two long newsletters which date from 1639.
39. PRO 30/53/7, no. 17, ff. 32–3.
40. Richard Baxter, *Reliquiae Baxterianae* (1696), 11.
41. Baxter, *More Reasons for the Christian Religion* (1672), A2^{r-v} (dedication dated 17 Jan. 1671/2).
42. Parish records published in J. R. Burton, *A History of Bewdley* (1883), appendix, pp. vi–vii.
43. Letter from Sir Henry to Scudamore, 2 Mar. 1632, PRO C115/N3/8548; extract printed in *Cambridge*, 637–8.
44. See George Herbert's letter to Sir Henry, XIV in Hutchinson, 377; the postscript to his letter to Nicholas Ferrar, Mar. 1631/2, ibid., XV, 378–9; and Hutchinson's summary of an unprinted letter from Woodnoth to Ferrar in the library of Magdalene College, Cambridge, ibid. 584.
45. NLW MS 5229E, no. 2. For more information see Warner, 20–7 and 193–204.
46. Warner, 25.
47. Ibid. 195.
48. Keeler, *Long Parliament*, 33.
49. For an account of him see ibid. 394.
50. Wallace Notestein, ed., *The Journal of Sir Simonds D'Ewes* (New Haven, 1923), 224; *JHC* ii. 64.
51. D'Ewes, *Journal*, 145.
52. Keeler, *Long Parliament*, 72–3.
53. D'Ewes, *Journal*, 415; *JHC*, ii. 94.
54. D'Ewes, *Journal*, 461–2.
55. *JHC* ii. 268 and 467.
56. *JHC* ii. 729.
57. Repr. in Bentley, ii. 690.
58. PRO SP23/186/534.
59. Warner, 30
60. James F. Larkin, ed., *Stuart Royal Proclamations*, Vol. 2 (Oxford, 1983), no. 425, 911–18.
61. Warner, 31–2.
62. Letters attempting to protect Ribbesford against royalist plundering and heavy local taxation were issued by Princes Rupert and Maurice and Jacob, Lord Astley, in 1645 (Warner, 32–6).
63. There are two namesakes with whom Sir Henry Herbert, Master of the Revels, can be confused. The more important is Colonel Sir Henry Herbert,

commander of an English regiment fighting in Holland. No biography of him exists, though there are brief references to him in Charles Dalton, *The Life and Times of General Sir Edward Cecil* (1885), ii. 15–16 and 314. His date of birth and family background are not known, but he seems to have belonged to a northern branch of the Herberts, and was probably the 'Henry Herbert, a Captain' knighted at Newark or York in 1617 (W. A. Shaw, *The Knights of England* (1906), ii. 162). He was named in a list of English officers serving in Holland in Sept. 1622 (PRO SP81/27/48ᵛ), and at least seven documents concerning him can be found in the State Papers Holland (SP84, 111/55, 118/211, 120/5, 146/105 and 113, 147/202, and 148/289), written between 1623 and 1634. In June 1635 his son, Philip Henry Herbert, born abroad, was granted denization (PRO SO3/11), and in 1635–6 a series of seven letters was exchanged between Elizabeth, Queen of Bohemia, and the Earl of Strafford, in which she asked him for unspecified services on behalf of Sir Henry (Strafford, *Letters*, i. 394, 444, 472, and 509, and ii. 7–8, 10–11, and 38). The House of Lords allowed Sir Henry to recruit and transport English volunteers for his company in Mar. 1642 (*JHL* ii. 659 and 677). He issued a warrant from The Hague in Jan. 1643 granting leave to two of his men to visit England to recruit (BL MS Add. 34253, no. 8, f. 17). He is almost certainly the soldier who acted as a patron to William Herbert, the Earl of Pembroke's illegitimate son by Lady Mary Wroth (Sir Thomas Herbert, *Herbertorum Prosapia*, Cardiff Central Library, Phillipps MS 5.7, 92). The two Sir Henrys knew each other: in a letter to Scudamore, 15 Aug. 1629, the Master of the Revels recorded having received a letter from the Colonel describing a military action (PRO C115/N3/8545).

The other namesake, Henry Herbert of Coldbrook, 1617–56, a parliamentarian soldier, was never knighted, and is less easily confused. There is a biography of him in the *Dictionary of Welsh Biography* (1959), 353.

64. PRO SP23/186/541–3. Sir Henry's compounding papers are calendared in two works edited by Mary A. E. Green: *Calendar of the Proceedings of the Committee for Advance of Money 1642–1656* (1888), i. 427 and ii. 832–3, and *Calendar of the Proceedings of the Committee for Compounding 1643–1660* (1890), ii. 1072–3 and 1295. The largest single group of papers is PRO SP23/186/518–43.

65. *JHC* iv. 431.

66. Ibid. 468.

67. This was certified by William Barton, minister of John Zecharies, London (SP23/186/538).

68. SP23/186/518.

69. *JHC* v. 516; *JHL* x. 532. Early in 1650 Sir Henry was accused of having undervalued his estate (SP23/186/528), but no action was taken.

70. This is established by a letter of 20 June 1648 from John Langley to Sir Richard Leveson, HMC, *Appendix to Fifth Report* (1876), 179.

71. Parish registers in the Guildhall Library, London, MS 4310.

72. Ibid.

73. PRO C10 13/42. He wrote her an angry letter on 3 Jan. 1651/2 (Warner, 46). But later there was a reconciliation, and he visited her in 1672 (see the letter dated 22 Aug. 1672 in Smith, 205).

74. 6 Feb. 1652; 1 July 1656; 8 Feb. 1665. Evelyn presented Sir Henry with an inscribed copy of his translation of *Another Part of the Mystery of Jesuitism* (1664), now in the BL (C53 bb 20).
75. PRO PROB 11/342, ff. 51ᵛ–55ᵛ.
76. The following list has been compiled from various sources, printed and manuscript, but full references have not been given at all points.

   1, 2. Elizabeth, Beatrice: twin daughters, born very late 1651. Elizabeth died young, probably before 1653, and Beatrice is almost certainly the 'Mrs. Betteris Herbert, daughter of Sir Henry Herbert' who was buried at Chelsea on 16 June 1657.

   3. Mary: possibly born 1653. Died 6 Aug. 1666 according to inscription printed in Warner, 5, but 'Mary Dau of Sᵗ Henry Herbert' was buried at St Paul's, Covent Garden, on 9 Jan. 1666/7.

   4. Henry: heir to title. Born 24 July 1654, christened at St Paul's, Covent Garden, on 10 Aug. Died 22 Jan. 1708/9, buried at St Paul's on 25 Jan. Biography in *DNB* and B. D. Henning, ed., *The House of Commons 1660–1690* (1983), ii. 530–1.

   5. Magdalen: born 12 July 1655, christened at St Paul's on 20 July. *DNB* asserts that she married George Morley, son of George Morley, Bishop of Winchester; but according to G. D. Squibb, ed., *The Visitation of Hampshire and the Isle of Wight 1686*, Harleian Society, NS 10 (1991), 16–17, she married Charles Morley, great-nephew of the bishop. She had a son, also Charles. Alive in 1698.

   6. Elizabeth: ?born 1656/7. Married Charles Hore of Cagford, Devonshire, 27 Aug. 1694. Died in childbed, 30 July 1695; buried at St Paul's, 2 Aug.

   7. Richard: baptized at Chelsea on 25 Feb. 1657/8. Ill in 1669; see letter of George Evelyn in NLW MS 5299E. Died on 10 Mar. 1669/70; buried at St Paul's on 12 Mar.

77. A draft of the warrant is in BL MS Egerton 2542, f. 361; see also PRO LC3/26/19 and LC3/73/9, where Sir Henry's name is first in lists of Gentlemen of the Privy Chamber.
78. PRO LC3/24 (unpaged roll).
79. For an account of his parliamentary career during the Restoration see Henning, ed., *House of Commons 1660–1690*, ii. 532.
80. *JHC* viii. 414–15.
81. See below, R48.
82. Printed in Smith, 202–9.
83. Any traces of his tomb were destroyed in a disastrous fire in 1798 which damaged the church so badly that it had to be rebuilt.

The Ribbesford Manuscripts

1. In his campaign against the Ireland forgeries Malone stressed that the first thing anyone who discovered a cabinet full of old documents would do would be to make 'an exact list of the whole' (Malone, *Inquiry*, 345).
2. In the pedigree of the descendants of Sir Henry printed in *Montgomeryshire Collections*, 7 (1874), 156–7, Francis Walker is shown as the great-grandson of

Mary Herbert (d. 1673), the youngest daughter of Sir Henry by his second marriage. But the pedigree has several errors and omissions, and the parish registers of Onibury, Shropshire, show that Mary, née Herbert, the wife of Richard Walker, gave birth to a daughter in July 1652, and cannot possibly be a child of the second marriage. Furthermore, all the evidence contradicts any suggestion that she was a child of the first marriage. The will of Lady Susan's first husband shows that this marriage was childless. There was obviously a link between the Walkers and the Herberts, but its exact nature remains to be determined.

3. See Evelyn H. Martin, 'History of Several Families connected with Diddlebury. II.—The Cornewalls', *Transactions of the Shropshire Archaeological Society*, 4th ser., 3 (1913), 291–9.

4. BL MSS Add. 7058–84; also Add. 37407, which was originally part of the collection but became detached from it accidentally.

5. Martin, 'History', 298.

6. Quaritch, *Catalogue of English Manuscripts*, no. 344 (May 1916), 7–9.

7. NLW, Powis Castle Correspondence, nos. 22150–1. What appears to be a list of the papers sent, in South's handwriting, survives in a chest of miscellaneous documents in Powis Castle. In 1928 the Powis Castle Papers were sent to the PRO, where they were sorted into chronological sequences. (One result of this operation was to make it harder to determine the provenance of individual documents.) The papers of national importance were later deposited in the PRO, where they constitute PRO 30/53/1–9. Papers of local and family importance were deposited in the NLW. There are still a few MSS at Powis Castle, including what seems to be the Herbert pedigree mentioned by Jonathan Scott.

8. In 1981 Messrs Aldridge of Bath put up for auction four miscellaneous collections of minor Herbert–Walker–Cornewall Papers, mainly from the eighteenth century and of a legal or financial nature (sale no. 234, 27 Mar. 1981, items 289–92). These had belonged to Mr C. A. South, son of Mrs Ada South, who in a private letter to the present editor dated 15 Apr. 1981 stated that he had no other Ribbesford papers.

9. These are set out in Bawcutt, 'The Manuscripts of Lord Herbert of Cherbury's *Autobiography*', *The Library*, 6th ser., 12 (1990), 133–6.

10. W. Page, ed., *The County of Worcester*, VCH, 4 (1924), 308.

11. BL MS Add. 42561, ff. 208^{r-v}.

12. Malone, iii. 59.

13. **201**.

14. See **231**, **291**, **350**, and **415**.

15. *Bibliotheca Boswelliana. A Catalogue of the Entire Library of the Late James Boswell, Esq.*, 24 May 1825, item 3129.

16. Thomas Thorpe, *Catalogue of Splendid and Valuable Manuscripts . . .* (2 Mar. 1826), item 299 (BL S.C.680.13).

17. *Catalogue of the . . . Library of the Late Joseph Haslewood* (Dec. 1833), item 1323 (BL 821.g.39); Thomas Thorpe, *Catalogue of Manuscripts* (1834), item 665 (BL S.C.568 (1834)); *Catalogue of the Kingsborough Sale* (Dublin, 1842), item 612 (BL P.R. 1b 30).

18. Chalmers, *Apology*, appendix II, 615.

19. Repr. below, **440**.

20. Printed on the verso of the title-page; see Adams, 'Office-Book', 3. Sir Henry was of course the brother, not the grandson, of the first Lord Herbert of Cherbury, and his house was in Worcestershire, not Shropshire (Salop).

21. Warner, *Illustrations*, iii. 58–60.

22. *Catalogue of a Valuable Collection of Books . . . Including the Remaining Articles of the Library of the Late Craven Ord, Esq.*, Evans, Pall-Mall (9 May 1832), 44, item 1048 (BL S.C. E44(4)).

23. Now in the Beinecke Library, Yale University Library, Osborn Shelves d1.

24. One of these, a small rectangle of paper gummed to p. 156, is a list of Masters of the Revels from Tyllney onwards in Herbert's hand. The other three are printed in the present volume: see **R38**, **A16**, and **B4**.

25. *Catalogue of . . . Autograph Letters of the Late Mr. Jacob Henry Burn*, Puttick and Simpson (2–4 Mar. 1870), item 523 (BL S.C. P. 135(4)); *Catalogue of a Collection of . . . An Amateur*, Sotheby, Wilkinson, and Hodge (24 June 1874), 8, item 89 (a cutting of this item is gummed into Burn).

26. 'Sir H. Herbert's MS Diary of Plays, 1621 to 1641', *Notes and Queries*, 6th ser. (24 Jan. 1880), 73–4.

27. Adams, 'Office-Book', 6–8.

28. Bawcutt, 'New Documents', 326–7.

29. Chalmers, *Apology*, 133 and 478; *Supplemental Apology*, 188.

30. Folger Shakespeare Library, MS S.b.31, p. 69.

31. Folger MS S.b.32, p. 59. Ord made a fuller transcript of the chamber accounts of Henry VII, which survives as BL MS Add. 7099.

32. Warner, 3.

33. Bodleian MS Eng. poet. d. 13, f. 117. The paper has the date 1795 as a watermark.

34. See **182** and **384**.

35. Malone did publish three entries of this kind in his commentaries to *The Winter's Tale* and *The Tempest*, **236**, **345**, and **369**; but Adams failed to include them.

36. E. A. B. Barnard, *The Prattinton Collections of Worcestershire History* (Evesham, 1931). This is a guide to the collection, not an edition of it.

37. Prattinton Collection, Library of the Society of Antiquaries, xxix. 48–9, 95–8, and 105–6.

38. Ibid. 93–4.

39. Burn gummed the list into his notebook, pp. 209–11, and claimed that he had compiled it for Thorpe.

40. Printed in Bawcutt, 'New Documents', 327–8.

41. Pages 251–60 of vol. iv, part iiB, in Barnard's numbering (*Prattinton Collections*). The Audit Office version of these accounts in the PRO is reprinted in *MSC* xiii. 139–48.

42. Letter to the present editor, 26 Feb. 1980, from Miss Margaret Henderson, Senior Assistant Archivist.

43. 'Sir Henry Herbert's Office-Book', *Notes and Queries*, 1st ser. (29 Dec. 1849), 143.

44. 'The Office of Master of the Revels', *Notes and Queries*, 1st ser. (2 Feb. 1850), 219.

45. 'Letters of the Herbert Family', *Notes and Queries*, 2nd ser. (23 Apr. 1859), 346.
46. Letter from the Earl of Powis to Sir Sidney Lee, 11 Jan. 1891, Bodleian MS Eng. misc. d. 179, f. 340. See also F. E. Hutchinson, 'Missing Herbert Manuscripts', *TLS* (15 July 1939), 421.
47. Sidney Lee, ed., *The Autobiography of Lord Herbert of Cherbury* (1886), 23, and Florentia C. Herbert, 'The Herberts of Cherbury', *Transactions of the Shropshire Archaeological Society*, 3rd ser., 7 (1907), 52. It looks as though F. C. Herbert borrowed her assertion from Lee, and Lee took his from Halliwell-Phillipps's 1880 note.
48. Adams, 'Office-Book', 5–6. Adams claimed that he proposed to incorporate this and other new evidence in a revised edn. of his *Dramatic Records*, but this second edn. never appeared, and the notes for it seem to have vanished.
49. W. Gifford, ed., *The Works of Philip Massinger*, 2nd edn. (1813), i, p. lvi n.

The Master of the Revels: The Office of Master

1. The standard historical accounts of the revels office are E. K. Chambers, *Notes on the History of the Revels Office under the Tudors* (1906), and Chambers, *ES* i. 71–105. For the early years of the revels, however, Chambers has been superseded by W. R. Streitberger, *Court Revels 1485–1559* (Toronto, 1994).
2. See W. P. Baildon, ed., *The Records of the Honorable Society of Lincoln's Inn. The Black Book*, i (1897), *passim*, and ii (1898), pp. xxviii, 28, and 169. After 1614 the names of persons appointed were not normally recorded, but there are later references to the office (ii. 291, 301, and 312).
3. C. T. Martin, ed., *Minutes of Parliament of the Middle Temple* (1904), i. 2, and F. A. Inderwick, ed., *A Calendar of the Inner Temple Records* (1896), i. 2.
4. Thomas Percy, ed., *The Regulations and Establishment of the Houshold of Henry Algernon Percy, The Fifth Earl of Northumberland* (1770), 346. He was paid 20*s*. annually.
5. Facs. in Williams, 'Laudian Imprimatur', 103.
6. Milton, *Areopagitica*, in D. M. Wolfe, ed., *Complete Prose Works* (New Haven, 1953–82), ii. 518.
7. See Streitberger, *Court Revels 1485–1559*, 62.
8. *MSC* xiii. 85.
9. The figure of twenty days occurs every year, and we might suspect that it was a nominal total, acceptable to the auditors of the revels accounts, which did not necessarily reflect reality.
10. *MSC* xiii. 144.
11. *Cambridge*, 637–8.
12. PRO LC5/132/140; printed in *MSC* ii. 351.
13. Chamberlain, *Letters*, ii. 602 (26 Feb. 1624/5); *CSPD 1623–5*, 481 and 485.
14. Letter from Garrard to Strafford, 23 Mar. 1636/7, in Strafford, *Letters*, ii. 56.
15. PRO E403/2562/18.
16. Cranfield Papers in Kent Archive Office, U269/1 OE602 (11 Nov. 1621). See Eccles, 480.
17. Kent Archive Office, U269/1 OE106; see Eccles, 480–1.
18. See A1 and 14.

19. PRO E403/2455/123–4. A copy of the grant was made for Sir Henry Herbert in 1660, A32–7.
20. Printed in Herford and Simpson, ed., *Works*, i. 237–9.
21. Chamberlain, *Letters*, ii. 404.
22. BL MS Harleian 389, f. 118.
23. Eccles, 482; Bentley, iv. 610.
24. Full version in PRO PSO2/50, no. 55, 9 May 1622; summary in SO3/7.
25. The documents are repr. in full in Appendix A.
26. Greg, *Bibliography*, i. 32.
27. Chamberlain, *Letters*, ii. 430.
28. *MSC* xiii. 85.
29. Malone sometimes mistakenly attributed these licences to Herbert, and Bentley in his chronology of theatrical events (vii. 44–8) inexplicably credited them all to Herbert; but there can be no doubt that Astley was responsible for them.
30. *MSC* xiii. 85.
31. Chalmers, *Apology*, 503.
32. Dutton, 222–5.
33. PRO SP16/261/39. See Peter Clark, *English Provincial Society from the Reformation to the Revolution: Religion, Politics and Society in Kent 1500–1640* (Hassocks, 1977), 368.
34. Longer version in PRO LC5/133/23–4; summarized in SO3/11, Mar. 1637/8.
35. The longer version is in the Audit Office Enrolment Books, PRO AO15/2/ ff. 352 ff. A shorter version, without the provision for yearly licences, is in the Exchequer Rolls, E406/45/ff. 82^v–83^v. Both were noted and briefly summarized by Wallace.
36. Printed in Cunningham, pp. xxii–xxiii, from PRO AO15/17/131.
37. PRO SP23/186/520. This is one of the papers drawn up early in 1646 when Herbert was negotiating with the parliamentary regime to compound (i.e. pay a fine on his estate) for having been a supporter of the royalist cause. His statements in this context need to be treated with caution.
38. Several versions of this are extant in the PRO: AO15/7/123–8, C66/2512 no. 5, and C82/2046/292.
39. See Shuttleworth, 14–15.
40. He was MP for Denbigh in 1593, and there is a brief biography of him in P. W. Hasler, ed., *The House of Commons 1558–1603* (1981), iii. 483–4.
41. See Hotson, 205, and **R34**.
42. See above, 4–5.
43. There is some uncertainty as to precisely how many plays were performed at court during the winter season of 1623–4; see *MSC* vi. 77–9.
44. See Collier, ii. 11 and 18–19. Warrants originating from the Lord Chamberlain's office were printed in Chalmers, *Apology*, 505–6, and Cunningham, p. xxiii, and more fully in *MSC* ii. 321 ff.
45. e.g. **251** and **A16**, which have not been printed before.
46. *MSC* xiii. 93.
47. Ibid., pp. xiii–xiv.
48. See **R21** and **R38**.

49. PRO SP23/186/520.
50. P. Morant, *The History and Antiquities of Essex* (1818 edn.), ii. 228.
51. W. Page, ed., *The County of Buckingham*, VCH, iv (1927), 354.
52. F. H. W. Sheppard, ed., *Survey of London XXXVI: The Parish of St Paul Covent Garden* (1970), 127 and n. 266.
53. Shuttleworth, 9.

The Master of the Revels: Licensing

1. See **380, 389, 408, 430**, and **437**. For courtier plays see Harbage, 99, repeated in Bentley, iv. 705, and Kevin Sharpe, *Criticism and Compliment* (Cambridge, 1987), 37, and for private performances Greg, *Aspects*, 105.
2. Bentley, iii. 137. Jasper Mayne's *The City Match*, intended for the same Oxford visit but not performed, was later put on at Blackfriars. No licence survives, but this does not necessarily prove that Herbert did not license it.
3. Warner, 3–5.
4. Bentley, i. 149–51.
5. Eccles, 459; Streitberger, 'Biography', 30–1. Chambers, *ES* i. 96, stated that Buc was acting as Master between 1603 and 1610, but Eccles and Streitberger do not agree. Buc was not Tyllney's nephew, though repeated assertions have been made to that effect, and the two men were not close friends.
6. *STC* 7757; printed in Arber, iv. 528–36. Williams, 'Laudian Imprimatur', 102, argues that Laud put pressure on Herbert to give up licensing for the press, but there is no evidence to put this beyond question.
7. See Williams, 'Laudian Imprimatur', 97–8.
8. Greg, *Aspects*, 111.
9. See H. J. C. Grierson, ed., *The Poems of John Donne* (Oxford, 1912), ii, p. lxxxvi.
10. This edn. printed only ten of the *Problems*, though more survive in MSS, and one of the *Problems*, 'Why have bastards best fortune?', was abbreviated (see John Donne, *Paradoxes and Problems*, ed. Helen Peters (Oxford, 1980), p. lxxxii). This may have been the result of censorship by Herbert.
11. See his 1637 petition to Laud, repr. in Grierson, ed., *Poems of John Donne*, ii, pp. lxvi–lxvii.
12. Malone, iii. 231; Greville, *The Remains*, ed. G. A. Wilkes (Oxford, 1965), 22–3 and 264. See also W. W. Greg, 'Notes on Old Books', *The Library*, 4th ser., 7 (1926–7), 217–19.
13. Printed in Bentley, i. 17–18.

The Master of the Revels: Censorship

1. Bentley, iii. 379.
2. Ed. J. H. Walter, MSR (1933), p. xi.
3. Herbert's demand to the bookkeeper to submit 'a fairer copy' in future suggests that he was dealing with a professional company.
4. See letters to Carleton by Locke and Chamberlain in *CSPD 1623–5*, 481 and 485 (the latter is more accurately printed in Chamberlain, *Letters*, ii. 602).

5. Out of the five items listed in the last two paragraphs all but one (lines 1477–9) are fairly directly versified from Thomas Mun's little pamphlet *A Discourse of Trade from Europe vnto the East-Indies* (1621), which includes a section relating to the Mint. Arguments that could appear in print in 1621 were not acceptable on the stage twelve years later.

6. References are to the edition by J. Gerritsen, *The Honest Mans Fortune: A Critical Edition of MS Dyce 9 (1625)* (Groningen and Djakarta, 1952).

7. Ed. Arthur Brown, MSR (1958), pp. vi–xii.

8. The recorder of London at the date of licensing was Robert Mason. The *DNB* account of him indicates that as an MP he had been an opponent of royal policies, and had taken part in the impeachment of Buckingham, but 'in October 1634, either to silence him, or because he had come to terms with the court, Mason was recommended by the king for the post of recorder of London'. Perhaps it was feared that the character in the play might be identified with Mason, though no attempt was made to satirize him.

9. The differences are recorded in the historical collation in Fredson Bowers's edn. of the play, in *The Dramatic Works in the Beaumont and Fletcher Canon*, gen. ed. Fredson Bowers (Cambridge, 1979), iv. 134–48. There is also a record in the textual apparatus of the separate edn. by G. B. Ferguson (The Hague, 1966). References here are to the Bowers edn.

10. W. W. Greg, ed., *Bonduca*, MSR (1951), p. xii. In the rest of this paragraph double references are given in parentheses, the first a through-line reference to the MS text as edited by Greg, the second an act, scene, and line reference to the Folio text as edited by Cyrus Hoy in *The Dramatic Works in the Beaumont and Fletcher Canon*, iv. 149–259.

11. *Demetrius and Enanthe* is quoted from the MSR edn. by Margaret Cook and F. P. Wilson (1951), *The Humorous Lieutenant* from Cyrus Hoy's edn. (*Dramatic Works*, ed. Bowers, v (Cambridge, 1982)).

12. Bald, *Studies*, 72.

13. Bentley, v. 1271–2.

14. R. C. Bald, 'Arthur Wilson's *The Inconstant Lady*', *The Library*, 4th ser., 18 (1937–8), 296–9.

15. References are to the edn. by Linda V. Itzoe (New York, 1980). Itzoe uses R as her copy-text, and gives variant readings from L, keyed to R line-numberings, in her textual apparatus.

16. *OED* gives *lantify*, *v.*, as a nonce-formation from *lant*, *sb.*, 'urine'.

17. See Itzoe's textual notes at the following lines: 1. 1. 225–34 and 242; 3. 1. 111 and 115–16; 4. 3. 68–70 and 74.

18. Howard-Hill, *Game*, 20 and 56, challenges this assumption, pointing out that the King left London on 14 July. He argues that the players were waiting for Sir Henry to be away from London, and uses the data found in Adams to show that there was a gap in Sir Henry's activity between 7 July and 3 Sept. But we know from the new entries in Burn that he licensed plays on 14, 24, and 26 July 1624; we are thus not entitled to assume that he was out of London while *A Game at Chess* was being performed.

19. Howard-Hill, *Game*, 17, points out that this might be an equivocation, meaning simply that they had not altered the play in performance, though passages could have been added in the MS since licensing. But Sir Henry

himself was available to check the prompt-copy, so this would have been a risky manœuvre (cf. what happened over Jonson's *Magnetic Lady*, **240** and n., **266**).

20. At least four copies of this poem survive; see Howard-Hill, *Game*, 211–13.
21. The Earl of Pembroke to the president of the Council, BL MS Egerton 2623, f. 28, quoted in Bald, *Game*, 165, and Howard-Hill, *Game*, 206–7.
22. Heinemann, ch. 10.
23. Cogswell, 'Middleton and the Court'. Cogswell provides a fuller historical background in *The Blessed Revolution: English Politics and the Coming of War, 1621–1624* (Cambridge, 1989).
24. John Woolley, letter to William Trumbull, 6 Aug. 1624, BL Trumbull Papers, alphabet. ser. XLVIII, no. 134 (quoted by Cogswell, 'Middleton and the Court', 281).
25. Heinemann, 164–5.
26. There are links between Herbert himself and Middleton's circle of city patrons. Middleton's pious compilation, *The Marriage of the Old and New Testament* (1620), was dedicated to Richard Fishbourne and John Browne. In his will dated 30 Mar. 1625 Fishbourne left money for the purchase of mourning clothes to Sir Henry (see above, pp. 5–6, n. 24), as well as money for mourning clothes and £5 for a mourning ring to William Hammond, to whom Middleton dedicated the Crane transcript of *A Game at Chess* now in the Bodleian (MS Malone 25). In his will dated 15 Aug. 1624 (PRO PROB 11/144/67), Edmond Plumer, Lady Susan Herbert's first husband, bequeathed mourning cloaks to Fishbourne, Browne, and Hammond.
27. Salvetti to Scudamore, 14 Aug. 1624, PRO C115/N1/8488 (noted by Cogswell, *Blessed Revolution*, 302).
28. Jane Sherman, 'The Pawns' Allegory in Middleton's *A Game at Chesse*', *RES* NS 29 (1978), 156–7.
29. Woolley to Trumbull, 28 Aug. 1624, BL Trumbull Papers, alphabet. ser. XLVIII, no. 137 (noted by Cogswell, 'Middleton and the Court', 281). In *MSC* vi. 79 David Cook stated that the King's men performed the play at court on 6 Aug., but there is no evidence to confirm this assertion.
30. Undated and unsigned newsletter to Scudamore, BL Add. 11043, f. 94.
31. Heinemann, 37, says that censorship was 'almost exclusively' political.
32. 412–13.
33. *MSC* ii. 395.
34. Edmond, 78–9 and 87–90.
35. Butler, 135–6 and 220.
36. Brome, *Dramatic Works* (1873), i. 218.
37. The complimentary poems to this collection, by Sir Aston Cokayne and Alexander Brome, do not present Brome as a radical critic of the monarchy; on the contrary, they show the theatre as hostile to Puritanism and suppressed by it.
38. Unfortunately the page on which Sir Henry wrote two crosses and the word 'buried' in the margin, f. 5a, is mainly torn or cut away, and what he objected to cannot be known (see the edn. by C. J. Sisson, MSR (1927), lines 173–6).
39. *MSC* i. 394–5; see also *CSPD 1639*, 529–30, repr. in Bentley, i. 314–15 and v. 1441–2.

40. Chamberlain, *Letters*, ii. 578; also Bald, *Game*, 163, and Howard-Hill, *Game*, 205.
41. *CSPD 1623–5*, 325; also Bald, *Game*, 159 and Howard-Hill, *Game*, 200.
42. Chambers, *WS* i. 239. 'Slight' is of course an abbreviation of 'By God's light'.
43. Bentley, *Profession of Dramatist*, 179.
44. Letter from Edmund Rossingham to Viscount Conway, PRO SP16/420/109 (also *CSPD 1639*, 140).
45. Assertions by such scholars as Heinemann and Butler that Puritans patronized the drama, and used it for ideological propaganda, substantially overstate the case, though there is not space here for a full rebuttal. It is true that some members of the gentry, who had strong Calvinist convictions and were later to become supporters of the parliamentary side in the civil war, were prepared in the 1630s to watch and read plays. But hard-core Puritan moralists and theologians maintained an unremitting hostility towards drama and did all they could to suppress it.

The Master of the Revels: Sights and Shows

1. Crosfield, 54. Crosfield was interested in actors; in July 1634 Richard Kendall, wardrobe-keeper to the Salisbury Court players, then in Oxford, gave Crosfield an account of the leading London companies and their personnel (ibid. 71–3).
2. Evans, 455.
3. *St. Pavles-Chvrch her Bill for the Parliament*, E4^{r-v}, quoted in Bentley, vi. 209.
4. Davenant, *The Shorter Poems*, ed. A. M. Gibbs (Oxford, 1972), 129.
5. Possibly he invented the phrase and gave it currency; *OED* quotes numerous citations from the seventeenth century, but none earlier than 1624. 'Hocus-Pocus Junior', who published a book of conjuring tricks in 1634 (*STC* 13545.5), was probably a disciple or admirer; see Trevor H. Hall, *Old Conjuring Books* (1972), 129.
6. Thomas Ady, *A Candle in the Dark* (1656), 29.
7. Crosfield, 71 and 79. In the 1634 entry Crosfield called him 'His maiesties Hokus Pokus'.
8. *Coventry*, 442.
9. Epitaphs, no. 111, M7^v; not in earlier edns.
10. *The Staple of News*, Second Intermean 15, in *Works*, vi. 323; *The Magnetick Lady*, Chorus I. 29 (ibid. vi. 528); *The Masque of Augures*, 268 (in *Works*, vii. 638).
11. B. Morris and E. Withington, eds., *The Poems of John Cleveland* (Oxford, 1967), 29.
12. Ibid. 77. This may not be by Cleveland.
13. Hugh Trevor-Roper, *Archbishop Laud* (1940), 357–8.
14. PRO SO3/9.
15. See Bentley, ii. 521–3, *MSC* vi. 47, 61, and 144, and **B3**.
16. *Coventry*, 397, 417, and 425. For Restoration examples see **R2** and n.
17. e.g. **212**, **309**, and **316**. For fuller discussion see Bentley, vi. 159 and 194–5 and vii. 5–9.
18. Crosfield, 26–9. For lists of puppet-show titles see Jonson, *Bartholomew Fair*, 5. 1. 8–12, Marston, *The Dutch Courtesan*, 3. 1. 127, and Buc's 1618 licence, quoted below.

19. *Bartholomew Fair*, 5. 1. 12–14.
20. *Coventry*, 429. It might have been a painting or a copy of a painting; in 1631 Charles I paid £210 for a Honthorst painting of the Elector and his family (*CSPD 1629–31*, 558).
21. Crosfield, 71.
22. *Coventry*, 434.
23. Crosfield, 71.
24. Ibid. 175.
25. *Norwich*, 146.
26. See above, n. 1.
27. *Coventry*, 440.
28. John Spalding, *Memorialls of the Trubles in Scotland and in England, A.D. 1624–A.D. 1645* (Aberdeen, 1850–1), ii. 125–6, quoted in Hyder E. Rollins, ed., *The Pack of Autolycus* (Cambridge, Mass., 1927), 9.
29. *Coventry*, 443.
30. Cf. **164**, *Coventry*, 425, *Cambridge*, 619, and Crosfield, 54 (quoted above, n. 1).
31. Arthur Freeman, *Elizabeth's Misfits* (New York, 1978), 138–9.
32. *MCB* 5, f. 161ᵛ.
33. *MSC* ii. 302.
34. Chambers, *ES* iv. 271.
35. Ibid. 273.
36. *MSC* ii. 316.
37. Murray, 247.
38. *Norwich*, p. xxxvi.
39. Bentley, vi. 212.
40. *Norwich*, 115. Galloway has not been able to identify this beast (396).
41. Printed in Bawcutt, 'New Documents', 327–8 and 331.
42. *Norwich*, 142 and 157.
43. For an example see *Norwich*, 173, entry dated 5 Oct. 1622.
44. All quotations in this paragraph are taken from the Quarter Sessions Order Book QSM: 1/1, f. 272ᵛ, in the Dorset Record Office. For earlier allusions to this affair see Murray, 206, and Kevin Sharpe, *The Personal Rule of Charles I* (1992), 748–9.
45. *Norwich*, 151–2.
46. Bentley, ii. 561.
47. Ibid. 617–18.
48. PRO SP16/238/49. Modernized and slightly abbreviated versions of the documents are printed in *CSPD 1633–4*, 47–9, and Murray, 163–7. The item in the Banbury Corporation Records, which Sharpe, *Personal Rule*, 748, interprets as a payment to players, is more likely to have been expenses incurred in relation to this incident.
49. *MSC* i. 384–5.
50. Speaight, 69–72.

The Master of the Revels: The Restoration

1. See above, 13. Herbert later submitted claims for official expenses, though the revels accounts for 1660–1 were not approved until 1665 (they are printed in Boswell, appendix B, 273–6).

2. Bentley, vi. 114, and Hotson, 108–12.

3. See R7 and Davenant's draft of 20 Aug., quoted in Hotson, 201.

4. Hotson, 202–3.

5. Bentley, vi. 305.

6. Ibid. 308.

7. Milhous–Hume, 7; Hotson, 400. References to Milhous–Hume are to item nos. not pages.

8. Milhous–Hume, 8; Hotson, 199–200; partial facs. in Edmond, 136.

9. Milhous–Hume, 15; Hotson, 200. Presumably Palmer felt that Davenant and Killigrew should be allowed to go ahead, but not be given what amounted to a perpetual monopoly.

10. Milhous–Hume, 18; Hotson, 201–2.

11. Hotson, 203–4.

12. There was probably a closure, of uncertain duration, due to mourning for the death of the King's brother, the Duke of Gloucester, who died 13 Sept. and was buried 21 Sept.

13. Freehafer, 19.

14. Hotson, 203–6, and 211–13.

15. PRO LC3/25/115 and LC3/26/151.

16. See n. 14.

17. Hotson, 212, quoting J. C. Jeaffreson, ed., *Middlesex County Records* (1888), iii. 322–3.

18. For full details see Milhous–Hume, 131 and 186.

19. From the patents as quoted in Fitzgerald, i. 74 and 78.

20. Freehafer's argument in *London Stage*, i. 38–9, that Herbert deliberately falsified the evidence in order to gain licence-fees that should have gone to Hayward, is over-ingenious and unconvincing.

21. PRO LC23/26/151 and LC3/73/149.

22. P. W. Thomas, *Sir John Berkenhead 1617–1679* (Oxford, 1969), 210–11.

23. Greg, *Aspects*, 106.

24. *CSPD 1664–5*, 67. The signature on this letter, SP29/104/98, is identical to that on R49. It is not clear how he managed to combine being a naval captain and an officer in the revels.

25. Matthews and Latham, v. 276.

26. A copy of the reversion made for Herbert is in A91–3.

27. *MCB* 4, f. 135.

28. Ibid., f. 135^v.

29. Ibid., f. 227.

30. Milhous–Hume, 534 and 536–7.

31. *MCB* 5, f. 131^v (not in Milhous–Hume). Neither the letters nor the copies seem to have survived.

32. 4 June 1664 (*MCB* 4, f. 217^v); 4 Oct. 1669 (*MCB* 5, f. 122); 6 Nov. 1669 (*MCB* 5, f. 124^v); and 11 Mar. 1670/1 (*MCB* 5, f. 168^v).

33. From the entry for 12 Oct. 1670 (*MCB* 5, f. 154).

34. *MCB* 5, f. 168^v.

35. Ibid., f. 167^v.

36. From Davenant's patent, as reproduced in Geoffrey Ashton and Ian Mackintosh, eds., *Royal Opera House Retrospective 1732–1982* (1982), facing p. 21.

37. References are to M. C. Nahm's edn. of the Worcester College Library MS (Oxford, 1935).
38. PRO SP44/10/54; Milhous–Hume, 195; *CSPD 1663–4*, 83.
39. PRO SP44/10/54–5; Milhous–Hume, 195; *CSPD 1663–4*, 83.
40. Wilson wrote a prologue, not in the MS but printed in the first Quarto of 1664, 'Intended, upon the revival of the Play, but not spoken' (also in Nahm, ed., 234–5), in which he complained of the way Scruple's part had been 'libb'd' (i.e. castrated), presumably by Denham and Waller.
41. Boas, 250.
42. Nahm, ed., 133–4.
43. *Diary*, 15 Apr. 1667; Matthews and Latham, viii. 167–8.
44. Milhous–Hume, 380.
45. Pepys, *Diary*, 16 Apr. 1667; Matthews and Latham, viii. 168.
46. Ibid.
47. It is written more neatly, and with a finer pen, than is usually the case with Herbert; compare Langhans's facs., 132, with the undoubtedly autograph licence for *The Ordinary*, Langhans, 337.
48. See Boas's edn., 5 (note by T. C. Skeat). Most of the new section deals with Asinello, but is not enclosed in rules, so it is presumably not the original version. Narrow stubs remain of the leaves which were removed; they contain a few letters, but not enough to reconstruct the text, as well as traces of rules used to enclose the text, similar to those found elsewhere.
49. Bodleian MS Rawlinson poet. 195, f. 49.
50. *OED* terms *Snigs* a 'minced oath', but does not explain its derivation.
51. Line references are to the facsimile in Langhans.

EDITORIAL PROCEDURES

Wherever possible, documents have been printed directly from manuscripts, and an attempt has been made to reproduce the original closely, though lineation has often been simplified. A few abbreviated forms have been expanded in contexts where they might cause difficulty; an example is 'p', which can have various significances ('per', 'par', 'pro', etc.). Deletions are enclosed in square brackets, interlinear additions or revisions in diagonal slashes. Double slashes indicate an insertion within an insertion. Angle brackets ⟨ ⟩ are used for text that is in varying degrees problematic. Brackets left empty indicate that the manuscript is defective or the surviving text illegible. Words in angle brackets with a question-mark are plausible but not certain reconstructions based on surviving letters or portions of letters, context, or the repeated use of formulas in a document. Words in brackets with no question-mark are not completely legible in the original, but there can be little doubt that this is what the scribe intended. Angle brackets are also used at points where Halliwell-Phillipps cut off parts of an Ord transcript and wrote in the missing words himself (e.g. 12, 15, 24–5, etc.; see above, 19–20).

Items are placed in chronological order; Herbert normally used the old style of dating, and it has been assumed that all dates before 25 March are old style; in other words, a date such as 12 February 1623 means 12 February 1623/4. When only the month or year of an item can be determined, the item is placed at the beginning of the relevant month or year. An asterisk is used to distinguish entries which appear to derive from the office-book, though in some cases they are clearly summary or paraphrase and not direct quotation. Descriptive titles for the Restoration documents are entirely editorial (the material before 1642 is usually so brief that titles did not seem necessary).

Because the office-book is lost, it is impossible to tell whether surviving copies follow precisely the wording and layout of the original. Where there is only one version of an entry, we have no choice but to follow it, but complications arise when there are multiple copies. Occasionally these are identical, but usually there are slight differences of wording and arrangement. To give one example only, Malone (iii. 230) printed the licence for Massinger's *The Renegado* (**97**) as follows:

> The Renegado, or the Gentleman of Venice, April 17, 1624.
> Acted at the Cockpit.

This does not correspond to the version he wrote into his own copy of the play, Bodleian Mal 236(5):

> "The Renegado or the Gentleman of Venise. by Messenger.
> Allowed to be playd this 17. of Aprill 1624" From the Office
> book of Sir Henry Herbert, Master of the Revels

The inverted commas suggest that Malone was quoting verbatim, but his version is not identical to Ord's (HP5, 150):

> For the Cockpit company
> The Renegado or the Gentleman of Venice by Messinger
> this 17th Apr 1624. 1^{li}.

Chalmers (p. 218) followed Ord, but with slight modifications and the omission of the licence-fee:

> 17 April—For the Cockpit; *The Renegado, or*
> *the Gentleman of Venice:* Writ-
> ten by Messinger

Burn (p. 202) rearranged the material in order to bring the title of the play to the beginning, and misread the date (all other authorities give April, not November):

> The *Renegado*, or Gent of Venice, by Massinger alld
> for the Cockpit Comp^{y} 17 Nov 1624   1^{li}

The choice for an editor seems to lie between Ord and Malone's manuscript version, but Ord has finally been chosen because it gives more information (the name of the company and the fee). Elsewhere what appears to be the fullest and most authentic version has been chosen; but as we have already seen, there can be no guarantee that it accurately represents what Sir Henry actually wrote. On a few occasions where there are substantially differing versions of the entry for a particular play (e.g. **56a** and **b**, **77a** and **b**, and **247a** and **b**), both have been printed. Some items have gaps where the transcriber evidently could not decipher a word or part of a word (e.g. **55** and **426**).

Cuttings from transcripts of the office-book made by Craven Ord survive in various places, and as the matter is somewhat complicated, it seemed best to give the sigla here rather than with the abbreviations and references.

Ord/Burn   Cuttings from Ord inserted by Burn into his *Collections* notebook, Osborn Shelves d1, Beinecke Library, Yale University Library.

Ord C1   Folded sheet of paper forming two leaves, with writing on one page only, inserted into a notebook of Chalmers, Bodleian Eng. poet. d. 13, f. 117. The paper bears a watermark in the form of the date 1795. See above, 20–1.

Ord C2   Single leaf gummed into a notebook of Chalmers, *Collectanea Shakespeariana*, iii. 59, Folger Shakespeare Library MS S. b. 32. See above, 20.

The remaining items are all found in notebooks compiled by Halliwell-Phillipps; the first two are half-page cuttings, the first containing seven items and the second ten, gummed into a notebook in Edinburgh University Library:

Ord HP1   Edinburgh University Library H-P Coll. 315, f. 55.
Ord HP2   Ibid., f. 57.

The rest are in notebooks in the Folger Shakespeare Library. The number of items per cutting varies from one to eight. The sigla given here are followed by the Folger pressmark and the title given to the notebook by Halliwell-Phillipps.

Ord HP3   W. b. 139   'Appliances'.
Ord HP4   W. b. 143   'Burbage'.
Ord HP5   W. b. 156   'Fortune'.
Ord HP6   W. b. 157   'Globe'.
Ord HP7   W. b. 158   'The Hope'.
Ord HP8   W. b. 160   'Kemp'.
Ord HP9   W. b. 163   'King's Servants after 1616'.
Ord HP10   W. b. 165   'Lowin'.
Ord HP11   W. b. 174   'Noble Companies'.
Ord HP12   W. b. 196   'Theatres of Shakespeare's Time'.

ABBREVIATIONS AND REFERENCES

Unless otherwise indicated, the place of publication is London. Certain books and articles mentioned briefly are not included here. A few items discussing Herbert which are not referred to in this book are listed for the sake of completeness.

A   BL Additional Manuscript 19256.

Adams   J. Q. Adams, ed., *The Dramatic Records of Sir Henry Herbert* (New Haven, 1917).

Adams, 'Office-Book'   J. Q. Adams, 'The Office-Book, 1622–1642, of Sir Henry Herbert, Master of the Revels', in P. E. Lawler, John Fleming, and Edwin Wolf, eds., *To Doctor R. Essays . . . in honor . . . of Dr. A. S. W. Rosenbach* (Philadelphia, 1946), 1–9.

Arber   Edward Arber, ed., *A Transcript of the Registers of the Company of Stationers of London, 1554–1640* (1875–94).

Bald, *Game*   Thomas Middleton, *A Game at Chess*, ed. R. C. Bald (Cambridge, 1929).

Bald, *Studies*   R. C. Bald, *Bibliographical Studies in the Beaumont & Fletcher Folio of 1647* (Oxford, 1938).

Bawcutt, 'Astley'   N. W. Bawcutt, 'Evidence and Conjecture in Literary Scholarship: The Case of Sir John Astley Reconsidered', *ELR* 22 (1992), 333–46.

Bawcutt, 'New Documents'   N. W. Bawcutt, 'New Revels Documents of Sir George Buc and Sir Henry Herbert', *RES* NS 35 (1984), 316–31.

Bawcutt, 'Ord Transcripts'   N. W. Bawcutt, 'Craven Ord Transcripts of Sir Henry Herbert's Office-book in the Folger Shakespeare Library', *ELR* 14 (1984), 83–94.

Bentley   G. E. Bentley, *The Jacobean and Caroline Stage* (Oxford, 1941–68).

Bentley, *Profession of Dramatist*   G. E. Bentley, *The Profession of Dramatist in Shakespeare's Time* (Princeton, 1971).

BL   British Library, London.

Boas   F. S. Boas, *Shakespeare and the Universities* (1923).

Boswell   Eleanore Boswell, *The Restoration Court Stage (1660–1702)* (Cambridge, Mass., 1932).

Burn   J. H. Burn, *Collections towards Forming a History of the Now Obsolete Office of the Master of the Revels*, Beinecke Library, Yale University, Osborn Shelves d1.

Butler   Martin Butler, *Theatre and Crisis 1632–1642* (Cambridge, 1984).

Cambridge   Alan H. Nelson, ed., *Cambridge*, REED (Toronto, 1989).

CCB   *Commissary Court Book 1656–82*, Cambridge University Archives Comm. Ct. V. 13, Cambridge University Library.

Chalmers   George Chalmers, *A Supplemental Apology for the Believers in the Shakspeare-Papers* (1799).

Chalmers, *Apology*   George Chalmers, *An Apology for the Believers in the Shakspeare-Papers* (1797).

Chamberlain, *Letters*   N. E. McClure, ed., *The Letters of John Chamberlain* (Philadelphia, 1939).

Chambers, *ES*   E. K. Chambers, *The Elizabethan Stage* (Oxford, 1923).

Chambers, *WS*   E. K. Chambers, *William Shakespeare: A Study of Facts and Problems* (Oxford, 1930).

Charles   Amy Charles, 'Sir Henry Herbert: The Master of the Revels as Man of Letters', *MP* 80 (1982–3), 1–12.

Charles, *Life*   Amy Charles, *A Life of George Herbert* (Ithaca, NY, 1977).

Clare   Janet Clare, *'Art made tongue-tied by authority': Elizabethan and Jacobean Dramatic Censorship* (Manchester, 1990).

Cogswell, 'Middleton and the Court'   Thomas Cogswell, 'Thomas Middleton and the Court, 1624: *A Game at Chess* in Context', *HLQ* 47 (1984), 273–88.

Collier   J. P. Collier, *The History of English Dramatic Poetry* (1831).

Coventry   R. W. Ingram, ed., *Coventry*, REED (Toronto, 1981).

Crosfield   F. S. Boas, ed., *The Diary of Thomas Crosfield* (Oxford, 1935).

CSPD   *Calendar of State Papers Domestic*.

CSP Venetian   *Calendar of State Papers Venetian*.

Cumberland, etc.   Audrey Douglas and Peter Greenfield, eds., *Cumberland, Westmorland, Gloucestershire*, REED (Toronto, 1986).

Cunningham   Peter Cunningham, ed., *Extracts from the Accounts of the Revels at Court, in the Reigns of Queen Elizabeth and King James I* (1842).

Cutts J. P. Cutts, 'New Findings with regard to the 1624 Protection List', *Shakespeare Survey 19* (Cambridge, 1966), 101–7.

Devon John M. Wasson, ed., *Devon*, REED (Toronto, 1986).

DNB *Dictionary of National Biography*.

Dutton Richard Dutton, *Mastering the Revels: The Regulation and Censorship of English Renaissance Drama* (1991).

Eccles Mark Eccles, 'Sir George Buc, Master of the Revels', in C. J. Sisson, ed., *Thomas Lodge and other Elizabethans* (Cambridge, Mass., 1933), 409–506.

Edmond Mary Edmond, *Rare Sir William Davenant* (Manchester, 1987).

Edwards and Gibson Philip Edwards and Colin Gibson, eds., *The Plays and Poems of Philip Massinger* (Oxford, 1976).

ELR *English Literary Renaissance*.

Evans G. Blakemore Evans, ed., *The Poems and Plays of William Cartwright* (Madison, 1951).

Eyre G. E. B. Eyre, ed., *A Transcript of the Registers of the Worshipful Company of Stationers 1640–1708* (1913–14).

Feil J. P. Feil, 'Dramatic References from the Scudamore Papers', *Shakespeare Survey 11* (Cambridge, 1958), 107–16.

Feuillerat Albert Feuillerat, ed., *Documents relating to the Office of the Revels in the time of Queen Elizabeth* (Louvain, 1908).

Fitzgerald Percy Fitzgerald, *A New History of the English Stage* (1882).

Fleay F. G. Fleay, *A Chronicle History of the London Stage 1559–1642* (1890).

Freehafer John Freehafer, 'The Formation of the London Patent Companies in 1660', *Theatre Notebook*, 20 (1965), 6–30.

Gildersleeve Virginia Gildersleeve, *Government Regulation of the Elizabethan Drama* (New York, 1908).

Greg, *Aspects* W. W. Greg, *Some Aspects and Problems of London Publishing between 1550 and 1650* (Oxford, 1956).

Greg, *Bibliography* W. W. Greg, *A Bibliography of the English Printed Drama to the Restoration* (London, 1939–59).

Greg, *Companion* W. W. Greg, *A Companion to Arber* (Oxford, 1967).

Greg, *Licensers* W. W. Greg, *Licensers for the Press, &c. to 1640* (Oxford, 1962).

Halliwell-Phillipps J. O. Halliwell-Phillipps, ed., *A Collection of Ancient Documents Respecting the Office of Master of the Revels* (1870).

Harbage Alfred Harbage, *Cavalier Drama* (New York, 1936).

Heinemann Margot Heinemann, *Puritanism and Theatre: Thomas Middleton and Opposition Drama under the Early Stuarts* (Cambridge, 1980).

Herefordshire, Worcestershire David N. Klausner, ed., *Herefordshire, Worcestershire*, REED (Toronto, 1990).

HLQ *Huntington Library Quarterly*.

HMC Historical Manuscripts Commission.

Hotson Leslie Hotson, *The Commonwealth and Restoration Stage* (Cambridge, Mass., 1928).

Howard-Hill, *Game* Thomas Middleton, *A Game at Chess*, ed. T. H. Howard-Hill (Manchester, 1993).

Hutchinson F. E. Hutchinson, ed., *The Works of George Herbert* (Oxford, 1941).

JHC *Journals of the House of Commons*.

JHL *Journals of the House of Lords*.

Lancashire David George, ed., *Lancashire*, REED (Toronto, 1991).

Langhans Edward Langhans, *Restoration Promptbooks* (Carbondale, Ill., 1981).

Lawrence W. J. Lawrence, 'New Facts from Sir Henry Herbert's Office Book', *TLS*, 29 Nov. 1923, 820; repr. in *Speeding Up Shakespeare: Studies of the Bygone Theatre and Drama* (1937), 159–178.

Limon Jerzy Limon, *Dangerous Matter: English Drama and Politics in 1623/4* (Cambridge, 1986).

London Stage William Van Lennep, ed., *The London Stage 1660–1700* (Carbondale, Ill., 1965).

Malone Edmond Malone and James Boswell, eds., *The Plays and Poems of William Shakespeare, with the Corrections and Illustrations of Various Commentators* (1821).

Malone 1790 Edmond Malone, ed., *The Plays and Poems of William Shakespeare* (1790).

Malone, *Inquiry* Edmond Malone, *An Inquiry into the Authenticity of Certain Miscellaneous Papers and Legal Documents* (1796).

Malone MS Office-book entries written by Malone into his own books and papers.

Matthews and Latham W. Matthews and R. Latham, eds., *The Diary of Samuel Pepys* (1970–83).

MCB *Mayor's Court Books*, Norwich: (1) 1615–24, Case 16 a 15; (2) 1624–34, Case 16 a 16; (3) 1634–46, Case 16 a 20; (4) 1654–66, Case 16 a 23; (5) 1666–77, Case 16 a 24; Norfolk Record Office.

Milhous–Hume   Judith Milhous and Robert D. Hume, *A Register of English Theatrical Documents 1660–1730* (Carbondale, Ill., 1991).

MP   *Modern Philology.*

MSC   *Malone Society Collections.*

MSR   Malone Society Reprints.

Murray   J. T. Murray, *English Dramatic Companies 1558–1642* (1910) (all references are to vol. ii).

NLW   National Library of Wales.

Norwich   David Galloway, ed., *Norwich 1540–1642*, REED (Toronto, 1984).

Ord   Transcripts of entries from the office-book made by Craven Ord (for a detailed list see Introduction, 126).

Patterson   Annabel Patterson, *Censorship and Interpretation: The Conditions of Writing and Reading in Early Modern England* (Madison, 1984).

PRO   Public Record Office.

REED   Records of Early English Drama.

RES   *Review of English Studies.*

RORD   *Research Opportunities in Renaissance Drama.*

Rossi   Mario Rossi, *La Vita, Le Opere, I Tempi di Edoardo Herbert di Chirbury* (Florence, 1947).

Shuttleworth   J. M. Shuttleworth, ed., *The Life of Edward, First Lord Herbert of Cherbury* (Oxford, 1976).

Smith   W. J. Smith, ed., *Herbert Correspondence* (Cardiff and Dublin, 1963).

Speaight   George Speaight, *The History of the English Puppet Theatre* (1955).

SR   Stationers' Register.

STC   *The Short-Title Catalogue.*

Strafford, *Letters*   William Knowler, ed., *The Earl of Strafford's Letters and Dispatches* (1739).

Streitberger, 'Biography'   W. R. Streitberger, 'On Edmond Tyllney's Biography', *RES* NS 29 (1978), 11–35.

TLS   *Times Literary Supplement.*

VCH   Victoria County History.

Wallace   Working papers of Professor C. W. Wallace in the Huntington Library, San Marino, California.

Warner   Rebecca Warner, *Epistolary Curiosities, Series the First* (1818).

White   Arthur F. White, 'The Office of Revels and Dramatic Censorship during the Restoration Period', *Western Reserve University Bulletin*, NS 34 (1931), 5–45.

Williams, 'Laudian Imprimatur'   Franklin B. Williams, 'The Laudian Imprimatur', *The Library*, 5th ser., 15 (1960), 96–104.

Williams, 'Licensing'   William P. Williams, 'Sir Henry Herbert's Licensing of Plays for the Press in the Restoration', *Notes and Queries*, NS 22 (June 1975), 255–6.

Wood   Chauncey Wood, 'George and Henry Herbert on Redemption', *HLQ* 46 (1983), 298–309.

Worden   A. B. Worden, 'Literature and Political Censorship in Early Modern England', in A. C. Duke and C. A. Tamse, eds., *Too Mighty To Be Free: Censorship and the Press in Britain and the Netherlands* (Zutphen, 1989), 45–62.

Revels Documents
to 1642

Sir George Buc, Master of the Revels 1610–1622

1613

1   From an extract taken by Sir Henry Herbert from the Office-book of Sir George Buc, his predecessor in the office of Master of the revels, it appears that the theatre in Whitefriars was either rebuilt in 1613, or intended to be rebuilt. The entry is: "July 13, 1613, for a license to erect a new play-house in the White-friers, &c. £20."

1616, 1618

2   "⟨Received⟩ of the King's players for a *lenten dispensation*, the other companys promising to doe as muche, 44s. March 23, 1616.

3   "Of John Hemminges, in the name of the four companys, for toleration in the holy-dayes, 44s. January 29, 1618."
Extracts from the office-book of Sir George Buc. MSS. Herbert.

1620

4   Sir Henry Herbert's office-book contains a few memorandums, extracted from that of his predecessor, Sir George Buck, and among them the following, "Oct. 6, 1620. For new reforming the *Virgin-Martyr* for the Red Bull, 40s."

Sir John Astley, Master of the Revels March 1622–July 1623

1622

5   *It appears from the office-book of Sir Henry Herbert, Master of the Revels to King James the First, and the two succeeding kings, that

1. Malone, iii. 52. Bentley, vi. 115–17. Herbert referred back to this item in **R38**.
2, 3. Malone, iii. 65. Bentley, vii. 3.
4. William Gifford, ed., *The Plays of Philip Massinger*, 2nd edn. (1813), i, p. lvii n. See Introduction, 26. Bentley, iii. 263–6. Gifford assumed that this was an old play re-licensed, but Bentley argues that the size of the fee indicates a new play.
5. Malone, iii. 57–60. It is odd that Cane and Greville appear twice; see Bentley, ii. 398 and 451.

very soon after our poet's death, in the year 1622, there were but five principal companies of comedians in London; the King's Servants, who performed at the Globe and in Blackfriars; the Prince's Servants, who performed then at the Curtain; the Palsgrave's Servants, who had possession of the Fortune; the players of the Revels, who acted at the Red Bull; and the Lady Elizabeth's Servants, or, as they are sometimes denominated, the Queen of Bohemia's players, who performed at the Cockpit in Drury Lane.

"1622. The Palsgrave's servants. Frank Grace, Charles Massy, Richard Price, Richard Fowler, —— Kane, Curtys Grevill" MS. Herbert. Three other names have perished. Of these one must have been that of Richard Gunnel, who was then the manager of the Fortune theatre; and another, that of William Cartwright, who was of the same company.

"The names of the chiefe players at the Red Bull, called the players of the Revells. Robert Lee, Richard Perkings, Ellis Woorth, Thomas Basse, John Blany, John Cumber, William Robbins." *Ibidem*.

"The chiefe of them at the Phoenix. Christopher Beeston, Joseph More, Eliard Swanson, Andrew Cane, Curtis Grevill, William Shurlock, Anthony Turner." *Ibidem*. Eliard Swanston in 1624 joined the company at Blackfriars.

That part of the leaf which contained the list of the king's servants, and the performers at the *Curtain* is mouldered away.

6   *The *Childe hath founde his Father*, for perusing and allowing of a New Play, acted by the Princes Servants at the Curtayne, 1622 1^{li}.

7 May

7   *⟨Middleton and Rowley's *The Changeling*⟩ Licensed to be acted by the Lady Elizabeth's servants at the Phoenix, May 7, 1622. by Sir Henry Herbert Master of the Revels.

---

6. Burn, 194. Licence not known to Bentley, v. 1021. An alternative title for William Rowley's *The Birth of Merlin*, published 1662. This has previously been dated either 1608 or 1620–2; Herbert's licence confirms the later date.

7. Malone MS in his copy of the play, Bodleian 246(9). Printed by Lawrence. Bentley, iv. 861–4. Malone must have been mistaken in attributing the licence to Sir Henry rather than Sir John Astley; all the evidence indicates that Sir Henry did not begin licensing until July 1623.

10 May

8   *A New Play called the *Black Lady*, all^d. 10 May 1622, by the Lady Elizabeth's Servants 1*li*.

9   *A New Play called the *Welsh Traveller*, alld 10 May 1622, acted by the Players of the Revells, 20/-.

14 May

10 *Fletcher's *The Prophetess*, a new play, licensed.

3 June

11 *Valiant Schollar, a New P. containing 10 sheets and three pages, alld. 3 June 1622; 1^li. Acted by the Lady Elizabeth's Servants.

10 June

12 *10th June for allow: of a new P. conteyn: 13 sheetes 2 ⟨pages ½ called the⟩ Duche painter & the French brank acted by the ⟨Princes pleyers at⟩ the Curtayne— 20^s.

22 June

13 *Fletcher's *The Sea Voyage* licensed. Acted at the Globe.

20 August

(see under 20 Aug. 1623, 45, *A license to Thos. Barrell)

6 September

14 *In the Office book of Sir Henry Herbert Master of the Revels is the following entry now before me, made by his predcess^r

    "Item 6 Sep. 1622, for perusing and allowing of a new play called *Osmond the Great Turk*, which Mr Hemmings and Mr Rice affirmed to me that Lord Chamberlain gave order to allow of it because I refused to allow it ⟨?at⟩ first, conteyning 22 leaves and a page— Acted by the King's players . . . 20^s"

---

8. Burn, 194; also Chalmers, 213. Anon., lost. Bentley, v. 1294.

9. Burn, 204; also Chalmers, 213. Anon., lost. Bentley, v. 1435–6.

10. Malone, iii. 226. Bentley, iii. 394–7.

11. Burn, 203; also Chalmers, 213. Anon., lost. Bentley, v. 1430.

12. Ord HP5, 85; also Chalmers, 213, and Burn, 195. Anon., lost. Bentley, v. 1324–5. The meaning of 'brank' has not been established; what appears to be a later version of the title reads 'brawle' (see Bentley).

13. Malone, iii. 226; also Burn, 202, where it is attributed to Beaumont.

14. Malone MS in his copy of David Baker's *Biographica Dramatica, or, A Companion to the Playhouse* (1782), Bodleian Mal 156, p. 268^*. Printed by Lawrence. By Lodowick Carlell. Bentley, iii. 119–22.

29 September

15   *A note of such P: & Shewes as have been ⟨perused and allowed from⟩ Midsommer tyll Michealmas

3 October

16   *_Love's Royall Rewarde_, all^d. 3 Oct. 1622 by Sir J. Astley himselfe; acted at the Curtayne, by the Prince's Players, 1_li_.

16 October

17   (_Norwich_) Iohn ffinlason did this day bringe an Instrument dated the xxix^th of May 1622 sealed by Sr Iohn Ashely knight maister of the Revills to shewe a monster haveinge six toes on a foote & six fingers on his hand / the said Iohn ffinlason ys not p⟨er⟩mitted to shew his said monster but inioyned to dept this Citty /

24 October

18   *Fletcher's _The Spanish Curate_ licensed. Acted at Blackfriars.

26 December

19   *"Revels and Playes performed and acted at Christmas in the court at Whitehall, 1622;" for the preservation of which we are indebted to Sir John Astley, then Master of the Revels:

20   *Upon St. Steevens daye at night The Spanish Curate was acted by the kings players.

27 December

21   *Upon St. Johns daye at night was acted The Beggars Bush by the kings players.

28 December

22   *Upon Childermas daye no playe.

29 December

23   *Upon the Sonday following The Pilgrim was acted by the kings players.

_15._ Ord HP5, 85. Not in Bentley. On the bottom half of a rectangular cutting, the top half of which contains _12_ above. Over this item Halliwell-Phillipps wrote 'Herbert MS. 1622.'

_16._ Burn, 199. Not in Bentley; not otherwise known. Anon., lost. The use of the phrase 'by Sir J. Astley himselfe', as though this was something unusual, suggests that Astley's duties were being performed by his deputy, Sir Francis Markham (**34**).

_17._ _Norwich_, 173.   _18._ Malone, iii. 226. Bentley, iii. 417–21.

_19._ Malone, iii. 146.   _20._ Ibid.   _21._ Ibid.   _22._ Ibid.   _23._ Ibid.

1623

24 *For a prise playd at the Red Bull by M^r. ⟨Allen & Mr. Lewkner⟩ gentlemen— 10^s. for the house 10^s.

25 *A license to William Sands Ric^d. Luke, & John ⟨Sands with nine⟩ assistants for a yeare Tis calld the ⟨Caos of the world, they⟩ have given 1^l. & have given bond for ⟨more 1.10.0⟩

26 *For a Prise playd at the Princes armes or ⟨the Swann by Thos⟩ Musgrave & Renton — 10^s.

1 January

27 *Upon New-years day at night The Alchemist was acted by the kings players.

6 January

28 *Upon Twelfe night, the Masque being put off, the play called A Vowe and a Good One was acted by the princes servants.

8 January

29 *The *Troublesome Statesman*, a new P. perused and alld Jan 8, 1622–3; to be acted at the Fortune, by the Prince Palatine's servants, 1^h.

19 January

30 *Upon Sunday, being the 19th of January, the Princes Masque appointed for Twelfe daye, was performed. The speeches and songs

24. Ord HP12, 53. Shorter version in Chalmers, 209 = **440(m)**. Bentley, vi. 221. This and the next item are undated, but occur together on the same cutting from Ord following the item dated 4 Oct. 1623 (**60b**). Two other cuttings on the same page of Halliwell-Phillipps's notebook, each with one item, are dated 19 Aug. 1623 (**42**) and 12 Sept. (**55**). The undated items would thus appear to date from the second half of 1623, and to have been issued by Herbert rather than Astley.
25. Ord HP12, 53. See previous note. Abbreviated version in Chalmers, 209 = **440(n)**. For information about William and John Sands see Introduction, 80 and 84–5. William Sands the elder died at Preston, Lancs, in 1638; he was a joiner, and presumably could make his own puppets. In his will he bequeathed to his son John 'my Shewe called the Chaos, the Wagon, the Stage, & all the Ioyners tooles & other ymplementes & appurtenances to the said Shewe belonging' (*Lancashire*, 87).
26. Ord HP12, 127. Bentley, vi. 250. Undated, but sandwiched between two items dated 1623 (**48** and **60a**).
27. Malone, iii. 147.   *28.* Ibid. Anon., lost. Bentley, v. 1432–3.
29. Burn, 203. Not in Bentley; not otherwise known.
30. Malone, iii. 147. The masque was Jonson's *Time Vindicated to Himself and to his Honours*; see Bentley, iv. 672–6. Mademoiselle St Luc was the niece of the French ambassador.

composed by Mr. Ben. Johnson, and the scene made by Mr. Inigo
Jones, which was three tymes changed during the tyme of the
masque: where in the first that was discovered was a prospective of
Whitehall, with the Banqueting House; the second was the Masquers in a cloud; and the third a forrest. The French embassador
was present.

The Antemasques of tumblers and jugglers.

The Prince did leade the measures with the French embassadors
wife.

The measures, braules, corrantos, and galliards being ended, the
Masquers with the ladyes did daunce 2 contrey daunces, namely
The Soldiers Marche, and Huff Hamukin, where the French
Embassadors wife and Mademoysala St. Luke did ⟨daunce⟩.

2 February

31   *At Candlemas Malvolio was acted at court, by the kings servants.

25 February

32   *At Shrovetide, the king being at Newmarket, and the prince out
of England, there was neyther masque nor play, nor any other kind
of Revells held at court.

21 March

33   *1622. 21 Martii. For a prise at the Red-Bull, for the howse; the
fencers would give nothing. 10s. *MSS. Astley*.

24 May

34   (*Norwich*) This day willm Perry brought into Court an Instrument
vnder his Maties privie Signet and Signed wth his Ma^ts hand
authorisinge him wth Robt Lee Philip Rossiter & their Company as
Servants to Quene Ann to play &c Test vltimo octobris Anno xv°
Iacobi Regis/
They Shewed also A Confirmacion vnder the hand of S^r ffrances
Markham Deputy to the Maister of the Revelles bearinge date in
Aprill last wch confirmeth the kinges authority for a yeare
They are denyed to play aswell for the Cause of the poore whose
worke cannot be wanted as for some Contagion feared to be begun
as also for feare of tumult of the people/

31. Malone, iii. 147. Shakespeare, *Twelfth Night*.
32. Malone, iii. 147. Prince Charles and Buckingham had begun their journey to Spain
on 18 Feb.
33. Malone, iii. 66. Bentley, vi. 221.   *34*. *Norwich*, 175; also Murray, 347.

9 July

35　*⟨Middleton and Rowley's *The Spanish Gipsy*⟩ Acted by the Lady Elizabeth's Servants at the Phoenix July 9, 1623:- as appears by the Office book of Sir Henry Herbert then Master of the Revels.

SIR HENRY HERBERT, MASTER OF THE REVELS
JULY 1623–AUGUST 1642

1623

26 July

36　*A note of such playes as have byn ⟨allowed by me since I⟩ came to the office of the Revells, the 26ᵗʰ ⟨July 1623⟩.

27 July

37　*The Palsgraves Players—A Trajedy of Richard the thirde or the English Prophett with the reformation contayninge 17 sheetes written by Samuell Rowleye for the companye at the Fortune this 27th July 1623—1ˡⁱ: o.

30 July

38　*The Princes Players—A french Tragedy of the Belman of ⟨Paris containyng 40⟩ sheetes written by Thomas Drickers & John ⟨Day, for the company⟩ of the Read-bull this 30 July 1623.　1ˡⁱ. o.

31 July

39　*⟨　⟩ for 6 monthes ensuing the date hereof this 31 July 1623.—10ˢ.

August

40　*A Tragedy of the Plantation of Virginia, the ⟨prophaness left out⟩ contayninge 16 sheets and one ⟨leaf⟩ may be acted ⟨els not for the⟩ companye at the Curtune

35. Malone MS in his copy of the play, Bodleian Mal 246(8). Printed by Lawrence. Bentley, iv. 892–5. The next item indicates that the play was licensed by Astley, not Herbert (cf. 7 above).
36. Ord HP12, 51. Not in Bentley. This entry establishes beyond question the date on which Sir Henry began his duties as Master.
37. Ord HP5, 41; also Chalmers, 214, reading 'Profit' for 'Prophett', and Burn, 202. Lost. Bentley, v. 1013–14.
38. Ord HP12, 51; also Chalmers, 214, and Burn, 194. 'Drickers' is Dekker. Burn gives the length of the play as '10 sheets', which sounds far more plausible than '40'. Bentley, iii. 246.
39. Ord HP1. The beginning of this licence is missing, but it was clearly for some kind of travelling entertainment. Cf. 41 below.
40. Ord HP5, 85; also Chalmers, 214, and Burn, 201. Anon., lost. Bentley, v. 1395–6.

Founde fault with the length of this playe & ⟨commanded a⟩ reformation in all their other playes.

14 August

41   *A License to Edward James with one man or boye to sett forthe a showe in glass called the worlds wonder for 6 monthes ensuing the date hereof 14ᵗʰ Augᵗ. 1623.—10ˢ

19 August

42   *For the Princes servants of the Rede Bull—An oulde ⟨play called the⟩ Peacable Kinge or the lord Mendall former⟨ly allowed of by Sir⟩ George Bucke & likewise by mee & because ⟨itt was free from adition⟩ or reformation I tooke no fee this 19ᵗʰ Augᵗ. ⟨1623⟩

43   *For the king's players. An olde playe called Winter's Tale, formerly allowed of by Sir George Bucke, and likewyse by mee on Mr. Hemmings his worde that there was nothing profane added or reformed, thogh the allowed booke was missinge; and therefore I returned it without a fee, this 19 of August, 1623.

20 August

44   *A licence to Mʳ. John Williams with foure more to make showe of an Elephant for a yeare after the date hereof 20 Augᵗ. 1623 \gratis./

45   *A license to Thoˢ. Barrell with one man his wife & children to toss a pike for a yʳ. 20ᵗʰ Augᵗ. 1622.—10ˢ

46   *A license to Marke Bradley with his wife to make shewe of a Ramme with 4 horns for a year 20ᵗʰ Augᵗ. 1623.   10ˢ.

41. Ord HP1; also Chalmers, 208 = **440(f)**, reading 'Showing Glass' for 'showe in glass'. A show called 'the Worlds wonder' was put on at Coventry by Richard Tompson in 1630 (*Coventry*, 429).

42. Ord HP12, 53; also Chalmers, 214, abbreviated, and Burn, 201. Anon., lost. Bentley, v. 1393.

43. Malone, iii. 229; also ii. 462–3.

44. Ord HP1; also Chalmers, 208 = **440(a)**. Early in July 1623 the King of Spain sent an elephant and five camels as a present to King James (Chamberlain, *Letters*, ii. 507). In Sept. a warrant was issued granting custody of the elephant to John Williams, with an annual allowance of £270 (PRO SO3/7). Several writers of the time allude to the elephant (e.g. Jonson, *Neptune's Triumph*, line 250; Middleton and Rowley, *The Spanish Gipsy*, 2. 2. 179, 4. 1. 99).

45. Ord HP1. This is the fourth of seven consecutive items on a cutting from Ord. All the others are dated July–Aug. 1623 (39, 41, 44, 46, 51, and 52), and it looks as though Ord's '1622' is a mistake. A 'soldier that tossed a Pike' was rewarded at Coventry in 1636 (*Coventry*, 439).

46. Ord HP1.

21 August

47 *⟨For the Lady Elizabeth's Servants of the Cockpit⟩
An Old Play called Matche mee in London formerley allowed by Sir
George Buck & now by mee freely & without fee this 21ˢᵗ. Augᵗ. 1623.

23 August

48 *A license to Thomas Blorern with 3 assis⟨tants to make shewe of
an⟩ Italien motion 23ᵈ Augᵗ. — 5ˢ.

49 *This was done by the La: Elizabeths servants att the Cockpitt—
An olde Playe called the Martir'd Soldier formerlye allowed by Sir
John Ashlye but called in & reallowed with reformations: which
were not observed, for to every cross they added a stet of their owne
& for this cause I have thought fitt to peruse itt & to keep the booke
for a president to the office and to take my fee this 23ᵈ Augᵗ. 1623.

26 August

50 *An olde Playe called the Escapes of Jupiter taken from the
Cockpitt upon the remove of some of the sharers & because they
had payde their parts thogh itt hath byn acted in the Kings house
I have allowed of itt this 26ᵗʰ Augᵗ. 1623 — 1ˡⁱ—
      It was not complained of by the company of the Cockpitt and that
moved mee likewyse to allowe of itt.
      I had not allowed of itt but that the Cockpitt gave way & that
they have byn sharers therin some of them.

47. Ord HP4, 146, with first line supplied from Chalmers, 214; also Burn, 200. By
Thomas Dekker. Bentley, iii. 256.
48. Ord HP12, 127. Also abbreviated in Chalmers, 208–9 = **440(h)**.
49. Ord/Burn, 199. By Henry Shirley; entry not known to Bentley, v. 1060–2. The
title-page of the 1638 edn. claims that the play was performed '*By the Queenes Majesties
Servants*', and there has been debate as to whether this referred to Queen Anne or
Queen Henrietta Maria. This new entry shows that it was Queen Elizabeth's (i.e. the
Queen of Bohemia's) company and, as Sir Henry calls it an old play, *The Martyred
Soldier* was presumably one of the earliest plays to be licensed by Sir John Astley. See
below, 53.
50. Ord/Burn, 196. Thomas Heywood's *The Escapes of Jupiter* survives only in MS
(BL MS Egerton 1994, repr. MSR (1978)), and consists of scenes from two earlier
plays by Heywood, *The Golden Age* and *The Silver Age*. Hitherto nothing has been
known about its stage history (Bentley, iv. 567–8). Possibly the sharers mentioned
belonged to Prince Charles's company, which moved to the Cockpit or Phoenix theatre
in 1619, but left it early in 1622 to go to the Curtain, when a totally new Lady
Elizabeth's company was formed to play at the Phoenix (Bentley, i. 183 and 205).
Mention of 'the Kings house' rather surprisingly suggests that the play was performed
at three separate theatres.

27 August

51   *A license to Barth: Cloys with 3 assistants to make shewe of a musicall organ with divers motions in itt for a year this 27th Aug[t]. 1623   1[li].

52   *A license to William Reece & Tho[s]. Gittins to make shewe of a strange Ratt for a yeare 27th Aug[t]. 1623—10[s].

28 August

53   *for the   Under another name that itt may pass the better Att
     Palsgraves   the Intreaty of M[r]. Gunnell who prevailed with mee to
     Players.   gett the consent of M[r]. Biston to the Cockpitt itt bears
                    the name of the Martir'd Soldier this 28th of Aug[t].
                    1623—— 1[li].

29 August

54   *Maid in the Mill, a New Com. containing Twelve sheets and a leaf, written by Fletcher and Rowley, all[d] for the King's Players 29 Aug. 1623.

12 September

55   *For the lady Eliz:[s] Players.   September

51. Ord HP1; also Chalmers, 208 = 440(g). See also 118, 174, and 296. In Apr. 1632 Cloyse was granted a royal warrant to show 'such water Engines Clockes Organes &c as are or shalbe by him inuented' (PRO SO3/10). In Sept. 1632 he put on shows at Sturbridge Fair, near Cambridge, and 'the schollers & other persons have resorted and thronged to them', but on 11 Sept. the university authorities ordered him to leave (Cambridge, 647). Evidently Cloyse played organs which had mechanical moving figures attached to them; Donne jeered at them in Satire II, 15–16, 'As in some Organ, Puppets dance above | And bellows pant below, which them do move'.
52. Ord HP1.
53. Ord/Burn, 199. Not in Bentley. See above, 49. The Palsgrave's players were desperate for new plays because of the loss of their play-texts when the Fortune theatre was destroyed by fire in 1622 (Bentley, i. 149–51). Possibly Gunnell learned that Sir Henry had confiscated The Martyred Soldier from Beeston, and begged to be allowed to put it on, provided that Beeston agreed.
54. Burn, 199; also Malone, iii. 226, stating that it was acted at the Globe, and Chalmers, 214–15. Bentley, iii. 376–80. See below, 58 and 66.
55. Ord HP12, 53; also Chalmers, 215. Lost. Bentley, iii. 30–2. Presumably the rest of the word Ord gives as 'Cra' was missing or indecipherable; a play called The Crafty Merchant was entered in the SR in 1653. The last sentence is puzzling: the Lady Elizabeth's players were definitely one of the four major companies, and did not play at the Red Bull. An identical sentence was attributed by Malone to the next item, John Day's Come See a Wonder, where it makes much better sense. Perhaps we could revive a conjecture of Fleay and Adams, rejected by Bentley because he assumed that Ord and Chalmers wrote independent transcripts, and suggest that Ord attached the sentence to the wrong entry. Cf. 69 below.

A new Comedy called the Cra ___ Marchant ⟨or come to my
3.0.0 Cuntry⟩ houss contayninge 9 sheetes may bee acted ⟨this 12th
Septr. 1623⟩ Written by William Bonen
It was acted at the Red Bull & licensed without ⟨my hande to itt
because⟩ they were none of the foure companys

18 September
56a *Come see a Wonder, a New Com: writt: by Jno Deye, for a
company of strangers: allowed by me 18 Sept. 1623, for 2 li. My
Clerk had 5s.

56b Sir Henry Herbert observes that the play called Come See a
Wonder, "written by John Daye for a company of strangers," and
represented Sept. 18, 1623, was "acted at the Red Bull, and licensed
without his ⟨?my⟩ hand to it, because they ⟨i.e. this company of
strangers⟩ were none of the *four* companys."

29 September
57 *Note of such playes as were acted at court in 1623 and 1624

58 *Upon Michelmas night att Hampton court, The Mayd of the Mill,
by the K. Company

2 October
59 *A new Comedy, a *Fault in Frendship*, by Young Johnson and
Broome all^d 2 Oct. 1623, for Princes Company, 1*li*.

4 October
60a *A license to Henry Momford, John Monford ⟨Hen . . .⟩

60b *Fines with 2 assistants for tumbling & ⟨vaulting with other⟩ trickes
of slight of hand for half an year ⟨4th Oct.⟩ ⟨1^{li}.⟩

56a. Burn, 194; also Chalmers, 215, abbreviated. *56b*. Malone, iii. 224. Bentley, iii.
240. See previous entry.
57–8. Malone, iii. 22.
59. Burn, 197; also Chalmers, 215. Lost. Bentley, iii. 69–70. 'Young Johnson' has not
been identified; there is no evidence to suggest that he was a son of Ben Jonson.
60a. Ord HP12, 127. *60b*. Ord HP12, 53. These two fragments are on widely separated
Ord cuttings in a Halliwell-Phillipps notebook, the first at the bottom of a cutting, the
second at the top. Chalmers's paraphrased and abbreviated version of a licence to
'Henry Momford and others', 440(l), indicates that they belong together. The second
name is clearly 'Monford', though he is probably the John Momford named in 318.
'Mumford ye Tumbler' was paid 50s. for performing in a Lord Mayor's pageant in 1639
(*MSC* iii. 130).

17 October

61 *For the King's Company, An Old Play, called, *More Dissemblers besides Women*: allowed by Sir George Bucke; and being free from alterations was allowed by me . . .

62 *New Play, the *Deuill of Dowgate*, or Usury putt to use, by Fletcher, King's Company, 17 Oct. 1623. 1*li.*

18 October

63 *A new play, The *Foolish Ambassader*, allowd Oct. 18, 1623, King's Company 1*li.*

29 October

64 *A New Com: *Hardshipe for Husbands*, or Bilboes the best blade, containing 13 sheets, written by Sam. Rowley all^d Oct 29, 1623, for the Palsgrave's company.

30 October

65 *Oct. 30th 1623. Gratuity— M^r. Shakerlye brought mee with a note of Playes for Christmas as a gratuitye from the Cockpit companye 2^li.

1 November

66 *Upon Allhollows night at St. James, the prince being there only, The Mayd of the Mill againe, with reformations.

5 November

67 *Upon the fifth of November att Whitehall, the prince being there only, The Gipsye, by the Cockpitt company.

61. Chalmers, 215–16; also Malone MS (paraphrased) in his copy of the play, Bodleian Mal 247(4), and Burn, 200. By Thomas Middleton. Bentley, iv. 888–9. Chalmers caused some confusion by joining together this and the next entry in one continuous sentence.

62. Burn, 195; also Malone, iii. 226, Malone MS in his copy of Langbaine's *Account*, Bodleian Mal 130, f. 208, wrongly giving date as 27 Oct., and Chalmers, 216. Lost. Bentley, iii. 328–9.

63. Burn, 197. Anon., lost. Not in Bentley; not otherwise known.

64. Burn, 197; also Chalmers, 216, reading '*Hardshifte*' for '*Hardshipe*'. Lost. Bentley, v. 1011–12.

65. Ord HP5, 149. Bentley, vi. 59. For other gifts from the Cockpit company see **87**, **91**, and **438**.

66. Malone, iii. 227. Bentley, iii. 379, speculates on the puzzling fact that 'reformations' were made to a play licensed two months earlier and played at court one month earlier (**54** and **58**); they can hardly have been caused by censorship. See Introduction, 50.

67. Malone, iii. 227. Presumably Middleton and Rowley's *The Spanish Gipsy*.

19 November

68 *For the Palsgraves Players   November
A new Tragedye called 2 kings in a cottage written by Bowen this
19th 1623 — 1^{li}.

28 November

69 *The *Fayre Fowle One*: or the Baytinge of the Jealous Knight, written
by Smithe, for a company of strangers, 28 Nov. 1623, 2*li*. Acted at
Red Bull, and licensed without my name to a strange Company.

3 December

70 *The *Noble Bondman*, written by Ph. Massinger, Gent. all^{d} 3 Dec.
1623 to the Queen of Bohemia's Company 1^{li}.

4 December

71 *The *Hungarian Lion*, written by Gunnell, licensed for the Palsgrave's Company 4 Dec. 1623. 1^{li}.

6 December

72 *Wandring Lovers*, written by Mr Fletcher, for the King's comp^{y}.
all^{d} 6th Dec. 1623. 1^{li}.

26 December

73 *Upon St. Stevens daye, the king and prince being there, The
Mayd of the Mill, by the K. company. Att Whitehall.

27 December

74 *Upon St. John's night, the prince only being there, The Bondman,
by the queene ⟨of Bohemia's⟩ company. Att Whitehall.

28 December

75 *Upon Innocents night, falling out upon a Sonday, The Buck is a
Thief, the king and prince being there. By the king's company. At
Whitehall.

68. Ord HP5, 149; also Chalmers, 216, reading 'Bonen' for 'Bowen', and Burn, 203.
Lost. Bentley, iii. 32.
69. Burn, 196; also Chalmers, 216, abbreviated. Lost. Bentley, v. 1177–8.
70. Burn, 201; also Malone, iii. 230, noting that it was acted at the Cockpit, and
Chalmers, 216. Bentley, iv. 765–70.
71. Burn, 198; also Chalmers, 216. Lost. Bentley, iv. 518.
72. Burn, 204; also Malone, iii. 226, summarized, noting that it was acted at
Blackfriars, and Chalmers, 216. Revised by Massinger and published in 1647 as *The
Lovers' Progress*. Bentley, iii. 359–63.
73. Malone, iii. 227.   74. Ibid. By Massinger. See above, 70.
75. Ibid. Anon., lost. Bentley, v. 1297.

1624

1 January

76   *Upon New-years night, by the K. company, The Wandering Lovers, the prince only being there. Att Whitehall.

77a *A new years Gift receiued of £2 from the King's Company by W. Hemings
     The other company paid New years gifts but more tardily.

77b *A new years gift—1623. Received as a Newyeares ⟨gift from the Kings Company⟩ by Mʳ. Hemings upon the daye itts selfe—2*li*.

2 January

78   *For the Palsgraves company.   January
     The history of the Dutchess of Suffolk by Mʳ. ⟨Drewe being full of dange⟩rous matter was much reformed & for my ⟨paines this 2ᵈ Jan. 1623 I had 2li.⟩

4 January

79   *Upon the Sonday after, beinge the 4 of January 1623, by the Queene of Bohemias company, The Changelinge, the prince only being there. Att Whitehall.

6 January

80   *Upon Twelfe Night, the maske being put off, More Dissemblers besides Women, by the king's company, the prince only being there. Att Whitehall.
     (*in margin*) The worst play that ere I saw.

81   *The *Four Sons of Amon*, att the intreaty of Worth, and another, being an olde Playe tho' never allowed of before, nor of a legible hand, with promise of my fee 6 Jan. 1623, for Prince's Company   1*li*.

---

76. Malone, iii. 227. See above, **72**.

77a. Ord C1. *77b.* Ord HP8, 153 (Halliwell-Phillipps has added the date 1624 at the top of the slip). Both entries appear to refer to the same transaction, but with slightly different wording. (a) is at the foot of a page containing Ord transcripts, but is not in Ord's handwriting, and seems to have been written in by Chalmers.

78. Ord HP8, 153; also Malone MS in his copy of the play, Bodleian Mal 190(3), Chalmers, 217, and Burn, 195, including printing licence (see **109** below). By Thomas Drue. Bentley, iii. 284–6.

79. Malone, iii. 227. By Middleton and Rowley. See above, **7**.

80. Ibid. By Middleton. See above, **61**. The masque, Jonson's *Neptune's Triumph*, was postponed and then abandoned (Bentley, iv. 660–3).

81. Burn, 197; also Chalmers, 217, abbreviated. Anon., lost. Bentley, v. 1337.

18 January

82   *To the Duchess of Richmond, in the kings absence, was given The Winter's Tale, by the K. company, the 18 Janu. 1623. Att Whitehall.

26 January

83   *The *Whore in Grain*, a Trag: may be acted 26 Jan. 1623–4. 1^{li}. For the Palsgrave's Company.

2 March

84   *Itt determins the 3^d March 1624. A license to John ⟨Townshend, Alexander⟩ Foster & in confirmation of their patent for a year after ⟨the date herof this⟩ 2^d. March 1623— £3: 1^s: 0^d

3 March

85   *Sun's Darling*, in the Nature of a Masque, by Decker and Forde, all^d to Cockpit Comp^y. 3 March 1623–4 1*li*.

86   *Itt determins the 4th March 1624. A license to Gilbert ⟨Reason, George Bosgrave and⟩ in confirmation of an exemplification from the Princes ⟨company patent⟩ for a yeare after the date herof the 3^d March 1623: 3^{li}. M^r. ⟨Biston gives his⟩ word for the payment of itt att Whitsuntyde. whereof ⟨remains 18^s.⟩

10 March

87   *A Newyeres gift this 10th March 1623—Received as a new-yeres gift from the Cockpitt company Sir Walter Rawleys booke worth 1^{li}:

12 March

88   *For the press—The Noble Bondman was allowed for the press this 12th March 1623.

---

82. Malone, iii. 228.

83. Burn, 204; also Chalmers, 217. Anon., lost. Bentley, v. 1440–1.

84. Ord HP11, 141. Not in Bentley. Townsend and Foster belonged to the Lady Elizabeth's company that travelled exclusively in the provinces (Bentley, i. 179–82).

85. Burn, 203; also Chalmers, 217, and Malone MS in his copy of the play, Bodleian Mal 238(8). Bentley, iii. 459–61.

86. Ord HP11, 121. Not in Bentley. This was presumably the 'Exemplificacon of a patent' that Gilbert Reason showed to the authorities at Norwich on 29 Jan. 1625 (*Norwich*, 187; Murray, 351). 'Biston' is Christopher Beeston.

87. Ord HP5, 150. Bentley, vi. 59.

88. Ord HP5, 150; also Chalmers, 216, and Burn, 201. See above, **70**.

16 March

89   *For the kings company. *Shankes Ordinarie*, written by Shankes himselfe, this 16 March, 1623,—1*l*. 0*s*. 0*d*.

20 March

90   (*Dover*) Itm' then p^d [him] for ye like given as a gratuity vnto the Players of the Lady Elizabeth having also his Ma^{tes} lycence, & the mr of Revells his Confirmacon   0—10—0

30 March

91   *From Mr. Blagrave, in the name of the Cockpit company, for this Lent, this 30th March, 1624. £2. 0. 0.

1 April

92   *For Lent— M^r. Hemings brought mee for Lent this 1st Apr. 1624—2^{li}.

6 April

93   *For the Fortune—   1624
A New Comedy called a Match or no Match written by M^r. Rowlye this 6th Apr: 1624—   1^{li}.

9 April

94   *It determines 9th March 1624— A license to Perrye & others in ⟨confirmation of a⟩ pattent from the Revels for a year after the date hereof this ⟨9th Apr. 1624. 3^{li}.⟩ He hath given his bonde for 6^{li}. more to bee payd in sixe ⟨months in respect of⟩ the weakness of his commission for the Revels their having ⟨a latter grant of⟩ more force; att the same tyme   dayes libertye to ⟨acte with his companye⟩ in this towne of London att the Curtin— 10^s.— Of this ⟨hath byn payd⟩ for the compisition by M^{rs}. Fleminge this 17th Apr. 1624—2^{li}.

89. Malone, iii. 221 (and 515); also Ord C1; Ord HP8, 152; Chalmers, 179; and Burn, 203. Bentley, v. 1050–1.

90. *MSC* vii. 51; also Murray, 266.   *91*. Malone, iii. 66. Bentley, vii. 4.

92. Ord HP8, 152. Bentley, v. 1050, vii. 3.

93. Ord HP5, 41; also Chalmers, 217, and Burn, 200. Lost. Probably by Samuel rather than William Rowley (Bentley, v. 1012–13).

94. Ord HP5, 85. Bentley, vi. 137–8. This puzzling document seems to refer to the licence which was copied into the Exeter records on 31 May 1624 (see Appendix B1), though it does not mention any right to act at the Curtain Theatre in London. Who precisely had the 'latter grant of more force' cannot be established.

10 April

95   *For the king's company. The Historye of Henry the First, written
by Damport; this 10 April, 1624,—1*l.* 0. 0.

17 April

96   *For the Fortune—
The Way to content all Women or how a man may please his wife
written by Gunnell this 17 Apr. 1624— 1^{li}.

97   *For the Cockpit company
The Renegado or the Gentleman of Venice by Messinger this 17th
Apr 1624. 1^{li}.

3 May

98   *For the Prince's Company; A New Play, called, *The Madcap:*
Written by *Barnes.*

99   *On the 3d of May 1624, Sir Henry Herbert states, that he had
licensed, without a fee, *Jugurth*, an old play, allowed by Sir George
Bucke, and *burnt, with his other books.*

15 May

100   *Nero*, all^{d} to be printed 15 May 1624, 10s. for the Press.

21 May

101   *Honour in the End*, Com: conteyninge 12 sheets and half, allowed
for the Palsgrave's company 21 May 1624 1*li*

---

95. Malone, iii. 229; also Malone, *An Inquiry*, 299. By Robert Davenport, lost. Bentley,
iii. 230–1.
96. Ord HP5, 41; also Chalmers, 217, and Burn, 204. By Richard Gunnell,
lost. Bentley, iii. 519–20. Burn gives an impossible date of 1641 (Gunnell died in
1634).
97. Ord HP5, 150; also Malone MS in his copy of the play, Bodleian Mal 236(5);
Malone, iii. 230; Chalmers, 218; and Burn, 202, giving date as Nov. By Philip
Massinger. Bentley, iv. 811–15. See Introduction, 125.
98. Chalmers, 218. Full name of author not known. Lost. Bentley, iii. 9–10.
99. Chalmers, 203; also Chalmers, 218, with title given as '*Jugurth*, King of Numidia',
and without the last six words. By William Boyle, surviving only in MS. Bentley, iii.
36–8, argues that the books destroyed by fire were those belonging to the Fortune
theatre, burnt down on 9 Dec. 1621, not those in the private library of Sir George
Buc.
100. Burn, 200; also Chalmers, 218. Anon. Bentley, v. 1379–82.
101. Burn, 198; also Chalmers, 218. Anon., lost. Bentley, v. 1351–2.

27 May

102 *For the King's Company; A Comedy, called, *A Wife for a Month*: Written by Fletcher.

103 *The *Parricide*, containing 13 sheets and a half, allowed for the Princes Company 27 May 1624.   41?

31 May

(*Exeter*. Licence to William Perry and others, dated 9 Apr. 1624, copied into Exeter records; see Appendix **B**1)

11 June

104 *A new play, called the *Fairy Knight*, written by Forde and Decker, all[d] 11 June 1624.   1*li*.

12 June

105 *"A new play called *A Game at Chesse*, written by Middleton," was licensed by Sir Henry Herbert, June 12. 1624. So his Office Book MS.

16 June

106 *The *Protecter*, a New P. written by Sunn, 16 June 1624.

23 June

107 *A license to James Tomson to make shew of *a Fishe* for half a yr 23[d]. June—gratis

July

108 *Love me or Love me not*, a new Comedy by Drew, alld for the Palsgrave's Company July 1624,   1*li*.

---

102. Chalmers, 218; also Malone, iii. 226, and Burn, 204, adding licence fee of £1. Bentley, iii. 422–5.

103. Burn, 201; also Chalmers, 218. Bentley, iv. 489–93, discusses this entry in connection with Henry Glapthorne's *Revenge for Honour*, entered in the SR in 1657 as 'The Paraside or Revenge for Honour'. He argues that this entry can hardly refer to Glapthorne, who was born in 1610, and must indicate an anonymous lost play. Burn's '41?' perhaps suggests that he had reservations about the accuracy of the date.

104. Burn, 196; also Chalmers, 218. Lost. Bentley, iii. 249–50.

105. Malone MS in his copy of the play, Bodleian Mal 247. First printed by Wilson, *The Library*, 4th ser., 7 (1926–7), 209; also Burn, 197, abbreviated but including licence-fee of £1. Bentley, iv. 870–9. See below, **114–15**.

106. Burn, 202. Not in Bentley; both play and dramatist not otherwise known.

107. Ord HP2.

108. Burn, 198. Not in Bentley; not otherwise known. 'Drew' is presumably Thomas Drue or Drew (Bentley, iii. 280–6).

2 July

109 *⟨*The Duchess of Suffolk*⟩ allowed to be printed 2 July 1624, brought by Drewe, the Poet.

7 July

110 *For the adding of a scene to The Virgin Martyr, this 7th July, 1624,—£0 10 0.

14 July

111 *The *Honest Citizen*, an English History, by Deye, alld for the Prince's Company, 14 July 1624   1*li*.

24 July

112 *False Alarm*, a new play, by Mr Decker, allowd for the Cockpit Company 24 July 1624, 1*li*.

26 July

113 *A Wedding, or a *Cure for a Cuckold*, by Webster, allowed July 26th. 1624, for the Princes Company   1*li*

20 August

114 The Spanish Amb^r. hath at last though wth much adoe, gott the Players to be silenst, and enter in a bond not to Play Gundomar ⟨i.e. *A Game at Chess*⟩ or any other till they know his Ma^ts. farther pleasure. Middleton the Poet is sought after, and it is supposed shall be clapt in prison, if he doe not cleere him selfe by the M^r. of the Reuells, who alowed of it; and it is thought not w^thout leaue, from the higher powers I meane the P. and D. if not from the K. for they were all loth to haue it forbidden, and by report laught hartely at it.

---

109. Burn, 195. Not in Bentley. See above, **78**; only Burn includes the printing as well as the acting licence. Not entered in the SR, with Sir Henry as licenser, until 13 Nov. 1629, and published in 1631.

110. Malone, i. 424; also Burn, 204. By Dekker and Massinger. See above, **4**.

111. Burn, 198. Not in Bentley; not otherwise known. 'Deye' is presumably John Day (Bentley, iii. 238–40).

112. Burn, 196. Not in Bentley; not otherwise known.

113. Burn, 195. Licence not known to Bentley, v. 1248–50.

114. Letter from John Woolley to William Trumbull, BL Trumbull Papers, alphabet. ser. XLVIII, no. 136. For the acting licence see above, **105**. Numerous contemporary documents referring to *A Game at Chess* are now known; this and the following item are included because they explicitly mention the Master of the Revels. The figures identified by initials are obviously Prince Charles, the Duke of Buckingham, and King James.

21 August

115 Wee haue called before vs, some of the principall Actors, and
demaunded of them, by what lycence and authoritie they haue
presumed to act the same ⟨A Game at Chess⟩, in answer whervnto
they produced a booke being an orriginall and p⟨er⟩fect Coppie
thereof (as they affirmed) seene and allowed by Sr Henry Herbert
knight M^r of the Reuells, vnder his owne hand, and subscribed in the
last Page of the said booke; We demaunding further, whether there
were no other parts or passages represented on the Stage, then those
expressely contained in the booke, they confidentlie protested they
added or varied from the same nothing at all . . . As for our
certifieing to his Matie: (as was intimated by yor lre) what passages
in the said Comedie we should finde to be offensiue and scandalous,
we haue thought it our dutie for his Ma^{ts} clearer informacon to send
herewth all the booke it self subscribed as aforesaid by the M^r of the
Reuells that so either yor self or some other whom his Matie: shall
appoint to peruse the same, may see the passages themselues out of
the orriginall and call Sr Henry Herbert before yo^u to know a reason
of his lycenceing thereof, who (as we are giuen to vnderstand) is
now attending at Court.

25 August

116 *A license to William Smith & Jane his wife with two assistants to
shew a birde called a Starr for 6 months 25th Aug^t.—10^s.

September

117a *A new Trag: call: a Late murther of the sonn upon the mother
writt: by Mr Forde Webster & this   Sept. 1624. 2^{li}.

117b *The same Trag: writt: M^r. Drew & allowed for the day after
theirs because they had all manner of reason

117c . . . He saieth that the saide Anne Ellesden wished this dep. to
repaire to the M^r of the Reuells deputy and to tell him that there

115. Letter from the Privy Council to Secretary Conway; text from PRO SP14/171/99.
A text from the Privy Council Register, with spelling differences only, is in MSC i. 380–1.
116. Ord HP2.
117a–b. Ord HP5, 149; 117a also in Chalmers, 218–19, and Burn, 198. Lost. Bentley,
iii. 252–6, 280–1, 286. For an account of the lawsuit provoked by this libellous play see
C. J. Sisson, Lost Plays of Shakespeare's Age (Cambridge, 1936).
117c. From the Information laid in the Court of Star Chamber by Benjamin Garfield,
26 Nov. 1624, PRO STAC8 31/16, f. 19^v. He was the son-in-law of Mrs Anne Ellesden
or Elsden, the widow whose mishaps gave the play its subtitle, Keep the Widow Waking.

was a rumo[r] that shee [was] \should be/ played \& acted/ vppon the stage at the redd bull & to desire him to interdicte \& forbidd/ the saide playe wch this depo: accordingly did & tendered him the saide deputy xx[j]ˢ the vsuall ffee for allowing of a play as this depo was informed & saieth that the saide Anne afterwards vnderstand-inge that the said play [was] had been acted since this depo: being w[th] the saide deputy & his p⟨ro⟩mise to interdicte \& forbidd/ the same sent this Depo: to the def worth & to the players there to wish them to forbeare to acte the saide play w[ch] notw[th]standinge was often acted afterwards . . .

117d . . . this Defend[t] sayth, that true it is, Hee wrote two sheetes of paper conteyning the first Act of a Play called The Late Murder in White Chappell, or Keepe the Widow waking, and a speech in the Last Scene of the Last Act of the Boy who had killed his mother w[ch] Play (as all others are) was licensed by S[r] Henry Herbert knight, M[r] of his Ma[ties] Reuells, authorizing thereby boeth the Writing and Acting of the sayd Play.

117e . . . this deft saith that he doth not know of anie suite made to the M[r] of the Revells or anie of the players to desist from acting the said play

118 (*Coventry*) Paid w[ch] was given to Bartholomew Cloys being allowed by the Maister of the Revells for shewing a musicall organ wth divers strang and rare motions in September last as appeareth by a Bill vnder M[r] Maio[rs] hand   v[s]

3 September
119 *For the Cockp: Comp:— A new P: call: the Captive or the lost recovered written by Hayward this 3[d] Sept. 1624—1[li].

6 September
120 *The *Bee*, a New play, written by Rowley. Alld 6 Sept. 1624 1*li*. For the King's Company.

117d. From Dekker's first deposition, dated 3 Feb. 1625, PRO STAC8 31/16, f. 30. Facs. and transcript by C. J. Sisson in *The Library*, 4th ser. 8 (1927–8), 257.
117e. From Dekker's second deposition, dated 24 Mar. 1626. STAC8 31/16, f. 49. Facs. and transcript, ibid. 258–9.
118. *Coventry*, 419; also Murray, 250.
119. Ord HP5, 149; also Chalmers, 218, and Burn, 194. By Thomas Heywood. Bentley, iv. 560–2.
120. Burn, 194. Not in Bentley; not otherwise known. As it was put on by the King's company, the author was probably William rather than Samuel Rowley.

15 September

121   *For the Palsg: comp:— A Trag: called the Faire Star of Antwerp 15th Sept. 1624   1^{li}.

18 September

122   *A license to Henry Sands, Alexander Baker & Robert Smedlyy to shew a motion called the *Creation of the World* for a y^r. 18 Sept.   3^{li}.

123   (*Norwich*) This day mr wambus shewed forth a Letter from Sr Henry Hobart Dated in Iune last purportinge that yt was my Lo Chamblyns pleasure that he should be set at liberty And should giue his owne security for payment of his Chardges in the begininge of August followinge

2 October

124   (*Norwich*) This day one Edward Knoffe brought into this Court a wrightinge vnder the Seale of Sr Henry Hobart knight maister of the Revells whereby Robt Skynn⟨er⟩ wth the said Edward Knoffe & one more his assistants ys authorised to shewe a bay nagge wch can shewe strange feats, he hath leaue for iij dayes & no longer at his p⟨er⟩ill /

14 October

125   *For the Cockp: comp: A new P. call: The city Nightcap writt: by Damport 14 Oct. 1624.   1^{li}.

15 October

126   *For the Palsg: comp:— A new P. call: The Angell King 15 Oct. 1624—1^{li}.

---

121. Ord HP5, 149; also Chalmers, 219, and Burn, 196. Anon., lost. Bentley, v. 1327–8.
122. Ord HP2; also in Chalmers, 209, much abbreviated = 440(o). See **129** below. A show with the same title was performed at Coventry by Christopher Tomson in Feb. 1639 (*Coventry*, 443).
123. Norwich, 182; also Murray, 350. Francis Wambus was imprisoned at Norwich on 26 Apr. for persisting in his efforts to perform a comedy called *The Spanish Contract* (anon., lost; Bentley, v. 1455–6), despite a letter from the Privy Council of May 1623 forbidding playing at Norwich (*Norwich*, 177–8, and Murray, 359–60, from Norwich records; *MSC* i. 378–9, from Privy Council Register). It is not clear why Wambus took so long to produce a letter written in June.
124. Norwich, 187; also Murray, 351.
125. Ord HP5, 149; also Chalmers, 219, and Burn, 194. By Robert Davenport. Bentley, iii. 227–8.
126. Ord HP5, 149; also Chalmers, 219, and Burn, 194. Anon., lost. Bentley, v. 1290–1.

19 October

127   *Fletcher's *Rule a Wife and Have a Wife* licensed.

22 October

128   *For the P. comp: A new P. call: The Bristowe Marchant writt: by Forde & Decker 22 Oct. 1624.   1^{li}.

25 October

129   (*Gloucester*) At wch tyme one Henry Sandes wth three others brought a comicon vnder Sr Henry Harberts hand & seale m^r of the revells & requested mr mayor to let them play according to their comicon, wch comicon was dated the xviijth day of Sept Anno R⟨egni⟩ R⟨egis⟩ Iacobi xxijth directed to the sayd Henry Sandes [Allexdin] Allexander Baker & Robert Smedley, & the sayd Allexander Baker confessed his name \was/ Barker & not Baker & they had wth them one Iarvis Gennat.\a mynstrell./

1 November

130   *Upon All-hollows night, 1624, the king being at Roiston, no play.

2 November

131   *The night after, my Lord Chamberlin had Rule a Wife and Have a Wife for the ladys, by the kings company.

3 November

132   *For the Cock: comp: A new P. call: The Parlam^t. of love writt: by Massinger   3^d Novr. 1624   1^{li}.

11 November

133   *For the Palsg: comp: A new P. call: the Masque   11th. Novr. 1624

---

127. Malone, iii. 226. See below, 131 and 135. Bentley, iii. 407–11.
128. Ord HP5, 149; also Chalmers, 219, expanding 'P: comp' to 'Palsgrave's company', and Burn, 194, expanding to 'Prince's company'. As most of Dekker's work at this period was either for the Prince's company at the Red Bull or for the Lady Elizabeth's company at the Cockpit, Burn's interpretation seems more plausible. For a Restoration puppet-show called 'The Merchant's Daughter of Bristol' see R73. Bentley, iii. 247–8.
129. *Cumberland, etc.*, 319–20.   *130*. Malone, iii. 228.   *131*. Ibid.
132. Ord HP5, 149; also Malone, iii. 230; Chalmers, 219; and Burn, 201. The MS of this play (Dyce MS 39, Victoria and Albert Museum), the only surviving text, has a portion cut from the last leaf which may have held Sir Henry's licence: see MSR, ed. K. M. Lea (1929), p. xi.
133. Ord HP5, 149; also Chalmers, 219. Probably by Richard Gunnell, lost. Bentley, iv. 518–19.

29 November

134 A certificate \grounted/ to Edward Shackerly not to bee arested or imprisoned dureinge the tyme of the Revells, the 29ᵗʰ of Nouembeʳ. 1624

20 December

(*Letter of submission to Sir Henry from the King's company, apologizing for having played an unlicensed play called *The Spanish Viceroy*. See under 19 Oct. 1633, 265d.)

26 December

135 *Upon St. Steevens night, the prince only being there, ⟨was acted⟩ Rule a Wife and Have a Wife, by the kings company. Att Whitehall.

27 December

136 *Upon St. John's night, ⟨the prince⟩ and the duke of Brunswick being there, The Fox, by the ———. (*sic*) Att Whitehall.

137 Theise are to Certefie yoᵘ. That Edward Knight, William Pattrick, William Chambers, Ambrose Byland, Henry Wilson, Jeffery Collins, William Sanders, Nicholas Vnderhill Henry Clay, George Vernon, Roberte Pallant, Thomas Tuckfeild, Roberte Clarke, [George Rickner,] John Rhodes, William Mago, [and] Anthony Knight ⟨and Edw: Ashborne, Will: Carver, Allexander Bullard, William Toyer, William Gascoyne. *in left margin*⟩ are all imployed by the Kinges Maᵗⁱᵉˢ: servantes in theire quallity of Playinge as Musitions and other necessary attendantes, And are att all tymes and howers to bee readie with theire best endevoʳs to doe his Maᵗⁱᵉˢ: service (dureinge the tyme of the Revells) In Which tyme they nor any of them are to bee arested, or deteyned vnder arest, imprisoned, Press'd for Souldiers or any other molestacon Whereby they may bee hindered from doeing his Maᵗⁱᵉˢ: service, Without leaue firste

---

134. See below, **137**.

135. Malone, iii. 228.

136. Ibid. Malone's dash presumably indicates a defect in the office-book; Jonson's *Volpone* would have been performed by the King's company.

137. Copy of a warrant protecting the musicians of the King's company from arrest, A44. For discussion and facs. see Cutts. Underneath the text given here are notes of two more protections, for Edward Shackerly (see above, **134**) and Richard Sharpe (below, **139**). The upper left-hand corner has an indentation suggesting that the document once bore a seal, but the marginal annotation indicates that it was retained as an office-copy.

had and obteyned of the Lo^r: Chamberlyne of his Maties: most
hono^{ble}: housould, or of the Maister of his Maties: Revells. And if any
shall presume to interrupt or deteyne them or any of them after
notice hereof given by this my Certificate hee is to aunswere itt att
his vtmost p⟨er⟩ ill. Given att his Maties Office of the Revells vnder
my hand and Seale the xxvijth day of Decemb^r. 1624.

To all Mayo^{rs}, Sheriffes, Iustices
of the Peace, Bayleiffes, Constables,
knight Ma^rshalls men, and all othe^r   HHerbert.
his Maties: Office^rs to whom
it may or shall apperteyne.

(*vertically in left margin*) A note of the Protections that haue byn
granted by mee.

28 December
138   *Upon Innocents night, the ⟨prince⟩ and the duke of Brunswyck
being there, Cupids Revenge, by the Queen of Bohemia's Servants.
Att Whitehall, 1624.

29 December
139   A certificate graunted to Richard Sharpe the 29° of Decemb^r. 1624.
not to bee arested or imprisoned dureinge the tyme of the Revells.

140   *The Masque book was allowed of for the press & brought me by
⟨M^r. Ion   29 Decr. 1624.⟩

1625

January
141   *New years gifts From Rice & Robinson in the name of the ⟨Kings
Comp.   iij^{li}.⟩

1 January
142   *Upon New-years night, the prince only being there, The First Part of
Sir John Falstaff, by the king's company. Att Whitehall, 1624.

138. Malone, iii. 228. By John Fletcher.
139. See above, **137**.
140. Ord HP10, 131; also Chalmers, 219, who expands 'Ion' to 'Jon[son]'. This refers
to the text of Jonson's masque, *The Fortunate Isles and their Union* (see below, **143-4**).
Bentley, iv. 519 and 642.
141. Ord HP10, 131. Not dated, but between items dated 3 Nov. 1624 and 25 Jan.
1624/5. Bentley, iv. 642.
142. Malone, iii. 228. Presumably *Henry IV, Part I.*

6 January

143   *Upon Twelve night, the Masque being putt of, and the prince only
       there, Tu Quoque, by the Queene of Bohemias servants. Att
       Whitehall, 1624.

9 January

144   *Upon the Sonday night following, being the ninthe of January
       1624, the Masque was performed.

25 January

145   *For the Prin: comp: A new P. call: the Widowes prize contay⟨ning
       much abusive⟩ matter was allowed by mee on condition my
       reformations ⟨were observed 25 Jan 1624⟩

2 February

146   *On Candlemas night the 2 February, no play, the king being att
       Newmarket

4 February

147   *George Wilson was sworne his Majesty (sic) servant & a Groome
       of his Majestys Revels in Ordinary 4.ᵗʰ Feb: 1624

8 February

148a   *For the Kgs comp: an olde P. call: The honests (sic) mans fortune
       the original being lost was reallowed by me att Mᵣ. Taylors intreaty
       & on condition to give me a booke 8ᵗʰ. Feb: 1624.   The Arcadia

148b   This Play, being an olde One and the Originall Lost was reallowd
       by mee. This. 8. febru. 1624 Att the Intreaty of Mᵣ ⟨Taylor⟩

---

143. Malone, iii. 228. John Cooke, *Greene's Tu Quoque, or the City Gallant.*
144. Ibid. Jonson's *The Fortunate Isles*, postponed from Twelfth Night. See above, **140.**
145. Ord HP10, 131; also Chalmers, 219–20. By William Sampson, lost. Bentley, v. 1046–7.
146. Malone, iii. 228.
147. Ord C1; also Ord HP11, 141, and Chalmers, 210. Bentley, ii. 620–1.
148a. Ord HP10, 71; also Malone, iii. 229, and Chalmers, 220. By Fletcher and others. Bentley, v. 1075–6. Malone puts 'The Arcadia' in square brackets, and Chalmers omits it. This is presumably the book Sir Henry was given (the enlarged edn. of Sidney's *Arcadia* was published in London in 1622 and 1623), but it has been unconvincingly suggested that the reference is to Shirley's play of that title.
148b. Licence written in at end of MS of play, Dyce MS 9, Victoria and Albert Museum, f. 34ᵛ. In Sir Henry's handwriting. Though the bottom of the page is badly worn, and the last word (obviously 'Taylor') is missing, there are no traces of Sir Henry's signature, and he seems not to have signed it.

11 February

149 *The Cock: comp: A new P. call. Love tricks with comp[ts]. 11th. Feb: 1624. 1[li].

9 March

150 *A license to John Townsend, Joseph Moore and Foster ⟨in confirmat: of their⟩ pattent for a year after the date herof 9th March 1624. ⟨3. [li].⟩

15 March

151 *From Mr. Gunnel, in the name of the dancers of the ropes for Lent, this 15 March, 1624. £1. 0. 0.

16 March

152 *A license to Ellis Gret Arthur Grimes & Rob[t]. Selbye with the rest of their comp: to playe for a yeare after the date herof 16 Mch 1624. 3[li].

19 March

153a *From Mr. Gunnel, to allowe of a Masque for the dancers of the ropes, this 19 March, 1624. £2. 0. 0.

153b *For Lent— From Mrs Gunnill to allowe of a masque for the dancers of the ropes 19th March 1624. 10[s].

28 May

154 (Norwich) This day Ellis Gest brought into this Court a lycence vnder the hand & seale of S[r] Henry Hobart maister of the Revelles bearinge date the xvj[th] of March Anno xxij° Iacobi nuper Regis, whereby the said Ellis & other of his Company are lycenced to play &c to whome was shewed the Letters from the lordes of the Counsell & his Ma[ties] p⟨ro⟩clamacon And therevpon they were not p⟨er⟩mitted to play But in regard of the honorable respect w[ch] this

---

149. Ord HP10, 71; also Malone, iii. 231 (giving date as 10 Feb.) and Chalmers, 220. By James Shirley; published in 1631 as *The School of Compliment*. Bentley, v. 1144–7.
150. Ord HP11, 141. Not in Bentley. Cf. 84.
151. Malone, iii. 66. Bentley, vii. 5.
152. Ord HP11, 2; also Ord C1. Not in Bentley. 'Gret' is a misreading of 'Gest' or 'Guest' (Bentley, ii. 453–4). He produced this licence at Norwich on 28 May (see below, 154). Bentley mentions Grimes (ii. 452) but not Robert Selbye.
153a. Malone, iii. 66. 153b. Ord HP11, 2. Bentley, vi. 159. It is not clear whether or not these entries are different versions of the same item. Bentley points out that £2 seems a large amount 'for such a short script as a rope dancers' masque must have been', and if Mrs Gunnell also paid 10s., the amount would be higher still. Possibly Ord's is the correct version.
154. Norwich, 189; also Murray, 352–3. See above, 152.

City beareth to the right ho^{ble} the Lo: Chamberlyn and Sr Henry
Hobart there ys given vnto them as a gratuety xx s /
A Letter ys to be written to the Lo: Chamberlyn touchinge players

1 July

155   *A confirmacon of the Kings companys patent to travell for a yeare
1st July 1625.   1^{li}.

6 July

156   Mr. *Snelling* moveth, that, where the Players, being restrained here,
will go into the Country, to the Danger of spreading the Infection;
to restrain these.
    Resolved, Sir *Ben. Rudyard* shall, from the House, move the Lord
Chamberlain to restrain these.

9 July

157   Sir *Ben. Rudyard* returneth Answer from the Lord Chamberlain;
That he hath given Order to the Master of the Revels, not to suffer
any Players to play in any Part of *England*, during the Time of this
Infection.
    Ordered, Thanks to be returned from this House to his Lordship,
for his Care therein.

1626

22 January

158   *Fletcher's *The Fair Maid of the Inn* licensed. Acted at Blackfriars.

3 February

159   *Fletcher's *The Noble Gentleman* licensed. Acted at Blackfriars.

9 February

160   *Shirley's *The Maid's Revenge* licensed.

---

155. Ord HP9, 49; also Ord C1 (two copies) and Chalmers, 185. Bentley, i. 19. The
next two items, not known to Bentley, ii. 654–7, show that the patent was almost
immediately nullified.
156. *JHC* i. 804. Theatres were closed at the end of Mar. 1625 because of the death
of James I, and remained closed because of the plague, not reopening until the
beginning of Dec.
157. *JHC* i. 807. For a later parliamentary petition to the Lord Chamberlain see
Bentley, vi. 21.
158. Malone, iii. 226. Bentley, iii. 336–9.
159. Malone, iii. 227. Bentley, iii. 387–91.
160. Malone, iii. 231. Bentley, v. 1132–4.

6 March

161   (*Leicester*) Item geuen to Ellis Geste, Thomas Swinerton, Arthuret Grimes, and others, going about with a Pattent from the M^r of the Revells the sixth of March   i^{li}

25 April

162a   Right Honorable

According to an order made by yor hono^r the 27th. day of Janua: last, whereby a Cause depending in Chauncery betweene *Worth* playntiffe and *Baskerville* defendant was referred vnto mee, I haue vpon the continuall solicitacon of the playntiffe appointed divers daies this vacacon for hearing of the Cause, all wch the playntiffe very diligently attended wth his Counsell who were also ready for him, but the defendant sometime pretending her Counsell was not in towne or some time that she could not gett them or by some other excuse hath still put of the hearing of the Cause: At last seeing the Terme drawe on, and how peremptory it was to ye playnetiffe to haue mee make some end or Certificate in the Cause before the Terme; At ye playnetiffs importunitie I appointed Satturday last, at wch time though in reguard of much weakenes by reason of sicknes I was vnfitt to be troubled, yet rather then the poore man should be preiudiced I was willinge to haue heard the Cause, for wch purpose the playnetiffe and his Counsell were ready, but the defendant as formerly (though shee had notice the Thursday before) excused her selfe alledging shee had no Counsell ready, but depended on Sarjeant Binge who was not then come to towne; Herevpon I told her, that I would take some other time the beginninge of this terme, assoone as my strength should serue not doubting but I should make some good end of the Cause; and at ye playnetiffs request moued her to forbeare to seeke a dismission for lack of my Certificate, her selfe only having bin in fault; but shee

---

161. Murray, 316.

162a. Letter from Sir Henry to the Master of the Rolls, PRO C38/52; first published in *The Athenaeum*, 29 Aug. 1885, 282. The main body of the letter, down to 'Court', is in a scribal hand, the remainder is by Herbert himself. Mrs Susan Baskerville was the widow of an actor in Queen Anne's company, which she sued in 1623 for failing to pay her a pension to which she was entitled. The company, in the name of Ellis Worth, counter-claimed in Chancery in 1626, but Mrs Baskerville seems to have deliberately avoided attending the court or the mediation of Sir Henry. For a fuller account see Bentley, i. 158–9, and C. J. Sisson, 'The Red Bull Company and the Importunate Widow', *Shakespeare Survey 7* (Cambridge, 1954), 57–68.

refused the same, and thereby gaue mee iust cause to beleiue that her former delayes haue bin of purpose to take aduantage thereof to the playnetiffs preiudice, All wch. I thought fitt to certifie to yor. hono^r. wthall assuring you that assoone as my strength shall serue mee I will this Terme heare the Cause and end it, or make Certificate to this hono^{ble}. Court.

this. 25. Aprill,
1626.
Whitehall.

Your honors humble
seruant,
HHerbert

Hauinge made use of my seruants penn I hope your honor will attribute itt rather to my weaknes then to any ill maners.

25 May

162b ... vppon the 24th daie of this instant moneth of Maye he repayred to Sr Henrye Herbert knight M^r of the Reuells at his lodginge at Chelsey vnto whome the cause in question betweene the plts and defendts hadd beene formerlie referred as he conceyveth to mediate an ende betwixt them and desieringe to vnderstand what the said Sr Henrye hadd done or determyned therein he the said Sr Henrye saide that indeede there hadd [beene] formerlie beene reference to suche purpose from this Courte vnto him to haue indevored therein before the firste daie of this laste Tearme and as he vnderstoode a contynewacon of the same order vntill the 10th of this monethe but by reason of greate sicknesses whereof he still languisheth he could not heare yt nor appointe anie tyme and that nowe yt did noe waie concerne him but the Courte to take order in yt wch he desiered and said he woulde rather gyve 20^{li} then be troubled anie further in yt.

17 July

163 *17 July, 1626, ⟨Received⟩ from Mr. Hemmings for a courtesie done him about their Blackfriers hous,—3*l*. 0. 0.

22 August

164 *A license to Philip Newsam & 2 assistants to shewe a Bay nag \dancinge/ for a year 22^d Augt 1626

11 October

165 *Massinger's *The Roman Actor* licensed for the king's company.

162b. Deposition in the Worth–Baskerville case by Francis Smith of Gray's Inn, Chancery Register of Affidavits, PRO C41/3, f. 601^v.
163. Malone, iii. 229. Bentley, i. 21–2.   *164*. Ord HP2.
165. Malone, iii. 230. Bentley, iv. 815–17.

4 November
166 *Shirley's *The Brothers* licensed.

1627

12 January
167 *Davenant's *The Cruel Brother* licensed.

24 February
168 (*Norwich*) This day a lycence was brought into this Court vnder the hand & seale of the maister of the Revelles Authorisinge him (*sic*) to shewe A rare portraycture or Sight wthin this City wch lycence beareth date the xxixth of March 1626 /

20 March
169 *March 20, 1626. From Mr. Hemminges, for this Lent allowanse, £2. 0. 0.

9 April
170 *For a warrant to the Musitions of the king's company, this 9th of April, 1627,—£1. 0. 0.

11 April
171 *From Mr. Heminge, in their company's name, to forbid the playinge of any of Shakespeare's playes to the Red Bull company, this 11th of Aprill, 1627,—5 0 0.

6 June
172 *Massinger's *The Judge* licensed for the king's company.

5 July
173 *The Great Duke was licensed for the Queen's Servants, July 5, 1627. This was, I apprehend, The Great Duke of Florence, which was acted by that company.

10 July
174 *11th. Jan 1627   A license to Bartholemew Cloyse & 4 assistants to
determines   shew an Organ for half a yeare 10th July 1627

166. Malone, iii. 231. Bentley, v. 1082–4, argues that this is not the play published as *The Brothers* in 1652 (see **423** n.).
167. Malone, iii. 284. Bentley, iii. 201.   *168.* *Norwich*, 195; also Murray, 353.
169. Malone, iii. 66.   *170.* Malone, iii. 112.
171. Malone, vii. 291; also iii. 229. Bentley, i. 270–1.
172. Malone, iii. 230. Lost. Bentley, iv. 793–4.
173. Malone, iii. 230. Bentley, iv. 786–8.   *174.* Ord HP10, 19.

10 October

175   *A license to Humfry Bromley & 3 assistants to show a childe with 3 heads for a y^r. 10 Oct. 1627.

1628

12 January

176   *The profitts for licensing of shewes being cast up from 26th. July 1623 to the 12th Jañy 1627—103$^{li.}$: 6^s. : o$^{d.}$

6 May

177   *The Honour of Women was licensed May 6, 1628. I suspect that this was the original name of The Maid of Honour, which was printed in 1631, though not entered for the stage in Sir Henry Herbert's book.

25 May

178   *The kinges company with a generall consent and alacritye have given mee the benefitt of too dayes in the yeare, the one in summer, thother in winter, to bee taken out of the second daye of a revived playe, att my owne choyse. The housekeepers have likewyse given their shares, their dayly charge only deducted, which comes to some 2l. 5s. this 25 May, 1628.

The benefitt of the first day, being a very unseasonable one in respect of the weather, comes but unto £4. 15. 0.

2 July

179   (*Norwich*) This day A lycence vnder the hand of Sr Henry Herbert dated the 7th of Iune 1628 Annoq^e 4° Caroli Regis was brought to this City Authorisinge Elis Guest Antony Burton Antony Grymes w^m Eyton Edward Bagly Iosias white w^m Haruye Nicholas Lowe

---

175. Ord HP2. On 5 June 1616 'Humfry Bromely' was permitted to show a child with two heads at Norwich. He was ordered to leave Norwich with his wife on 12 June 1616 (*Norwich*, 146–7).

176. Ord HP2.

177. Malone, iii. 230. Bentley, iii. 790–2, argues that this is a lost play by Massinger, not an alternative title for an existing play. Edwards and Gibson, i, pp. xxiii–xxv, xxxi, treat it as a lost play. In the version of the licence which Malone wrote into his own copy of *The Maid of Honour*, Bodleian Mal 236(8), he gave the date as 26 May.

178. Malone, iii. 176. Bentley, i. 23–4. Malone follows this with a list of similar payments up to 6 June 1633 (**181, 189, 197, 211, 219, 226, 242,** and **256**). On 30 Oct. 1633 (**268**) it was agreed that two fixed payments of £10, in summer and winter, should be made.

179. *Norwich*, 197–8; also Murray, 353

Tho: Doughton Richard Hauly Richard Bromefild Richard willis & Antony Gibes to play &c To whome is given xx^s for a gratuety vpon their request & so they are to dept wthout playinge.

3 October

180   *Shirley's *The Witty Fair One* licensed.

22 November

181   *The benefit of the winters day, being the second daye of an old play called The Custome of the Cuntrye, came to 17*l*. 10*s*. 0*d*. this 22 of Nov. 1628. From the Kinges company att the Blackfryers.

24 November

182   *Ford's play ⟨*The Lover's Melancholy*⟩ was exhibited at the Blackfriars on the 24th of November, 1628, when it was licensed for the stage, as appears from the Office-book of Sir Henry Herbert, Master of the Revels to King Charles the First, a manuscript now before me.

1629

19 January

183   *Jonson's *The New Inn* licensed.

9 February

184   *Very soon indeed after the ill success of Jonson's piece ⟨*The New Inn*⟩, the King's Company brought out at the same theatre a new play called The Love-sick Maid, or the Honour of Young Ladies, which was licensed by Sir Henry Herbert on the 9th of February, 1628–9, and acted with extraordinary applause. This play, which was written by Jonson's own servant, Richard Brome, was so popular, that the managers of the King's Company, on the 10th of March, presented the Master of the Revels with the sum of two pounds, "on the good success of The Honour of Ladies;" the only instance I have met with of such a compliment being paid him.

10 March
(See under 9 Feb.)

---

180. Malone, iii. 231. Bentley, v. 1166–7.   *181.* Malone, iii. 176.
182. Malone, i. 421. Bentley, iii. 448–51.
183. Malone, i. 421. Bentley, iv. 622–4.
184. Malone, i. 421. Bentley, iii. 77–80. Lost. Bentley is surprised that a play apparently so successful was not printed.

9 May

185   (*Norwich*) . . . xx s given to certain players who brought
lycence from the Maister of the revelles By warrant of the ix[th] of
May 1629

13 May

186   *For allowing of a new act in an ould play, this 13th May,
1629,—£0 10 0.

8 June

187   *Massinger's *The Picture* licensed for the king's company.

27 June

188   (*Norwich*) This day Elias Guest one of the Company of Ioseph
Moore Alex ffoster Rob[t] Guylman & Iohn Towneshend sworne
servantes to the Kinge brought into this Court a warrant signed w[th]
his Ma[ties] privie signett & a lycence from the M[r] of the Revells dated
the eight day of this instant Iune whereby they are lycenced to play
Comedies &c The said Elias affirmed that the residue of his
Company are still at Thetford wherevpon he did Consent to accept
such a gratuety as this Court should thinke fitt to give And
therevpon this Court did thinke fitt to giue him & his Company a
gratuety of fforty shillinges w[ch] hee thankfully accepted./

21 July

189   *The benefitt of the summers day from the kinges company being
brought mee by Blagrave, upon the play of The Prophetess, comes
to, this 21 of July 1629,—6*l*. 7*s*. 0*d*.

22 July

190   *Davenant's *The Colonel* licensed.

29 July

191   *Brome's *The Northern Lass* licensed for the king's company.

2 October

192   *Davenant's *The Just Italian* licensed.

---

185. *Norwich*, 200, also Murray, 371.   *186*. Malone, i. 424.
187. Malone, iii. 230. Bentley, iv. 808–10.   *188*. *Norwich*, 201. Murray, 353.
189. Malone, iii. 176.
190. Malone, iii. 284. Bentley, iii. 215–16. No play of this title survives; possibly an
early version of *The Siege*, published in 1673.
191. Malone, i. 431. Bentley, iii. 81–4.   *192*. Malone, iii. 284. Bentley, iii. 204–5.

3 November

193   *Shirley's *The Faithful Servant* licensed.

194   *Massinger's *Minerva's Sacrifice* licensed for the king's company.

4 November

195   *For the allowinge of a French company to play a farse at Blackfryers, this 4 of November, 1629,—*2l. os. od.*

22 November

196   *For allowinge of the Frenche ⟨company⟩ at the Red Bull for a daye, 22 Novemb. 1629,—⟨*2l. os. od.*⟩

197   *The benefitt of the winters day from the kinges company being brought mee by Blagrave, upon the play of The Moor of Venise, comes, this 22 of Nov. 1629, unto—*9l. 16s. od.*

30 November

198   (*Reading*) William Perrye and Richard Weekes, his Majestie's sworne servantes, licensed with the rest of their company, John Kerke, Edward Armiger, Hughe Tatterdell, Deavid Ferris, Robert Hint and george Williams, all of the Red Bull company, by the Master of the Revells, dated the tenth of November, 1629.

14 December

199   *For allowinge of a Frenche companie att the Fortune to play one afternoon, this 14 Day of Decemb. 1629,—*1l. os. od.*

      I should have had another peece, but in respect of their ill fortune, I was content to bestow a peece back.

1630

200   **Merry Marriage* allowed to Fortune Company. Com. 1630

201   *⟨Thomas May, The Old Couple⟩ Acted first in 1630, as appears by the Office book of S[r] Henry Herbert, Master of the Revels, of which I have made a copy. June 22. 1789.

---

193. Malone, iii. 231. Bentley, v. 1114–18. Published in 1630 under the title *The Grateful Servant.*
194. Malone, iii. 230. Bentley, iv. 799–800. Lost.
195. Malone, iii. 120 (date misprinted as 1639; 1629 in Malone 1790). Bentley, i. 25–6.
196. Malone, iii. 120. Bentley, vi. 225–7.   *197.* Malone, iii. 177.
198. Murray, 386.   *199.* Malone, iii. 120.
200. Burn, 200. Not in Bentley; not otherwise known.
201. Malone MS in his copy of Langbaine's *Account*, Bodleian Mal 131, p. 364*. Printed by Lawrence, who mistakenly read the date as 1636. In his transcript of

(*Worcester*. Indictment of John Jones for using a counterfeit licence; see Appendix **B2**)

202   (*Leicester*) Item geven to an other Companie of Players
wth a Comission from the Master of the ⟨Revells⟩   vi^s viii^d
Item geven to an other Com⟨pany of Players⟩ with
Comission from the M^r of ⟨his Ma^{ts} Revels⟩   i^{li}
Item geven to another Companie of Players w^{th}
Comission from the Master of his Ma^{ts} Revells   i^{li}

April

203   *I suspect he ⟨John Heminges⟩ died of the plague, which had raged
so violently that year ⟨1630⟩, that the playhouses were shut up in
April, and not permitted to be opened till the 12th of November,
at which time the weekly bill of those who died in London of that
distemper, was diminished to twenty-nine. (MS. Herbert)

17 April

204   Haueing receiued order from the L^{ds} &c' in regard of the great
appear^rance & app^rhension of the increase of the sicknesse to
cause all stage playes & all other Assemblyes for sports or pas-
times to bee prohibited & suppressed, Theis are to pray & require you to take effectuall order that their Lo^{ps} Order therin
bee duly obserued & put in execution by all those that are
vnder your subordination. And for soe doeing Theis shall bee
yor warr^t. Aprill 17. 1630. To S^r H Herbert./

M^d the like warraunt was sent to *Gabriell Marssh* for ye suppressing of bear & bull baitings

(*in margin*) A warr^t for supp^rssing of stage playes &c'.

12 November

205   (*Reading*) Memorandum, Robert Kimpton, Nathaniell Clay,
Thomas Holman, and others named in the licence from the
Master of the Revells, dated the 30th of December 1629, tendred
themselues to play in Towne, but did not, and were here in Lent
last.   5^s.

Aubrey's *Lives*, Bodleian MS Eng. misc. d. 26, f. 35, entry for Thomas May, Malone
added a list of his plays with dates, and that for *The Old Couple* is unmistakably 1630.
Bentley, iv. 839–40.

202. Murray, 318.   *203*. Malone, iii. 190–1.
204. PRO LC5/132/182; also *MSC* ii. 352.   *205*. Murray, 386.

25 November

206   *⟨Randolph's⟩ The Muses' Looking-Glass was not printed till 1638
(at Oxford by Leonard Lichfield & Francis Bowman) & the
title-page has only By T. R. without any preface or mention of the
theatre where it was acted. But it was acted by the Children of
the Revels under the title of the *Entertainment* in the summer of
1630; and licensed by Sir Henry Herbert Nov. 25. 1630.

26 November

207   *⟨Randolph's⟩ Amintas was licensed by Sir Henry Herbert, Nov.
26. 1630. It was acted by The Children of the Revels. See his
Office-book MS.

1631

10 January

208   A petition of *William Measure* agst Wm *Hurt* debt 7^{li} Answered (vizt)
I desire Sr *Henry Herbert Kn^t*. to make stay of soe much money as
shall appeare to bee iustly due vnto the pet^r [out of the] from his
Ma^{tye} out of the first moneys payable vnto Wm *Hurt* & to make
payment therof vnto the pet^r or his Assigne Accordingly And This
shall bee his warr^t. Jan. 10. 1630.

11 January

209   *This day being the 11 of Janu. 1630, I did refuse to allow of a play
of Messinger's, because itt did contain dangerous matter, as the
deposing of Sebastian king of Portugal, by Philip the ⟨Second,⟩
and ther being a peace sworen twixte the kings of England

---

206. Malone MS in his copy of Langbaine's *Account*, Bodleian Mal 131, p. 414*^{v}.
Printed by Lawrence. Malone wrote a shorter version of this note in his copy of the
play, Bodleian Mal 184(3). Bentley, v. 986–9.

207. Malone MS in his copy of Langbaine's *Account*, Bodleian Mal 131, p. 414*.
Printed by Lawrence. Bentley, v. 969–71.

208. PRO LC5/183/93. Bentley, ii. 463, reads the name as 'Hart', and assumes that
he was the actor William Hart. But the reading is clearly 'Hurt', and he is much more
likely to have been William Hurt the wire-drawer (see Introduction, 28). Measure had
already petitioned on 24 Sept. 1630 for a debt of £67 owed to him by Hurt
(LC5/183/87). See *MSC* xiii. 163.

209. Malone, iii. 229–31. Bentley, iv. 762–5. This is clearly the play licensed in May
under the title *Believe As You List*; it was thoroughly revised and reset in ancient Rome,
but traces of the original version survive in the MS (MSR, ed. C. J. Sisson (1927), p.
xvi). The 'peace sworen' refers to the Treaty of Madrid between England and Spain
concluded on 5 Nov. 1630.

and Spayne. I had my fee notwithstandinge, which belongs to me for reading itt over, and ought to be brought always with the booke.

210   A warrant for the app^rhension of *Henry sharpe* of *Bricklewell* in *Essex* vpon the complaint of *Sr Henry Herbert.* Ianuar. 11. 1630. (*in margin*) App^rhension./

18 February

211   *Received of Mr. Taylor and Lowins, in the name of their company, for the benefitt of my winter day, upon the second day of Ben Jonson's play of Every Man in his Humour, this 18 day of February, 1630,—12*l. 4*s.* 0*d.*

212   *Reced of M^r. Lowins for allowinge of a Dutche vaulter att their house 18th ffeb: 1630

11 March

213   *Massinger's *The Emperor of the East* licensed for the king's company.

4 May

214   *Shirley's *The Traitor* licensed.

6 May

215   This Play, called Beleiue as you liste, may bee acted, this 6. of May. 1631. Henry Herbert.

7 May

216   *Massinger's *Believe as You List* licensed for the king's company.

17 May

217   *Shirley's *The Duke* licensed.

---

210. PRO LC5/132/226; also *MSC* ii. 353.   *211.* Malone, iii. 177.
212. Ord HP10, 19. Bentley, vi. 194, vii. 6. Other Dutchmen received licences on 7 Jan. and 16 Mar. 1635 (**309**, **316**). It is not clear whether they are all the same person.
213. Malone, iii. 230. Bentley, iv. 777–81.
214. Malone, iii. 231. Bentley, v. 1150–3.
215. BL MS Egerton 2828, f. 27^v. This famous licence at the end of the MS has often been reproduced (e.g. Adams, 48; MSR, ed. Sisson (1927)).
216. Malone, iii. 230. The discrepancy of a day between the previous entry and this hardly seems large enough to demand an explanation.
217. Malone, iii. 232. Bentley, v. 1120–1. This is generally accepted to be the play published in 1640 under the title *The Humorous Courtier.*

10 June

218 *Received of Mr. Benfielde, in the name of the kings company, for a gratuity for ther liberty gaind unto them of playinge, upon the cessation of the plague, this 10 of June, 1631,—3*l*. 10*s*. 0*d*. This was taken upon Pericles at the Globe.

12 June

219 *Received of Mr. Shanke, in the name of the kings company, for the benefitt of their summer day, upon ye second daye of Richard ye Seconde, at the Globe, this 12 of June, 1631,—5*l*. 6*s*. 6*d*.

13 June

220 *Massinger's *The Unfortunate Piety* licensed for the king's company.

21 June

221 *Received of Turnor 5: 10: 0 as so much money layd out by me in a peice of Clarett wyne given to S^r. William Uvedale for their courte money for three yeares this 21st. June 1631.

18 July

222 (*Reading*) Then Ellys Guest, Richard Errington and their company, players, shewed their licence under the seale of the Master of the Revells, dated the 15th of July 1631, to endure six monethes, vizt., the xvj^th of January next, desired leave to playe, but did not.

29 August

(Licence prepared for Sisley Peadle, Thomas Peadle, Elias Grund-ling and three others to exercise rope-dancing, tumbling, vaulting, etc. See Appendix B3)

18 October

223 A warr^t for ye app^rhension of *Iohn Platt* a Cunstable in *Ware* for forbidding players to show there beeing lycensed by Sr *Henry Herbert Kn^t*./ Octob. 18. 1631./
(*in left margin*) App^rhension

---

218. Malone, iii. 177. Bentley, ii. 658–9.   *219*. Malone, iii. 177.
220. Malone, iii. 230. Lost. Bentley, iv. 820–1.
221. Ord C2. Not in Bentley. 'Turnor' seems to be Anthony Turner, an actor in Queen Henrietta's company (Bentley, ii. 607–8). Sir William Uvedale was Treasurer of the Chamber (see *MSC* vi, pp. ix–x, and also 81, where Turner received payment on behalf of his company for court performances by a warrant dated 4 July 1630). It looks as though Herbert gave Uvedale a cask of claret on behalf of the players, who then reimbursed him.
222. Murray, 386–7.   *223*. PRO LC5/132/269; also *MSC* ii. 355.

14 November
224   *Shirley's *Love's Cruelty* licensed.

December
225   *The play of Holland's Leaguer was acted six days successively at Salisbury Court, in December, 1631, and yet Sir Henry Herbert received on account of the six representations but *one pound nineteen shillings*, in virtue of the *ninth* share which he possessed as one of the proprietors of that house.

1 December
226   *Received of Mr. Blagrave, in the name of the kings company, for the benefitt of my winter day, taken upon The Alchemiste, this 1 of Decemb. 1631,—13*l*. 0*s*. 0*d*.

1632
227   *Shakerley Marmion, *Country Gentleman*, allowed to be acted 1632.

10 January
228   *Shirley's *The Changes* licensed.

12 January
229   *For allowing of an ould play, new written or forbisht by Mr. Biston, the 12th of January, 1631,—£1 0 0.

20 April
230   *Shirley's *Hyde Park* licensed.

25 April
231   *Love yields to Honour — played at the Globe — This the earliest that I have found of The Queen's going to Blackfriars

224. Malone, iii. 232. Bentley, v. 1129–32.
225. Malone, iii. 178. Written by Shakerley Marmion. Bentley, iv. 745–8. The printing licence (**C41**) shows that Sir Henry censored the play.
226. Malone, iii. 177.
227. Burn, 195. Not in Bentley; not otherwise known. It probably had no connection with the later play of the same title, by Sir Robert Howard and George Villiers, Duke of Buckingham, suppressed in 1669 but surviving in MS (see A. H. Scouten and Robert Hume, eds., *The Country Gentleman: A 'Lost' Play and its Background* (Philadelphia and London, 1976)).
228. Malone, ii. 232. Bentley, v. 1091–4.
229. Malone, i. 424 (not in Adams). Bentley, iii. 17.
230. Malone, iii. 232. Bentley, v. 1121–3.
231. Malone MS in an interleaved copy of vol. Iii of his 1790 edn. of Shakespeare, Bodleian Mal 1046, p. 144*[v]*. Not mentioned in Bentley, v. 1369, who notes that the

25 May

232   *Massinger's *The City Madam* licensed for the king's company.

13 June

233   *⟨For a prise from⟩ Blagrove playd at ye Hope ye 13th. June 1632

20 June

234   *⟨1632. For a warrant to⟩ Grimes for shewing ye Camell for a yeare from 20th June

235   *⟨. . .⟩f Ovids Epistles translated into English to ye press 20th June 1632

3 September

236   *A license to James Seale to shew a *strange fish* for half a yeare, the 3d of September, 1632.

5 September

237   *A license to John Pitcher and three assistants to shew a live Beavr (*sic*) & a Racoon for a y[r]. 5 Sept. 1632.

8 September

238   (*Norwich*) This day Robt Kempston and others of his Company of the Revelles vpon their shewinge of the lycence of the Maister of the Revelles are lycenced to play in this City by the space of two dayes.

5 October

239   (*Norwich*) A Patent vnder the Seale of the Revelles Dated the vth of March 1631 was this day shewed wherein Henry Miller and ffower

---

play was hitherto known only as a title in Malone's list of unprinted plays (Malone, ii. 438–9). The reference to the Globe is puzzling, as the King's company normally played at Blackfriars, their winter theatre, in Apr. (Bentley, i. 3, referring to **452**). This entry and **291** may be added to the list of Queen Henrietta's visits to Blackfriars given in Bentley, i. 48–9.

232. Malone, iii. 230. Bentley, iv. 771–4. It has been argued that Herbert's date may be inaccurate, or the play may have been written several years earlier, but recent scholars accept the date of 1632 (Edwards and Gibson, iv. 1–3).

233. Ord HP7, 46. Bentley, vi. 212.

234. Ord HP7, 46; also in Chalmers, undated, 208 = **440(e)**.

235. Ord HP7, 46; also Chalmers, 209, paraphrased and with no date = **440(v)**. See C47 and 52.

236. Malone, xv. 95 (not in Adams).

237. Ord HP2; also Chalmers, 208, much abbreviated = **440(b)**.

238. Norwich, 208; also Murray, 354.   *239. Norwich*, 210; also Murray, 354.

Assistants are lycensed to shewe feates and sleight of hand &c one of the said Company said that they payd dere for their patent./

12 October

240   *Received of Knight, for allowing of Ben Johnsons play called Humours Reconcil'd, or the Magnetick Lady, to be acted, this 12th of Octob. 1632, 2*l.* 0. 0.

17 October

241a   *Received from Henry Seyle for allowinge a booke of verses of my lord Brooks, entitled Religion, Humane Learning, Warr, and Honor, this 17 of October 1632, in mony, 1*l.* 0*s.* 0*d.* in books to the value of 1*l.* 4*s.* 0*d.*

241b   More of Seyle, for allowinge of two other small peeces of verses for the press, done by a boy of thirteen called Cowley, at the same time, 0*l.* 10*s.* 0*d.*

6 November

242   *Received for the summer day of the kings company ye 6 Novemb. 1632,—1*l.* 5*s.* 0*d.*

Received for the winter day upon The Wild Goose Chase, ye same day,—15*l.* 0*s.* 0*d.*

12 November

243   A petition of *William Blagraue* & *William Beeston* that his Lo^p would restore vnto them a boy named *Stephen Hamerton* inveigled from them by one *Christopher Babham* & by him imployed at the

240. Malone, iii. 231. Bentley, iv. 618–20. Feil, 109, quotes a letter of 17 Nov. 1632 from John Pory to Viscount Scudamore, not quoted by Bentley: 'The Players of the Black fryers were on Thursday called before the high Commission at Lambeth, and were there bound over to answere such articles as should be objected against them. And it is said to be for uttring some prophane speaches in abuse of Scripture and wholly thinges, which they found penned, for them to act and playe, in Ben Jonsons newe comedy called the Magnetique lady' (PRO C115/M35/8418). It looks as though at first the players tried to put the blame for what had happened on Jonson and Sir Henry. But the affair dragged on, and a year later the players took the blame on themselves, and exonerated Sir Henry (see below, **266**). Possibly they failed to observe deletion-marks Sir Henry had made in the text.

241a–b. Malone, iii. 231. 241a also Malone MS in his copy of Langbaine's *Account*, Bodleian Mal 129, f. 88. Chalmers, 209, very briefly notes a printing licence for Fulke Greville's *Caelia* (*sic* for *Caelica*) and the licence for Cowley = **440(w)** and (x). Chalmers's reading of 'thirteen' in **241b** has been substituted for Malone's 'this town'.

242. Malone, iii. 177.

243. PRO LC5/183/128; also *MSC* ii. 408. Bentley, i. 35–6, ii. 460–1.

Blackfryars playhouse Answered vizt I desire Sr *Henry Herbert Kn^t*. M^r of the Reuells to his Matie to take this petition into his consideration & to make such an accommodacon of the difference therin mentioned as may bee best for his Ma^{ts} service & the satisfaccon of the pet^{rs}. Or certifie mee the true state therof & what hee conceaveth fitt to bee done therin./ Nou. 12. 1632 (*in left margin*) Blagraue & Beeston.

14 November

244 Ordered that Sr Hen Herbert giue accompt to the board on [thursday] fryday to giue accompt (*sic*) why hee warranted the booke of D. Dns paradoxes to bee printed. By the kings comand delivered by the Bishop of London

16 November

245 *Shirley's *The Ball* licensed.

18 November

246 *18 Nov. 1632. In the play of The Ball, written by Sherley, and acted by the Queens players, ther were divers personated so naturally, both of lords and others of the court, that I took it ill, and would have forbidden the play, but that Biston ⟨Christopher Beeston⟩ promiste many things which I found faulte withall should be left out, and that he would not suffer it to be done by the poett any more, who deserves to be punisht; and the first that offends in this kind, of poets or players, shall be sure of publique punishment.

1633

14 January

247a *1633, Jan. 14. *The Corporal* was licensed for acting at Blackfriars by the King's men.

247b *In Sir Henry Herbert's Office Book, under date of January 14, 1632, there is an entry of a payment of £2, or 40s., to the King's

---

244. PRO SP16/225/39; also *CSPD 1631–3*, 437.

245. Malone, iii. 232. Bentley, v. 1076–9.   *246.* Malone, iii. 231–2.

247a. Fleay, 278; *247b.* W. C. Hazlitt, *A Manual for the Collector and Amateur of Old English Plays* (1892), 50. Not in Adams. Bentley, v. 1270–1. These licences do not occur elsewhere, and no one has been able to explain how Fleay and Hazlitt got hold of them. The second is puzzling; as Bentley comments, if the household servants of the Earl of Essex paid the King's men £2 to be allowed to put on an amateur performance, why should Sir Henry have bothered to record it?

Company, for allowing the performance of it ⟨Wilson's *The Corporal*⟩ by my Lord of Essex his servants.

21 January

248 *Shirley's *The Bewties* licensed.

1 February

249 *A license to Peter Wise a German to shew certaine feates of charging & discharging a Gun for a y^r. 1st Feb. 1632.—1.

5 February

250 *A license to Balthazer Ursty to shew \Ann Christi/ a female childe \of 70 y^{rs}. of age/ overgrown with Heare \from the face to the foote/ for a y^r. 5th feb. 1632.—1

22 February

251 . . . wee are given to vnderstand by Sr Henry Harbert M^r of the Revells that euer since our Maske two yeares ago their hath ben existing vn payed the summe of fiftie pounds for which he is much Importuned by the workmen and others to whom it is due . . .

March

252 *⟨William Heminges⟩ produced in March, 1632–3, a comedy entitled The Coursinge of a Hare, or the Madcapp, which was performed at the Fortune theatre, but is now lost. MS. Herbert.

6 May

253a (*Banbury*)

Right hono^{ble}

Our humble service to yor Lo^{ps} p⟨re⟩mised Wee make bold to send to yor Lo^{ps} herewithall a Pattent of license pretended by the bearers

---

248. Malone, iii. 232. Bentley, v. 1080–1. Published later in 1633 under the title *The Bird in a Cage*.

249. Ord HP2; also abbreviated in Chalmers, 209 = 440(p), where 'feates' is given as 'freaks'.

250. Ord HP2. See Crosfield's *Diary* for 11 July 1631, item 4, quoted in the Introduction, 81.

251. PRO LR5/65. Part of a warrant issued on behalf of Queen Henrietta Maria for payment of £50 out of her household accounts; attached is a receipt by Sir Henry signed and dated 6 Apr. 1633. The masque was Jonson's *Chloridia*, performed at court on 22 Feb. 1630/1.

252. Malone, iii. 189 (misprinted 198). Bentley, iv. 542–3.

253. SP16/238/44–6; rewritten and modernized version in *CSPD 1633–4*, 47–9. The civic authorities at Banbury, a town notorious for its Puritan sympathies, arrested a

of it to be graunted by his Matie, and a comission from the m^r of the Revells, the pattent we suspect, the comission wee find Rased, how soever wee find the p⟨ar⟩ties (who haue gone abroad into divers countyes wth the same) wandring Rogues, if not more dangerous p⟨er⟩^{sons} as may appeare by their exami⟨na⟩cons (wch we haue also sent to yor Lo^{ps}) in which is apparent howe they haue chaunged their names &c Their be six of them all wch wee have comitted to the prison of o^r Burrough where wee shall kepe them safe till yor Lo^{ps} pleasure be signified to vs . . .

253b ⟨Bartholomew Jones⟩ saieth that the Comission from the M^r of the Reuells was raysed by one of their company that is gon from them and that the m^r of the Reuells will giue allowaunce [for it] to the said Raysinge yf he may be paied for it.

253c ⟨Richard Whitinge⟩ confesseth that the Comission from the Master of the Reuells to his knowledge was out of date in Ianuary last and that it was raised, and made Iune . . .

7 May

254 *R. for allowinge of The Tale of the Tubb, Vitru Hoop's parte wholly strucke out, and the motion of the tubb, by commande from my lorde chamberlin; exceptions being taken against it by Inigo Jones, surveyor of the kings workes, as a personal injury unto him. May 7, 1633,—2l. o. o.

11 May

255 *For a play of Fletchers corrected by Sherley, called The Night Walkers, the 11 May, 1633, £2. o. o. For the queen's players.

6 June

256 *R. of ye kings company, for my summers day, by Blagrave, the 6 of June 1633, ye somme of 4l. 10s. od.

group of six players led by Richard Bradshaw because their licences were not in order. After taking depositions from the players, the authorities notified the Privy Council, enclosing the depositions and licences. Item (a) is the covering letter from the mayor and justices of Banbury, dated 6 May; (b) is from the second deposition of Bartholomew Jones, dated 3 May; and (c) is from the second deposition of Richard Whiting, dated 3 May. The licences seem to have disappeared. On 22 May the Privy Council replied, sending a messenger to take the arrested players to London for further examination. But on 8 June the players were released, and there is no evidence to suggest that they were punished (*MSC* i. 384–5). See Bentley, ii. 387–8, 418–19, 480, 484–5, 608–9, and 617–19.

254. Malone, iii. 232. Bentley, iv. 632–6.
255. Malone, iii. 236; also i. 424. Bentley, iii. 384–6.   *256.* Malone, iii. 177.

19 June

257 (*Norwich*) Robt Kympton and Richard Erington and their Company lycenced players by the maister of the Revells had a reward of Thirty Shillinges given them And so they are to depart and forbeare to play.

27 June

258 This Play, called ye Seamans Honest wife, all ye Oaths left out In ye action as they are crost In ye booke & all other Reformations strictly obserud, may bee acted not otherwyse. this .27. Iune. 1633.   Henry Herbert

I commande your Bookeeper to present mee with a fairer Copy hereafte⟨ ⟩and to leaue out all Oathes, prophaness, & publick Ribaldry, as he will answer it at his perill.   HHerbert.

3 July

259 *The comedy called The Yonge Admirall, being free from oaths, prophaness, or obsceanes, hath given mee much delight and satisfaction in the readinge, and may serve for a patterne to other poetts, not only for the bettring of maners and language, but for the improvement of the quality, which hath received some brushings of late.

When Mr. Sherley hath read this approbation, I know it will encourage him to pursue this beneficial and cleanly way of poetry, and when other poetts heare and see his good success, I am confident they will imitate the original for their own credit, and make such copies in this harmless way, as shall speak them masters in their art, at the first sight, to all judicious spectators. It may be acted this 3 July, 1633.

I have entered this allowance, for direction to my successor, and for example to all poetts, that shall write after the date hereof.

---

257. Norwich, 210.

258. BL MS Egerton 1994, f. 349. Walter Mountfort, *The Launching of the Mary, or the Seaman's Honest Wife*. Bentley, iv. 922–4. In the second sentence 'fairer' is normally transcribed as 'faire' (e.g. MSR, ed. J. H. Walter (1933), line 2978), but see note J in W. W. Greg's *The Shakespeare First Folio* (Oxford, 1955), 103. Herbert is not asking for a second copy of the play, but that in future the bookkeeper present him with tidier manuscripts. For Herbert's censorship of this play see Introduction, 53–7.

259. Malone, iii. 232–3. Bentley, v. 1168–70.

6 July

260 (*Norwich*) This day willm Perry brought to this Court a Bill signed wth his Maties hand & privy Signett Dated the last day of Aprill in the nynth yeare of his Maties Reigne Confirmed by the Master of the Revells vnder his seale the 24th of May last to play Comedies &c wth a non obstante all restreint to the Contrary./ There is gyvne vnto them Thre poundes as a gratuety And therevpon the said w^m Perry p⟨ro⟩mised to desist

13 July

261 (*Norwich*) This day Adrian Provoe & his wife brought into this Court A lycence vnder the Seale of the Revells dated the xij^th day of November 1632 whereby she beinge a woman w^thout hands is licenced to shew diverse workes &c done wth her feete, they are lycenced to make their shewes fower dayes./

15 August

262 *Received of Biston, for an ould play called Hymens Holliday, newly revived at their house, being a play given unto him for my use, this 15 Aug. 1633, 3*l*. 0. 0. Received of him for some alterations in it, 1*l*. 0. 0.

Meetinge with him at the ould exchange, he gave my wife a payre of gloves, that cost him at least twenty shillings.

28 September

263 (*Norwich*) Thomas Gibson brought into this Court a lycence vnder the hand and seale of the master of the Revelles for licence to shewe the pictures in wax of the Kinge of Sweden & others, And hee & his three Assistantes haue lycence for fower dayes.

October

264 *Octob. 1633. Exception was taken by Mr. Sewster to the second part of The Citty Shuffler, which gave me occasion to stay the play,

260. *Norwich*, 210–11; also Murray, 354, dated 3 July.
261. *Norwich*, 211; also Murray, 354.
262. Malone, iii. 233. William Rowley, *Hymen's Holiday, or Cupid's Vagaries*, lost. Bentley, v. 1023–4. See below, **277**.
263. *Norwich*, 211. See also **440(u)**.
264. Malone, iii. 172. Anon., lost. Bentley, v. 1309–10. It may be relevant that in Nov. 1623 Edward Sewster, a goldsmith, received a royal pardon for 'deceipt in false waighing of some syluer plate by him bought of the goodes of Sr John Sames knight and George Browne gent' (PRO SO3/7). In Apr. 1626 he was paid £1,500 for a ring given by the King to the Queen (SO3/8).

till the company ⟨of Salisbury Court⟩ had given him satisfaction; which was done the next day, and under his hande he did certifye mee that he was satisfyed.

18 October

265a   *On friday the nineteenth of October, 1633, I sent a warrant by a messenger of the chamber to suppress The Tamer Tamd, to the Kings players, for that afternoone, and it was obeyd; upon complaints of foule and offensive matters conteyned therein.

They acted The Scornful Lady instead of it, I have enterd the warrant here.

265b   These are to will and require you to forbeare the actinge of your play called The Tamer Tamd, or the Taminge of the Tamer, this afternoone, or any more till you have leave from me: and this at your perill.

On friday morninge the 18 Octob. 1633.

To Mr. Taylor, Mr. Lowins, or any of the King's players at the Blackfryers.

265c   On saterday morninge followinge the booke was brought mee, and at my lord of Hollands request I returned it to the players ye monday morninge after, purgd of oaths, prophaness, and ribaldrye, being ye 21 of Octob. 1633.

Because the stoppinge of the acting of this play for that afternoone, it being an ould play, hath raysed some discourse in the players, thogh no disobedience, I have thought fitt to insert here ther submission upon a former disobedience, and to declare that it concernes the Master of the Revells to bee carefull of their ould revived playes, as of their new, since they may conteyne offensive matter, which ought not to be allowed in any time.

The Master ought to have copies of their new playes left with him, that he may be able to shew what he hath allowed or disallowed.

All ould plays ought to bee brought to the Master of the Revells, and have his allowance to them for which he should have his fee, since they may be full of offensive things against church and state;

265a–f. Malone, iii. 208–10. Bentley, i. 36–8. The date in the opening sentence of **265a** is incorrect, as is shown by the warrant. *The Spanish Viceroy*, a lost play mentioned in the letter of submission, **265d**, was included by Malone, iii. 230, in a list of Massinger's plays, and was also entered in SR on 9 Sept. as by Massinger; but Bentley, v. 1412–13, prefers to regard it as anonymous.

ye rather that in former time the poetts tooke greater liberty than is allowed them by mee.

The players ought not to study their parts till I have allowed of the booke.

265d   To Sir Henry Herbert, K^t. master of his
Maties Revels.

After our humble servise remembered unto your good worship, Whereas not long since we acted a play called The Spanishe Viceroy, not being licensed under your worships hande, nor allowd of: wee doe confess and herby acknowledge that wee have offended, and that it is in your power to punishe this offense, and are very sorry for it; and doe likewise promise herby that wee will not act any play without your hand or substituts hereafter, nor doe any thinge that may prejudice the authority of your office: So hoping that this humble submission of ours may bee accepted, wee have therunto sett our hands. This twentiethe of Decemb. 1624.

Joseph Taylor.	John Lowen.
Richard Robinson.	John Shancke.
Elyard Swanston.	John Rice.
Thomas Pollard.	Will. Rowley.
Robert Benfeilde.	Richard Sharpe.
George Burght.	

(*in margin*) 'Tis entered here for a remembrance against their disorders.

265e   Mr. Knight,

In many things you have saved mee labour; yet wher your judgment or penn fayld you, I have made boulde to use mine. Purge ther parts, as I have the booke. And I hope every hearer and player will thinke that I have done God good servise, and the quality no wronge; who hath no greater enemies than oaths, prophaness, and publique ribaldry, wh^{ch} for the future I doe absolutely forbid to bee presented unto mee in any playbooke, as you will answer it at your perill. 21 Octob. 1633.

265f   This was subscribed to their play of The Tamer Tamd, and directed to Knight, their book-keeper.

The 24 Octob. 1633, Lowins and Swanston were sorry for their ill manners, and craved my pardon, which I gave them in presence of Mr. Taylor and Mr. Benfeilde.

24 October

266 *Upon a second petition of the players to the High Commission
court, wherein they did mee right in my care to purge their plays
of all offense, my lords Grace of Canterbury bestowed many words
upon mee, and discharged mee of any blame, and layd the whole
fault of their play called The Magnetick Lady, upon the players.
This happened the 24 of Octob. 1633, at Lambeth. In their first
petition they would have excused themselves on me and the poett.

27 October

267 A Warraunt for paym^t of 240^{li} vnto the Queenes Players for 14
playes by them Acted. their bill signed by Sr Henry Herbert.
(in margin) Queenes Players

30 October

268 *On the 30th of October, 1633, the managers of the king's company
agreed to pay him the fixed sum of ten pounds every Christmas,
and the same sum at Midsummer, in lieu of his two benefits, which
sums they regularly paid him from that time till the breaking out of
the civil wars.

31 October

269 *Massinger's The Guardian licensed for the king's company.

11 November

270 *Shirley's The Gamester licensed.

16 November

271 *On Saterday the 17th of Novemb. being the Queens birth-day,
Richarde the Thirde was acted by the K. players at St. James, wher
the king and queene were present, it being the first play the queene
sawe since her M.^{tys} delivery of the Duke of York. 1633

19 November

272 *On tusday the 19th of November, being the king's birth-day, The
Young Admirall was acted at St. James by the queen's players, and
likt by the K. and Queen.

266. Malone, iii. 233. See above, 240.   267. PRO LC5/132/348; MSC ii. 361.
268. Malone, iii. 177–8.   269. Malone, iii. 230. Bentley, iv. 789–90.
270. Malone, iii. 232. Bentley, v. 1110–12. See below, 289.
271. Malone, iii. 233–4. Herbert has misdated the entry; the Queen's birthday was the
16th.
272. Malone, iii. 234. See above, 259.

23 November

273 *The Kings players sent me an ould booke of Fletchers called The
Loyal Subject, formerly allowed by Sir George Bucke, 16 Novemb.
1618, which according to their desire and agreement I did peruse,
and with some reformations allowed of, the 23 of Nov. 1633, for
which they sent mee according to their promise 1l. 0. 0.
(*In margin*) The first ould play sent mee to be perused by the K.
players.

26 November

274 *On tusday night at Saint James, the 26 of Novemb. 1633, was
acted before the King and Queene, The Taminge of the Shrew.
Likt.

28 November

275 *On thursday night at St. James, the 28 of Novemb. 1633, was acted
before the King and Queene, The Tamer Tamd, made by Fletcher.
Very well likt.

10 December

276 *On tusday night at Whitehall the 10 of Decemb. 1633, was acted
before the King and Queen, The Loyal Subject, made by Fletcher,
and very well likt by the king.

16 December

277 *On Monday night the 16 of December, 1633, at Whitehall was
acted before the King and Queen, Hymens Holliday or Cupids
Fegarys, an ould play of Rowleys. Likte.

21 December

278 (*Norwich*) This day Iohn Stone brought into this Court a Lycence
vnder the hand of the Maister of the Revelles to shewe an Italian
Motion.

1634

1 January

279 *On Wensday night the first of January, 1633, Cymbeline was acted
at Court by the Kings players. Well likte by the kinge.

273. Malone, iii. 234. Bentley, iii. 370–3.   *274*. Malone, iii. 234.   *275*. Ibid.
276. Ibid.   *277*. Ibid. See above, **262**.   *278*. *Norwich*, 213.
279. Malone, iii. 234.

6 January

280   *On Monday night the sixth of January and the Twelfe Night was presented at Denmark-house, before the King and Queene, Fletchers pastorall called The Faithfull Shepheardesse, in the clothes the Queene had given Taylor the year before of her owne pastorall.

The scenes were fitted to the pastorall, and made, by Mr. Inigo Jones, in the great chamber, 1633.

9 January

281   *This morning, being the 9th of January, 1633, the kinge was pleasd to call mee into his withdrawinge chamber to the window, wher he went over all that I had croste in Davenants play-booke, and allowing of *faith* and *slight* to bee asseverations only, and no oathes, markt them to stande, and some other few things, but in the greater part allowed of my reformations. This was done upon a complaint of Mr. Endymion Porters in December.

The kinge is pleasd to take *faith*, *death*, *slight*, for asseverations, and no oaths, to which I doe humbly submit as my masters judgment; but under favour conceive them to be oaths, and enter them here, to declare my opinion and submission.

The 10 of January, 1633, I returned unto Mr. Davenant his playe-booke of The Witts, corrected by the kinge.

The kinge would not take the booke at Mr. Porter's hands; but commanded him to bring it unto mee, which he did, and likewise commanded Davenant to come to me for it, as I believe: otherwise he would not have byn so civill.

12 January

282   *The Guardian, a play of Mr. Messengers, was acted at court on Sunday the 12 January, 1633, by the Kings players, and well likte.

14 January

283   *The Tale of the Tub was acted on tusday night at Court, the 14 Janua. 1633, by the Queenes players, and not likte.

16 January

284   *The Winters Tale was acted on thursday night at Court, the 16 Janua. 1633, by the K. players, and likt.

280. Malone, iii. 235. Bentley, i. 39.   *281.* Malone, iii. 235. Bentley, iii. 222–5.
282. Malone, iii. 235. Bentley, iv. 789–90.   *283.* Malone, iii. 236. See above, 254.
284. Malone, iii. 236.

19 January
285   *Davenant's *The Wits* licensed.

28 January
286   *The Witts was acted on tusday night the 28 January, 1633, at Court, before the Kinge and Queene. Well likt. It had a various fate on the stage, and at court, though the kinge commended the language, but dislikt the plott and characters.

30 January
287   *The Night-Walkers was acted on thursday night the 30 Janu. 1633 at Court, before the King and Queen. Likt as a merry play. Made by Fletcher.

3 February
288   *The Inns of court gentlemen presented their masque at court, before the kinge and queene, the 2 February, 1633, and performed it very well. Their shew through the streets was glorious, and in the nature of a triumph.—Mr. Surveyor Jones invented and made the scene; Mr. Sherley the poett made the prose and verse.

6 February
289   *On thursday night the 6 of Febru. 1633, The Gamester was acted at Court, made by Sherley, out of a plot of the king's, given him by mee; and well likte. The king sayd it was the best play he had seen for seven years.

18 February
290   *On Shrovetusday night, the 18 of February, 1633, the Kinge dancte his Masque, accompanied with 11 lords, and attended with 10 pages. It was the noblest masque of my time to this day, the best poetrye, best scenes, and the best habitts. The kinge and queene were very well pleasd with my service, and the Q. was pleasd to tell mee before the king, 'Pour les habits, elle n'avoit jamais rien vue de si brave'.

285. Malone, iii. 284. See above, **281.**   *286.* Malone, iii. 236.
287. Ibid. See above, **255.**
288. Malone, iii. 236. Bentley, v. 1154–63. The masque was Shirley's *The Triumph of Peace.* Bentley points out that Herbert's date of 2 Feb. is clearly a mistake; all other records date the performance as 3 Feb.
289. Malone, iii. 236. See above, **270.**
290. Malone, iii. 236–7. Bentley, iii. 106–10. The masque was Thomas Carew's *Coelum Britannicum.*

April

291 *The Queen, Sir Henry Herbert mentions, likewise went to Black-friars in the preceding month of April to see "*The Spartan Ladys* written by Lodowick Carlyle"

7 April

292 *Bussy d'Amboise was playd by the king's players on Easter-monday night, at the Cockpitt in court.

8 April

293 *The Pastorall was playd by the king's players on Easter-tusday night, at the Cockpitt in court.

7 May

294 *Massinger's *The Tragedy of Cleander* licensed for the king's company.

13 May

295 *"The 13 May, 1634, the Queene was at Blackfryers, to see Messengers playe."—The play which her majesty honoured with her presence was The Tragedy of Cleander, which had been produced on the 7th of the same month, and is now lost, with many other pieces of the same writer.

17 May

296 (*Norwich*) This day Bartholmew Cloysse wth Six Assistants did bringe into this Court a lycence vnder his Maties privie Signett and signed wth his Maties Royall hand Dated the xxvth of Aprill 1634 Giveinge warrant to the said Bartholmew Cloyse to shew diu⟨er⟩se rare engins, wch lycence is Confirmed by the Master of the Revilles for one yeare after the xvth of Aprill 1634, They haue liberty to shewe the same till wednesday come sevenight.

---

291. Malone MS in an interleaved copy of vol. Iii of his 1790 edn. of Shakespeare, Bodleian Mal 1046, f. 145. Not known to Bentley, iii. 124. This new entry makes it certain that the play was performed at Blackfriars, and therefore by the King's company. Malone wrote it to follow on from **295** below.

292. Malone, iii. 237. By George Chapman.

293. Ibid. Bentley, vii. 92, suggests that 'The Pastoral' is probably Fletcher's *The Faithful Shepherdess*, already performed on 6 Jan. (**280**).

294. Malone, iii. 230. This is generally accepted as a revision by Massinger of an early Fletcher play, subsequently published under the title of *The Lovers' Progress* in the Beaumont and Fletcher Folio of 1647; see Bentley, iii. 359–63, and iv. 774.

295. Malone, iii. 167. See previous note. Bentley, i. 39.   *296*. *Norwich*, 214–15.

6 June

297   *Massinger's *A Very Woman* licensed for the king's company.

10 June

298   (*Exeter*) This day it is agreede that Mr Maior shalbe repaid by Mr Rec⟨eiver⟩ of xl s latelie disbursed by hym for freeing the Cittie of certayne stage players wch came to this Cittie wth A licence vnder the Seale of the Office of Revells.

24 June

299   *Shirley's *The Example* licensed.

19 July

300   (*Norwich*) Mathew Duphen, Conrade Blantes & Iohn Cappemaker did this day bringe into this Court a lycence vnder the Seale of the office of the Revells Dated the Second of Iuly 1634 to shewe Two Dromedaries, They haue leaue to shewe the same this day, Monday, Tuseday wednesday & Thursday next, & no longer and they are to be gone on Thursday night.

20 July

301   A peticon of the Kings Players complayning of intermingleing some passages of witches in old playes to ye p^riudice of their designed Comedy of the Lancashire witches, & desiring a prohibition of any other till theirs bee allowed & Acted. Answered p Reference to *Blagraue* in absence of Sr *H. Herbert.*/ Iuly 20. 1634
(*in margin*) Players peticon about ye Witches

16 August

302   *An ould play, with some new scenes, Doctor Lambe and the Witches, to Salisbury Courte, the 16th August, 1634,—£1 0 0.

13 September

303   (*Norwich*) A lycence vnder the seale of the office of Revells dated the xxv^th of Iune Anno Decimo Caroli was brought into this Court

297. Malone, iii. 230. Bentley, iv. 824–8.   *298. Devon,* 197–8.
299. Malone, iii. 232. Bentley, v. 1108–10.
300. Norwich, 215; also Murray, 355. See also **440(d)**.
301. PRO LC5/183/148; also *MSC* ii. 410. Bentley, i. 40–2, iii. 73–6, v. 1455. Bentley argues that the old play referred to was the anonymous *Doctor Lamb and the Witches* (see next entry); the new play for the King's players was Heywood and Brome's *The Late Lancashire Witches.*
302. Malone, i. 424. Anon., lost. See previous note. Bentley, v. 1455.
303. Norwich, 215; also Murray, 355–6.

by Elias Guest one of the players in the said Lycence mencioned, yt is thought fitt to giue to them fforty Shillinges.

22 October

304 (*Norwich*) This Day Iohn Tandy one of the assistantes vnto Robt Tyce Iames Gentleman & Thomas Galloway did bringe into this Court a lycence vnder the hand and seale of the maister of the Revilles to shew feates &c desired (*sic*) leaue to shewe &c This Court beinge Informed & takeinge into their Consideracon that many howses at this tyme are visited wth the Contagion of the small pox, m^r Maior therefore offered them some mony toward their Charges wch they refused to accept And for the reason of the said Contagion they are forbidden to shewe their feates for the cause before mencioned, yet afterward there was leave granted to him to shewe his feats till satterday night next, And he p⟨ro⟩misseth to stay no longer but to be gone on monday morninge

20 November

305 *Davenant's *Love and Honour* licensed. Originally called The Courage of Love. It was afterwards named by Sir Henry Herbert, at Davenant's request, The Nonpareilles, or the Matchless Maids.

24 November

306 *The Proxy, or Love's Aftergame, was produced at the theatre at Salisbury Court, November 24, 1634.

29 November

307 *Shirley's *The Opportunity* licensed.

1635

308 (*Bristol*) Item paide to one that came with a licence from the maister of Revells to shewe tumblinge trickes   ij s. vi d.

7 January

309 *Received of a Dutchman for liberty to dance on the Ropes for Christmas holydaies 7 Jan. 1634—2^{li}.

304. Norwich, 217–18; also Murray, 356.
305. Malone, iii. 284. Bentley, iii. 205–6.
306. Malone, iii. 238. Anon., lost. See below, 341. Bentley, v. 1399.
307. Malone, iii. 232. Bentley, v. 1134–7.
308. *Bristol*, REED, forthcoming, by courtesy of the editor.
309. Ord HP 12, 166. Halliwell-Phillipps noted that this took place at the Salisbury Court Theatre.

10 January

310 *Massinger's *The Orator* licensed for the king's company.

24 January

311 A Warr^t for paym^t of xxx^{li} vnto Wm Blagraue for himselfe & the rest
of his Company for three playes Acted by the Children of the
Reuells at Whitehall in Anno 1631. M^d their Bill was signed by S^r
Henry Herbert M^r of the Reuells & passed Ian 24. 1634
(*in margin*) Children of the Reuells.

6 February

312 *Shirley's *The Coronation* licensed.

16 February

313 *I committed Cromes a Broker in long lane 16 ffeb: 1634 to ye
Marshalsey for lending a church Robe with the name of Jesus upon
it to ye players in Salisbury Court to present a Flamen a priest of
the Heathens. Upon his petition of submission & acknowledgment
of his faulte I released him 17 feb: 1634.

17–20 February

314 *On tuesday night the 17 of February, 1634, a Frenche company of
players, being approved of by the queene at her house too nights
before, and commended by her majesty to the kinge, were admitted
to the Cockpitt in Whitehall, and there presented the king and
queene with a Frenche comedy called Melise, with good approbation: for which play the king gives them ten pounds.

This day being Friday, and the 20 of the same monthe, the kinge
tould mee his pleasure, and commanded mee to give order that this
Frenche company should playe the too sermon daies in the weeke,
during their time of playinge in Lent, and in the house of
Drury-lane, where the queenes players usually playe.

The kings pleasure I signifyed to Mr. Beeston the same day, who
obeyd readily.

310. Malone, iii. 230. Lost. Bentley, iv. 803–4.
311. PRO LC5/134/39; *MSC* ii. 375.   *312.* Malone, iii. 232. Bentley, v. 1098–9.
313. Ord HP12, 166; also Malone, iii. 237. Bentley, i. 294, ii. 417. He may have been
the William Crome who twice petitioned the Lord Chamberlain in Dec. 1632 (*MSC* ii.
408). For a similar incident, cf. *The Cardinal's Conspiracy* (Bentley, v. 1300–1).
314. Malone, iii. 121. Bentley, vii. 4–5. See *MSC* ii. 376, and vi. 85. Bentley, vii. 96–7,
identifies the three plays as *La Melise, ou les Princes Reconnus*, by R.-M. Du Rocher,
Le Trompeur Puni, ou Histoire Septentrionale, by Georges de Scudery, and *Alcimedon*,
by Pierre Du Ryer.

The house-keepers are to give them by promise the benefit of their interest for the two days of the first weeke.

They had the benefitt of playinge on the sermon daies, and gott two hundred pounds at least; besides many rich clothes were given them.

They had freely to themselves the whole weeke before the weeke before Easter, which I obtaynd of the king for them.

The 4 Aprill, on Easter monday, they playd the Trompeur puny, with better approbation than the other.

On Wensday night the 16 Aprill, 1635, the French playd Alcimedor with good approbation.

(*In margin*) The Frenche offered mee a present of 10*l*.; but I refused itt, and did them many other curtesys, *gratis*, to render the queene my mistris an acceptable service.

7 March

315   *From Vincent—For dancing on the Ropes this Lent at ye Fortune by Blagrave 7 March 1634—2^{li}.

16 March

316   *From the Dutchman————at ye Globe by Blagrave 16th March 1634.— 2^{li}.

28 March

317   (*Norwich*) w^m Gostlynge brought into this Court a lycence vnder the seale of the master of the Revelles dated the 9th day of August in the Tenth yeare of kinge Charles to shew the portraiture of the City of Ierusalem in all places for a yeare, hee hath leaue to make shew of the said portraiture for this whole weeke nowe to come./

4 April
(see under 17 Feb.)

6 April

318   *Received of John Momford dancer on the Ropes by the hands of M^r. Berry the somme of 30^{li}. which monyy is in consideration for the makinge him ye Kings servant & gaininge for him the libertye of travaylinge into the Cuntrye this Monday in Easter weeke being the 6th. Apr. 1635.—30^{li}.

315. Ord HP5, 46. Bentley, vi. 164, ii. 6.   *316*. Ord HP6, 133. Bentley, vi. 194.
317. *Norwich*, 219; also Murray, 356–7.   *318*. Ord HP6, 133.

13 April

319 (*Coventry*) Paid to the kinges players who brought a Comission from
Sir Henry Harbert 13. Aprill. last   ij^{li} x^d

16 April
(see under 17 Feb.)

29 April

320 *Shirley's *Chabot, Admiral of France* licensed.

5 May

321 *A warrant granted to Josias D'Aunay, Hurfries de Lau, and others,
for to act playes at a new house in Drury-lane, during pleasure, y^e
5 May, 1635.

The king was pleased to commande my Lord Chamberlain to direct
his warrant to Monsieur Le Fevure, to give him a power to contract
with the Frenchemen for to builde a playhouse in the manage-
house, which was done accordinglye by my advise and allowance.

"Thes Frenchmen," Sir Henry adds in the margin, "were
commended unto mee by the queene, and have passed through my
handes, *gratis*."

They did not, however, pass quite free, for from a subsequent
entry it appears that "they gave Blagrave three pounds for his paines."

6 June

322 (*Norwich*) This day Richard Weekes and Iohn Shanke brought into
this Court a Bill signed wth his Maties hand and privie signett Dated
the last day of Aprill in the nynth yeare of his Maties Reigne, and a
lycence vnder the seale of his ma^{ties} Revelles dated the second of
March last & contynuinge till the Second of September next, They
haue leaue to play here till the xviijth of this moneth

1 August

323 *Davenant's *News of Plymouth* licensed.

324 A peticon of *Iohn Shankes* to my Ld Chamberlaine shewing that
according to his Lo^{ps} order hee did make a proposition to his

319. *Coventry*, 437; also Murray, 252, reading 'v^d'.
320. Malone, iii. 232. Bentley, v. 1088–91. Published as by Chapman and Shirley;
probably a revision by Shirley of an earlier play by Chapman.
321. Malone, iii. 122. Bentley, ii. 437.   *322*. *Norwich*, 219; also Murray, 357.
323. Malone, iii. 284. Bentley, iii. 209–10.
324. PRO LC5/133/51; also *MSC* ii. 372–3. The dispute leading to this arbitration is
summarized in Bentley, i. 43–7 and vi. 36–7.

fellowes for satisfaccon vpon his assigening (*sic*) of his parts in ye seuerall houses vnto them but they not onely refused to giue satisfaccon but restrained him from the Stage. that therfore his lo^p would order them to giue satisfaccon according to his propositions & computation. Answered (vizt) I desire Sr *H. Herbert* & Sr *Iohn Finett* & my sollicitor *Daniell Bedingfield* to take this petition & the seuerall papers heerunto annexed into their serious considerations & to speake wth the seuerall parties interested, & therupon, & vpon the whole matter to sett downe a proportionable & equitable sume of money to bee payd vnto *Shankes* for the two parts which hee is to passe vnto *Benfield, Swanston* & *Pollard* & to cause a finall agreem^t & convayances to bee settled accordingly & to giue mee an account of their whole proceedings in writing. / Aug 1. 1635. / (*in margin*) M^d all concerning this & here entred were deliuered, annexed

3 September

325 (*Norwich*) A Patent vnder the hand & seale of Sr Henry Herbert master of the Revelles bearinge date the 28th of November 1634 made to willm Danyell willm Hart Iohn Townesend Samuell Minion Hugh Haughton Thomas Doughton and the rest of their Company not exceedinge the number of ffiftene p⟨er⟩sons to play Comedies &c was this day brought & shewed by the said willm Daniell who prayed leaue to play in this City, But his sute beinge not granted hee had in liew thereof a gratuety of tenn shillinges

16 September

326a *Received of Blagrove from the King's Company, for the *renewing* of Love's Pilgrimage, the 16th of September, 1635,—£1 0 0.

326b *Shirley, who had the revisal of some of those pieces which were left imperfect by Fletcher, (as appears from Sir Henry Herbert's Office-book,) finding The New Inn unsuccessful, took the liberty to borrow a scene from it, which he inserted in Love's Pilgrimage, when that play was revived, or as Sir Henry Herbert calls it, *renewed*, in 1635.

325. Norwich, 220; also Murray, 357.
326a–b. Malone, i. 424. Bentley, iii. 366–70. By Fletcher. Bentley points out that Shirley was working for Queen Henrietta's company in 1635, and would not have revised plays for the King's company.

26 September

327 (*Norwich*) This day Christofer Townson and Edward Day brought into this Court a writinge vnder the Seale of the master of the Revelles to shew waterworkes bearinge date the 25th of Aprill in the Eleaventh yeare of his Ma[ties] Reigne they haue tyme till the vth of October next.

10 October

328 (*Norwich*) This day Martyn Backhust brought into this Court a licence vnder the Seale of the master of the Revelles bearinge date the 23th of March in the xth yeare of his Ma[ties] Reigne, hee is licenced to shewe this day & to dep⟨ar⟩t on monday morninge.

15 October

329 *Shirley's *The Lady of Pleasure* licensed.

330 This Play Call'd the Lady-mot⟨h . . .
       (the Reformacons obseru'd) may ⟨b . . .
       Acted. October the xv[th]. 1635
              Will: Blagrau⟨e
              Dep[t] to the M⟨
              of the Reuoll⟨

13 November

331 (*Norwich*) A warrant signed by his Ma[tie] vnder his highnes privie Signett bearinge date the xiij[th] day of December in the Third yeare of his Reigne & Confirmed by the master of the Revelles vnder his hand & seale was yesterday shewed to m[r] Maior & diu⟨er⟩se Iustices & Aldermen by willm Vincent one of the patentees, hee hath tyme to exercise his feates till wednesday night next

16 November

332 *Davenant's *The Platonic Lovers* licensed.

10 December

333 A warr[t] for y[e] paym[t] of 100[li] to y[e] Princes Comedians vizt 60[li] for 3 Playes Acted at Hampton Court. at 20[li] for each Play in Sept. and October. 1634 & 40[li] for 4 playes at Whitehall & the Cockpitt in

327. *Norwich*, 220; also Murray, 357.   *328.* *Norwich*, 222; also Murray, 357.
329. Malone, iii. 232. Bentley, v. 1125–7.
330. BL MS Egerton 1994, f. 210. First published from manuscript in 1883 by A. H. Bullen, who assigned the play, *The Lady Mother*, to Henry Glapthorne. Facs. in MSR, ed. Arthur Brown (1958 (1959)), facing p. 1.
331. *Norwich*, 222; also Murray, 358.   *332.* Malone, iii. 284. Bentley, iii. 211–12.
333. PRO LC5/134/84; *MSC* ii. 377.

Ianuary Febr. & May following. at 10^{li} for each Play, M^d their bill was signed by Sr H. Herbert. Dec. 10. 1635. Ioseph Moore Andre Kayne & Ellis Worth. mentioned only.
(*in margin*) Princes Players.

14 December

334 *The pastorall of Florimene with the description of the sceanes and interludes, as it was sent mee by Mr. Inigo Jones, I allowed for the press, this 14 of Decemb. 1635. The pastorall is in French, and 'tis the argument only, put into English, that I have allowed to be printed.

21 December

335 *Le pastorale de Florimene fust representé devant le roy et la royne, le prince Charles, et le prince Palatin, le 21 Decem. jour de St. Thomas, par les filles Françoise de la royne, et firent tres bien, dans la grande sale de Whitehall, aux depens de la royne.

23 December

336 (*Norwich*) Thomas Maskell did this day bringe a lycence from the master of the Revelles Dated the xxth of Iune last past to sett forth an Italian motion, hee hath leaue so to doe till Tuseday night next & no longer

1636

18 January

337 *Shirley's *The Duke's Mistress* licensed.

16 February

338 *The Second part of Arviragus and Philicia playd at court the 16 Febru. 1635, with great approbation of K. and Queene.

18 February

339 *The Silent Woman playd at Court of St. James on thursday ye 18 Febr. 1635.

22 February

(?Shirley, *The Duke's Mistress*, played at St. James — see 25 Feb. below)

334. Malone, iii. 122. Bentley, v. 1333–5. See C77.
335. Malone, iii. 122. See previous item.   *336. Norwich*, 222; also Murray, 358.
337. Malone, iii. 232. Bentley, v. 1107–8.
338. Malone, iii. 237. By Lodowick Carlell. See below, 347 and 353–4. Bentley, iii. 113–15.
339. Malone, iii. 237. By Ben Jonson.

24 February

340 *On Wensday the 23 of Febru. 1635, the Prince d'Amours gave
a masque to the Prince Elector and his brother, in the
Middle Temple, wher the Queene was pleasd to grace the enter-
taynment by putting of⟨f⟩ majesty to putt on a citizens habitt,
and to sett upon the scaffold on the right hande amongst her
subjects.

The queene was attended in the like habitts by the Marques
Hamilton, the Countess of Denbighe, the Countess of Holland, and
the Lady Elizabeth Feildinge. Mrs. Basse, the lace-woman, leade in
this royal citizen and her company.

The Earl of Holland, the Lord Goringe, Mr. Percy, and Mr.
Jermyn, were the men that attended.

The Prince Elector satt in the midst, his brother Robert on the
right hand of him, and the Prince d'Amours on the left.

The Masque was very well performed in the dances, scenes,
cloathinge, and musique, and the Queene was pleasd to tell mee at
her going away, that she liked it very well.

Henry Lause
William Lause } made the musique.

Mr. Corseilles made the scenes.

341 *Loves Aftergame, played at St. James by the Salisbury Court
players, the 24 of Feb. 1635.

25 February

342 *The Dukes Mistres played at St. James the 22 of Feb. 1635. Made
by Sherley.

---

340. Malone, iii. 237–8. Bentley, iii. 218–20. Davenant's *The Triumphs of the Prince
D'Amour*. Herbert's date must be mistaken. Wednesday fell on the 24th, and the title-
page of the 1636 edn. says that it was performed on 24 Feb. Bentley suggests that
Herbert's muddle indicates a postponement.
    In the second paragraph Malone incorrectly reads 'law-woman'. Bentley quotes a
letter from George Garrard to Strafford, 15 Mar. 1635/6 (Strafford, *Letters*, i. 525),
referring to 'Mrs. *Basset* the great Lace-Woman of *Cheapside*', and in another letter,
not in Bentley, of 28 Apr. 1637 (ibid. ii. 72), Garrard refers to 'Mr. *Basse*, the great
Lace-man in *Cheapside*'.
341. Malone, iii. 238. See above, 306.
342. Malone, iii. 238. Bentley, v. 1107–8. 'Since Herbert is giving a continuous account
of Court performances in chronological order, and since this entry follows the entry of
February 24 and precedes the entry of February 28, I believe that the correct date is
February 25.' (Adams, 56 n.).

343   *The same day at Whitehall I acquainted king Charles, my master, with the danger of Mr. Hunts sickness, and moved his Majesty, in case he dyed, that he would be pleasd to give mee leave to commend a fitt man to succeed him in his place of Yeoman of the Revells.

The kinge tould me, that till then he knew not that Will Hunt held a place in the Revells. To my request he was pleasd to give mee this answer. Well, says the king, I will not dispose of it, or it shall not be disposed of, till I heare you. *Ipsissimis verbis.* Which I enter here as full of grace, and for my better remembrance, sinse *my master's custom affords not so many words, nor so significant.*

28 February

344   *The 28 Feb. The Knight of the Burning Pestle playd by the Q. men at St. James.

10 March

345   *A licence to Francis Sherret, to shew a *strange fish* for a yeare, from the 10th of Marche, 1635.

12 March

346   *For the Queen's Company.— For a new play called Love's Tryal or the *Hollander* this 12 march 1635 — 2. 0. 0

18, 19 April

347   *The first and second part of Arviragus and Philicia were acted at the Cockpitt, before the Kinge and Queene, the Prince, and Prince Elector, the 18 and 19 Aprill, 1636, being monday and tusday in Easter weeke.

9 May

348   *Massinger's *The Bashful Lover* licensed for the king's company.

---

343. Malone, iii. 238. On 29 Oct. 1611 letters patent were issued appointing William Hunt as Yeoman of the Revels (*MSC* ii. 339–41), but he did not take over from his predecessor Edward Kirkham until Oct. 1616 (*MSC* xiii. 79). Letters patent to appoint Joseph Taylor as Hunt's successor were issued on 11 Nov. 1639 (*MSC* ii. 339–41). Taylor was a leading actor in the King's company (Bentley, ii. 590–8).

344. Malone, iii. 238. By Beaumont.   *345.* Malone, xiv. 368. Not in Adams.

346. Malone MS in his copy of Glapthorne's play, Bodleian Mal 171(2). Printed by Lawrence. Bentley, iv. 482–3.

347. Malone, iii. 238.   *348.* Malone, iii. 230. Bentley, iv. 760–2.

12 May

349 *Received of ould Cartwright for allowing the ⟨Fortune⟩ company to add scenes to an ould play, and to give it out for a new one, this 12th of May, 1636,—£1 0 0.

350 *Sr Hen H. had the benefit of the second day of Hannibal & Scipio — played at [the] Sal. Court by the Princes Servants amounting to £2. 14. 12 May 1636 as a satisfaction for a debt due by Gunnel

351 *At the increase of the plague to 4 within the citty and 54 in all.—This day the 12 May, 1636, I received a warrant from my Lord Chamberlin for the suppressing of playes and shews, and at the same time delivered my severall warrants to George Wilson for the four companys of players, to be served upon them.

14 October

352 (Dorchester) Will: Gosling coming to this Towne with a license vnder the hand of the Master of the Revelles, signed Henry Herbert, and sealed with the seale of the office of Revelles with a Cinquefoyle, authorizing the said Gosling to shew the portraiture of the City of Jerusalem dated 15 June, xij Caroli, and denied to make his shew heere by reason of the dangerous tyme of sicknes.

26 December

353 *At Hampton Court, 1636.
The first part of Arviragus, Monday Afternoon, 26 December.

---

349. Malone, i. 424. Bentley, i. 276–7 and vi. 165.

350. Malone MS in an interleaved copy of vol. Iii of his 1790 edn. of Shakespeare, Bodleian Mal 1046, p. 136*. Not in Bentley's account of Thomas Nabbes's play with this title (iv. 934–6). This item is puzzling. Nabbes's play was published in 1637 with a statement that it was acted in 1635 at the Phoenix by Queen Henrietta's company, which was managed by Christopher Beeston, and its printed cast-list clearly refers to that company (Bentley, i. 246). The company broke up partly because of the plague closure of 1636–7, and several players went to Salisbury Court (see **367**), but Herbert's phraseology suggests that this took place in Oct. 1637. Furthermore, Richard Gunnell died before 7 Oct. 1634 (Bentley, vi. 94). A rather desperate solution would be that some of the actors from the Queen's company seceded to the Salisbury Court early in 1636, managing to take a copy of Nabbes's play with them, and that Gunnell, who managed the Salisbury Court, left a debt behind him which Sir Henry insisted on being paid.

351. Malone, iii. 239; also in Chalmers, 211, abbreviated. Bentley, ii. 661. George Wilson was Groom of the Revels (see **147**).

352. The Municipal Records of the Borough of Dorchester, Dorset, ed. C. H. Mayo (Exeter, 1908), 667.

353. Malone, iii. 239.

27 December

354 *The second part of Arviragus, tusday 27 December.

1637

1 January

355 *Love and Honour, on New-years night, sonday.

5 January

356 *The Elder Brother, on thursday the 5 Janua.

10 January

357 *The Kinge and no Kinge, on tusday yᵉ 10 Janua.

12 January

358 *The Royal Slave, on thursday the 12 of Janu.—Oxford play, written by Cartwright. The king gave him forty pounds.

17 January

359 *Rollo, the 24 Janu.

31 January

360 *Julius Caesar, at St. James, the 31 Janu. 1636.

7 February

361 *Cupides Revenge, at St. James, by Beeston's boyes, the 7 Febru.

9 February

362 *A Wife for a Monthe, by the K. players, at St. James, the 9 Febru.

14 February

363 *Wit without Money, by the B. boyes at St. James, the 14 Feb.

---

354. Ibid.   *355.* Ibid. By William Davenant. See above, **305**.
356. Ibid. By John Fletcher. Bentley, iii. 332–6.
357. Malone, iii. 239. By Beaumont and Fletcher. Bentley, i. 51.
358. Malone, iii. 239. Bentley, iii. 134–41. Performed by the King's company at Hampton Court.
359. Malone, iii. 239. *Rollo, Duke of Normandy, or the Bloody Brother*, by Fletcher and others. Bentley, iii. 401–7. Herbert or Malone made a mistake with the date; in the list of court performances 1636–7 submitted by the King's company as part of the revels accounts, it is made clear that *Rollo* was performed on 17 Jan., *Hamlet* on 24 Jan. (Adams, 76, from PRO AO3/908/22).
360. Malone, iii. 239.
361. Ibid. By Beaumont and Fletcher. Bentley, i. 324–5.
362. Malone, iii. 239. By Fletcher. See above, **102**.
363. Malone, iii. 239. By Fletcher. Cf. **361** above.

17 February

364 *The Governor, by the K. players, at St. James, the 17 Febru. 1636.

21 February

365 *Philaster, by the K. players, at St. James, shrovtusday, the 21 Febru. 1636.

23 February

366 *On Thursday morning 23ᵈ feb: 1636 The Bill of the Plague made the number at 44 upon which decrease the king gave the players ther liberty & they began 24 feb: 1636
     The plague increasinge the players laye still until the 2 of Oct. 1637 when they had leave to play

367 *Mr. Beeston was commanded to make a company of boyes, and began to play at the Cockpitt with them the same day.
     I disposed of Perkins, Sumner, Sherlock and Turner, to Salisbury Court, and joynd them with the best of that company.

21 May

368 (*Coventry*) . . . to them that had a shew vnder the Maister of the Revelles seale the 21ᵗʰ of May,   6ˢ 8ᵈ

2 October
(see above, under 23 Feb.)

4 November

369 *A license for six months granted to Lazaras, an Italian, to shew his brother Baptista, that grows out of his navell, and carryes him at his

364. Ibid. Possibly by Sir Cornelius Formido; see Bentley, iii. 464–8. In the list of court performances referred to above (359), 'the Governour' is assigned to 16 Feb.

365. Malone, iii. 239.

366. Ord HP3, 127; also Malone, iii. 239. The theatres opened on 24 Feb., but the number of plague victims went up again, and they were closed on 1 Mar., not reopening until Oct. (Bentley, ii. 662).

367. Malone, iii. 240. Bentley, i. 237–40, 324–6.

368. *Coventry*, 440; also in Murray, 253.

369. Malone, xiv. 368 (not in Adams); also incomplete version in Ord HP2, reading 'consideration' for 'confirmation'. Lazarus and Baptista Colloretti, or Colloredo, were Siamese twins from Genoa. Martin Parker's ballad about them, 'The Two Inseparable Brothers', is repr. by Hyder Rollins, *The Pack of Autolycus* (Cambridge, Mass., 1927), 10–14. Rollins also assembles a number of seventeenth-century allusions to them (ibid. 7–9, 237). They appeared at Norwich in Mar. 1638 and Dec. 1639 (*Norwich*, 227 and 233), and at Aberdeen in 1642 (see Introduction, 81).

syde. In confirmation of his Majesty's warrant, granted unto him to make publique shewe. Dated the 4. Novemb. 1637.

1638

370   *Arcadian Shepherdess*, all^d. Salisbury Courte 1638

371   *Devil and Collyer*, allowed 1638. Bull company — second part all^d. same year.

372   *Broome, *Florentine Frend*, allowed 1638   Queen's Company.

373   *Love Sick Courtier*, all^d for Salisbury Court, 1638

374   *Messanissa*, allowed to fortune's Comp. 1638

375   *More Fields*, alld Fortune Company 1638

376   *New World in the Moon*, allowed Bull's Comp. 1638.

377   *Princely Lovers*, allowed Cockpit Company 1638

378   *Seven Stars*, allowed Fortune Company 1638

8 January

379   *Davenant's *Britannia Triumphans* licensed for the press.

26 January

380   *⟨Suckling's⟩ Aglaura was licenced by the Master of the Revels, Sir Henry Herbert, 26 Jany 1637–8, and printed in that year.

28 February

381   (*Norwich*) Danyell Abbot brought into this Court a lycence vnder the seale of the maister of the Revells Dated in November last to

370. Burn, 194. Not in Bentley; not otherwise known.
371. Burn, 195. Not in Bentley; not otherwise known.
372. Burn, 197. In Bentley, v. 1333, only as an anonymous entry in the SR, 29 Dec. 1653. Apparently a lost play by Richard Brome.
373. Burn, 198. Not known elsewhere with this precise title; possibly Richard Brome's *The Lovesick Court, or the Ambitious Politique* (Bentley, iii. 76–7).
374. Burn, 200. Not in Bentley; not otherwise known.
375. Ibid. Not in Bentley; not otherwise known.
376. Ibid. Not in Bentley; not otherwise known. Burn suggests that the play was inspired by John Wilkins's *The Discovery of a World in the Moone* (1638).
377. Burn, 202. Not in Bentley; not otherwise known.
378. Ibid. Not in Bentley; not otherwise known.
379. Malone, iii. 284. Bentley, iii. 199–200.
380. Malone MS in his transcript of Aubrey's *Lives*, Bodleian MS Eng. misc. d. 26, f. 27^v. Another version is in his copy of Langbaine's *Account*, Bodleian Mal 132, p. 496*^v. Not known to Bentley, v. 1201–7.
381. *Norwich*, 227.

shewe sightes &c. Mr Maior offered him xxij s for a gratuity to forbeare his shewes wch hee refused And in the end Mr Maior gaue him leaue to shewe on munday tuesday and wednesday next till noone./

16 April

382 *Davenant's *The Unfortunate Lovers* licensed.

23 April

383 *Shirley's *The Royal Master* licensed.

3 May

384 *One of the leaves of Sir Henry Herbert's Manuscript, which was missing, having been recovered since the remark in the text ⟨that Ford's *The Ladies' Trial* does not appear to have been licensed by Sir Henry Herbert⟩ was made, I find that the Ladies Trial was performed for the first time at the Cockpit theatre in May, 1638, on the 3d of which month it was licensed by the Master of the Revels.

2 June

385 *Received of Mr. Lowens for my paines about Messinger's play called The King and the Subject, 2 June, 1638, 1*l*. o. o.

5 June

386a *The name of The King and the Subject is altered, and I allowed the play to bee acted, the reformations most strictly observed, and not otherwise, the 5th of June, 1638.

At Greenwich the 4 of June, Mr. W. Murray gave mee power from the king to allowe of the play, and tould me that hee would warrant it.

> Monys? Wee'le rayse supplies what ways we please,
> And force you to subscribe to blanks, in which

---

382. Malone, iii. 284. Bentley, iii. 220–2.
383. Malone, iii. 232. Bentley, v. 1139–42.
384. Malone, i. 424. Bentley, iii. 446–7.
385. Malone, iii. 240. Bentley, iv. 794–6. Bentley accepts Greg's conjecture that the fee of £1 represents an extra fee, in addition to Herbert's normal fee of £2, because Herbert had been obliged to take special pains about the play, which is lost.
386a. Malone, iii. 240. *386b.* Malone, iii. 230. See previous item. Malone offers no evidence to support his conjecture that the play was retitled *The Tyrant*, also lost, and Bentley is sceptical. Bentley, i. 61, identifies 'W. Murray' as William Murray, Gentleman of the Bedchamber, later the first Earl of Dysart, and a person of great influence with the King. For other theatrical connections of Murray see Bentley, iv. 477–8 and vii. 58.

We'le mulct you as wee shall thinke fitt. The Caesars
In Rome were wise, acknowledginge no lawes
But what their swords did ratifye, the wives
And daughters of the senators bowinge to
Their wills, as deities, &c.

This is a peece taken out of Phillip Messingers play, called The
King and the Subject, and entered here for ever to bee remembered
by my son and those that cast their eyes on it, in honour of Kinge
Charles, my master, who, readinge over the play at Newmarket,
set his marke upon the place with his owne hande, and in thes
words:

This is too insolent, and to bee changed.

Note, that the poett makes it the speech of a king, Don Pedro
king of Spayne, and spoken to his sujects.

386b *I suspect it was new named The Tyrant. The play is lost.

9 June
387   *⟨A licence⟩ to make showe of an outlandish creature, called a
Possum

17 November
388   *Davenant's _The Fair Favourite_ licensed.

1639

389   *_Claricilla_ — Thomas Killigrew, allowed 1639

390   *The _Courte and the Cuntrye_, by Damport, all^d. 1639, Pastoral.

391   *_Dido and Æneas_, all^d Queen's Company 1639

392   *_Hogshead_, an olde play, a new scene, alld Princes Company 1639

393   *The _Jewell_, a Com. Fortune, lic. 1639

_387._ Chalmers, 208 = 440(c).   _388._ Malone, iii. 284. Bentley, iii. 203–4.
_389._ Burn, 194. Not known to Bentley, iv. 698–700, who presents evidence suggesting
that the play was written in Rome in the first half of 1636, though the Castle Howard
MS is dated June 1639.
_390._ Burn, 195. Not in Bentley; not otherwise known. Presumably a lost play by Robert
Davenport.
_391._ Ibid. Not in Bentley. Probably a new play rather than a re-licensing of the
anonymous lost play with this title performed in 1598.
_392._ Burn, 198. Not in Bentley; not otherwise known.
_393._ Ibid. Not in Bentley; not otherwise known.

394   *Massinger, History of Will: *Longesword*, son to Rosamund, lic. to the bull 1639.

395   *A Queen and No Queen*, all^d to Fortune Comp. 1639

396   *Spanish Purchas*, all^d to Salisbury Court Comp. 1639

397   *Walstein, Duke of Fredland*, Traj. all^d Globe, 1639

398   *Woman Monster*, alld Fortune Comp. 1639

25 September

399   *Massinger's *Alexius, or The Chaste Lover* licensed for the king's company.

9 October

400   (*Norwich*) Robert Browne and George Hall Did this Day exhibit a lycence from Sr Henry Herbert master of the Revelles to shewe an Italian motion but because he sayth his motion is noe Italian motion but made in London this Court thinkes fitt not to suffer them to shewe.

12 October

401   (*Norwich*) Vpon Thursday last was sent to London to be deliu⟨er⟩ed to m^r Alderm' Anguish or m^r Edmond Burman at the Grene Dragon at Bishipsgate streete London sealed vp in a letter and deliu⟨er⟩ed to Young Sotherton a lycence granted vnto one Iohn Rawlyns and his assistance to play and shewe his skill vpon instruments vnder the seale of the office of the Revells now because it appeared playnely that the Date of the same and the yeare of the kings reigne were amended and altered and the said Rawlings vpon his Examinacon confessing that one Long that keeps the Swan in Newington Iustice Long his brother had mended & altered the same because he could not haue yt renewed by m^r walter Sr Henry

---

394. Ibid. Not in Bentley; not otherwise known.

395. Burn, 202. Not in Bentley. Possibly Brome's *The Queen and Concubine* (Bentley, iii. 85–6).

396. Burn, 203. In Bentley, v. 1410, only as the title of an anonymous MS play which Warburton claimed to have owned but which cannot now be traced.

397. Burn, 204. Licence not known to Bentley, iv. 477–9; presumably Henry Glapthorne's *The Tragedy of Albertus Wallenstein, late Duke of Fridland* (1639).

398. Burn, 204. Not in Bentley; not otherwise known.

399. Malone, iii. 231. Bentley, iv. 758–9.

400. *Norwich*, 232; also Murray, 359.

401. *Norwich*, 232.

Herbertes Secretary that Dwells in Shoe Lane vnder 30ˢ and that the said Long had xiiᵈ. for his paynes, mʳ Maior seized the patent and sent yt as aforesaid to mʳ Anguish & mʳ Burman or in their absence to mʳ Birch to shewe to Sʳ Henry Herbert and to compleyne of the abuse of theise false lycenses, and of the great number of other of the like quality, and to desire his helpe and furtherance to redresse this abuse./

30 October

402   *Shirley's *The Gentleman of Venise* licensed.

30 November

403   *Spanish Lovers*, by Davenant, allᵈ to Kings Comp. 1639

1640

404   *The *Challenge*, alld 1640; it was acted without license by Beeston at Cockpit

405   *The *Humours of Rome*, made by a Schollar, allᵈ Fortune Company, 1640

406   *The *Noble Ryveles*, T. C. by Coxe, allᵈ Cockpit Company 1640.

407   *The *Noble Thief*, by Younge Clifton, allᵈ Bull Comp. 1640.

408   *Abington, *Q. of Aragon*, allᵈ to Kings Comp. 1640

26 January

409   *Massinger's *The Fair Anchoress of Pausilippo* licensed for the king's company.

---

402. Malone, iii. 232, with date misprinted as 1629. Bentley, v. 1112–14.

403. Burn, 203, giving year only; also Malone, iii. 284, giving day and month. Malone suggested that this is the play now entitled *The Distresses*, and the identification has been generally accepted. Bentley, iii. 202–3.

404. Burn, 194. Not in Bentley; not otherwise known. This may have been the play that got Beeston into trouble (see below, 412–13).

405. Burn, 198. Not in Bentley; not otherwise known.

406. Burn, 201. Not in Bentley; not otherwise known. The dramatist may be the Robert Coxe who was an actor in the Cockpit company in 1639 (Bentley, ii. 414–15), but he was not known as a dramatist before the closing of the theatres (Bentley, iii. 182–3).

407. Burn, 201. Not in Bentley; not otherwise known. 'Younge Clifton' has not been identified.

408. Burn, 202. By William Habington. Licence not known to Bentley, iv. 522–3. The play was entered in the SR on 2 Apr. 1640. See below, 411.

409. Malone, iii. 231; also Burn, 196. Lost. Bentley, iv. 781–2.

April

410   *At Easter 1640, the Princes company went to the Fortune, and the
       Fortune company to the Red Bull.

9 April

411   *On thursday the 9 of Aprill, 1640, my Lord Chamberlen bestow'd
       a play on the Kinge and Queene, call'd Cleodora, Queene of
       Arragon, made by my cozen Abington. It was performd by my lords
       servants out of his own family, and his charge in the cloathes
       and sceanes, which were very riche and curious. In the hall at
       Whitehall.
            The king and queene commended the generall entertaynment, as
       very well acted, and well set out.
            It was acted the second tyme in the same place before the king
       and queene.

3 May

412   Wheras William Bieston and the Company of Players \of the
       Cockpitt/ in Drury Lane haue lately Acted a new play wthout any
       Licence from the M^r of his Ma^{ts} Reuells & beeing comaunded to
       forbeare playing or Acting of the same play by the sayd M^r of the
       Reuells & commaunded likewise to forbeare all manner of playing
       haue notwithstanding in contempt of the Authority of the sayd M^r
       of the Reuells & the power graunted vnto him vnder the great seale
       of England Acted the sayd Play & others to ye p^{r}iudice of his Ma^{ts}
       seruice & in contempt of the office of the Reuells ⟨?by which⟩ hee
       & they & all other Companyes euer haue beene & ought to bee
       gouerned & regulated. Theis are therfore in his Ma^{ts} name, &
       signification of his royall pleasure to comaund the sayd Willm
       Bieston & the rest of that Company of the Cockpitt Players from
       henceforth & vpon sight heerof to forbeare to Act any Playes
       whatsoeuer vntill they shall bee restored by the sayd M^r of the
       Reuells vnto their former Liberty. Wherof all partyes concernable
       are to take notice & to conforme accordingly as they and euery of
       them will answere it at their (sic). Giuen &c' at Whitehall the 3^d. of
       May 1640/

---

410. Malone, iii. 241; also i. 485. Bentley, i. 279–80 and 315–16.
411. Malone, iii. 240–1; first two paragraphs also in Ord/Burn, 194.
412. PRO LC5/134/392; also MSC ii. 393–4. Bentley, i. 332–4. See next item.

To William Bieston. George
Estoteville & the rest of the Company of the Players at the Cockpitt
in Drury Lane./
(*in margin*) Vnlicensed Playes restrayned.

4–7 May

413 *On Monday the 4 May, 1640, William Beeston was taken by a
messenger, and committed to the Marshalsey, by my Lord Cham-
berlens warant, for playinge a playe without license. The same day
the company at the Cockpitt was commanded by my Lord Cham-
berlens warant to forbeare playinge, for playinge when they were
forbidden by mee, and for other disobedience, and laye still
monday, tusday, and wensday. On thursday at my Lord Chamberlen's entreaty I gave them their liberty, and upon their petition of
submission subscribed by the players, I restored them to their
liberty on thursday.

The play I cald for, and, forbiddinge the playinge of it, keepe
⟨?kept⟩ the booke, because it had relation to the passages of the K.s
journey into the Northe, and was complaynd of by his M.^tye to mee,
with commande to punishe the offenders.

1 June

414 *Shirley's *Rosania*; or Love's Victory, all^d King's comp^y. 1640

11 September

415 *re^d from 23 Octob 1637 to 11 Sep 1640
In three years Sr H. Herbert rec^d from his 9th Share in Sal. Court
House

90.	13.	8
87.	12.	8
112.	1–	–

near 97 p Ann.   £290.   7.   4.

10 November

416 *Shirley's *The Impostor* licensed.

413. Malone, iii. 241. See Introduction, 70–1.
414. Burn, 202; also Malone, iii. 232. Published in 1652 as *The Doubtful Heire*. Bentley,
v. 1105–7.
415. Malone MS in an interleaved copy of vol. Iii of his 1790 edn. of Shakespeare,
Bodleian Mal 1046, f. 148***. Not in Bentley.
416. Malone, iii. 232. Published in 1652 as *The Imposture*. Bentley, v. 1123–5.

25 November

417   *All^d for the press a Masque called *Masquerade du Ciel* for Mr. Thompson, gratis, 25 Nov. 1640.

1641

418   *The *Chevallers*, allowed to Cockpit Company 1641.

419   *Mad for a Head.* alld for the Bull, 1641

420   *Variety Com: with several.reformations made by Shirley 1641. My Lo^d Newcastle, as is said hath some hand in it. 1641 allowed upon review without exception.

421   *Youths Figaries* all^d upon several reformations and not otherwise 1641. Made by Jordan for the Bull Comp^y.

15 March

422   (*Norwich*) Mr Maior

Wheras I am enformed by yor worthey Burgesses for p⟨ar⟩liament that yor Cittie of Norwich is much offended and molested with players to the p^riudice of yor manufactures & the disturbance of the peace Theise are therfore In his Ma^t name to charge & require all players within yor said Citty vpon sighte hereof to forbeare playinge and to departe yor Citty in convenient time and incase of disobedience to giue yo^u the Maior and other officers full power and authority to punnishe the foresaid players or aney of them so offendinge and them or any of them to committ to warde vntill they or aney of them shall conforme to this my warrant and likewise to take from the said players or any of them [shall] any Lycence they or any of them shall produce in that behalfe   Dated this 15 of March 1640

                                   Henry Herbert

To the Maior & [f] the other officers of
the Citty of Norwich or to any of them

---

417. Burn, 200. Not in Bentley. A closet play probably by John Sadler, a Cambridge academic (Bentley, v. 1037–9). Herbert's printing licence is included in the 1640 Quarto opposite the title-page (C83).

418. Burn, 194. Not in Bentley; not otherwise known.

419. Burn, 199. Not in Bentley; not otherwise known.

420. Burn, 203. By William Cavendish, at this time Earl of Newcastle. Licence not known to Bentley, iii. 149–51.

421. Burn, 204. Not in Bentley; not otherwise known. Presumably a lost play by Thomas Jordan.

422. *Norwich*, 235; also in Murray, 360.

26 May

423 *The *Politique Father*, by Shirley, kings company, 1641

23 June

424 *23^d. June 1641 Reced for the licensinge a booke for the Fortune comp. called the Doge & the Dragon. 2^{li}.

2 August

425 This Comedy, called, *The Walks of Islington and Hogsdon, With the Humours of Woodstreet-Compter*, may be Acted: This 2. August, 1641.

         Henry Herbert.

5 August

426 *5th Augt 1641 upon conferense with the Earle of Essex Lord chamberlen to his Maty concerning the encrease of the plague to a hundred & I sent out warrants to the severall Playhouses for their restraynt & deliverd them to Mr Lovens to bee sente accordingly

25 November

427 *Shirley's *The Cardinal* licensed

12 December

428 *12 Decr 1641. the plague decreased to 86 my Lord Chamberlen gave the Players leave to play & they began the same day

1642

429 *Fatal Friendship* Tragedy alld 1642, kings company

430 *The *Sophy*, by Sir John Denham, all^d to kings Comp. 1642.

423. Burn, 202; also Malone, iii. 232. It is now accepted that this is the play published under the title of *The Brothers* in 1652, but is quite distinct from the play licensed as *The Brothers* in 1626 (**166**). For discussion of this complicated problem see Bentley, v. 1082–4.
424. Ord HP5, 48. Anon., lost. Bentley, v. 1321–2, vi. 173.
425. Printed on H4 of Thomas Jordan, *The Walks of Islington and Hogsdon* (1657). Bentley, iv. 688–90.
426. Ord HP10, 23; also Ord C1 and Chalmers, 212, paraphrased. Bentley, ii. 666–7.
427. Malone, iii. 232. Bentley, v. 1084–7.
428. Ord HP10, 23; also Chalmers, 212, paraphrased. Bentley, ii. 667, notes that the figure of eighty-six deaths does not correspond to the totals given in contemporary records.
429. Burn, 197. Licence not given in Bentley, iii. 98, where the play is known only from entries in the SR, in which the author is named as 'Mr Burroughes'.
430. Burn, 203. Licence not known to Bentley, iii. 276–9, who tentatively dated the play 1641.

6 January

431   *On Twelfe Night, 1641, the prince had a play called The Scornful Lady, at the Cockpitt, but the kinge and queene were not there; and it was the only play acted at courte in the whole Christmas.

26 April

432   *Shirley's *The Sisters* licensed.

June

433   *Received of Mr. Kirke, for a new play which I burnte for the ribaldry and offense that was in it, 2*l.* o. o.

8 June

434   *Received of Mr. Kirke for another new play called The Irishe Rebellion, the 8 June, 1642, 2*l.* o. o.

August

435   *Here ended my allowance of plaies, for the war began in Aug. 1642.

DOCUMENTS NOT PRECISELY DATABLE

436   *Rowley, *Foole without Booke*; full of faults, and must be Corrected, if allowed   1*li.* for the Princes Company

437   *18th. Feb: for allow: of a certayne P. called the *Resolute Queene* upon S[r]. Robert Cottons letter who had perused the booke the sayd P. to be acted only one night by certayne young men of the Strand & others no profec't players. — 12[s].

431. Malone, iii. 241. By Beaumont and Fletcher. Bentley, i. 67.
432. Malone, iii. 232. Bentley, v. 1147–9.
433. Malone, iii. 241. Bentley, ii. 492–3 and iv. 710–15 argues that 'Mr. Kirke' was the actor John Kirke, and he brought this play and the next item to be licensed in his capacity as manager of the Red Bull theatre and not as the author of the plays.
434. Malone, iii. 241–2. Anon., lost. Bentley, v. 1355–6.
435. Malone, iii. 242.
436. Burn, 197. Bentley, v. 1022, only as an entry in SR, 9 Sept. 1653, identifying the author as William Rowley. As Rowley died early in 1626, and the Prince's company seems to have broken up in 1625, the play probably dates from 1623 or 1624.
437. Ord/Burn, 202. Not in Bentley; not otherwise known. Sir Robert Cotton died in 1631.

438   *For a daye in Lent from the Cockpitt companye when their tyme
       was out   10^s.

439   *M^r. Biston sent mee for Lent by M^r. Blagrave in the name of the
       company this 5th April 2^{li}.

440   *(a) Sir Henry Herbert granted, on the 20th August 1623, a license
       gratis, to John Williams, and four others, to make *showe* of *an
       Elephant*, for a year; (b) on the 5th of September to make showe of
       a *live Beaver*; (c) On the 9th of June 1638, to make showe of an
       outlandish creature, called a *Possum*; (d) a license to a Dutchman to
       show two *Dromedaries*, for a year, for which, the licenser received
       one pound; (e) a warrant to Grimes, for showing *the Camell*:
       (f) —On the 14th of August 1624, a license was granted to Edward
       James to sett forth a *Showing Glass*, called the *World's Wonder*: (g)
       On the 27th of August 1623, a license was granted to Barth. Cloys
       with three Assistants to make show of a *Musical Organ*, with divers
       motions in it; (h) to make show of an *Italian Motion*; (i) to show *a
       Looking Glass*; (j) to show the *Philosopher's Lanthorn*; (k) to show *a
       Virginal*: (l) —A license was granted to Henry Momford, and others,
       "for tumbling, and vaulting, with *other tricks of slight of hand*;" (m)
       for *a prize* at the Bull by Mr. Allen, and Mr. Lewkner; (n) to
       William Sands and others to show "the *Chaos of the World*;" (o) to
       show a motion called *the Creation of the World*; (p) to show certain
       freaks of *charging* and *discharging a gun*; (q) a license to Mr. Lowins,
       on the 18th of February 1630, for allowing of *a Dutch vaulter*, at
       their Houses, ⟨the Globe, and Blackfriars.⟩ (r) A warrant was given
       to Francis Nicolini, an Italian, and his Company, "to dance on the
       ropes, to use *Interludes*, and *masques*, and to *sell his powders, and
       balsams*:" (s) —to John Puncteus, a Frenchman, professing *Physick*,

438. Ord HP3, 127. This and the next item form a single cutting from Ord.
Halliwell-Phillipps gave no hint of the year to which they apply. Bentley, vii. 3.
439. Ord HP3, 127.
440. Chalmers, 208–10. Of the twenty-one show licences and three printing licences
given here fourteen can be found elsewhere, usually in fuller and more accurate
versions: (a) = **44**, (b) = **237**, (e) = **234**, (f) = **41**, (g) = **51**, (h) = **48**, (l) = **60a–b**, (m)
= **24**, (n) = **25**, (o) = **122**, (p) = **249**, (q) = **212**, (v) = **235**, and (x) = **241b**. Clearly they
are not in chronological order. For (d) cf. **300**, and for (u) cf. **263**. For John Puncteus
(s) see Introduction, 98–9, and an anonymous pamphlet published in 1642, *A Great
Robbery in the North, Neer Swanton in Yorkshire*, BL Thomason Tracts E108(12), 3,
which mentions 'one *Knowles*, who was heretofore a dancer on the ropes, and also a
jester to Master *John Punteus* the French Mountebanke, which travelled throughout
this Kingdom'.

in prison in the Poultry Counter in London where he still re-
mayneth.

458   Peticion of Dorothy Blagrove Widdowe. That the Company of
Players of the Cockpitt playhouse in Drury Lane graunted to Sir
Henry Harbert under theire hands a play share dureing the time of
theire enioying the Queenes Service, and Sir Henry Harbert for one
hundred pounds consideracion to him paid graunted his said share
to William Blagrove (since deceased) his deputy and assignes. And
afterwards one Mr. Beeston being Master of the said playhouse who
alsoe subscribed with the rest takes occasion to quarrell with the
Company to the end hee might have a Company that would take
what hee would be willing to give them, And uppon this falling out
some of them goe to Blackfriers, and some to Salisbury Court
Playhouses and those of Salisbury Court are made the Queenes
Company.

459   And this def.[t] also saieth that afterwards the sicknes still contynue-
ing the said ffifteene shillings per weeke was still stopped from
this def.[t] whereby this def.[t] was in a kind enforced to treate againe
and to make some agreement wth the said William Beeston touching
the premises wherevpon the comp.[lts] or some of their Company
became suitors to S[r] Henry Herbert knight Master of the Revells to
here and examine the cause betweene them and the said Master of
the Revells taking the trouble vpon him did afterwards Award that
the def.[t] should bee paied six shillings weekly and ffive pounds for
every new play which hee should bring vntill such tyme as the
sicknes should cease and the p.[lts] should have leave to play againe
which Award the p.[lts] and Company did but in parte performe for
when they began to play againe which was in the month of October

458. Ibid. 243. Dated ?1640. Mrs Blagrave then petitioned to be allowed to receive the
benefit of the share inherited from her husband. Precisely when Herbert was given
the share and then sold it to Blagrave is not clear, but it seems to have been before the
breaking up of Queen Henrietta's company in 1636–7 (Bentley, i. 236–9 and vi. 64).
459. Extract from PRO Req. 2/723, as transcribed by Ann Haaker, 'The Plague, the
Theater, and the Poet', *Renaissance Drama*, NS i (1968), 304. The document is part of
a 1640 lawsuit between Salisbury Court theatre and the dramatist Richard Brome, the
defendant in the case. Brome had contracted in 1635 to write plays exclusively for
the Salisbury Court, but (according to Brome) during the closure of the theatres in the
plague years 1636–7 the company did not pay him the sums due to him under the
contract, and he was forced to turn to William Beeston for help. The company
thereupon asked Sir Henry to arbitrate, late in 1636 or early in 1637. For a full account
see Haaker.

with ten in his Company, to exercise *the quality of playing*, for a
year, and to *sell his drugs:* (**t**) On the 6th of March, a license was
given *gratis* to Alexander Kukelson to teach the *art of musick* and
dancing, for one year; (**u**) A license to Thomas Gibson, to make
shew of *pictures in Wax:* And, the master of the Revels appears also
to have licensed books, during the reigns of King James, and
Charles the 1st; (**v**) he received a fee, for allowing Ovid's Epistles,
translated into English; (**w**) he received a fee, for a book of verses
of my Lord Brook's, called *Caelia*; (**x**) he received of Sayle, the
Bookbinder, *ten* shillings, for allowing to be printed two other small
pieces of verses, done by *a boy* of *thirteen*, called *Cowley*.

441   *It appears from Sir Henry Herbert's Manuscript . . . that Fletcher
produced eleven new plays in the last four years of his life . . . ⟨and⟩
that the new plays which Fletcher had brought out in the course of
the year, were generally presented at court at Christmas.

442   *The Fatal Dowry does not appear to have been licensed for the
stage under that title, but was printed in 1632. A new Way to pay
old Debts does not appear to have been licensed for the stage, but
was printed in Nov. 1632.

443   *This play ⟨The Unnatural Combat⟩ ought to have been placed as
Massinger's first play, now extant, for it was acted before the year 1622.

444   *Plays in the time of King James the First, (and probably afterwards,) appear to have been performed every day at each theatre
during the winter season, except in the time of Lent, when they
were not permitted on the sermon days, as they were called, that
is, on Wednesday and Friday; nor on the other days of the week,
except by special licence: which however was obtained by a fee paid
to the Master of the Revels. In the summer season the stage
exhibitions were continued, but during the long vacation they were
less frequently repeated. However, it appears from Sir Henry
Herbert's Manuscript, that the king's company usually brought out
two or three new plays at the Globe every summer.

441. Malone, iii. 225.
442. Malone, iii. 230.
443. Malone MS in his copy of the play, Bodleian Mal 237(3). The item implies that
Malone found no entry for the play in his office-book; but Bentley, iv. 823–4, is
sceptical, and argues for a date between 1621 and 1625. Edwards and Gibson argue for
a date of 1624–5 (ii. 181–4).
444. Malone, iii. 151–3. Bentley, vii. 3.

445   *After Sir Henry Herbert became possessed of the office of Master of the Revels, fees for permission to perform in Lent appear to have been constantly paid by each of the theatres. The managers however did not always perform plays during that season. Some of the theatres, particularly the Red Bull and the Fortune, were then let to prize-fighters, tumblers, and rope-dancers, who sometimes added a Masque to the other exhibitions.

446   *Heminges, . . . it appears from Sir Henry Herbert's MS., took some concern in the management of the theatre, and used to present Sir Henry, as Master of the Revels, with his New Year's gift, for three or four years afterwards ⟨i.e. from 1624 onwards⟩.

447   *The Master of the Revels required . . . a Christmas Box of forty shillings, from each of the established theatres.

448   *He possest what seems to have been a necessary appendage of his office, an appropriate box in the established theatres.

449   *From Sir Henry Herbert's Manuscript I learn, that the musicians belonging to Shakespeare's company were obliged to pay the Master of the Revels an annual fee for a licence to play in the theatre.

450   *The [boxes attended by] money received at the theatre by *women* who were called boxholders. See Sr H. H Mss. p. 66.

451   *It appears from Sir Henry Herbert's Office-book that the king's company between the years 1622 and 1641 produced either at Blackfriars or the Globe at least four new plays every year.

452   *As the Globe was partly exposed to the weather, and they acted there usually by day-light, it appeared to me probable (when this essay was originally published) that this was the summer theatre; and I have lately found my conjecture confirmed by Sir Henry Herbert's Manuscript. The king's company usually began to play at the Globe in the month of May.

445. Malone, iii. 66. Malone then illustrated this generalization by quoting 33 and 151. Bentley, vii. 5.

446. Malone, *Inquiry*, 251. Bentley, ii. 468.   *447*. Chalmers, 210.

448. Chalmers, *Apology*, 520–1.   *449*. Malone, iii. 112.

450. Malone MS in Bodleian MS Mal 43, a collection of MS memoranda on the manners of Shakespeare's time. See Bentley, *The Profession of Player in Shakespeare's Time, 1590–1642* (Princeton, 1984), 93–7, who presents evidence to show that gatherers or box-holders, who collected admission money, were frequently though not invariably women.

451. Malone, iii. 166.   *452*. Malone, iii. 70–1.

453   *After the year 1620, as appears from Sir Henry Herbert's book, they ⟨the Swan and Rose theatres⟩ were used occasiona the exhibition of prize-fighters.

454   *I suppose he ⟨Sir William Davenant⟩ appointed her ⟨Mrs Eliz Beeston's⟩ son Mr. William Beeston his deputy, for from Sir H Herbert's office-book, he appears for a short time to have ha management of that theatre.

455   *I have learned from Sir Henry Herbert's office-book, that betw the year 1625 and 1641, ⟨authors'⟩ benefits were on the second of representation.

456   *From the time when Sir Henry Herbert came into the office of Revels to 1642, when the theatres were shut up, his Manuscr does not furnish us with a regular account of the plays exhibited court every year. Such, however, as he has given, I shall n subjoin.

457   Peticion of Robert Davison, his Majesty's servant, to John, Bisho of Lincoln, Lord Keeper. That your peticioner and one Grubb being bayle for one William Rowly att the suite of Robert Lewes The said Grubb was for the same in execucion taken and im- prisoned, and there dyed, After which the said Rowly was alsoe taken in execucion and imprisoned for the same debt. Whereupon a Composicion was made before Sir Henry Herbert and Mr. Ouldsworth, Secretarie to the Lord Chamberlaine (with both parties consentes) for the paiement of the debt att severall daies, which hath beene accordingly performed, and the whole debt is satisfied saving onely 7 li. odd money which by the agreement is not yet due. Nevertheles the said Robert Lewes by the instigacion of his uncle Samuell Lewes, did on Mondaie last arrest your peticioner alsoe in execucion for all the same debt, and hath thereupon layed him

453. Malone, iii. 56.   *454*. Malone, iii. 242. Bentley, vi. 74–6.

455. Malone, iii. 158.

456. Malone, iii. 228. The office-book provides lists of plays at court for the winter seasons of 1622–3, 1623–4, 1624–5, 1633–4, 1635–6, 1636–7, and 1641–2. These are conveniently assembled in Adams, 49–58.

457. *The Manuscripts of the House of Lords*, Vol. XI NS, *Addenda 1514–1714*, ed. Maurice F. Bond (1962), 170. Dated 11 Mar. 1624/5. Davison went on to petition that he might be set free, and in subsequent documents (ibid. 170–1) the Lord Keeper ordered his release. It is not clear precisely when Herbert and Oldsworth made arrangements for the repayment of the debt. 'William Rowly' is presumably William Rowley the dramatist.

1637. they were then Indebted vpon that Award and Accompt to this def.ᵗ the sume of Eleaven pounds Eleaven shillings six pence or thereaboutes.

460 That such of the Company as will not be ordered and governed by me as their governoʳ \ or shall not by the Mʳ of his mᵗˢ Revells and my selfe \\bee// thought fitt Comedians for her mᵗˢ service / I may haue power to dischardge from the Company, and wᵗʰ the Advice of the mʳ of the Revells to putt new ones in their places, and those who shalbe soe discharged not to haue the honoʳ to be her mᵗˢ servants, butt only those who shall Continew at the foresaid playhouse, And the said Company not to play at any tyme [at] \in/ any other place, but the forsaid playhouse wᵗʰout [the] \my/ Consent [of me] and my hand in wryting, (lest his Maᵗˢ service might be neglected) except by speciall Comand from one of the lo: Chamberlaines, or the mʳ of his mᵗˢ Revells &c.

460. BL Add. Charter 9292B. Extract from a draft patent drawn up by Richard Heton in the autumn of 1639, but never issued. Heton wanted to give himself dictatorial powers over the company at the Salisbury Court theatre, but could not ignore the authority of the Master of the Revels. See Bentley, ii. 684–7 and vi. 103–5.

Revels Documents
1660 to 1673

?late June 1660

(Sir Henry's warrant to William Beeston at the Salisbury Court theatre)

R1 *Whereas* the allowance of Playes the ordering of Players and Playmakers and the Permission for Errecting of Playhouses; Hath time out of minde whereof the memory of man is not to the Contrary belonged to the Master of his Maties Office of the Revells

And whereas M^r. William Beeston hath desired Authority and Lycence from mee to Continue the house called Salsbury Court Play house, In a Playhouse which was formerly built & Errected into a Playhouse by the Permission and Lycence of the Master of the Revells

These are therefore by vertue of a Grante vnder the Greate Seale of England and of the Constant Practice thereof to Continue and Constitute the said house called Salisbury Court Play house, into a Play house and to Authorize and Lycence the said M^r. Beeston to Sett Lett or vse it for a Play house, wherein comedies tragedies or Trage Comedies Pastoralls and Interludes may bee Acted, *Prouided* that noe persons be admitted to Act in the said Play house but such as shall be allowed by the Master of his Maties. Office of the Revells, Given vnder my hand and Seale at the office of the Revells this

(Endorsed:) For Mr W. Beeston

30 July 1660

(Warrant for fencers at the Red Bull)

R2   *Copy of a Warrant granted to Fencers.*

With the favour and priviledge of his Highnes the Duke of Yorke, it is agreed upon, by and betweene Francis Burges and

---

R1. A100 (Milhous–Hume, 6); scribal copy, undated. References to Milhous–Hume are to item nos., not pages.

R2. Warner, 183 (Milhous–Hume, 10). On 16 June 1669 Robert Gray and John Crighton were allowed at Norwich to show their skill with a very similar list of weapons, 'paying Twenty shillings to ye poore of ye City' (*MCB* 5, f. 112^v).

William Tubb, to play a tryall of skill at eight severall weapons, which are hereunder expressed, on the thirteenth day of August next, being Monday, at the Red Bull Playhouse.—30th July. 1660.

The Weapons of Francis Burges	The Weapons of Wm. Tubb
Backe Sword	Single Rapier
Sword and Gantlet	Rapier and Dagger
Sword and Dagger	Halfe Pike
Sword and Buckler.	Quarter Staffe.

Whereas his Highnes the Duke of Yorke hath been pleased to comende unto me Francis Burges and Wm. Tubb, for a warant to playe a prize.

These are to authorize the said Frances Burges and William Tubb to playe a prize at the weapons above named, at the House called the Red Bull, and for so doinge this shall be their warant.

Dated the 30th July, 1660.   H. HERBERT.

?August 1660

(*List of Red Bull plays*)

R3   Names of the plays acted by the Red Bull actors

The Humorous Lieutenant.	Elder Brother.
Beggars Bushe.	The Silent Woman.
Tamer Tamed.	The Weddinge.
The Traytor.	Henry the Fourthe.
Loves Cruelty.	Merry Wives of Windsor.
Wit without Money.	Kinge and no Kinge.
Maydes Tragedy.	Othello.
Philaster.	Dumboys.
Rollo Duke of Normandy.	The Unfortunate Lovers.
Claricilla.	The Widow.

4 August–14 September 1660

(*Sir Henry's petition against the grant to Davenant and Killigrew*)

R4   To the Kings most Excellent Maiestie
The humble peticon of S^r. Henry Herbert kn^t Ma^r of yor
Maiesties Office of the Revells Sheweth

R3. Malone, iii. 272–3 (Milhous–Hume, 12). The sequence of plays given here follows Malone 1790. For identification of plays and dramatists see Index.
R4. A48 (Milhous–Hume, 13). This appears to be the original document, with the signatures of Nicholas and Palmer. A second copy, entirely in a scribal hand, is on A49.

That whereas yor pet^r by vertue of seuerall graunts vnder the great seale of England hath executed the said Office as a Ma^r. of the Revells for about 40 yeares in the times of King Iames & of King Charles both of blessed memory with exepcon only to the time of the late horrid rebellion

And whereas the ordering of plaies, players and play makers, and the permission for erecting of playhouses are Peculiar branches of the said Office and in the constant Practice thereof by yor pet^{rs} Predecessors in the said Office and himselfe with excepcon only as before excepted, and authorised by graunt vnder the said great seale of England & that no person or persons haue erected any Playhouses or raised any Company of Players without Licence from yor pet^{rs} said Predecessors or from yor pet^r. But S^r. William Davenant knight who obtained Leaue of Oliuer and Richard Cromwell to vent his Operas in a time when yor pet^r owned not theire Authority

And whereas yor Ma^{ty} hath lately signified yor. pleasure by warrant to Sr Jefferry Palmer Kn^t and Barr^t yor Ma^{ts} Attorney Generall for the drawing [of a draught] of a graunt for yor Ma^{ts}. signature to pass the greate seale thereby to enable and impower M^r. Thomas Killegrew and the said S^r. William Davenant to erect two New Playhouses in London Westm^r or the Subburbs thereof, and to make Choice of Two Companies of Players to bee vnder theire sole regulacon, and that noe other players shalbee authorized to play in London Westm^r or the Subburbs thereof but such as the said M^r. Killegrew and S^r. William Davenant shall allow of

And whereas yor pet^r hath been represented to yor. Ma^{ty}. as a person consenting to the said powers expressed in the said Warrant, yor pet^r vtterly denies the least Consent or foreknowledge thereof but looks vpon it as an vniust surprize and distructiue to the powers graunted vnder the said great seale to yor pet^r and to the Constant practice of the said Office [vnder the said great seale] and exercised in the said Office ever since Players were first admitted by authority to act plaies, and cannot legally bee done as yor pet^r is advised & it may bee of very ill consequence as yor pet^r is advised by a new graunt to take away & cut off a braunch of ye antient powers graunted to the said Office vnder ye great seale.

Your pet^r. therefore humbly praies that yor Ma^{ty} would be iustly as graciously pleased to revoke the said Warr^t. from yor. Maties. said Attorney Generall, Or to referr the p^{r}mises to the consideracon of yor Ma^{ts} said Attorney Generall to Certify yor Ma^{ty}. of the truth of them and his Iudgment, on the whole matters in question betwixt the said M^r. Killigrew S^r. William Davenant and yor pet^r in relacon to the Legallity and Consequence of theire demaunds & yor pet^{rs} rights And yor pet^r shall ever pray &cr

At the Court at Whitehall 4° Augusti 1660
His Matie is pleased to referre this Peticon to Sr Jeffery Palmer Kn^t and Baronet his Maties. Atturney generall; who, hauing called before him all Persons concerned, & examined ye Peticoners right, is to certefy what hee finds to bee the true State of ye matters in difference, together with his opinion thereupon. And then his Matie will declare his further pleasure.

Edw. Nicholas
(*Written in left margin, at right angle to petition:*)
May it please yor most excellent Ma^{ty}
Although I haue heard the Parties concerned in this Peticon seuerally and apart, yet in respect M^r. Killigrew and S^r. William Dauenant haueing notice of a time appointed to heare all parties together did not come, I haue forborne to proceede further; haueing \alsoe/ receaued an intimacon by Letter from Sr William Dauenant that I was freed from further hearing this matter

JPalmer
14° Sept 1660

(*In right margin:*)
Sir Henry Herbert his Peticon
Petition Referred 4. Aug. 60

7 August 1660

(*Petition of John Rogers to be authorized to guard the theatres*)
R5   To the Kings Most Excellent Maiesty
The humble Peticon of John Rogers.
Most humbly sheweth
That yor Pet^r at the begining of the late Callametys lost thereby his whole estate & during the wars, susteyned much detrim^t & Imprisonm^t. & Lost his Limbs & the vse thereof who served his Excell: the now Lord Generall both in Engl: & Scotland and p⟨er⟩formed good & faithfull Service, In Consideracon whereof & by being Soe much decreapitt as not to act any more in the wars, his Excellency was fauorably please'd for yor Pet^{rs}. future Subsist-

ance without being further burthensome to this Kingdom or to yor
Majesty for a Pencon, To grant him a Tolleration, to erect a
playhouse or to haue a share out of them already Tollerated, yor
Pet.^r thereby vndertaking to Supres all Riotts Tumults or Molesta-
cons that may thereby arise And for that the said Graunt Remains
Imp⟨er⟩fect, vnles Corroborated by yor Majesty.

He therfore humbly Implors yor most Sacred Maiesty in Tender
Compassion, out of yor Kingly Clemency to Confirm vnto him a
share out of the Profitts of the said Playhouses or such allowance,
by them to be giuen, as formerly they vsed to alow to p⟨er⟩sons,
for to keepe the Peace of the same, that he may wth his wife &
famely be thereby Preserved & Releiued in his mamed aged yeares.
And he shall Dayly pray &c

At the Court at Whitehall the 7th of August 1660
His Majesty is Graciously pleased to Refer this Peticon to Sr Henry
Herbert Master of his Majesties Revells to take such order therein
as shalbe agreable to Equety w^thout further trubling his Majesty

J. Holles.
a true Copye

(*Vertically in left margin:*)
The Copy of Rogers Petition and the Reference

14 August 1660

(*Submission of Burt and others to Sir Henry*)

R6 Wee whose names are here vnderwritten doe hereby p⟨ro⟩mise &
Covenant to pay or cause to be paid vnto Sr Henry Herbert Kn^t
Master of his ma^is office of the Revells or to his deputy or agent the
sume of tenn pounds on Saterday next after the date hereof and
what playes soever wee shall act for the future to pay or cause
to be paid to the said Sr Henry Herbert his deputy or agent for
eu⟨er⟩^y new play forty shillings & for eu⟨er⟩^y reviued play twenty
shillings as fees aunciently belonging to the master of the Revells
and wee doe hereby furthermore p⟨ro⟩mise & Covenant to pay or
cause to be paid fower pounds to the said Master of the Revells his
deputy or agent on eu⟨er⟩^y Saterday successiuely next after the
date hereof In witnes whereof wee haue herevnto set our hands &
seals the fowerteenth day of August one thousand six hundred &

R6. Text from PRO CP40/2751/Mem. 317, discovered by Hotson, 202; damaged and
partially illegible copy in A64 (Milhous–Hume, 16).

sixty These Covenants are to be made good dureing the time of acting vnder the said master of the Revells Mic Mohum Robt Shatarall Willm Cartwright Willm Wintshall Walt Clunn Charles Hart & Nich Burt

20 August 1660

(*Sir Henry's reply to the petition of John Rogers*)

R7   August 20. 1660 From the Office of the Reuells

[In obedience to His Maties. Reference I Haue taken the matter of the Petit^rs Request Into Consideration, And conceiue it reasonable That the Pet^r. should haue the same Allowance weekly from you for Guardinge y^r Playhouse which you doe allowe Other Persons for the same worke.

To the Actors at the Redbull and to euery of them]

In obedience to his Maties Comands I haue taken the Matter of the peticone^rs request into Consideration and doe therevppon Conceiue it very resonable y^t the peticoner should haue the same allowance weekely from yo^u. & euery of yo^u. for himselfe and his men for Guarding yor. playhouses from all Molestations and Iniuries which yo^u. formerly did or doe allow or pay to other persons for the same or such like seruice, and y^t it be duly and truely paid him w^thout deniall And the rather for that the Kings most excelent Matie. vpon the Lord Generall Monks recomendation, And the Consideracon of the peticone^rs Losses and Sufferings, hath thought fitt to Commisserate the peticone^r John Rogers his sad Condicon and to refferr vnto me, the releife of the said peticone^r. Given at his Maties office of the Revells vnder my hand & the Seale of the said office the twentith day of August in the twelueth yeare of his Maties. Raigne.

To the Acto^rs. at the Playhouses called the Redd bull Cockpitt and Theatre in Salesbury Co^rt & to euery of them in & about the Citties of London & westm'ster

21 August 1660

(*The King's grant to Killigrew and Davenant*)

R8   Charles the Second by the Grace of God, of England Scotland ffrance and Ireland, King deffender of the ffayth &c, To all to

R7. A46^v (Milhous–Hume, 17). The opening seven lines, mostly deleted with diagonal pen-strokes, are in Herbert's hand; the fuller version is scribal.
R8. A47 (Milhous–Hume, 19). The original from which this was copied has not been discovered.

whome these p^{r}sents shall Come Greeting, Whereas wee are giuen
to vnderstand that Certaine persons In and about Our Citty of
London or the Suburbs thereof, Doe frequently assemble for the
performing and Acting of Playes and Enterludes for Reward, To
which diuers of Our Subiects, doe for theire Entertainm^t Resort,
which said playes, As wee are Informed doe Containe much Matter
of Prophanation and Scurrility, soe that such Kind of Entertainments, which if well Mannaged might serue as Morrall Instructions
In Humane life, As the same are now vsed doe for the most part
tende to the Debauchinge of the Manners of Such as are present at
them, and are very Scandalous & offensive, to all pious and well
disposed persons, Wee takeing the p^{r}mises into our Princely
Consideration, yett, not holding it necessary totally to Supresse the
vse of theatres, because wee are assured that if the Evill & Scandall
In the Playes that now are or haue bin acted, were taken away, the
same might serue as Innocent and Harmlesse diuertisements for
many of our Subiects, And Haueing Experience of the Art and skill
of our Trusty and welbeloued Thomas Killegrew esq^r. one of the
Groomes of our Bedchamber and of S^r. William Dauenant Knight
for the purposses hereafter menconed, Doe hereby giue & Grante
vnto the said Thomas Killegrew and S^r. William Dauenant full
power & authority to Erect two Companies, of Players Consistinge
respectiuely of such persons, As they shall chuse and appoint, And
to purchase builde and Erect or hire at theire Charge, As they shall
thinke fitt, Two Houses or Theaters, withall Convenient Roomes
and other Necessaries therevnto appertaining for the Representation of Tragydies Comedyes, Playes, Operas & all other
Entertainments of that nature In Convenient places And likewise to
Setle and Esstablish such payments to be paid by those that shall
resort to see the said Rep^{r}sentations performed As either haue bin
accustomely Giuen and taken in the like Kind or as shall be
reasonable In regard of the Great expences of Scenes musick and
such new Decorations as Haue not bin formerly used with further
power to make such allowances out of that which they shall soe
receiue to the Actors and other persons employed In the said
Representations in both houses Respectiuely As they shall thinke
fitt, the said Companies to be vnder the Gouernement and Authority of Them the said Thomas Killegrew and S^r. William Dauenant And In regard of the extraordinary Licentiousnes that hath ben
lately used In things of this nature, Our Pleasure, Is, that there shall
be noe more Places of Representations nor Companies of Acto^{rs}. of

Playes or Operas by Recitatiue, musick or Representations by
danceing and Scenes or any other entertainments on the stage In
our Citties of London and Westminster or In the [suburbs]
\liberties/ of them, then the two, to be now erected by vertue of
this Authority, Neuertheless wee doe Hereby by our Authority
Royall strictly enioine the said Thomas Killegrew and S^r. William
Dauenant that they doe not at any time Hereafter cause to be acted
or represented any Play, Enterlude or opera Containing any Matter
of Prophanation, Scurrility or Obscenity, And wee doe further
Hereby authorize and Command them the said Thomas Killegrew
and S^r. William Dauenant to peruse all playes that haue ben
formerly written and to expunge all Prophanesse and scurility from
the same, before they be represented or Acted, And this Our
Grante and Authority made to the said Thomas Killegrew and S^r.
William Dauenant, shall be effectuall and Remaine in full force and
Vertue, Notwthstanding any former order or direction by vs Giuen,
for the suppressing of Playhouses and playes or any other entertainments of the Stage,
Given August 21th. 1660

(*Endorsement:*)
Copy of the Grante the. 21. August, 60/ made to mr Thomas
Killigrew and Sir will: Dauenant by the K^s maiesty under the Priuy
signett

?late August 1660

(*Draft arguments against the grant to Davenant and Killigrew*)

R9   Abstracte of the Powers granted to M^r. Thomas Killigrew and
Sir William Dauenant by warant directed to His Mat^{tes}: Aturney
Generall

To erecte two new Playhouses In London Westminster or the
suburbes therof

To raise two new Companies and to haue the sole Regulation of
them

That noe Other Playhouses shallbe allowed of nor any Other
Players but such as shallbe Authorized by them.

Sir Henry Herberts Answer
Master of His Maties. Office of the Reuells.

R9. A61 (Milhous–Hume, 20); in Herbert's hand.

That the licensinge and Orderinge of Playes, Players and Playmakers and for Erectinge of Playhouses Is an Antient Branche of His
Mat[ies]. Office of the Reuells and Hath ben soly exercised by the
present Master of the Reuells and His Predecessors [for a Hundred
yeares at least] \tyme out of minde/, with exception only to the
time of the late Horrid Rebellion when Sir Henry Herbert owned
not their uniust & Tyranicall Authority, thogh Sir William Dauenant did and obteyned then leaue to Vente His Operas.
That the Grante of the forenamed Powers Is Destructiue to the Powers
granted under the Great Seale to Sir Henry Herbert by the late Kinge
of Blessed Memory. And to the constant practise of the said Office.
That It is Destructiue to a Hundred Persons at least that depende
upon the Quality and the Houses & Haue noe Other liuelyhood
That It cannot legally be done As Councell doth aduise & being
granted begets a suite at law upon the Validity of the Grantes.

30 August 1660

(*Letter from Humphrey Moseley to Sir Henry*)

R10 S[r]

I haue bene very much solicited by the Gentlemen Actors of the Red
Bull for a Note under my hand to certifie unto your Wor[p]. what
Agreement I had made with M[r] Rhodes of the Cock-Pitt Playhouse;
Truly (S[r]) I am so farr from any Agreement with him, that I neuer so
much as treated with him, nor wth. Any from him; neither did I euer
consent Directly or Indirectly, y[t] hee, or any others should Act any
Playes that doe belong to mee without my Knowledge, and Consent
had & Procured. And the same allsoe I doe Certifie concerning The
Whitefryers Playhouse, & Players. S[r]. This is all I haue to trouble you
withall att Present, & Therefore I shall take the Boldnesse to,
                                        Remaine
August 30. 60   Your Wor[p]. most Humble Seruant
                                 Humphrey Mosley

28 September 1660

(*Second petition by John Rogers*)

R11   To the Kings Most Excellent Ma:[ty] &[c]:
        The humble Peticon of John Rogers

R10. Harvard Theatre Collection TS992.31.7, no. 39 (Milhous–Hume, 22). Facs. in
Alwin Thaler, *Shakspere to Sheridan* (Cambridge, Mass., 1922), facing 122.
R11. BL MS Egerton 2549, f. 88 (Milhous–Hume, 27).

Humbly Sheweth

That yo[r] Pet[r]. Haveing bin a very Great Sufferer in the late
Callametyes, both through the Loss of his estate & vse of his Limbs,
& Continued Loyall & ffaithfull to yo[r] Sacred Ma[ty]: As by the Duke
of Albemarl[s] & other Certificats doth appeare, Did Humbly Peticon
yo[r] Ma[ty]: that for his Livelehood he might Have an Order to
Receiue 1[s] in twenty taken at every of the Publique Playhouses in
this Citty of London or adjacent therto, And did p⟨ro⟩pound 3
Reasons to Induce yo[r]. Majesties Clemencie thereto, the first for
that it was noe more then a Crum from the Players Trencher They
being at p[r]sent better able to spare it, then yo[r] Majestye a Pencon,
& 2:[dly] that he would vndertake to maintaine men out of that Triveall
alowance to keep yo[r] Ma[tys]: Peace & to Guard their Playhouses from
all Molestacons, by Reason men haue bin maintained, for that
Purpose And lastly; that yo[r]. Pet[r]. would maintaine such men for
that Purpose, As hath bin Reall Sufferers for yo[r] Majestye, To
Which equetable Request of yo[r] Pet[r]. yo[r] Majesty was Graciously
pleased to Refer him to the Master of the Revells for his aprobacon,
who did Graunt yo[r] Pet[r]. an Immediate Order, authorizeing him to
Receiue such \like/ an allowance as aforesaid vpon the said
Considerations, But yo[r]. Pet[r]. Having bin at very Great Charg &
Truble, Cann as yett Reap no Benefitt vnles It is yo[r] Majesties most
Gracious Pleasure, to Graunt him yo[r]. Majesties warrant, for the
same, He having already the Generalls, to y[e] same effect

May It therfore pleas Yo[r] sacred Ma[ty]: there being a Necessety for
the same To Graunt vnto yo[r] Pet[r]. yo[r] Majesties Order, to the same
Purpose as is above alleaged, and in Order thereto, to Refer Yo[r]
Pet[r]. to one of yo[r] Majesties Right Hono[ble]. secretarys of State, for
the same That he may be in a Capacety to desist from further
Trubling yo[r] Majesty for the future, And in much bounden duty,
He shall wth his whole ffamely Perpetually Pray &c.

White Hall Sept: 28th: 1660

His Ma[tie] is graciously pleased to referre this peticon to the right
hono[ble] his Ma[ts]: Secretarys of State or either of them to take the
peticoners request into Consideracon and to prepare him a warrant
accordingly if they shall think fitt, and that such Grant doe not
interfere with any authority all ready given to any other person or
persons

Ricffanshawe

6 October 1660

(*Letter from Sir Henry to the mayor of Maidstone*)

R12 S‌ʳ

By the Kings Maties Authority that corp⟨or⟩acon is constituted & by the same Authority The Bearer Jacob Brewer & his company are Authorised to exercise what is conteyned in my License vpon the Condicons therein menconed. And as you would be obeyed in the execucon of youre Office so you ought to give obedience And therefore you are desired to give him leaue to exercise accordinge to his warrant That legall proceedings may be avoyded And the same liberty taken that you would have given to his Ma:^ties Authority And herein you may put a civility vpon

Oct: 6. 60.   youre Affecconate freinde
Courte.   Hen: Herbert
ffor the wor^ll the Mayor of
Maydstone.

8 October 1660

(*Order from Sir Henry to John Rhodes at the Cockpit*)

R13 **Whereas** by vertue of a Grante vnder the Greate Seale of England, Playes Players and Playmakers and the Permission for Errecting of Play houses haue been allowed Ordered and Permitted by the Masters of his Maties. Office of the Revells my Predecessors successiuely time out of minde whereof the memory of man is not to the Contrary, And by mee for almost fforty yeares with exception only to the Late times./

These are therefore in his Maties. name to require yo^u. to attende mee concerning yor. Playhouse called the Cockpitt Play-house in Drury Lane, And to bring wth yo^u. such Authority As yo^u. haue for Errecting of the said house, Into a Playhouse at yor p⟨er⟩ill, Given at his Maties. Office of the Revells the 8th. day of October 1660

To M^r. John Roades at the   Henry Herbert
Cockpitt Playhouse in Drury Lane.

R12. BL MS Add. 37157, f. 64 (Milhous–Hume, 31); scribal copy. Jacob Brewer may be the 'Jacobus Brower', a vaulter and rope-dancer probably of Dutch or German origin, who petitioned the King, possibly in Apr. 1660, *CSPD 1659–60*, 423 = SP18/220/118.

R13. A50^r–v (Milhous–Hume, 32). The signature and endorsement are in Herbert's hand.

(*Endorsement:*)

Warrant sent to Rhodes and brought backe by him the 10th. of Oct. 60, wth this Answer That the Kinge did authorise Him

(*Letter from the mayor and recorder of Maidstone to Sir Henry*)

R14   *Maidstone, 8th Oct.* 1660.

HONORABLE SIR,—We received youres of the sixth instant by these bearers, and question not your commission, as Master of his Majestie's Revells, or your licence granted to these persons, Jacob Brewer, &c.; nor them, so farre as they shall use the same according to lawe, to which your license doth prudently and carefully tye them. One particular of which theyre lawfull exercise we conceive to be within the verge of his Majestie's courte, wherever it shall be, in any parte of Englande, where they may be under your eye and care, for the reforminge and regulating any abuses of their license, which might be committed by them. But we doe not finde that you doe, and presume you did not intend to, grant them a licence to wander abroade all England over, at what distance soever from you. And we finde that the wanderinge abroad of such persons is expresslye cautioned by the statut of the 39th of the Queen, in the case of players of interludes and minstrels, (except it be by expresse license under the hande and seale of such Baron, or other noble person, of greater degree, to whome they doe particularly belonge); and however we knowe no lawe or statut that requires the magistrates of any place to give them any particular leave or license of theyre owne, by way of addition to any other. And indeed the mischiefe and publicke disorders by the practices of such kinde of persons, in wanderinge abroade from countye to countye, is such, that we cannot think it reasonable to give them any further countenance than the lawe provides; which we hope will not be displeasing to you, who, we presume, do take the observance of his Majestie's lawes to ⟨?be⟩ the best obedience to his Majestie's authoritye. In which assurance we take leave, and rest, Honourable Sir, youre most humble servants,

RICHARD BILLS, Maior
LAMBARDE GODFREY, Recorder.

To the Hon. Sir Henry Herbert, knight, Master of his Majestie's Revells, these humbly present.

R14. Warner, 59–61 (Milhous–Hume, 33).

(*Endorsed:*)—From the Maior of Maydstone, and the Recorder, concer. Jacob Brewer, dancer on the ropes.

9 October 1660

(*Letter from Sir Henry to the mayor of Maidstone*)

R15   *Oct. 9,—60, from the Office of the Revells.*

SIR,—Yours of the 8th comes to my hande the 9th of this monthe, and makes out an acknowledgment and submission to his Majestie's grante, as Master of his Majestie's Revells, and to the powers of lycencinge the persons in question, and to their exercise of the said powers, so farr as they shall use the same accordinge unto law: but you restraine the exercise thereof to the verge of his Majestie's court, and then restraine the Master of the Revells to the said limits, as to his jurisdiction; which is, in some sort, a contradiction; and such an interpretation as was never given before by any learned gentlemen. The license is granted upon the conditions of good behaviour to the lawes and ordinances of superiors. But you are not taken to be in a capacity, by virtue of your charter, to suppresse them, they bearinge themselves as they ought to doe. And there is *non obstante* in the concession, which provides against the penall lawes, which being under the greate seale of England, and corroborated by a constant practice, whereof the memorie of man is not to the contrarie, I conceive you will not be the sole infringer of his Majestie's grante, and the constant practice thereof in all his Majestie's dominions and liberties in England. And you may be assured by me, that you are the first mayor or other officer, that ever did dispute the authority, or the extent of it; for to confine it to the verge of the Court, is such a sense as was never imposed upon it before, and contrary to the constant practice; for severall grantes have been made by me, since the happy restoration of our gracious sovereign, to persons in the like quality; and seriously, therefore, admitted into all the counties and liberties of England, without any dispute or molestation.

You are, therefore, desired to give them leave to exercise their qualities, according to the conditions of their license, the rather that they have suffered muche in lyinge still, and are in their waye to the sea syde for transportation: and I have given them order to stay noe longer than they have raysed their necessarye charges. But

R15. Warner, 61–3 (Milhous–Hume, 34).

in case you doe delyghte in opposition and obstinacy to lawfull authority, and yet would be obeyed in yours without dispute; then you may take this from me, that I shall forthwith sende a message from his Majestie's chamber, to fetche you and Mr. Recorder Godfrey hither, to answer your disobedience to his Majestie's authority derived unto me under the great seale of England, and in exercise of the said powers by me for almost forty yeares, with exception only to the late times. And if you have endangered your charter by this refracteriness, and doe put charges and displeasures on your corporation and persons, you will remember that you were faierly invited to the contrary, and admonished thereof by your very affectionate friend,

HENRY HERBERT.

Respects to Mr. Recorder Godfrey, of whom I have hearde well by my cosen Lambert, and for whom I have a particular kindnes.

13 October 1660

(*Order from Sir Henry to Michael Mohun at the Cockpit*)

R16 WHEREAS seuerall complaints haue been made against you to the Kinges most excellent Maiesty by M^r. Killegrew and S^r. William Dauenant concerning the vnusuall and vnresonable rates taken at yor. play house doores of the Respectiue Persons of quality that desire to refresh and Improue themselues by the sight of yor. Morrall Entertainments which were Constituted for profitt and delight And the said Complaints made vse of by the said M^r. Killegrew and S^r. William Dauenant as part of theire Suggestions for theire pretended power and for your Late Restrainte./

And Whereas Complaints haue been made thereof formerly to me wherewith you were acquainted as Innouations and Exactions not allowed by mee; And that the like Complaints are now made that yo^u doe practice the said Exactions in takeing of Excessiue & vnaccustomed rates vppon the Restitution of yo^u. to yor. Liberty. These are therefore in his Maties. name to require yo^u and Euery of yo^u to take from the persons of qualitie and others as dayly frequent

R16. Original in the possession of Messrs Bernard Quaritch (see Catalogue 1103, *English Literature in Manuscript*, Apr. 1989, item 32). Milhous–Hume, 35. Sold at Sotheby's on 25 July 1978; facs. and transcript in Catalogue, 246–7. Last ten lines only (beginning 'And you are . . .') in Herbert's own hand. The lines dealing with censorship are squashed together; Herbert signed the letter, and then decided to insert them.

yo[r]. Play:house, Such vsuall and accustomed rates only as were
formerly taken at the Black-fryers, by the late Company of Acto[rs]
there & noe more, nor otherwise for euery new or old Play that shall
be allowed you by the Master of the Revells to be Acted in the said
Playhouse or any other playhouse; And you are Hereby further
required to bringe or sende to me All such old Plaies As you doe
Intende to Acte \at y[e] saide playhouse,/ that they may be reformed
of Prophanes & Ribaldry, \at yo[r] perill/ giuen at y[e] office of y[e]
Revells

To m[r]. Michael Mohan   Henry Herbert
and y[e] rest of y[e] Acto[rs]
of y[e] Cockpitt play house
in Drury Lane
The 13th of october 1660
(*Endorsed*:) [Copy of] y[e] Warant sent to the Actors at y[e] Cockpit In
Drury Lane by Tom Browne the. 13. Oct. 60/

(*Petition from Michael Mohun and others to the King*)
R17   To the Kings Most Excellent Maiestie
The Humble petition of Mich: Mohun Rob[t]: Shutterell Charles
Hart Nich: Burt W[m]. Cartwright Walter Clunn & W[m]. Wintersell

Humbly sheweth
That yo[r] Ma[ties]. humble Pet[rs]. haueing bene supprest by a warrant
from yo[r] Ma[tie], Sir Hen: Herbert informed vs it was M[r]. Killegrew
had caused it and if wee would give him soe much a week, he would
protect them against M[r] Killegrew and all powers: The Complaint
against vs was Scandalous Plaies, raising the Price, and acknowledging noe Authority. All which ended in so much ye weeke to
him; for which wee had his leaue to Play & p⟨ro⟩mise of his
Protection. The which yo[r]. Ma[tie] Knowes he was not able to
performe; Since M[r]. Killegrew haueing yo[r]. Ma[ties]. former Grante
supprest vs vntill wee had by covenant obleiged our selues to Act
with Woemen a new Theatre and Habitts according to our Scaenes,
And according to yo[r]. Ma[ties]. approbation from all the Companies
wee made Election of one Company; And soe farre Sir Hen:
Herbert hath bene ⟨from⟩ Protecting vs; that hee hath bene a
continuall disturbance vnto vs, who ⟨?were then⟩ est⟨a⟩blisht by
yo[r] Maties. Comand vnder M[r]. Killegrew as M[r]. of yo[r] Ma[ties].

R17. A71 (Milhous–Hume, 36); scribal copy made for Herbert. Left-hand side
damaged and water-stained.

⟨?Company;⟩ Wee haue annext vnto our Petition the date of the warrant by ⟨w⟩:ᶜʰ ⟨w⟩ee were Supprest and for a Protection against that Warrant he forct ⟨?fees⟩ at so much a weeke; And if yoʳ Maᵗⁱᵉ. be gratiously pleased to cast yoʳ eye vpp⟨on⟩ the date of the warrant hereto annext yoʳ. Maᵗⁱᵉ. shall find the date to o⟨?ur Contr⟩act succeeded; wherein hee hath broke the Covenants and not your ⟨Petʳˢ.⟩; haueing abused yoʳ. Maᵗⁱᵉ. in giueing an ill Charecter of yoʳ Petʳˢ. only to force a sume from theire poore endeavours; who neuer did nor shall refuse him all the respects and iust profitts that belong to his Place; Hee haueing now obtaind Leaue to Arrest vs only to giue trouble and Vexation to yoʳ Petʳˢ. hopeing by that meanes to force a summe of money illegally from vs.

The pʳmises considered yoʳ Petʳˢ. humbly beseech yoʳ Maᵗⁱᵉ. to be Gratiously Pleasd to Signify yoʳ Royall Pleasure to the Lord Chamberlaine that yoʳ Petʳˢ. may not bee molested in theire Calling

And As in duty bound yoʳ Petʳˢ. shall Pray &c.

Nich: Burtt

William Wintershall   Rob.ᵗ Shutterell

Charles Hart

(*Endorsement*:)

⟩ the. 13. of ⟨

⟩ence Had with th⟨

⟩cerninge Killigrew

⟩layers

(*In modern hand*:) 13 Octob. 1660

5 November 1660

(*Articles of agreement between the players and Davenant*)

R18   Articles of Agreement Tripartite Indented made and agreed vppon this fifth day of Nouember in the xijᵗʰ yeare of yᵉ reigne of our Souereigne Lord Kinge Charles the second Annoqe dni 1660 Betweene Sir Wᵐ. Davenant of London Kᵗ. of the first part And Tho: Batterton Tho: Sheppey Robert Noakes James Noakes Thomas Lovell John Moseley Caue Vnderhill Robert Turner & Thomas Lilleston of the second part And Henry Harris of yᵉ Citty of London painter of the third part as followeth/Imprimis the said Sir

R18. A53–60 (Milhous–Hume, 44). Copy made for Herbert of the original, BL Add. Charter 9295.

William Davenant doth for himselfe his Exec⟨uto⟩ʳˢ adm⟨inistra-
to⟩ʳˢ & ass⟨ign⟩ᵉˢ Couenant promise grant & agree to & wᵗʰ the
sd Thomas Batterton Thomas Sheppey Robert Noakes James
Noakes Thomas Louell Jo: Moseley Cave Vnderhill Robert Turner
and Thomas Lilleston that hee the sd Sir Wᵐ. Davenant by vertue
of the authority to him deriued for that purpose doe ⟨*read* doth⟩
hereby constitute ordeine and erect them the said Thomas Batterton Thomas Sheppey Robert Noakes James Noakes Thomas Louell
John Moseley Caue Vnderhill Robert Turner and Thomas Lilleston
and their Associates to bee a company publiquely to act all manner
of Tragedies Comedies and playes whatsoeuer in any Theatre or
Playhouse erected in London or Westmʳ or the Suburbs thereof and
to take the vsuall rates for the same to the vses hereafter expresst
vntill the said Sir Wᵐ. Davenant shall p⟨ro⟩uide a newe Theatre
with Scenes/
Item It is agreed by and betweene all the said parties to these
presents that the sd Company (vntill yᵉ sd theatre bee prouided by
yᵉ sd Sir Wᵐ. Davenant) be authorized by him to Act Tragedies
Comedies & playes in the Playhouse called Salisbury Court Playhouse or any other house vppon yᵉ Condicons onely hereafter
followeinge vizt/
That yᵉ generall receipts of money of yᵉ sd playhouse shall (after
the houserent hirelings and all other accustomary and necessary
expences in that kind bee defrayed) bee devided into fowerteene
p⟨ro⟩porcons or shares whereof Sir Wᵐ. Davenant shall haue foure
full proporcons or shares to his owne vse and the rest to the vse of
the said Companie/
That dureing yᵉ time of playeinge in the said Playhouse (vntill the
aforesaid Theatre bee prouided by the sd Sir Wᵐ. Davenant) the
said Sir Wᵐ. Davenant shall depute the said Thomas Batterton
James Noakes and Thomas Sheppey or any one of them perticulary
for him and on his behalf to receiue his proporcon of those shares
and to survey the accompts conduceinge therevnto and to pay the
sd p⟨ro⟩porcon euery night to him the said Sir Wᵐ. or his assignes
wᶜʰ they doe hereby Couenant to pay accordingly/.
That the said Thomas Batterton Thomas Sheppey and the rest of
the said Company shall admitt such a Consort of Musicians into the
said Playhouse for their necessary vse as the said Sir William shall
nominate and provide dureinge their playeinge in the said Playhouse not exceeding the rate of 30ˢ the day to be defrayed out of

the generall expences of ye house before the said fowerteene shares
bee devided.

That the said Thomas Batterton Thomas Sheppey and the rest of
the said Companie soe authorized to play in ye Playhouse in
Salisbury Court or elsewhere as aforesaid shall at one weekes
warneinge giuen by the said Sir W^m. Davenant his heires or assignes
dissolue and conclude their Playeinge at the ˺house &/ place
aforesaid or at any other house where they shall play and shall
remove and Joyne with the said Henry Harris and with other men
and women prouided or to bee prouided by the sd Sir W.^{m}
Davenant to performe such Tragedies Comedies Playes & representacons in that Theatre to be publiquely p⟨ro⟩uided by him the
said Sir W^m as aforesaid/

Item It is agreed by and betweene all ye sd. parties to these p^{r}sents
in manner and forme followeinge (vizt) That when the said
Companie together with the said Henry Harris are ioyned with the
men and women to bee prouided by the said Sir William Davenant
to Act and performe in the sd Theatre to bee prouided by the said
Sir Wm Davenant That then the generall receipts of the said
Theatre (the generall expence first beinge deducted) shalbee
deuided into fifteene shares or proporcons whereof two shares or
p⟨ro⟩porcons shalbee paid to the said Sir W^m. Davenant his Exec^{rs}
adm^{rs} or ass^s. towards the house rent buildinge scaffoldinge and
makeinge of fframes for Scenes And one other share or p⟨ro⟩por-
con shall likewise bee paid to the said Sir William his exec^{rs} adm^{rs}
and assignes for provision of Habitts Properties and scenes for a
supplement of the said Theatre.

That the other twelue shares (after all expences of men hirelings
and other customary expences deducted) shalbee deuided into
seauen and fiue shares or p⟨ro⟩porcons whereof the sd Sir W^m.
Davenant and his Exec^{rs} adm^{rs} & assignes shall haue seauen shares
or proporcons to mainteine all ye Women that are to performe or
represent Womens parts in the aforesaid Tragedies Comedies
Playes or representacons And in consideracon of erectinge and
establishinge them to bee a Companie and his the said Sir W^{ms}
paines and expences to that purpose for many yeeres And the other
fiue of the said Shares or p⟨ro⟩porcons is to bee deuided amongst
the rest of the persons to theis presents whereof the said Henry
Harris is to haue an equall share wth the greatest p⟨ro⟩porcons in
the said fiue shares or p⟨ro⟩porcons

That the generall receipts of the said Theatre (from and after such
time as the said Companie haue p⟨er⟩formed their playeinge in
Salisbury Court or in any other Playhouse accordinge to and noe
longer then the tyme allowed by him the said William as aforesaid)
shall bee by Ballatine or ticketts soulled for all doores & boxes./

That Sir Wm Davenant his Exec^{rs} or asses shall at ye gen⟨er⟩all
Chardge of the whole Receipts prouide three persons to receiue
money for the said Ticketts in a roome adioyninge to the said
Theatre And that the Acto^{rs} in the said Theatre nowe parties to
these presents who are concerned in the said ffiue shares or
p⟨ro⟩porcons shall dayly or weekely appoint two or three of
themselues or the men hirelings deputed by them to sitt with the
aforesaid three p⟨er⟩sons appointed by him the said Sir Willm that
they may survey and giue an accompt of the money receiued for
the said Ticketts, That the said seauen shares shalbee paid nightly
by the said three p⟨er⟩sons by the said Sir W^m deputed or by anie
of them to him the said Sir W^m his Exec^{rs} adm^{rs} or assignes

That the said Sir Wm Davenant shall appoint half the number of
the Doorekeepers necessary for ye receipt of the said Ticketts for
doores and Boxes, the Wardrobe Keeper barber and all other
necessary persons as hee the said Sir W^m shall thinke fitt and their
Sallary to bee defrayed at the publique Chardge.

That when any Sharer amongst the Acto^{rs} of the aforesd fiue shares
and partyes to these p^{r}sents shall dye that then the said Sir W^m.
Davenant his Exec^{rs} adm^{rs} or assignes shall haue the denominacon
& appointm^t of the Successo^r and successo^{rs}. And likewise that the
Wages of the men hirelings shalbee appointed and established by
the said Sir W^m. Davenant his Exec^{rs} adm^{rs} or assignes.

That the said Sir Wm Davenant his exec^{rs} adm^{rs} or ass^s shall not bee
obliged out of the shares or p⟨ro⟩porcons allowed to him for the
supplyeinge of Cloathes Habits and Scenes to prouide eyther Hatts
feathers Gloues ribbons swords belts bands stockings or shoes for
any of the men Acto^{rs} aforesaid Vnles it be to Properties

That a priuate boxe bee prouided and established for the vse of
Thomas Killigrewe Esqr one of the Groomes of his Maties Bedchamber sufficient to conteine six persons into which the said M^r.
Killigrewe and such as he shall appoint shall haue liberty to enter
without any Sallery or pay for their entrance into such a place of
the said Theatre as the sd Sir Wm Davenant his Exec^{rs} adm^{rs} or ass^s
shall appoint.

That the said Thomas Batterton Tho Sheppey Robert Noakes James Noakes Tho: Louell Jo: Moseley Cave Vnderhill Robert Turner and Tho: Lilleston doe hereby for themselues Couen⟨a⟩nt p⟨ro⟩mise gr⟨an⟩t & agree to & wth the sd Sir Wm D. his exec^{rs} adm^{rs} & ass^s by these p^rsents That they & euery of them shall become bound to the said Sir W^m. Dauen⟨a⟩nt in a bond of 5000^{li}. condiconed for the [paym^t of] performance of these presents And that euery Successor to any part of the said fiue shares or p⟨ro⟩porcons shall enter into ye like bond before hee or they shalbe admitted to haue anie part or porcon of the said shares or proporcons

And the said Henry Harris doth hereby for himself his Exec^{rs} adm^{rs} and assignes Couenant p⟨ro⟩mise gr⟨an⟩te and agree to and wth the said Sir W^m. Dauenant his Exec^{rs} adm^{rs} & ass^s by these p^rsents That hee the said Henry Harris shall within one weeke after ye notice giuen by Sir W^m. Dauen⟨a⟩nt for ye Concludinge of ye playeinge at Salisbury Co^{rt}. or any other house else abouesaid become bound to the said Sir W^m. Davenant in a bond of 5000^{li} condiconed for the performance of these ⟨presents⟩ And that euery Successo^r to any of the said ffiue shares shall enter into ye like bond before hee or they shalbee admitted to haue any part or porcon in the said ffiue shares

Item It is mutually agreed by and betweene all the parties to these presents That ⟨hee⟩ the said Sir W^m. Dauenant alone shalbee Master and Superior & shall from time to time haue the sole gouerm^t of the said Thomas Batterton Thomas Sheppey Robert Noakes James Noakes Thomas Louell John Moseley Caue Vnderhill Robert Turner and Tho. Lilleston & allsoe of the said Henry Harris and their Associates in relacon to the Playes by these p^rsents agreed to be erected

In Wittnes &c

Examinatur Cum Originali
Per W^m. Moseley.
et
Ric⟨ard⟩um Crupp

14 November 1660

(*Letter from Thomas Killigrew to unknown correspondent*)
R19 Right Worsh:^{ll}

R19. BL MS Egerton 2537, f. 273 (Milhous–Hume, 25).

The Bussines of Mr John Rogers (the bearer hereof) I desire yo^u will expedite as soone as possibly yo^u can, I being fully satisfied therewith and hereby giveing my full Consent thereto, it being noe damage vnto mee and herein you will obleige

Whitehall: 14°: 9bis.   Yo^r Worshipps very humble
          1660   and faithful servant
                                          Thomas Killigrew

?November 1660

(*Draft for warrant for John Rogers*)

R20 **Charles ye Second** by the Grace of God King of England Scotland France & Ireland Defend^r of the Faith &c Whereas wee haue beene Credibly informed that the Bearer hereof John Rogers our servant hath alwayes bin loyall to vs and Our Interest & a very great Sufferer in the losse of his estate and Limbes in the late Distraccons Insomuch That hee is altogether disabled to prosecute any Calling or obteyne a Livelihood. Which Wee in pietie and pittie takeing into Our Royall Clemencie Aswell for his future mainetainance, as for the Conservacon of Our Peace against all Violacon and Interrupcon Do hereby signifie, That it is Our Will and Pleasure, and doe expressly Order That the sd John Rogers, haue and doe receiue to himselfe and his Menn for Guarding [all] \the/ Publique \shews/ Playhouses [& Showes] by what Name or Title soeuer distinguished or Called) from all molestacons (in as much as in him lyes) of all or any p⟨er⟩son or persons whatsoeuer) One Shilling of every twentie shillings taken and receiued in each of the sd Playhouses or Showes wthin Our Realme of England, And that the sd Allowance therefore bee truly and duly paid vnto him, the said John Rogers or his Assignes dureing his n⟨atu⟩rall life

[And in case Refusall bee made of payment of the said Allowance, becoming justly due in manner aforesd That then it shall and may bee lawfull for him the sd John Rogers to putt a stopp to all and every such Playhouse or Show, vntill they and every of them doe and shall pay & satisfie him]

And y^t shall, & may be lawfull to and for the sd John Rogers his deputie or deputies to apprehend all and euery such p⟨er⟩son and

---

R20. BL MS Egerton 2537, f. 275 (Milhous–Hume, 25). No evidence has been discovered to show that Rogers actually received his warrant, but there is a reference to 'Mr Rogers and his soldiers' in **R47**, item 6.

p⟨er⟩sons whatsoeuer, that shall soe disturbe Our Peace and ye p⟨er⟩sons soe Acting as aforesd & carry him and them before any of our next Justices of ye Peace to ⟨?be⟩ procedded against as disturbers thereof according to the Lawes of this Our Realme Requiring all Mayors Sheriffs Justices of the Peace Constables and all other officers Civill & Military to bee Ayding and Assisting vnto him the sd John Rogers or his Assignes in ye Execucon hereof Given &c

(*Alternative conclusion to first paragraph squeezed into left margin, beginning opposite* Guarding:)

in & about the Citties of London westm^r & suburbs therof the allowance formerly Granted them for the Guarding of all their Playhouses and showes by what name or title soeuer called or distinguished wth in our Realme of England one shilling of euery twenty shalbe taken & received in euery of the sd Playhouses or showes

17 December 1660

(*Sir Henry's memoranda*)

R21   ⟩Decemb
        ⟩60/

To proue the Allo⟨?wance of Pla⟩yes & the allowance of ⟨

To proue the Licensinge ⟨of⟩ Playhouses & of Players to Acte

To proue the suppressinge of Players & their Obedience

To proue the allowances made by the Players to my Predecessors and my selfe, besids the Fees

To proue the Lord Chamberlins Grantes & declarations In ayde of ye master of the Reuells

To produce ye Comissions granted to my Predecessors

To proue my practice by the Grants made by me for 40. yeares to seuerall Companies of Players to Trauell

To proue the suppressinge of them by warants Executed by Constables & Messingers of ye K^s. Chamber

To proue a sumers day & winters day of cleere profits allowed by the Company of the Blackfryers and that they payd 40^s. for a new Play & 20^s. for reuiuinge of an Olde.

To proue that m^r Beeston payd me 60^li per ann besids vsuall Fees & allowances for Court Plaies.

R21. A51–2 (Milhous–Hume, 49). In Herbert's hand; damaged, with small portions missing at top and sides. The day of the month is not certain.

To proue a share payd by ye Fortune Plaiers and a share by the Bull
Plaiers & a share by Salsbry Court Play. (*sic*)

To produce the[ir] Acknowledgments of ye Red Bull Actors & of y^e
Cockpit Company

To produce my Grante

That the De.^{ts} Acted under the Authority & were twise suppressed
by my warrants & did not Acte till they had leaue from me.

The Grant under the signet ⟨   ⟩ll to Killegr⟨   ⟩
Dauenant and giues them n⟨   ⟩ to authorize ⟨   ⟩
It restraines to the Cities of London & Westminster and ⟨   ⟩
Liberties thereof which cannot be good In Law, when the Master of
the Revells Hath tyme out of minde Exercised the powers ouer y^e
Players In allowinge of Plaies \&/ reforminge and orderinge of Players
And that y^e present master of y^e Reuells doth au⟨
seuerall Companies of Players to trauell Int⟨
and acte by vertue of Authoritie from y^e Off⟨
Reuells.

The Authoritie giuen to Killigrew & Dauenant Is not exclusive to
y^e Master of y^e Reuells, nor any mention of him therein, so that the
Intention of y^e Grante if good was not to take \away/ any Rights
or proffits due to the Master of the Reuells.

(*Endorsed, possibly in a modern hand:*) 17 Decr 1660

29 December 1660

(*Norwich*)

R22 It is ordered & agreed by the Court that Thomas Knowles & other
p⟨er⟩sons that came to this City to sett vp a playe in y^e same &
did beate vp there drummes wthout allowance & have played twice
or thrice shall not from henceforth act any playe any more in this
City vpon payne of incurringe the vtmost penalty the lawe will
inflict & that they dep⟨ar⟩t the City vpon mondaye morninge next

7 January 1660/1

(*Norwich*)

R23   The viith daye of January 1660
Wheras we whose names are here vnderwritten haue a Comission
vnder the hand of Sr Henry Harbart knight master of the Revells

R22. *MCB* 4, f. 138* (Milhous–Hume, 52).
R23. *MCB* 4, f. 138^{*v} (Milhous–Hume, 55). This must refer to the previous item,
though Thomas Knowles is not mentioned.

& his seale of office for the shewenge & excerisenge of playes in the
seu⟨er⟩all Corporacons & places in this Kingdome & repayeringe
to the Citty of Norw^ch wth the said Comission & appearinge before
[the said] Sr Joseph payne knight Maior & the rest of the Court of
Aldermen ther vpon the nyne & twentith daye of December last for
some miscariages of o^rs were then by the said Court p⟨ro⟩hibited
from playeinge in the said City we doe hereby humbly confesse and
acknowledge o^r error therin & desire that it maye be forgiven &
passed by & doe p⟨ro⟩mise that we shall from henceforth readely
and willingly submitt & conforme o^rselfes & be obedient to the
Comandes of the said Maior & Court wittnes o^r hands the day &c
aboue said

> Robert Williams
> Samberlain Haruey
> Nicholas Caluert

20 February 1660/1

(*Norwich*)

R24 This daye Gabrael Shad & other players who came to this City w^th
a Comission vnder Sr Henry Harberts hand maister of the Revells
& Seale of office hath Liberty to play in this City till Tuesdaye
night next & they are to give ffive pownds for the poore of the City
for that liberty.

4 May 1661

(*Warrant for the arrest of John Tradescant*)

R25 *Whereas* Information is giuen me that John Traduskyn doth make
shew of seuerall strainge Cretures without Authority from his
Maiesties office of the Revells
These are therefore in his Maties. name to will and require you to
bring before me the said John Traduskyn to answere for the said
Contempt, And this shall be yor. Sufficient warrant.
Dated at the office of the Revells this 4th day of May 1661.
To M^r. Ralph Nutting officer to
his Maties. office of the Revells.   Henry Herbert

R24. *MCB* 4, f. 141^v (Milhous–Hume, 62). Shad became a stage-keeper at the Theatre
Royal, Bridges Street, in 1670 (Milhous–Hume, 24).
R25. PRO SP29/38/154; summary in *CSPD 1661-2*, 27.

June 1661

(Draft of the King's authorization for Tradescant)

R26 Complaint being made unto Us by John Tredeskyn that hee hath been lately serued by a Warrant from Sr Henry Herbert for a contemptuous practice (as is pretended) in taking the confidence to shew his rarities (to the inuading of the rights wch doe belong to the Master of ye Revells) And Wee being satisfied, that the fact, in it selfe, is not onely of very harmelesse import, & not found p^{r}judicial to any person; but that it hath been practised & continued, vninterruptedly, by him & his Father, with the Allowance or good Liking (at least) of Our Progenitors, for many yeares past. Our expresse pleasure & Comand is, That the said Tredeskyn bee suffered, freely & quietly to proceed, as formerly, in entertaining & receauing all persons, whose Curiosity shall inuite them to the delight of seing his rare & ingenious Colleccons of Art and nature: and to this purpose that the said Warrant bee recalled and noe proceeding had against him for or by occasion of the same. And hereof all Persons whome it doeth or may concerne are to take notice and to conforme themselues. Giuen at Our Court at White-hall the   of June 1661.

By his Ma^{ts}. Comand

1 July 1661

(Letter from William Bickford to Sir Henry)

R27 hon S^r:

Acordin to your desiear I haue sent you a trow s^{r}tificate of the buaryall of S^r. John Ashley.

S^r. I am you⟨r⟩ faithfull frind
& Searuant to Command.

from maydston   Will: Bickford

ye. 1. of Iuly. 1661

Christopher Balldwin Caryor of maidstone Logeth at the Sine of the pide doge one St Mary hill nere Billenegate

---

R26. PRO SP29/38/152; summary in *CSPD 1661–2*, 27.

R27. A65 (Milhous–Hume, 79). In BL MS Add. 37157, f. 65, is another letter from Bickford to Herbert, dated 20 Dec. 1660, complaining that those unfavourable to the King have rigged the local elections at Maidstone to put themselves in power. They have forced out the previous recorder, and in his place put 'one Godfrey a Sequestrator & one of the same faction who hath lately punished some of your servants' (cf. **R13–15**).

(*Endorsements:*)

ffor ye Right worshfull S.ʳ henry herbert thes.

Mʳ Bickfords Letter ⟨fr⟩om Madstone wth a certificate ⟨of⟩ ye deathe of Sir John Ashley R. the 2. July. 61

31 July 1661

(*Proclamation by the Lord Chamberlain*)

R28 To all Mayors Sherriffs Justices of the peace Bayliffs Constables, and other his Maᵗˢ. Officers, True Leigemen & Subjects whom it may concerne & to every of them *Whereas* I am credibly informed that there are manie & very great disorders & abuses comitted by divers and sundry Companies of Stage Players Tumblers, vaulters Dauncers on the Ropes, and alsoe by such as goe about wᵗʰ. motions & Shewes & other like kind of persons by reason of certeyne Grants Comissions & Lycenses, which they have by secret means p⟨ro⟩cured from the Kings Maᵗⁱᵉ. by vertue whereof they do abusesively claime unto themselves a kinde of Lycentious freedome to travell as well to Shew plaie & exercise in Eminent Citties & Corporacons wᵗʰin this Kingdome as alsoe from place to place without the Knowledge & App⟨ro⟩bacon of his Maᵗˢ. Office of the Revells, and by that means doe take uppon them att their owne pleasure to act & sett forth in many places of this Kingdome divers & sundry plaies & Shews which for the most p⟨ar⟩ᵗᵉ are full of scandall & offence both against the Church & State and doe likewise greatlie abuse their authoritie in lending, letting & selling their said Comissions & Lycenses unto oth⟨ers⟩ By reason whereof divers lawless & wandring persons are suffered to have free passage, unto whom such grants & Lycenses were never intended Contra⟨ry⟩ to his Maᵗˢ. pleasure yᵉ. Lawes of this Land his Majesties grant & Comission to the Master of the Revells and the first institucon of the sᵈ Office, Theis ar⟨e⟩ therefore in his Maᵗˢ. name straightly to charge & comand you & every of you, That whosoever shall repaire to any of your Citties Borroughs, Towne⟨s⟩ Corporate, Villages, Hamletts, or p⟨ar⟩ishes, & shall there by vertue of any Comission warrant or Lycence whatsoever act, sett forth, Shew, or present anie Play, Shew, Motion, feats of activitie & sights, whatsoever; not

---

R28. A69 (Milhous–Hume, 85). This seems to be the original document, with Manchester's signature. A printed version is in PRO SP29/39/110. It is almost identical with the proclamation issued by Pembroke on 20 Nov. 1622 on behalf of Astley (A8).

haveing a Lycense now in force under the hand & seale of Office of
S^r: *Henry Herbert* Kn^t. now M^r. of his Ma^{ts}. office of the Revells or
under the hand of his Deputy & sealed likewise with the said Seale
of the office, That you & every of you att all tymes for ever
hereafter, doe Seize & take away all & every such grant pattent,
Comission, or Lycence, whatsoever from the bringer or bearer
thereof, and that you forthwith cause the said Graunt or Lycence
to be conveyed & sent unto his Ma^{ts}: said offic⟨e⟩ of the Revells
there to remaine at the disposicon of the foresaid M^r. of the said
Office, And that to the uttermost of yor. power you do⟨e⟩ from
henceforth forbidd and suppresse all such Plaies, Shewes, Motions,
feates of Activitie, Sights and every of them, vntill the⟨y⟩ shall be
approved Lycenced and authorized by the said S^r. *Henry Herbert* or
his said Deputy in manner aforesaid, Who are appointed by his
Matie: under the great Seale of England for that end and purpose;
Herein faile you not as you will answer the contrary at your perrills,
And for your more certeintie I advise you to take an exact Coppy
of this \my/ Mandate, Given at Whitehall under my hand and
Seale this one and Thirtieth day of July in the yeare of our Lord
God one Thousand six hundred sixty and one.

EManchester

?1661/2

(*Breviat, Sir Henry and Simon Thelwall v. Davenant*)

R29 That the Office of the Reuells was Instituted by the Saxons
That Kinge Henry. 8. by his Letters Patents under His Great Seale
bearinge date at Westminster the. ii. Marche In the .36. of His
Reigne did giue and Grante to Thomas Cawerden K^t the said
Office. Habend. et Exercend. for His Life. & 10^{li}. a yeare Fee. with
power to Constitute a Deputye.

116. y^{rs}. This Grante was not produced at
former tryalls Copy proued by R. Grainge

That Q. Elizab. made the like Grante to Edmond Tilney Esqr.
24. July In the [36] \21/ yeare of Her Reigne

82 y^{rs}. since. Copy proued

R29. A106 (Milhous–Hume, 92). This is the only breviat (i.e. summary of legal
arguments to be used in a lawsuit) in Herbert's own hand, with corrections, and may
be the original from which the others were taken and modified by scribal copyists. For
the licence to Robert Lea or Lee see *MSC* i. 284 and for that to Andrew Cane see
A17 n. Here and in R30 and R33 side-notes which in the original are in the left margin
have been transferred below and to the right of the item they refer to.

That K. James made the like Grante to George Buck Esqr. 21.
June In ye 1°. y^r. of his Reigne

Copy proued

That K. James made the like Grante to John Ashley K^t. 3.
Aprill In ye 10 y^r of his Reigne

Copy proued

That K. James made the like Grante to Beniamin Johnson .5.
Oct. In ye 19. y^r of his Reigne

Copy proued

That K. Charles the first made ye like Grante to Henry Herbert K^t.
And to Symon Thelwall Esqr. for their liues & the Longest Liuer
of them. [5 Carol] 25. August In ye 5. y^r. of His Reigne.

Great Seale

The words of the Grant are Officium Magistri Jocorum Reuellorum
et Mascorum Omnium et singulorum suorum cum Omnibus
Domibus Manscionib Regard Profic Jurib^s Librt' et Aduant' eidem
Officio quouis modo pertinent siue spectant uel tali officio pertiner
siue spectar debent'.

[That] It apeares by these wordes and by the wordes of Dedimus
et Concessimus et Facimus Ordinamus et Constituimus, That It
was not the Creation of the Office but the Continuance of it and
that Houses & proffits could not belong to a New Created office

> Stat. 9. Eli. C. 5.
>
> New erected Mills must paye Tythes but if a mill was
> erected a 100 y^{rs} agoe so that noe man can proue when
> erected it shall paye noe Tythes and shall be supposed to be
> Erected In Ed. 2. tyme/

That the Allowance of Playes, the Orderinge of Players and the
permittinge of Playhouses Haue tyme out of minde ben In the
Exercise and Allowance of ye Masters of ye Reuells respectiuely

Michael Oldsworthe   Richard Hall   William Hall
Rhodes   William Beeston   Sir John Treuor

That the Playes made by sir William Dauenant acted at y^e
Blackfryers by the then K^s. Company were allowed for the stage by
the Playnt.

A Grante from K. James dated ye 24 Febr. 17. of His Reigne to Robert
Lea to exercise the Quality of Playinge, &c. Prouided that all Authority
proffits. &c. belonging to ye mast^r of ye Reuells shall remaine

See ye Grante

The like Grant made by K. Ch. first. 7. y^r of his Reigne To Andrew
Cane &c. With the like Prouiso.

A declaration under William Earle of Pembrokes Hande of the Antient powers of the Office dated the 20th of Nouemb. 1622.
Seuerall Plays allowed by Mr Tilney In 1598. which is .62. years since.
 Sir William Longsword allowed to be Acted the. 24. May. 1598
 The Faire Mayd of London
 And Richard Cordelyon.
Kinge and noe Kinge to be Acted In 1611 & y^e same to be printed, Allowed by Sir George Bucke
And Hogg Hath Loste His Pearle by Sir George Buck.

             Richard Hall
That y^e de^t erected a Company of Players at Salsbery Court London the 5th. Nouemb. 1660. by his owne pretended Authority & Authorized them to play playes \and tooke the proffits/. &c. In defyance of y^e Authority of y^e Master of the Reuells. As apeares by Articles made between y^e de^t and Batterton & others. &c.

 See y^e Articles proued by Thomas Shippey William Beeston
That y^e Fees payd by the then K^s. Company at y^e Blackfryers about 40 y^{rs} agoe were for a new Playe 40^s. for a reuiued Play. 20^s. besids other Fees. And ye proffits of a sumers day & winters day And ye like fees from other Companys.

        Richard Hall William Hall
That all sortes of Players actinge In London [or In y^e] Westminster or Cuntrye, obeyed ye Authority of ⟨y^e⟩ Playnt. till ye de^t set up a new Jurisdiction & protected His pretended Company ag^t ye Playnt
That the K. cannot grante away an Incident to an Office thogh the office be In the K^s. Guifte.

      1°: Elizab. fo. 175. Dier Skrogs case
What a good Prescription Is? The tyme wherof the memory of man Is not to the Contrarie. Brac. Lib. 4. p. 230/

            Cok. Lit. fol. 115

Yonge and Steels Case

            Crok. 1. part

Stat. 9. Eliz. Cap. 5.

?1661/2

(*Breviat, Sir Henry and Simon Thelwall v. Sir William Davenant*)
R30 That King Hen. 8 by his letters Pattents under the Great Seale of England dated at Westm^r. the 11th. of March in the 36th. yeare of

---

R30. A101 (Milhous–Hume, 91). There are two more copies of this breviat, with a few very minor differences, on A102 and A103.

his Reigne did giue and graunt to Thomas Cawarden K^t the said
Office habend &c for his life and 10^l. p⟨er⟩ Annum Fee with power
to Constitute a Deputy &c.

p^r. by R. Grainge

That Q. Eliz. made the like grante to Edmond Tilney Esqr. 24th Jul
in the 21th. yeare of her Reigne

p^r. by R. Grainge

That K. James made the like Grante to G. Buck Esqr. 21th. Jun in
the first yeare of his Reigne

p^d. by R. Grainge

That K. James made the like Grante to John Ashley K^t. 3. Aprill
in the 10th. yeare of his Reigne

p^d. by R. Grainge

That K. James made the like Grante to Benjamin Johnson 5. Oct.
in the 19th. yeare of his Reigne

That K. Charles the first made the like Grante to Henry Herbert
K^t and S. Thelwall Esqr. 25. Aug. 5to of his Reigne

p^d. by the Grante

A praescription is the time whereof the Memory of man is not to the
Contrary, As 60 yeares {Yong and Steeles Case {Stat. 9 Eliz. Cap. 5

Cook Litt. fol. 115 Crok. 1. part.

The words of the Grante Are Officium Magistri Jocorum Reuellorum et Mascorum omniu et singulorum suorum Cum omnibus
domibus Mancionib. regard. Profic. Jurib. Libert et Aduant' eidem
officio quouis modo pertinentib' siue spect' debent. &c.

It appeares by these words And by the words of Dedimus et
Concessimus et Facimus ordinamus et Constituimus That at the
tyme of the Grante by H. 8. to Cawarden it was not the Creation
of the office but the Continuance of it And that houses profitts &c.
Could not belong to a new Created office, And that the house the
Earle of Elgen now liveth in at St Johness did belong to the office
of the Reuells

> New erected Mills must pay Tithes but if a Mill was erected
> 100. y^{rs}. since so that no man can proue when. It shall pay
> no tithes and bee supposed to be erected in Ed. 2. time

A declaration under William Earle of Pembrokes hand of the
Ancjent Powers of the Office 20. Nou. 1622

That the respective Masters of the Reuells successiuely haue
Authorized All shewes that Are to be p⟨re⟩sented by Any Persons
in England

That the def^t. prohibited diuers persons from taking their Authority from the p^{lt} as they ought to doe for Publishing of shewes, And threatned others and warranted others Against the p^{lt}. which made them refuse to take their Authority from the p^{lt}. to the p^{lts}. damage

> Edw. Thomas   John Rogers   John Millard

That George Harman was by the def^t. prohibited to take Any Authority from the Office of the Reuels And Trauelled into the Country without Any Authority from the office of the Reuells

> Edw. Thomas   John Rogers.

That D^r. Lambert was by the deft prohibited to take Authority from the Office of the Reuells And trauelled into the Countrey by Comission from John Pointz

> Edw. Thomas   John Rogers

That the King cannot grante Away an Incident to an office, though the office bee in the Kings Guift

> 1°. Eliz, fol. 175   Dier. Skrogs Case

That Nicholas Spencer haueing Authority from the p^{lt}. was disturbed by the def^t. from exercising his quality by threats and Arrests and by payeing of fiue and Twenty shillinges in Money

> See the Authority to Nicholas Spencer

(*Endorsed*:) Breviat   Sir H. Herbert v. Sr W. Davenant

16 January 1661/2

(*Petition to the King of Killigrew and Davenant*)

R31   To the Kings most Excellent Matie

The humble peticon of Thomas Killegrew one of you^r Maties Groomes of your Maties Bedchamber and Sr William Davenant one of ye gent of your Maties Privie Chamber:

Sheweth

That your Royall Father of blessed memory 22° Augustj in the fifth yeare of his Reigne by his Letters Patents under his great seale did graunt ye office of his Revells and Maskes together with ye fee of ten poundes p⟨er⟩ ann^u to Sr Henry Herbert Kn^t and Symon Thelwell whereby (with all submission to your Maties Judgm^t) your pet^{rs} conceave they ye said Sr Henry Herbert and Symon Thelwell are for their Lives seized of ye said Fee & of ye Office of M^r of ye Revells within your Maties howshold onely

R31. PRO SP29/49/95; summary in *CSPD 1661–2*, 244 (Milhous–Hume, 115).

That your sayd Royall Father by Letters Patents vnder ye great seale of England did giue power to your pet^r Sr William Davenant to erect a Playhouse, and to entertaine one Company of Players

That your Matie ye 20th of August in ye 12th yeare of your Maties Raigne vnder your Maties privie seale & signe Manuall for ye Reasons therein alledged were gratiously pleased to Comand Sr William Wilde Recorder of London and diverse other Justices of ye peace therein named to prohibite all publique actinges of Comedies and Tragedies in any of ye Playhouses in or neare ye Cittie of London. And by another Warrant vnder your Maties signe manuall were gratiously pleased to give warrant to Sr Jeffery Palmer your Maties Atturney generall to prepare a Bill for y^r Maties signature to passe ye great seale of England conteyning a grant to your pet^{rs} to give them full power and authority to erect two Companyes of Players consisting of such persons as they shall choose and appoint and to purchase build and erect such two houses or Theatres for ye Representation of Comedies and tragedies as shallbee thought fitt by ye Surveyor of your Maties workes &c Vpon which graunt your pet^{rs} have to their great charge erected two Play houses and made some progresse without any infringement to ye grant of ye said Sr Henry Herbert and Simon Thelwell (as your pet^{rs} humbly conceave:) yet notwithstanding haue ye sayd Sr Henry Herbert and Symon Thelwell presumeing that they have ye power over Tragedy and Comedy (thinges not so much as menconed in their Patent) in Easter Terme last past brought their accon at Comon law against your Pet^{rs} thereby pretending that they are disturbed in ye execucon of their office

May it please your Matie to heare and determine ye said difference or to referre ye examination thereof to ye Com^{ttee} which your Matie hath lately been gratiously pleased to constitute for inspection into ye encroachments of your Maties servants into ye respective offices of each other or any three of y^e said Committee to heare both parties and Report y^e true State thereof to your Matie that thereupon your Matie may be pleased to determine y^e same

And your pet^{rs} shall as in duety bound ever pray for your Maties long and happy Raigne. &c.

Att y^e Court at Whitehall Jan 16$^{th.}$. 166 $\frac{1}{2}$
His Ma^{ty} is graciously pleased to referre this Peticon & y^e matter in controversy to y^e Committee intimated in y^e Prayer, or any three or

more of them: who are to examine y^e whole businesse, & upon a full hearing of y^e Partyes concerned to endeauo^r an amicable composure of y^e difference between them; or otherwise, to certify his Ma^{ty} the state of ye businesse, & what hinders why such a composure cannot be effected. Whereupon his Ma^{ty} will declare his further Pleasure.

EdwNicholas

14 April 1662

(*Licence for George Bayley to perform* Noah's Flood, *signed by J Poyntz*; see Appendix B5)

26 April 1662

(*Record of Lord Chamberlain's warrant to arrest John Poyntz*)

R32 Whereas John Poyntz hath giuen out Commissions for the authorizing of Playes without any Just Authority for the same These are therefore to will and require you to take into your Custody the same John pointz and him safely keepe vntill you receaue further order And this shalbe your Warr^t Giuen vnder my hand and seale this 26th day of Aprill 1662

M

To any of his Maties Messengers of the Chamber

Possibly May 1662

(*Breviat of Sir Henry and Simon Thelwall v. Thomas Betterton*)

R33 That K. Hen. 8. by his Lett^{rs} Pattents under the Greate Seale dated at Westm^r. the 11th: March in the 36. yeare of his Reigne did giue and grant to Thomas Cawarden K^{nt}: the said Office Habend &c for his life and 10^l. p⟨er⟩ Annum Fee with Power to Constitute a Deputy

p^d by R. Grainge

That Q Eliz. made the like Grante to Edmund Tilney Esqr. 24. Jul. in the 21. yeare of her Reigne

p^d by Grainge

That K James made the like Grante to George Buck Esqr. 21. Jun. in the first yeare of his reigne

p^d by Grainge

R32. PRO LC5/184/60^v (Milhous–Hume, 132). This is not the actual warrant but a copy of it entered into the Lord Chamberlain's records (cf. R36, R42, etc.).
R33. A105^{r-v} (Milhous–Hume, 134). A second copy, virtually identical, is on A104, without the list of Masters of the Revels, which is in Herbert's own hand.

That K. James made the like Grante to John Ashley K^{nt}. 3. Apr. in the 10. yeare of his Reigne

p^d by Grainge

That K. James made the like Grant to Benjamin Johnson 5. Octob. in the 19. yeare of his reigne

p^d by Grainge

That K. Charles the first made the like Grant to Hen. Herbert K^t and S. Thelwall Esqr. 25. Aug. in the fift y^r. of his reigne

p^d by the Great Seale

A Praescription is the time whereof the Memory of man is not to the Contrary, As 60. yeares {yong and steeles Case {Stat. 9. Eliz. Cap. 5

Cook. Lit. fol. 115   Crok. 1. Part

That Sr John Ashley and Benjamin Johnson are dead proued by

Michael Beauer   Samuel Hooper

The wordes of the Grante Are Officium Magistri Jocorum Reuellorum et Mascorum omnium et Singulorum Suorum Cum omnib. Domib. Manconib. Regard Profic Jurib Libert et Aduant' eidem Officio quouis modo pertinent' siue spectare debent' etc.

It appeares by these words and by the words of Dedimus et Concessimus et Facimus Ordinamus et Constituimus That at the time of the Grante by Hen. 8 to Cawarden it was not the Creation of the office but the Continuance of it And that houses profitts &c could not belong to a New Created office

> Mills newly erected must pay Tithes but if a Mill was erected a 100 years since so that noe man Can proue when erected it shall pay noe tithes and bee supposed to bee erected in Ed. 2^d. time.

That the Allowance of Playes the Ordering of Players and Permitting of Playhouses haue time out of minde been in the exercise and Allowance of the Masters of the Reuells respectiuely.

George Bosgrove   Mich. Oldsworth   Rich. Hall   Will:
Hall   Will: Beeston   Rhodes   Sr John Trevor

That the Playes made by Sr William Dauenant Acted at Blackfryars by the then K^s. Company were Allowed for the stage by the Plaint. A Grant under the Signett from K James dated the 24. Feb: 17. of his reigne to Robert Lea and others to exercise the quality of Playing &c. Prouided that All Authority Profitts &c due to the master of the Reuells shall remaine

See the Grante

The like Grante made by K Charles the first \7 yeare of his reigne/ to Andrew Cane And others with the Like Prouiso

A Declaration under William Earle of Pembrokes hand of the Ancient Powers of the Office Dated Nouember 20. 1622.

Seuerall Playes Allowed by Mr Tilney in 1598. As

Sr William Longsword Allowed to bee Acted in 1598.

The Fair Maid of London

Richard Cor de Lyon

See the Bookes

Allowed by Sir George Buck

King and Noe King to bee Acted in 1611. and the same to bee Printed

Hogg hath lost his Pearle and hundreds more

Richard Hall

That the Great house in S^t. Johnes's where the Earle of Elgyn liueth did antiently belong to the office of the Reuells and was giuen away by K. James to the Lord Aubigny and an Allowance of fifty pounds a yeare made to the respectiue Masters of the Reuells in Lieu of the said house which to this day is in Charge with the Auditor

That the def^t Articled with Sr William Dauenant the 5. Nou. 1660 to Acte with the said Dauenant and under his p⟨re⟩tended Authority at Salsebery Court Playhouse and at the Theatre in Portugall Row to the p^{r}judice of the office of the Reuells and in disturbance of the Priuiledges and Profitts thereof and to the p^{lts}. Damage.

That all Sorts of Players Acting in London Westminster Suburbs thereof and Countrey obeyed the p^{lts} Authority till the def^t and others of their Company did joyne with the Said Dauenant to Acte under the said Dauenants p^{r}tended power and that the def^t till that time did acte at the Cockpitt Playhouse under the p^{lts}. Authority and owned the same and none other

That the King Canot grante away an Incident to an Office though the Office bee in the Kings Guift

1° Eli. fo. 175.   Dier Skrogs Case

Sir Henry Herbert

Breviat Sr H. Herbert v. Betterton

Not on Record	{Sir Richard Guilford
36. H. 8	{Sir Thomas Cawarden
Not on Record	{Sir Thomas Beneger

Not on Record   {Sir John Fortescu
24 Jul. Eli. 21   {Edmond Tilney Esqr
23 Jun. 1. Ja.   {Sir George Buck
10. Jacob.   {Sir John Ashley
19. Jaco.   {Beniamin Johnson
25. Aug. 5.   {Sir Henry Herbert and Simon
   Car. 1.   Thelwall Esqr.

6 May 1662

(*Statement of Sir Henry and Simon Thelwall v. Thomas Betterton*)

R34 Sr Henry Herbert K^nt & Symon Thelwall Esqr p^lts &
Thomas Betterton def^t in an Accon of the case

The plaintiffs declare that whereas w^thin this realme of England to
witt \at London/ in the parish of St Mary Bowe in the ward of
Cheape there is & time out of minde hath been an office of the
Master of the Revells & Masks of o^r Lord the King his heires &
successors To wch said office & to wch said Master or Masters by
vertue of that office the licenceing alloweing overseing & correction
of all & singuler Comon Actors of Playes & of all stage Playes by
them Acted by the whole time aforesaid haue belonged & apper-
teined & doe yett belong & apperteine for the executing of wch said
office the Masters of the Revells & Masks aforesaid for the time
being from time to time dureing the whole time aforesaid haue had
& receiued & haue accustomed to haue & receiue of the Comon
Actors of Playes aforesaid for the time being diu⟨er⟩s fees
p⟨ro⟩fitts & emoluments for the licenceing & allowing the said
stage Playes wch said office togeather wth all fees p⟨ro⟩fitts &
emoluments to the same office belonging & apperteining by the
whole time aforesaid was given & graunted & hath been accustomed
to be giuen & graunted by our Lord the King now & his p^rdecessors
Kings & Queens of England for the time being to any p⟨er⟩son or
persons willing to exercise the said office: And whereas Queen
Elizabeth by her letters Patents vnder the great seale dated at
Westm the 24th of July in the 21th yeare of her Reigne did graunt
the said office to Edmond Tilney Esqr h⟨ab⟩end⟨um⟩ the said
office to the said Edmond for his life to be exercised by him or his
deputy: By vertue whereof the said Edmond was seized of the said

R34. A67–8 (Milhous–Hume, 135); in a scribal hand. Herbert's dates are unreliable:
Tyllney was buried on 6 Oct. 1610, and Buc died on 31 Oct. 1622, Jonson on 6 Aug.
1637, and Astley on 26 Jan. 1639/40.

office as of his franktenem[t] for his life And being soe seized King
James by his letters Patents vnder the great seale the 23th of June
in the first year of his Reigne over England did graunt to George
Bucke then Esqr & afterwards Kn[t] the said office H⟨ab⟩end⟨um⟩
the said office to him for his life to be exercised by \himself or/
his deputy from the time of the death of the said Edmond Tilney
or assoon as the said office should become void by [the] surrender
[or] forfeiture or oth⟨er⟩ legall manner And that afterwards the
20th of August. 1610 the said Edmond Tilney died after whose
death the said George Bucke by vertue of the said graunt of the
office was thereof seized as of his freehold for the terme of his life
And being soe seized King James by his Lres Patents vnder the
great seale the 3[d] of Aprill in the 10th year of his Reigne did graunt
the said office to John Ashley Kn[t] H⟨ab⟩end⟨um⟩ to him [for his
life] from the death of the said George Bucke or assoone as the said
office by resignacon surrender or oth lawfull way should become
void for the terme of his life to be exercised by himselfe or deputy
And whereas alsoe King James by his other Lrs Patents the 5th of
October in the 19th year of his Reigne graunted the said office to
Beniamin Johnson gent' for his life from the death of the said
George Bucke & John Ashley or assoon as the said office by
resignacon or surrender or other lawfull manner should become
void after w[ch] graunt to witt the 20th of September 1623 the said
George Bucke dyed after whose death John Ashley by vertue of the
said graunt of the office was seized thereof as of his freehold for his
life And being soe seized & the said Beniamin Johnson then alive
the late King Charles by his Lrs Patents vnder the great seale the
22th of August in the 5th year of his Reigne of his c⟨er⟩taine
knowledge & mere mocon for himself his heirs & successors did
giue & graunt to the plaintiffs the said office H⟨ab⟩end⟨um⟩ to
them for their lives & the [lives] life of the longer liver of them after
the death of the said John Asheley & Beniamin and assoon as the
said office by resignacon surrender [or ot] forfeiture or other lawfull
meanes should become void wth all mancon houses Regards pfitts
libties & advantages to the same office belonging or apperteining
And that afterwards to witt the 20th of November 1635 Beniamin
Johnson dyed & on the 13th of January 1640 the said John Ashley
dyed after whose deaths the plaintiffs tooke vpon them the said
office & from thence hith⟨er⟩to haue indeavoured faithfully &
diligently to exercise the same & to haue & receiue the vails fees

p⟨ro⟩fitts & advantages to the said office belonging And that the defend^t intending to hinder the pl^{ts} in the vse & exercise of their said office and to deprive & exclude them of the vailes \fees/ regardes p⟨ro⟩fitts & advantages to the same office belonging between the 15th of November in the 12th year of the Reigne of o^r now Lord the King & and the day of the bringing the pl^{ts} Originall writt—to witt the sixth of May in the 14th year of this King at London aforesd in the parish & Ward aforsd the said defend^t wth divers others p⟨er⟩sons vniustly & wthout the licence or allowance of the said pl^{ts} or either of them and against their wills \did Act/ diuers stage Playes aswell new Playes as revived Playes to witt 10 new playes & 100 revived Playes the ffees for the licenceing & allowing thereof due to the plaintiffs or either of them not being paid And this they lay to their damage C.^{li} The defend^t by Henry Salman his Attorney hath pleaded not guilty.

4 June 1662

(Draft of an agreement between Sir Henry and Thomas Killigrew)

R35   Articles of Agreement \Indented/ made and Agreed upon this [fifth] \fourth/ day of June In the 14. yeare of the Reigne of our Souueraigne Lord Kinge Charles the Second And In the yeare of our Lord. 1662. Betweene sir Henry Herbert of Ribsford In the County of Worcester Knight of the One parte and Thomas Killegrew of Couent Garden Esqr on the Other Parte.

As followeth:

Imprimis It is Agreed, That a firme Amity be concluded for life betweene the said sir Henry Herbert and \the said/ Thomas Killegrew [Esqr]

Item the said Thomas Killegrew Esqr doth for Himselfe Couenant promise grant and Agree to paye or cause to be payd unto Sir Henry Herbert or to His Assignes on or before the fourthe day of August next, All monies due to the said sir Henry Herbert from the Kinge \and Queens/ Company of Players, called Mychaell Mohun William Wintershall Robert Shaterell William Cartwright Nicholas Burt Walter Clunn Charles Hart and the rest of that Company, for the New Plaies at fortie shillinges a Play, and for the Old Reuiued Plaies at twentie shillinges a Play, they the said Players

---

R35. A66 (Milhous–Hume, 139). A draft in Herbert's own hand, with several revisions. The two uses of 'Out' in the margin and the square brackets immediately facing them are in the original, though the text has not in fact been deleted.

Haue Acted since the Eleuenthe of August In the yeare of our Lord
1660.

Item the said Thomas Killegrew Esqr doth for Himselfe Couenant
promise grante and Agree to paye or cause to be payd unto the said
sir Henry Herbert or to His Assignes on \or before/ the fourthe
day of August next such monies as are due to Him for Damages
and Costes obteyned at Law ag^t mychaell mohun william wintershall Robert Shaterell William Cartwright Nicholas Burt walter
Out Clun and Charles Hart [upon An Action of the Case brought by the
said sir Henry Herbert [ag^t y^e] In the Courte of Comon Pleis agt y^e
said mychaell mohun william Wintershall Robert Shaterell William
Cartwright Nicholas Burt Walter Clunn and Charles Hart] Wher-
upon a Uerdict Hath ben obtayned as aforesaid agt them. And
likewise doe promise and Agree that the Costes and charges of suits
upon another Action of the Case brought \by the said sir Henry
Herbert/ agt the said mychaell mohun & y^e rest of y^e Players aboue
named shall be also payd to the said sir Henry or to His Assignes
on or before the said fourthe day of August next.

Item the said Thomas Killegrew [Esqr] doth for Himselfe Couenant
promise grante and Agree; That the said Mychaell Mohun and the
rest of the Kinge \and Queens/ Company of Players shall on or
before the said fourthe day of August next paye or cause to be payd
unto the said Sir Henry Herbert or to His Assignes the sume of
fiftie pounds As a [noble] present from them for His great damages
susteyned from them and by their means.

Item that the said Thomas Killegrew Esqr doth Couenant promise
gr⟨   ⟩ Agree to be aydinge and Assistinge unto the said sir
Henry Herbert I⟨   ⟩ due execution of the office of the Reuells,
and neither directly nor Indirectly to Ayde or Assiste sir William
Dauenant Knight or a⟨   ⟩ His pretended Company of Players or
Out any other Company of Play⟨ers⟩ [to be raysed by him or any other
Company of Players] whatsoe⟨uer⟩ In the due execution \of the
said office/ as aforesaid [otherwise then In the due ⟨   ⟩ of y^e
Kinges \and Queens/ Company of Players,] soe as y^e \[ayd soe to
bee]/[sd kings and qu' players] ayd soe to be required of y^e sd
Thomas Killigrew extend n⟨o⟩t to y^e silencing or oppression of y^e
sd King & Queenes comp^y.

(*Corrected editorial version of last paragraph, ignoring deletions:*)

Item that the said Thomas Killegrew Esqr doth Couenant promise
grant and Agree to be aydinge and Assistinge unto the said sir

Henry Herbert In the due execution of the office of the Reuells, and neither directly nor Indirectly to Ayde or Assiste sir William Dauenant Knight or any of His pretended Company of Players whatsoeuer In the due execution of the said office as aforesaid, soe as y^e ayd soe to bee required of y^e sd Thomas Killigrew extend not to y^e silencing or oppression of y^e sd King & Queenes comp^y.

And the said sir Henry Herbert doth for Himselfe Couenant promise grant and Agree not to molest ye said Thomas Killegrew Esqr or His Heires In any suite at Lawe \or otherwise/ to the preiudice of the Grants made unto him by His Matie. or to Disturbe the Receiueinge of y^e proffits arysinge by Contract from the Kinge \and Queens/ Company of Players to Him, but to ayd and Assiste the said Thomas Killegrew [Esqr] In the d⟨ue⟩ execution of the legall powers granted unto Him by His Matie. fo⟨r the⟩ orderinge of [His Mat^s] the said Company of Players, and In the leuyinge and Receiuinge of y^e monies due to Him the said Thomas Killegrew [Esqr] or which shall be due to Him from y^e said Company of Players by Any [said] Contract \made or to be made between them concerninge the same/ and neither directly nor Indirectly to Hinder the payment of y^e said monies to be made weekly or otherwise by y^e said Company of Players to y^e said Thomas Killegrew Esqr or to His Assignes but to be aydinge and Assistinge to the said Thomas Killegrew Esqr And His Assignes therein if there be cause for it and that the said Thomas Killegrew [Esqr] desire it of y^e said sir Henry Her⟨bert⟩.

And the said sir Henry Herbert doth for Himselfe Couenant promise gran⟨t⟩ and Agree upon the performance of the Matters which are Herein contayned and \to be/ performed by the said Thomas Killegrew [Esqr] Accordinge to the daies of payment and other things lymited and expressed in these Articles to deliuer Into the Handes of y^e said Thomas Killegrew [Esqr] the Deede of Couenants sealed and deliuered by the said mychaell mohun & y^e others Herein named bearinge date the. 11. August. 1660. To be cancelled by the said Thomas Killegrew [Esqr] or Kept as He shall thinke fitt or to make what further Aduantage of the same In my name or Right As He shall be aduised

(*Left margin folded over and endorsed*:)

Copy of the Articles sealed and deliuered the 4th. June. 62 Between Sir H.H. & Tho: Killegrew

Bonds of 5000. for the performance of Couenant.

18 June 1662

(*Record of another warrant to arrest Poyntz*)

R36 A Warr^t to apprehend John Pointz for still continueing to giue out Commissions for the authorizing of playes without any iust authority for the same And &c. June 18th. 1662

30 June–7 July 1662

(*Davenant's petition against Sir Henry*)

R37   To the Kings most Sacred Majesty

The humble Petition of Sir William Davenant Knight

Sheweth,

That your Petitioner has bin molested by Sir Henry Harbert with severall prosecutions at Law.

That those prosecutions have not proceeded by your Petitioners default of not paying the said Henry Harbert his pretended Fees (he never having sent for any to your Petitioner) but because your Petitioner hath publiquely presented Plaies; notwithstanding he is authorizd thereunto by Pattent from your Majesties most royall Father, and by severall Warrants vnder your Majesties royal hand and Signet.

That your Petitioner (to prevent being out lawd) has bin enforcd to answere him in Two Tryals at Law, in one of which, at Westminster, your Petitioner hath had a Verdict against him, where it was declard that he hath no Jurisdiction over any Plaiers nor any right to demand Fees of them. In the other (by a London Jury) the master of Revels was allowd the correction of Plaies, and Fees for soe doeing; but not to give Plaiers any licence or authoritie to play, it being provd that no Plaiers were ever authorizd in London or Westminster, to play by the Commission of ye Master of Revels, but by authoritie immediately from the Crowne: Neither was the proportion of Fees then determined or made certaine because severall witnesses affirmd that variety of payments had bin made; sometimes of a Noble, sometimes of Twenty, and afterwards of Forty shillings for correcting a new Play, and that it was the custome to pay nothing for supervising revivd Plaies.

That without any authoritie given him by that last Verdict, he sent, the day after the tryall, a prohibition under his hand and seale (directed to the Plaiers in Litle Lincolnes Inn fields) to forbid them to act Plaies any more.

R36. PRO LC5/184/64 (Milhous–Hume, 141).

R37. A74^{r-v} (Milhous–Hume, 137, 141); a scribal copy made for Herbert.

Therefore your Petitioner humbly praies that your Majesty will graciously please (Two Verdicts having passd at Common Law contradicting each other) to referre the Case to the examination of such honorable persons as may certify your Majesty of the just authoritie of the Master of Revells, that so his Fees (if any be due to him) may be made certaine to prevent extorsion; and time prescribed how long he shall keep plaies in his hands; in pretence of correcting them; and whether he can demand Fees for revivd Plaies; and lastly, how long Plaies may be layd asyde ere he shall judge them to be revivd.

And your Petitioner (as in duty bound) shall ever pray &c.

At the Court at Hampton Court the 30ᵗʰ of June 1662. His Majesty being graciously inclind to have a just and friendly agreement made betweene the Petitioner and the said Sir Henry Harbert, is pleasd to referre this Pet⟨it⟩ion to the right honorable the Lord high Chancellor of England, and the Lord Chamberlaine, who are to call before them, as well the Petitioner, as the said Sir Henry Harbert, and upon hearing and examining their differences, are to make a faire, and amicable accomodation between them, if it may be, or otherwise to certify his Majesty the true state of this business together with their Lordᵖˢ. opinions.

Edward Nicholas

Wee appoint Wednesday morning next before Tenn of the Clock to heare this businesse of which Sir Henry Harbert and the other Parties concerned are to have notice my Lord Chamberlaine having agreed to that hower.

Clarendone

July 7 1662.

11 July 1662

(Sir Henry's statement listing his fees)

R38   To the Rᵗ. Honnʳᵇˡᵉ. Edward Earle of Clarendon Lord High Chancellor of England, and Edward Earle of Manchester Lord Chamberlain of his M.ᵗⁱᵉˢ Household.

In Obedience to your Lordshippes comandes signifyed unto mee on the Ninth of this Instant July, To make a remembrance of the fees, profittes, and Incidents, belongeinge to yᵉ Office of the Reuells.

R38. Original inserted in Burn, 227–30 (Milhous–Hume, 146); it appears to be entirely in a very neat scribal hand.

They are as followeth:

	l	s	d
For a new play, to bee brought with the Booke — — — —	002	00	00
For an old play, to be brought with the Booke — — — —	001	00	00
For Christmasse fee — —	003	00	00
For Lent fee — — —	003	00	00
The profittes of a sumers day Play at the Blackfryers Valued at	050	00	00
The profittes of a winters-day, at Blackfryers — — —	050	00	00

Besides Seuerall Occasionall Gratuityes from the late K^s. Company at B: fryers.

For a Share from Each Company of four Companyes of Players (besides the late Kinges Company) valued at a 100^l. a yeare, one yeare with Another, besides the usuall fees, by the yeare   400—00—00

That the Kinges Company of Players Couenanted the 11th: of August 60 to pay Sr Henry Herbert per week from that tyme Aboue the Usuall fees   004—00—00

That Mr William Beeston Couenanted to pay weekly to Sr Henry Herbert the Summe of   004—00—00

That Mr Rhodes promised the like per weeke   004—00—00

That the 12^l. per weeke from the three forenamed Companyes hath been totally deteyned from Sr Henry Herbert Since the said 11th: Aug: 60, by Illegal and unjust Meanes. and all Usuall fees. And Obedience due to the Office of the Revells.

That Mr Thomas Killegrew drawes 19^l–6^s per week from the Kinges Company As Credibly Informed.

That Sr William Dauenant drawes 10. Shares of 15. Shares which is valued at 200^l. per week, Cleer profitt, one week with Another, As Credibly Informed.

Allowance for Charges of Suites at Law, for that Sr Henry Herbert is unjustly putt out of possession and profittes. And could not obtaine an Apparance Gratis.

Allowance for Damages susteyned in Creditt and profittes for aboue two yeares since his Maties: happy Restauration.

(*next two sentences in left margin, omitted by Malone:*)

Sr George Buck had 20^l: for Alloweing a Play house in Whitefryers

Sr Henry Herbert Allowed the Play house for the K^s Company.

Allowance for their New Theatre to bee used as a playhouse.

Allowance for New and old playes acted by Sr William Dauenantes pretended Company of Players at Salesbery-Court, the Cockpitt, and now at Portugall-Rowe, from the 5th. Novemb^r: 60. the tyme of their first Conjunction with Sr William Dauenant.

Allowance for the fees at Christmasse and at Lent from the said tyme. A boxe for the Master of the Reuells and his Company. Gratis. As Accustomed.

A Submission to the Authority of the Revells for the future, And that Noe playes New or old bee acted, Till they are Allowed by the Master of the Reuells.

That Rehearsall of Playes \to bee acted at Court/ be made as hath been Accustomed before the Master of the Reuells or Allowance for them.

Wherefore it is humbly pray'd That Delay being the said Dauenantes best Plea, wh^{ch}: he hath Exercised by Illegall Actinges for allmost two yeares, He may noe longer keep Sr Henry Herbert out of Possession of his Rightes: but that your Lordshippes would Speedily Assert the Rightes due to the Master of the Reuells. And Ascertaine his fees and Damages. And Order Obedience and payment Accordingly. And In Case of Disobedience by the said Dauenant and his pretended Company of players, That Sr Henry Herbert may bee at Liberty To pursue his Course at Law, In Confidence that hee shall haue the Benefitt of his Ma^{ts}: Justice, As of your Lordshippes fauour and Promises in satisfaction, or Liberty to proceed at Law.

And it may bee of ill Consequence That Sr Henry Herbert, dateing for 45. yeares Meniall service to the Royall Family, And haueing purchased Sr John Ashleys Interest in the said Office, And obtained of the Late Kings Bounty A Grante under the Greate Seale of England for two Liues, should haue noe other Compensation for his Many yeares faithfull Services and Constant Adhaerence to his Ma^{tys}: Interest Accompanyed with his Great Sufferinges and Losses, Then to bee outed of his \Just/ Possession Rightes and Profittes by Sr William Dauenant, A Person, who exercised the Office of Master of the Reuells to Oliuer the Tyrant, And wrote the first and second parte of *Peru*, Acted at the Cockpitt, in Oliuers Tyme, and soly in his fauour; Wherein hee sett of the Justice of Oliuers Actinges by Comparison with the Spaniards And Endeauoured thereby To make Oliuers Crueltyes appeare Mercyes, in Respect of the Spanish Crueltyes. *But the Mercyes of the wicked are Cruell.*

That the said Dauenant published a Poem in Vindication and Justification of Oliuers Actions and Government, And an *Epith-*

alamium in praise of Olivers Daughter M^s Rich. As Credibly Informed

That Matters of Difference betweene Mr Thomas Killegrew and Sr Henry Herbert are upon Accomodation.

My Lordes: Your Lordshippes very humble
                                                          Servant,

July 11th: 62.   Henry Herbert
Cary-house:

(*Endorsed:*)

Originall of what was deliuerd to the Lord Chanceller and Lord Chamberlin the 11. July. 62

14 July 1662

(*Killigrew's promise to pay Sir Henry's costs*)

R39 Mr. KILLEGREWE'S *Promise to pay the Costes of Suite against the Players.*

Julley 14, 1662.

I, Thomas Killigrew, doe by this presentes obleige myselfe to paey to Sir Henry Herbert all the costes and charges he shall apr, othe make apear, to be expendded in the sute betwixt him and the Kinges companye of acters, in the axion of the caes which he had a werdict for against them, in Ield Hall, woen (owing); and a part thereof, fortey pound, I hafe paid him. Witness my hande and seale the day and date over saide,

THO. KILLIGREWE.

Witness,

   JO. CAREW,
   L. KIRKE.
   WALTER GYLES.

After 23 July 1662

(*List of plays performed by Killigrew's company*)

R40 November. 60.

Monday the .5. Nouember. 60.   Wit without money
Tusday the .6. No.   The Traitor

R39. Warner, 184–5 (Milhous–Hume, 147).
R40. A62–63^v (Milhous–Hume, 45); in Herbert's hand. This is a folded sheet of paper attached at the hinge, but folded in the wrong direction, so that the order of pages is not 1, 2, 3, 4, but 3, 4, 1, 2. The entries are arranged here in correct chronological sequence. For identification of plays and dramatists see Index. It is not clear why some play-titles have single or double crosses in front of them.

Wensday the .7. No.	The Beggers Bushe
Thursday the .8. No.	Henry the fourthe. First Play
	Acted at ye new Theatre
Friday the .9. No.	The merry wifes of Windsor
Saterday the .10. No.	The sylent woman
Monday the .12. No.	× [Loues Mistres]
Tusday the .13. No.	Loue lies a Bleedinge
Wensday the .14. No.	
Thursday the .15. No.	Loues Cruelty
Friday the .16. No.	The widowe
Saterday the .17. No.	The mayds Tragedy
Monday the .19. No.	The Unfortunate Louers
Tusday the .20. No.	× The Beggars Bushe
Wensday the .21. No.	The scornfull Lady
Thursday the .22. No.	× The Traytor
Friday the .23. No.	The Elder Brother
Saterday the .24. No.	The Chances
Monday the .26. No.	The Opertunity
⟨Tus⟩day the .27. No.	
⟨Wen⟩sday the .28. No.	
⟨Thurs⟩day the .29. N⟨o.⟩	The Humorous Lieutenant
⟨Friday the⟩ .30. No.	
⟨Sater⟩day the 1. De	Claricilla
Monday the .3. De	A Kinge and no Kinge
Tusday the .4. De	
Wensday the .5. De	
Thursday the .6. De	Rollo, Duke of Normandy
Friday the .7. De	
Saterday the .8. De	The moore of Venice
Wensday the .9. Jan.	The weddinge
Saterday the .19. Jan	The Lost Lady
Thursday the .31. Jan	Argalus and Parthenia
	Loyall subject
Fe ⟨?26⟩	Mad Louer
	The Wildgoose chase
	Alls Loste by Luste
March. 61	The mayde In the mill
Aprill	A wife for a monthe
	The Bondman

May

July

Aug

Sept

Oct

Nouemb.

	The dancinge Mas⟨ter⟩	⟨ ⟩
	Vittoria Corumbona	11. ⟨ ⟩
	The Cuntry Captaine	13. ⟨Decemb⟩
	The Alchymist	16. Decemb
	Bartholmew Faire	18. Decemb
	The spanishe Curate	20. Decemb
	The Tamer Tamed	23. De
	Aglaura	28. De
	Bussy Dambois	30. De
	mery Deuill of Edmonton	6. Janu
	The Virgin martire	10. Jan.
××	Philaster	11. Jan.
	Jouiall Crew	21. Jan.
	Rule a wife and Haue a wife	28. Jan.
×	Kinge & noe Kinge	15. Febr.
×	The mayds Tragedy	25. Febr.
	Aglaura yᵉ Tragicall way	27. Febr.

	Humorous Lieutenant	1 March 62
A new Play	Selindra	3. March
×	The French dancing Masʳ	11. March
	The Litle Theefe	15 M.
	Northern Lasse	4. Aprill
	Fathers owne son	19. Aprill
New Play	The Surprisall	23. Apr.
	Kᵗ of yᵉ Burnige Pestle	5. May
Sir JSuckling's	Brenoralt	12. May
	Loue In a Maze	17. May
		June
		July.
	Loues mistres	26. Oct. 61
	⟨Discon⟩tented Collonell	
	⟨Loue a⟩t first sight	

June .1. 62	Cornelia A New Play.	sir W. Bartleys
June .6. 62	Renegado.	
July .6. 62	The Brothers	
	The Antipodes	
July .23. 62	The Cardinal	

(*At the beginning of this item is a note in the left margin, possibly by Malone:*)
This is a List of plays acted [by Davenant's Company at Salisbury Court & the Cockpit in D.L.] by the kings company at the Red Bull [& Gibbons] and the new house in Gibbon's Tennis C^t. near Clare market.

1 August 1662

(*Licence for William Lyde to show a blank book*; see Appendix **B6**)

1 January 1662/3

(*Licence for George Jolly*; see Appendix **B7**)

6 March 1663

(*Licence for John Wilson's* The Cheats)
R41 This Comedy, of the Cheates, may be Acted, As Allowed for the stage, the Reformations strictly obserued, to the Kings Company of Actors by Henry Herbert. Master of the Reuells
       Marche. 6. 1662

6 May 1663

(*Record of Lord Chamberlain's warrant to arrest unlicensed showmen*)
R42 A Warrant to app: paul Reames for setting vp Modells and dumb Shewes without leaue first obteyned of the Master of the Reuells May 6th. 1663.

30 June 1663

(*Record of Lord Chamberlain's warrant to arrest unlicensed showmen*)
R43 *Whereas* diverse persons doe sett forth dumbshowes, Dancing vpon the Ropes, and keepe Lotteries and also play and Exercise the part of a Montebanke without leaue of the Mast^r of the Revells These are therefore to require you to apprehend and take into y^r Custody the Bodyes of such persons as aforesaid that doe sett forth dumb

---

R41. From MS in Worcester College Library, Oxford, f. 44^v.
R42. PRO LC5/185/21 (Milhous–Hume, 204). 'Reames' is probably identical with the 'Paul Ryemes' mentioned in **R74**.
R43. PRO LC5/185/46^v (Milhous–Hume, 217).

Showes, Dancing vpon the Ropes and that keepe Lotteries, and play and Exercise the part of Montebankes, and that you bring them before me to answere to such things as shalbe Objected ag^t them And all Majors Sheriffs Bayliffs and Constables and all other persons are required to be ayding and assisting in the Execution of this Warr^t And this Shalbe yor Warr^t. Given vnd^r my hand and Seale this 30th day of June 1663

11 July 1663

(*Letter from the King to the city of Norwich*)

R44   Charles R

Trusty and wellbeloved we greet you well. Whereas you have humbly represented vnto vs the greate inconveniences and ill consequences wch are brought vpon that o^r Citty by the frequency of Lotteries Puppet playes and other showes resorting thether wherby the meaner sort of people are diverted from their labo^rs & manufactures & tempted to a vaine expence of their time & money to the great impoverishment of that o^r Citty and the sensible disadvantage of the trade and manufactury there . . . Wee have thought fitt to authorise and empower . . . you & yor Successo^rs . . . so to limit & determine the stay and abode of all such lotteryes Puppet plays & showes in that o^r Citty as you and they shall iudge fitt & reasonable, & that they may not or shall not remaine any longer time in that o^r Citty then you shall permitt and allow of, any licence or permission from vs or the Maister of our Revells or any other power liberty matter or thing to the contrary in any wise not with standing . . .

By his Maties Comand
Henry Bennet

To our Trusty & wellbeloved the Maior Sheriffes & Aldermen of o^r Citty & County of Norwich

23 July 1663

(*Instructions from Hayward and Poyntz to Edward Thomas*)

R45 Instructions to Edward Thomas, one of the Messengers belonging to his Ma^ts office of the Revells, xxiij^th. of July. 1663.

R44. From copy in Norwich City Records, City Revenue and Letters, Case 17b, f. 93 (Milhous–Hume, 219), slightly abbreviated. The original has vanished. Another copy is in PRO SP29/76/118, summarized in *CSPD 1663–4*, 200.

R45. A75 (Milhous–Hume, 225). Originally written for use in Bristol; 'London or' later added in margin. This and **R46–8**, 51–2, and 57, are all in the same hand, apparently Hayward's.

1. You are forthw[th]. to make yo[r] repaire to the Citie of \London or/ Bristoll, (the ffaires approaching,) and soe soone as yo[u] come thither, acquaint the Maior of the said Citie, wth. his Ma[ts]. Grants to vs, and the Lord Chamberleines mandate, touching musick, Cockfightings, maskings, prizes, Stageplayers, tumblers, Vaulters, Dancers on the ropes, such as act, sett forth, shew or present any play, shew, motion, feats of actiuity, or sights whatsoever; as also the authoritie yo[u] haue from this office;

2. You are to enquire out the names of all such persons, as are come, or shall come to the said Citie during the time of the faire, wth. an intention to present any of the things abouementioned, & having found the Master, or cheife person of each company, to Demand his Commission, & in case hee hath any vnder the seale of this office, & the time not expired, then yo[u]. are to suffer him to proceed, after yo[u]. haue taken notice when the said Commission did commence and Determine; But if yo[u] find any (as noe Doubt yo[u] will) who haue not authority from this office, to act as aforesaid, yo[u] are to acquaint the cheife Magistrate wth. it, that all such persons may bee suppressed, and kept in safe custody by yo[u], vntill they shall become bound, wth good security to the master of his Ma[ts] office of the Revells, to appeare at this office w[th].in ten Daies after such apprehension, vpon the penaltie of twentie Pounds, to answere their contempt, and if they haue not by their obstinacy or abuse forfeited the fauour of the Office, to receiue respectiue Commissions for their future acting, and to bee limitted, that they doe nothing thereby offensiue against the lawes of God, or the land.

3[ly]. Notw[th].standing the premisses, if yo[u] find any persons there, w[ch]. are Inhabitants in Wales, or other remote places, who seldome or never come to London, and w[th].out very great preiudice cannot attend the office, yo[u]. are to permitt them for the faire time onely, provided they keepe good rule, and pay a present acknowledgement to the office, w[ch]. yo[u] are to receiue, & become engaged in a bond of twenty pounds, to the master of his Ma[ts]. Office of the Revells, that they will not act or shew any more w[th].out lycence from the said office either there or in any other place.

4[ly]. and lastly, yo[u] are required soe to order yo[r] busines as to render a punctuall accompt in writing at yo[r] returne to London, as to each particular contained in these instruccons, or what els may bee omitted through hast, as Mountebankes, Lotteries or the like relating in any kind to the office of the Revells, And this shall warrant yor soe doing. Given vnder our hands and seales, at his Ma^{ts}. office of the Revells.

E Hayward

J Poyntz

(*Left margin folded over and inscribed:*)

23th. July. 1663. Instruccons to Edward Thomas, in order to his [Journey to Bristoll]

25 July 1663

(*Hayward's arguments that the Master of the Revels should issue press-licences*)

R46 the 25th July 1663 Arguments to proue, that the Master of his Ma^{ts}. office of the Revells, hath not onely the power of lycencing all playes, Poems, & ballads, but of appointing them to the Press.

That the M^r. of his Ma^{ts}. office of the Revells, hath the power of lycencing all playes whether Tragedies, or Comedies before they can bee acted, is wth.out Dispute and the Designe is, that all prophanenes, oathes, ribaldry, and matters reflecting vpon piety, and the present gouernement may bee obliterated, before there bee any action [vpon] in a publiq⟨ue⟩ Theatre.

The like equitie there is, that all Ballads, songs & poems of that nature, should pass the same examinacon, being argued a Majore ad Minus, and requiring the same antidote, because such things presently fly all over the Kingdome, to the Debauching & poisoning the younger sort of people, vnles corrected, and regulated.

The like may bee said as to all Billes for shewes, Stage playes, Mountebankes, Lotteries &c. because they all receive Commissions from the M^r. of the Revells, who ought to inspect the same, that their pretences may agree wth. what is granted by their Commissions, otherwise many of them may Divide their companies & by way of cheat (as hath beene vsuall) make one Commission serve for two Companies, if not for three.

Now from the premisses, it may bee concluded but rationall, that hee who hath the power of allowing & lycencing (as the M^r. hath) should likewise bee authorised to appoint & order the press, least after such examination and allowance, alterations should bee made, and the abuse proue a scandall & reflection vpon the master, and therefore all sober, considerate persons must from the premisses

R46. A76^v–77^v (Milhous–Hume, 226).

conclude, that the ordering of the Press doth of right belong to the M^r. of the Revells; and in order to the regulating of this busines, and to make it knowne to the world, that not onely the power of it, but the care of well ordering, bounding, and correcting all vnsauoury words, & vnbecomming expressions, (not fitt to bee lycenced in a Christian Commonwealth,) belongeth solely and properly to the M^r of the Revells, all Poetts and Printers, and other persons concernd, are to take notice, after this manifestation shall come out, or a precept Drawne from thence, bee sent vnto them, that they and every of them, doe for the future, forbeare their poetry & printing, soe farre as may concerne the premisses, wth.out lycence first obteined from the office of the Revells, over against Petty Cannons hall in S^t. Pauls churchyard, where they may certainly find one or more of the officers every day.

(*Endorsement:*)

25th. July. 1663 Arguments to proue that the Master of his Ma^{ts} Office of the Revells, hath not only the power of Lycenceing all Playes, poems and ballads, but of appointing them to the press.

27 July 1663

(*Hayward's memoranda for a meeting with Sir Henry*)

R47 27th. July. 1663. Remembrances when I waite vpon S^r. Henry Herbert.

1. To call vpon him for the Records, wch. hee promised, having asyet onely half a dozen loose Presidents.

2. To desire him to appoint a time for the making of mee knowne to the Lord Chamberleine, S^r. William Davenant, Mr Killegrew, Sr Edward Griffin Thre⟨sure⟩r of the Chamber, & the Lord Chamberleines secretaries, that in Sr Henryes absence I may haue free access to them either personally or by letters.

3. To know of Sr Henry what Dutie or attendance is required of mee at Whitehall, that I may not bee wanting therein, & charged wth. neglect, when time shall come to demand my quarterly allowances and wages. & likewise to know from whom it is to be p^d. & ye times when.

4. To bee informed what allowances Capt. Poyntz can by ancient or moderne custome Demand, as Clerke Comptroller & Clerk, over and aboue the rates and fees sett Downe by Sr Henry Herbert as

R47. A78–79^v (Milhous–Hume, 227).

the M^{rs}. Fees and what Capt. Poyntz his Dutie is as to such demands, & what the opinion of Councell hath beene, at the close of contests betweene Sr Henry & him, & whether S^r. Henry did ever waue any of his trialls, out of a feare or Doubtfulnes of being cast.

5. To \be/ informed by Sr Henry, whether it Doth not as equally belong to him to lycence all Poems and Ballads as playbookes, wch I may not omitt to enquire after, for the enlarging & extending of my proffitts, if the thing in it self proue feasable, & it wilbe the better for Sr Henry, if hee survive mee, for I intend to make a Diligent enquiry after the rights of the office, & to contend soberly and cautiously for them;

6. To bee informed whether it may bee prudentiall and safe to make vse of Mr Rogers and his Soldiers, vpon any private accompt saue at Bartholemew faire, and other faires wth.in the Cities of London & Westminster, & the liberties thereof.

7. To know of S^r. Henry Herbert, what playes haue beene lycenced or allowed vpon or since the 11th. of this instant July.

8. To know what is Done about Mr Pagett, & whether it bee necessary for mee to attend the Lord Chamberleine about it.

9. To enquire whether Sr Henry did not (as a branch of his office, sometimes lycence Billiard tables, Nine pinnes &c. and what fee hee vsually tooke for the same, what president or footsteps there was for it, and why hee Declined it.

10. Whether particular musitians are not to bee lycenced aswell as companies, for that if they bee left free, they may gather into companies wth.out a Commission, and the M^r. may loose his fees.

11. Whether new playes or reviu'd playes being once lycenced, shall pay noe further Duties to the M^r. my meaning is, what duration of time, brings either of them wth.in the compass of a new allowance by the Master.

12. To know how farre I may proceed (quasi M^{rs}. Dep^{ty}.) against such as shall not render themselues vpon summons, or warr^{ts}. whereby they may bee reduced to an obedience & conformitie to the M^{rs}. iust commands, my Designe is to avoid too frequent troubling of my Lord Chamberleine, vnles in extraordinary cases.

13. To entreat soe much fauo^r from Sr Henry, as that his Clerke may search the bookes, & informe mee what numbers of the severall companies vnderwritten are in England, & how many of them by name are out of Commission; & when; because none haue asyet appeared.   vizt.

Mountebankes
Lotteries.
Clockwork Mocons
Ordinary Motions.
extra. Motions.
Dancing horses & mares.
Ropedancers.
Slights of hand.

14. To know if I haue not the priuiledge of a box in each playhouse, being told that Sr Henry had one at Command when hee pleased, for himself or friends.

15. To bee informed whether Capt. Poyntz hath the like, or any priuiledge at all, as Clerk Comptroller and Clerk, because hee affirmes soe much in many respects, & resolues to contend for them.

16. To know how to blazon Sr Henryes coat of armes, & what the Crest is, because I intend to haue it in the office out of respect to him vnder whom I act.

To know whether Cockfighting, belongs not to the Master of the Revells.

17. To propound vnto Sr Henry the willingnes of Capt. Poyntz (that all former Differences may bee buried in oblivion) to giue a generall release to Sr Henry, & the like is Desired from Sr Henry to him.

18. To enquire of Sr Henry, whether the vestures belonging to the severall stageplayers, are not to be provided by the M^r of the Revells, for that some records wth. Capt. Poyntz, wch were Mr Walkers & others concernd in King James his time, doe manifest soe much.

M^d. old Mr Whitehead affirmes, that all Comedies, Tragedies, Poems, Ballads, half sides, drolleries, and all billes relating to Jokes belongs to the Revells, & were soe accompted in the times of Q. Elizabeth and King James, and further sayes that to his knowledge Edward Walker formerly servant to Sr Henry tooke moneyes for concealing many of the particulars last mentiond.

19. To desire of S^r. H. H. a copie of the articles betweene him & Mr Killegrew, that I may know what further to expect, and because it is reported, that great matters are to bee expected from ye duke of Yorks playhouse, I desire to know what that may probably bee.

(*Cover note, written vertically between items 17 and 18*:)
Remembrances when I waite vpon S^r H H.
M^d. to desire a copie of Sr Henryes Patent.

28 July 1663

(*Letter from Edward Hayward to Sir Henry*)

R48 Honourd S^r

I came this Day purposely to waite vpon yo^u and to dine wth. yo^u. that I might \take/ yor advice as to many particulars, & was vnwilling to trouble yo^u before now, by reason of yor much attendance at the parliament house. But being come in vaine I made bold to transmitt the enclosed, and to beg yor resolucon in the margent to each particular therein mentiond, and to returne it by the first safe opportunity, for till then I resolue not to close wth. capt Poyntz; but to keepe my distance as I haue done hitherto. & to preserve the reputacon of the Master in myselfe, if I may receiue countenance.

Another paper of my owne drafting, I haue made bold also to send, craving yor advice in it, I see I must vse my witts in an honest way, or els I shall fall much short of my expectacon, & therefore beg yor concurrent helpe and advice.

Thus wishing yo^u a good journey & safe returne I remaine honourd S^r

yor most humble servant

Lincolne house 28th. July. 1663.   E Hayward

(*Address on back:*)
To the right worp^{ll}. Sr Henry Herbert kn^t. at Ribsford neere Bewdley, in Worcestershire these humbly present.

15 August 1663

(*Letter from John Pointz to Sir Henry*)

R49 Sr Henry

I make bold by theis lines to acquaint yor: Wo^{rpp}. That on Tuesday last I Was sumoned before the Kings Majesty & Counsell by S^r: Richard Hubbard, who accused me there with officiating the Ma^{rs}: office of the Revells & licenceing of Games to his great prejudice. To which I pleaded, that the right of Licecencing (*sic*) of all manner of Games & playes did belonge to yor. Pattent, Wherevpon his Majesty being present did Comand that Neither S^r:

R48. A80 (Milhous–Hume, 227).   R49. A83 (Milhous–Hume, 235).

Richard Hubbard nor yor Deputy should licence any manner of Games for the future. M^r: Hayward not being sumoned as I was, would not appeare; wherefore I am very Jealous he will loose that branch of yor Pattent for want of pleading: Therefore beseech you stand in the Gapp and vse some meanes by letters to the Lord Chamberlaine who is yor: Wo^{rpps}: great freind in this Case, and he is displeased with S^r: Richard Hubbard for bringing a matter before the Counsell, that he is only Judge of, (the Law excepted). I very much feare wee shall be much streightned in payeing the yearely Sallary to you Except you helpe vs in this matter: This favour I begg of you, that you will please to approve & allowe of the Method that I have formerly given vnder my hand as Concerning Gameing, of which I have sent yor. Wo^{rpp}: a blancke. I did with M^r: Hayward give the same with his Licence, but before the time of M^r: Hayward I did assume it alone, And therefore hope now you will rather Ratify & Confirme what I did formerly, seeing that I am at present Complying with him, who is yor: Deputy: I begg yor: favour herein, if possibly it may be obteined of you. One favour more I begg of you, that you would obliviate all differencies & provocacons that I have given you. And that yor: Wo^{rpp}. would be pleased to send vs the heads of every officers duty, That wee May bring in moneys into the said office to pay you from time to time as it growes due. Pardon me that I make this offer to yor: Wo^{rpp}: of giveing you a generall Release; I desire heartily to doe it, and begg the favour that yor: Wo^{rpp}: will send me the same. So begging yor favour not to take exceptions for what I have writt, With my humble service presented to yor: selfe, & all yo^{rs}: in generall. I remaine

Yo^r: dutifull humble & obliged
Servant to Comaund to my
power till death seperates

London the 15th: day of August
    1663   J Poyntz

(*Address on back*:)

To the right Wo^{rppll}: S^r: Henry Herbert Kn^t: at his house in Ripsford neere Budely in Worcestershire.

(*Licence for a shovelboard, perhaps enclosed with above letter*)

R50   By Vertue of His Majesties Letters Pattents granted unto *John Lloyd* Gent. to be Clerke Comptroller of the Revels in *England* and

---

R50. A88 (Milhous–Hume, 236). The bulk of this document is printed, with gaps left for MS insertions. In this particular case, angle brackets are used to indicate portions in MS.

elsewhere; and by Assignment of the said place unto me by Deputation, and by virtue of the same, I have Examined, Inrolled, and Approved of ⟨Thomas Rogers— ⟩ in the Parish of ⟨White Chapple— ⟩ to make use of ⟨one Shovelbord and no other——— For the Moderate Exersise and Recreation of Civill Persons Such as the Statute Lawes Allowes of and none other and this to Continue for the space of one whole yeere After yᵉ Date hereof and noe longer⟩ And to the intent the said ⟨Thomas Rogers⟩ should not intrench upon the Laws and Liberties of His Majesty, or His Powers and Dominions, he hath given security. In testimony hereunto I set my Hand and Seal this   day of   166 ⟨And in the fifteenth yeere of his Maᵗˢ. Raigne

J. Poyntz.⟩

28 October 1663

(*Hayward's proposals to Sir Edward Nicholas*)

R51 To moue Sʳ. Edward Nicholas to write to one of the Secretaries of state, about the following concernment.

Edward Hayward gent. Deputie to Sʳ Henry Herbert Knᵗ. Mʳ of his Maᵗˢ. Office of the Revells, finding by some monethes experience & observation, that the validitie and power of that office is much enervated and weakned by the many yeares forced absence of the royall authority, insoemuch that hee concludes it impossible to recover the lost power anciently belonging, and proper to the Mʳ of the Reuells, vnles his gracious Maᵗʸ. shalbe pleased to grant a warrᵗ for maintaining and reuiuing the respect and dignitie of the office; it is the humble suit of the said Edward Hayward, that his Maᵗʸ. may bee moued touching the premisses, for an especiall warrᵗ. as to the p⟨ar⟩ticulars following, in order to a right settlement.

1. To enioyne all Magistrates and whom els it may concerne, to render Due obedience to all Commissions that shalbe granted from the said office, according to ancient custome, and the tenoʳ of the Patent, & vpon their Dissobedience of his Maᵗˢ. prerogatiue royall in that particular from good testimonialls, that the said Edward Hayward may haue power to send a messenger for them from his Maᵗˢ office of the Reuells, to answere their contempt, before the right honᵇˡᵉ. Edward Earle of Manchester, Lord Chamberleine of his Maᵗˢ. household.

R51. A86 (Milhous–Hume, 253). The date has been altered from 26 to 28.

2. That hee the said Edward Hayward may haue such further power touching offenders, and refractory persons, as was granted to Geruase Price Esq[r], Sergeant trumpett, by his Ma[ts] warr[t]. bearing date the 7th. of October. 1662.

3. That hee may enioy all ancient priuiledges at Court, the ordering of maskes in the Innes of law, halls, houses of great personages, and societies, all Balls, Dancing schooles, and musick, except his Ma[ts]. & the priuiledges of the Corporation touching freemen, if it extend so farre; Pageantry and other publiq⟨ue⟩ tryumphes, the rurall feasts comonly called Wakes, where there is constantly revelling & musick; Cockpitts, fencing & fencing schooles, nocturnall feasts and banquettings in publiq⟨ue⟩ houses, when attended wth. minstrelsy, singing & Dancing, together wth. the ordering of all momeries, fictions, Disguises, scenes and masking attire, all w[ch] (in the iudgment of an able lawyer) are w[th].in the verge and comprehension of the M[r] of the Reuells Patent, from the words Jocorum, Reuelorum et Mascorum.

From his Ma[ts] office of the
Revells in S[t]. Pauls churchy[d]   EHayward
28th. October. 1663

(*Vertically in left margin:*)
my humble proposalls to S[r]. Edward Nicholas

21 December 1663

(*Letter from Edward Hayward to Sir Henry*)

R52 Honourd S[r]

I am vnder many Discouragements at present, having paid 226[li]. and received onely 70[li]. from the beginning of my busines to this Day, 50[li]. I reckoned to receiue from M[r] Poyntz, and resolued to pay it to yo[u] at the end of November last, but his Domineering carriage was such in the office, that I was constrayned rather to part w[th]. him then to comply vpon vnreasonable tearmes such as would not bee pleasing either to yo[r]self or mee, by w[ch] meanes I am forced to Disappoint yo[u] & humbly begge yo[r] patience for a time, and rather then giue offence I will pay interest for the forbearance, not Doubting but that I shalbe reimbursed and encouraged when the busines is in a more setled way, and that the royall oake Lotteries, & Musick are reduced to obedience, wherein I hope to haue yo[r] vtmost furtherance.

R52. A85 (Milhous–Hume, 261).

S^r. I make it my work and study to improue every thing to the best aduantage, & I hope ere long to reape the fruits of my endeavo^{rs}. In the meanetime I begge yor tender regard, however as money comes in, it shalbe secured for yo^u. in the hands of M^r. Baker.

Thus presenting my service to yo^{r}self and my lady I remaine, worthy S^r

Yo^r most humble servant

E Hayward

From ye office, the
21th xber. 1663
(*Address on back:*)
To the right Worp^{ll}. S^r. Henry Herbert knight, these present

29 March 1664

(*Hayward's proposals to Thomas Killigrew*)

R53 *The heads of what I gave to Mr.* THO. KILLEGREW *the 29th of March,* 1664.

1. To have a generall warrant for musick throughout England, which is practised already, but many are very obstinate, and refuse to take lycences, especially in cities and townes corporate, under the pretence of being freemen.

2. There being many complaints of abuses in dancing schooles, for want of a due inspection and regulation, an order is desired (as it is a most proper branch of the Revells) that I may bee impowered to lycence all the dancing schooles, and to bind them respectively against *mixt* dancing in the schooles, and other practises, which at present begette a scandalous report of them. This work is already began, and submitted to by some; but it cannot bee done generally, unles countenanced by regall authority.

3. Touching wakes or rurall feasts, (another proper branch of the Revells,) which are annually observed in the greatest part of England, it is humbly desired, that some countenance may be putt upon the lycencing of them, by which means many disorders may bee prevented; and though there bee but 10s. from the most eminent towns, and 5s. from the meaner parishes, (to bee paid annually by the churche wardens,) it will not only bee a good advancement to the office of the Revells, but will much civilize the

---

R53. Warner, 185–7 (Milhous–Hume, 276). For E. F. Rimbault's possession of a copy of this document see Introduction, 24–5.

people, who are commonly dissordered at those feasts, which are constantly attended with revelling and musick.

4. All quack salvers and empyrickes, under the denomination of mountebankes, are properly belonging to the Revells, but will not come in (notwithstanding several summons) untill compelled by regall authority.

5. The royall oake lottery, which is a modell or dumb shew, and sortition, and as cleerely belonging to the Revells as the small lottery or pricking book, which have (*ab antiquo*) been commissioned by the office, the persons herein are obstinate, and will not come in, unles compelled by his Majestie's authority.

6. For gaming, though the justices throughout England (amongst other things) bind the victuallers in recognizances of £20 apiece, not to tolerate gaming in their houses; yet, nevertheless, under their noses, and to the knowledge of most justices, gaming is sett up and tolerated. Now in regard it is against the letter of the law to lycence gaming, (though to do the same is consistent with the Master of the Revells' patent,) it is desired, with some cautious lymitation, that his Majesty would countenance this particular, as to the lycencing all upon easy termes, by which meanes every victueller may bee bound to observe lawfull seasons, and good orders, otherwise it will become a common custome to play on fast days, in time of divine service, and at other seasons prohibited; and therefore some expedient to bee used that may please his Majesty, and support the power of the Revells, which hath been very much enervated, and weakened (*sic*) by the late times of trouble and distraction.

7. Though to grant lycences for gaming, hath been practised ever since his Majesty's happy returne, by the groome porter, and Poyntz, yet as to my particular, (who have not enjoyed the employment above nine months,) I doe act under many feares, and with much tenderness, to those few who have submitted, least I should offend the law of the land; and therefore once againe humbly desire, that some safe expedient may bee found out to reconcile the law and the King's prerogative.

19 April 1664

(*Copy of Lord Chamberlain's warrant suppressing shows in Lincoln's Inn Fields*)

R54 Whereas the tyme is Expired wherein leaue was granted To dance
R54. PRO LC5/185/148ᵛ (Milhous–Hume, 280). Several residents of Lincoln's Inn

vpon the Roapes & shew puppet playes & dumb shewes in Lyncolnes Inn fields These are therefore to pray and require you to giue speedy Order that they forbeare any longer to dance vpon the Roapes, or shew any Puppett playes or dumbe shewes or other Sports in that place: And they forthwith pull downe ye howses & Stages that are erected there And this shalbe yor Warrant Given vnd^r my hand this 19th of Aprill 1664

To Sr Henry Herbert kn^t: Mast^r of

ye Revells or to his deputy.

21 April 1664

(*Hayward's announcement that he is now acting as Master*)

R55 The whole Power belonging to the Master of the Revels, and of his Majestyes Sergeant Trumpeter, (as to that Concernment) being by Deputations vested in, and devolv'd upon *Edward Hayward* Esquire, Servant in Ordinary to his Sacred Majesty; whose Office is kept in *St Pauls Church-yard London*: This is to notify, that all *Travailing Stage-Players*, such as use *Pricking-Books*, with 12 *Blanks* or less to One *Prize*; *Jugglers*; *Mountebanks*; *Prize-Players*; *Shew-keepers*; *Tumblers*; *Rope-Dancers*; and all other Persons whatsoever being subject to the Authorities aforesaid, who have not their Commissions now in force under the Seal of the *Revells-Office*, and the hand of the said *Edward Hayward*, are Offenders, and Counterfeits, and to be proceeded against accordingly. Under which Notion there are Two persons now abroad under the Names of *Avis*, and *Trippus* with a Lottery, and a Counterfeit Commission.

20 May 1664

(*Norwich*)

R56 Joseph Chidley had liberty to sell Balsome drawe teeth & Cutt Cornes (wherunto he is Licensed by ye M^r of ye Reuells) soe that he continues not heere aboue   daies & giue   to ye poore of y^s City

---

Fields petitioned the Lord Chamberlain early in 1664, protesting against the nuisance caused by these shows (Milhous–Hume, 264)

R55. The Newes, no. 72 (21 Apr. 1664), 261 (Milhous–Hume, 281).

R56. MCB 4, f. 216^v.

11 June 1664

(*Letter from Hayward to George Johnson*)

R57 M^r. Johnson

When yo^u see S^r. Henry Herbert, present my humble service to him, & acquaint him that it is onely want of money, that protracts my waiting on him; wth. some odde Dribletts receiued in 6 weekes time, I haue onely beene enabled to quitt the rent of my office, & to discharge the stationer for parchment, paper &c. That soe soone as money comes in, that may encourage mee to see his face, I shalbe sure to attend vpon him, but I am vnder soe many discouragem^{ts}. & soe hopeles of my expectations, that I should reckon it the happiest dayes work that euer I made in this world to bee quitt of Sr Harry and the office, the hopes I had by musick is quite lost, I haue beene cheated of money vpon 3 prizes, haue 30^{li}. in debts & cannot receive one farthing; represent this, & lett the issue bee what it will I must stand to it, but at the rate that I haue observed, I am confident wth court allowances and all, it will never amount to 500^{li}. a year   I am

yor loving friend

11th. June. 1664   EHayward

(*Address on back*:)

This ffor M^r. George Johnson at the Lam tavern atthe backside of S^{an} Clemons Church

(*Endorsed by Sir Henry*:)

Hayward To Johnson. deliuer⟨ed⟩ to me by Johnson the 13. June 64

24 August 1664

(*Copy of Lord Chamberlain's warrant to arrest unlicensed showmen*)

R58 Whereas diverse persons doe sett forth dumbe shewes, Danceing vpon the Roapes & keepe Lotteryes and alsoe play & Exercise the part of Montebanks And likewise some other persons doe take vpon themselues to Authorize Dumbe shewes Danceing vpon the Ropes & Lotteryes & other sports without leaue of ye Mast^r of the Revells These are therefore to require ⟨?you⟩ to app^rhend and take into yor Custody the Bodyes of such persons as aforesd doe sett forth dumb Shewes Danceing vpon the Ropes and y^t keepe Lotteryes and play & Exercise the Part of Montebankes and likewise those persons

---

R57. A87 (Milhous–Hume, 282). George Johnson was Groom of the Revels from 1662 to his death in 1671 (PRO LC3/24).

R58. PRO LC5/186/10^v (Milhous–Hume, 291).

that doe authorize those sports without Lycence as aforesd And all Majors Sheriffs Bayliffs Constables and all other persons are required to bee ayding and Assisting in ye Execution of this Warr^t Dated ye 24th of August 1664

?October 1664

(*Rough accounts and list of plays*)

R59

michelmas	63	—	163.
christmas.	63	—	163.
lady day.	64	—	163.
midsomer.	64	—	163.
mihelmas.	64	—	163.

815   815

305

                                 Whereof payd — 142

510   260

250   250   673

        510   815

Deducte out of .673. the sume of   252

And remaines [523]   —   421

                             673

142   142

163   163

305   Deducte — 305   out of —   652

                             Re   347

                                  305

                                  652

252 out of — 347. And Rem.   815

For 5. quarters at 163. ye quarter   —   815

Receiued   ———   305

Allowed   ——   250

                                  555

                                  260

                                  815

R59. A73 (Milhous–Hume, 245). Milhous and Hume term these Hayward's accounts, but the handwriting seems to be Sir Henry's. Some of the plays belonged to the King's company, others to the Duke's. For identification of plays and dramatists see Index.

```
                  423–
                  163
                  ———
             260
 305.        163
             ———
             423
```

```
292–    4–
 29–   10–
 16–   10–
  5–   00–     Charged on Thewer
[29–   10] –
[16–   10] –
 ———
343–    4
 14–   00–     charged on Pointz
  1–   15–     From Aris— Owinge
  4–   00.     On ⟨?Burowes⟩
  3–   00–     On Harmer
 50–   00–     More on Izard.
 ———
[65    19–]
415–   19–
———
 72–   11–   6
———
488–   10–   6
```

Novemb. 3. 63 — Floras Figarys		2–
A Pastorall called the Exposure		2–
8. more	———	16–
A Re. Play	———	1–
H. yᵉ 5ᵗʰ	———	2–
Re Play Taminge yᵉ shrew	—	1–
The Generall	———	2–
Parsons Wedinge	———	2–
R. Play. Mackbethe	———	1–
H. 8. R. Play	———	1–
House to be let	———	2–
More for Plays whereof		
Eluira the last	———	9–
	For Playes	41–

16 January 1664/5

(*Announcement by Sir Henry that he has dismissed Hayward*)

R60   *Tuttill-street, Westminster, Jan.* 14.

Edward Hayward late Deputy to Sir *Henry Herbert* Knight, Master of the Revels, is ejected out of that Imployment, and all persons concerned are to forbear any further Address unto the said *Hayward* for Commissions, and to apply themselves as formerly to *Lincoln-house* in *Tuttill-street Westminster.*

5 March 1664/5

(*Norwich*)

R61 Mr Rich: Bourne was allowed to make shew of twoe Camells an Eagle & a Vulture for 14 daies. He haueinge authority from ye M^r of ye Reuells.

8–9 March 1664/5

(*Second announcement by Sir Henry that he has dismissed Hayward and Poyntz*)

Tuttill-street, March 8

R62 This is to notify that *Sir Henry Herbert Master* of the *Revells* desires his *Majesties Officers* in their respective places to take notice, that the *Commissions* granted by *Mr. Edward Hayward* and *Mr. John Points*, or either of them are void and of no effect. And that where they shall take away any of the said *Commissions*, they are desired to returne them to the *Office* of the *Revells* kept at *Lincoln-House Tuttill-street Westminster.*

18 March 1664/5

(*Copy of Lord Chamberlain's warrant for costumes for court musicians, to be supervised by Sir Henry*)

R63 These are to signifie unto yor Lo^{pp} his Maties pleasure That you prepare & make up Habitts of sev^{ll}. colrd. rich taffatas for foure and twenty Violins like Indian Gownes but not So full wth. short Sleeues

---

R60. The Intelligencer, no. 5 (16 Jan. 1664/5), 34; repeated in *The Newes*, no. 6 (19 Jan. 1664/5), 44 (not in Milhous–Hume).

R61. MCB 4, f. 241^v.

R62. The Newes, no. 20 (9 Mar. 1664/5), 155; repeated in *The Intelligencer*, no. 20 (13 Mar. 1664/5), 164 (Milhous–Hume, 309).

R63. PRO LC5/61/224 (Milhous–Hume, 315). Another version with slightly different wording is in LC5/138/46.

to the Elboes & trimed wth. Tinsell about the Neck ⟨&⟩ bottome & at the Sleeues. And also that yor Lo^{pp} provide twenty fowre Garlands of flowers of sev^{ll}. sorts to weare upon their heads all of the fashion & manner as Sr *Henry Herbert* Ma^r of his Maties Revells shall informe yor Lo^{pp} All wch p⟨ar⟩ticul^{rs}. are to be deli^d unto Sr Henry Herbert for his Maties. extraordinary Service And this shalbe yor Lo^{pps} warr^{tt} **Giuen** under my hand this 18th day of March 1664

EManchester

the right hon^{ble} Edwd. Earle of Sandwich
Ma^r. of his Maties great Wardrobe Or to
his Deputy   there

(*Note*: The theatres were closed by order of the Lord Chamberlain on 5 June 1665 (LC5/153/147), and not reopened until late Nov./early Dec. 1666)

13 April 1667

(*Licence for Edward Howard's* The Change of Crowns)

R64   This Tragicomedy called The Change of
            Crownes May be Acted: Aprill 13:th 1667.
Lyncoln house in   Henry Herbert
Tuttill street Westm^r.   M R

9 September 1667

(*Sturbridge Fair*)

R65 Whereas Edward Izatt hath exhibited in this Court a Patent vnder the hand and Seale of Henry Herbert Master of the Reuells to Licence him to make vse of one Blank Booke containeing Twelve Blankes to a Prize, Wee the Comissary aforesd for good reasons vs thereunto moveing, haue licenced, and doe hereby Licence the foresaid Edward Izatt to make vse of the said Blank Booke in this faire, dureing the continuanse of the said faire.

R64. From MS, f. 34; facs. in Langhans, 132, ed. F. S. Boas (1949), 89. The MS is now in the Folger Shakespeare Library, Washington (MS V.b. 329).
R65. CCB, f. 120. A year later, 10 Sept. 1668, Izatt was fined £1/3/8 for showing a lottery contrary to the statutes (f. 129). Sturbridge Fair was one of the largest in England, running from late Aug. to end of Sept. (*Cambridge*, 706). It was held near Cambridge, and the visiting entertainers were controlled by a Commissary Court set up by the university authorities.

(Sturbridge Fair)

R66 Whereas Willia⟨m⟩ Almond hath exhibited in this Court a Patent vnder the hand and Seale of Henry [Almond] \Harbert/ Master of the Revells to License him to make shew of one Danceing Mare performing extraordinary Feates; Wee the Comissary for good causes vs therevnto moveing, haue licensed the aforesd William Almond to shew the aforesd Danceing Mare performing extraordinary Feates, in this faire ⟨during⟩ the continuance of the sd faire.

10 September 1667

(Sturbridge Fair)

R67 Whereas Anthony Manning hath exhibited in this Court a Patent vnder the hand and Seale of Henry Harbert Master of the Revills to License him to make shew of one Blanke Booke containeing twelve Blankes to every Prize, Wee the Comissary aforesd, at the request of Anthony Manning aforesaid, for good causes vs therevnto moueing haue Licensed and by these p⟨re⟩sents doe License the said Anthony Manning to make vse of the said Blank booke in this faire dureing the continuanse of the said faire.

20 September 1667

(Norwich)

R68 William Almond produced a lycence vnder the hande & seale of office of Sr Henry Herbert Master of the Reuells to shew a Dauncinge Mare, and he had liberty tyll further Order to shew the sd Order (*sic*)

6 November 1667

(Norwich)

R69 Mrs Rose ffleming wid⟨ow⟩ wth her servant have licence to make shew & vse by her selfe & deputy one Blanck booke conteyning twelve or fewer blankes to eu⟨er⟩y prize of plate plush ware & other ware according to a pattent vnder ye hand & seale of

---

R66. CCB, f. 120. See **R68** below. At Norwich on 20 May 1664 Almond was allowed 'to shew twoe daunceinge horses At the Signe of the Angell' (*MCB* 4, f. 216^v).

R67. CCB, f. 121. 'Anthony Manning' is probably identical with the 'Anthony Manwaring' of **R70**.

R68. MCB 5, f. 45^v.

R69. MCB 5, f. 49^v. On 13 Nov. Rose Fleming and Anthony Manwaring were ordered to cease showing 'after monday next', i.e. 18 Nov. (f. 51).

Sr Henry Herbert [Marshall] \Master/ of the Revells vntill further order

11 November 1667

(*Norwich*)

R70 Mr Anthony Manwaring wth his servants is licenced to make shew of a blanke lottery booke according to a patent vnder the hand & seale of Sr Henry Herbert Master of the Revells vntill further order

13 November 1667

(*Norwich*)

R71 It is ordered that Stephen Scudamore shall haue liberty to make shew of ability of boddy by vaulting tumbling & feates of activity on the ground wth his servants vntill further order according to his patent vnder ye hand & seale of Sr Henry Herbert Master of the Revells

31 December 1667

(*Record of Lord Chamberlain's warrant to arrest unlicensed showmen*)

R72 A Warr^t to App: Jacob Hall &   Carter for vseing Danceing on ye Roapes & Dumbshewes without leaue from Sr Henry Herbert Mast^r of ye Reuells Dated Decemb^r 31th 1667 To Mr Harrison

4 January 1667/8

(*Norwich*)

R73 Robt. Bradford whoe brought a Lycence vnder the Seale of Sr Cha: Harbert M^r of the Reuells, to show a motion of ye Merch^{ts} daughter of Bristol, was p⟨er⟩mitted to make shew therof vntill further Order

---

R70. MCB 5, f. 50. See notes on **R67** and **69**.

R71. MCB 5, f. 51. See **R84** below.

R72. PRO LC5/186/183 (Milhous–Hume, 412). Jacob Hall was the famous rope-dancer mentioned by Pepys. He was allowed to perform at Norwich on 13 June 1673 (*MCB* 5, f. 244^v), but was fined for acting 'unlawfull games' at Sturbridge Fair on 11 Sept. 1673 (*CCB*, f. 167).

R73. MCB 5, f. 56. *Maudlin, the Merchant's Daughter of Bristol*, an 'ancient celebrated droll', was performed in London in 1720 and 1729 (*London Stage 1700–29*, 589 and 1043). Possibly on the same theme as Dekker and Ford's lost play, *The Bristowe Merchant*, licensed by Herbert on 22 Oct. 1624 (**128**).

20 January 1667/8

(Record of Lord Chamberlain's warrant to arrest unlicensed showmen)

R74 Warr^t. to App George Jolliffe John Russell Paul Ryemes & Peter Gryen for acting playes Erecting Stages & Publishing dumbshewes with out leaue from S^r H Herbert Master of His Maties Revells Dated January 20th 1667

10 October 1668

(Norwich)

R75 This daie Rose the wyffe of John Scudamore produced a Lycence vnder the Seale of the Office of ye Reuells to shew and make vse of a pricking Booke in Nature of a Lottery, and she had leaue giuen to vse the same in y^s City vntill further order from Mr Maior, shee giueinge to ye reliefe of the poore. *(sic)*

16 December 1668

(Norwich)

R76 Richard Lancashire according to a Patent from ye Master of ye Reuells to shew daunceinge vpon the Ropes had Licence giuen them tyll further Order

(Norwich)

R77 Charles Prynn had leaue to make vse of a Trumpet Marine accordinge to a Patent from ye M^r of his Ma^{tys} Reuells vntill further Order.

23 December 1668

(Norwich)

R78 Rich: Shore produced a Patent from ye Master of the Reuells to make shew of a motion & he is lycenced tyll further order

---

R74. PRO LC5/186/184^v (Milhous–Hume, 417). 'Jolliffe' is undoubtedly the well-known actor George Jolly (see Hotson, ch. 4). For Russell see **R79** n., and for 'Ryemes' see **R42** n.

R75. MCB 5, f. 91. On 7 Dec. 1668 'The Court gaue no certayne answer to John Scudamore to make shew of his Drollery' (f. 96).

R76. MCB 5, f. 97.

R77. MCB 5, f. 97^v. *OED* (*trumpet*, 2b) defines *trumpet marine* as 'a large obsolete musical instrument of the viol kind, played with a bow, and having a single thick string passing over a bridge fastened at one end only, the other vibrating against the body, and producing a tone like that of a trumpet'.

R78. MCB 5, f. 98.

9 January 1668/9

(*Norwich*)

R79 It is ordered that Mr Russell shall haue the liberty of the stage noe longer then thys day, and that his ser^{ts}. that pretend to act Drolls, doe not presume to act any longer in y^s City, ther beinge Comp^{lt} made of the obscenity of their speaches & actions, and also the Master of ye Reuells disownes their Authority

. · . · . · . · . ·

The s^d Mr Russell requested to abide 10 dayes, which is assented to, but not to vse dauncing vpon the ropes.

18 January 1668/9

(*Copy of Lord Chamberlain's warrant for musicians' costumes*)

R80 These are to signifie vnto yor Lord^{pp} his Maties Pleasure, That you forthwith make vpp *Habitts* of severall coloured rich Taffatas, ⟨for⟩ Twenty ffowre *violins like Indian Gownes*, but not so full with short sleeues to the Ellbowe, and trymmed with Tyncell about the Neck, and bottome, and at the Sleeues, after the same manner and fashion as formerly And to bee delivered to the Master of his Maties Revells for his Maties Extraordinarie service. And alsoe ffowre, and Twenty *Garlands* of severall culloured flowers for each of them. And this shalbee yor Lod^{pps} Warrant. *Giuen* vnder my hand this xviijth Day of *Januarie* 1668. In the xxth of his Maties Reigne./

E Manchester

To the right hono^{ble}. Edward Earl of
Sandwich Master of his Maties Great
Wardrobe, and to the Officers there

3 February 1668/9

(*Norwich*)

R81 Mr Russell had (vpon his humble request) the liberty of appearinge vpon the Stage vpon Satterday next.

R79. MCB 5, f. 98^v. See **R74** above and **R81** and **84** below. On 17 Oct. 1668 'John Russell Pratitioner in Phisicke was p⟨er⟩mitted to erect a stage and sell his Medicines accordingly to his Ma^{tys} pleasure signified by his lrs vnder his Roial signett' (*MCB* 5, f. 91^v). On 11 Dec. 1672 he again produced his royal patent (but no revels licence), and was permitted to show for a month (ibid., f. 225^v).
R80. PRO LC5/62/52 (Milhous–Hume, 477).
R81. MCB 5, f. 100^v. See **R79** n.

15 July 1669

(Letter from Sir Henry to the Lord Chamberlain)

R82   *Mill Bridge, Westminster, July* 15, 1669.

MY LORD,—The bearer hereof, Anthony Devotte, informs me that Mr. Price, the sergeant trumpett, demandes of him twelve pence a day, as due to him from every player; whereas Devotte is not in the notion of a player, but totally distinct from that quality, and makes shewe of puppettes only by virtue of his Majestie's commission, granted to the Master of the Revells, under the greate seale, for authorizing all publique shewes. And the said serjeant ought not to impose upon the said Devotte, and putt him to great trouble and charges, but should have proceeded legally against him, in case he had refused to pay what was legally due. But the sergeant having arrested Devotte upon his pretended clayme of twelve pence a day, and declared against him, was nonsuited for not proceedinge, which is a matter of great vexation to a stranger, and a stronge argument against the validity of the sergeantes grante. Your Lordship, therefore is humbly intreated on behalf of the said Devotte to appointe a day and houre when he shall attende your Lordship with his counsell, to be hearde before he be concluded in your Lordship's judgement. And that he may have the benefit of the law for his protection against the Sergeante's unjust demandes. This from your Lordship's very humble servant,

HENRY HERBERT.

To the Right Hon. Edward Earle of Manchester, Lord Chamberlayne of his Majestie's household.

22 February 1669/70

(Abingdon)

R83   The Informacon of John Parker of London watchmaker taken before Simon Hawkins gent Mayo^r & Justice of the peace wthin the said Borough the 22th. of ffebruary 1669 as followeth

---

R82. Warner, 74–5 (Milhous–Hume, 505). Anthony De Voto (his name appears in various forms) was a celebrated Italian puppeteer who worked in London between 1667 and 1677; he had a booth at Charing Cross, and performed at Bartholomew Fair (Speaight, 75–7, 282). On 18 June 1669 the Lord Chamberlain issued a warrant to arrest 'Anthony Devant' and others who had not paid a fee to Gervase Price, Sergeant Trumpeter to the King, for using music at their shows (Milhous–Hume, 499). 'Devant' was almost certainly De Voto, and in this letter Herbert intervened on his behalf against Price.

R83. Berkshire Record Office D/EP7/136 (Milhous–Hume, 546).

Saith vpon oath that Robert Hopkins of Abingdon aforesaid did assault and beate him this depon[t]. and teere in peeces his clothes and treated him in opprobrious language

    The Informacon of Roger Allcroft of London musitian taken the day & yeare abouesaid

who saith vpon oath that by virtue of a Comission from the M[r] of the Revells he was acting his shewe and in the midst of the Shew one Robt Hopkins did assault \&/ beate [and wo] this Informant and hinder him in the p⟨re⟩senting of the Shewe

    The Informacon of Edward Clements taken vpon oath the day and yeare abouesaid

who saith that [Robert] Robt Hopkins forced himselfe into the Roome where the Shewe was acted and saith that Robt Hopkins did kick John Parker one of the Players of the Shew out of a Roome in the same howse

    The Informacon of Willm Clarke

Saith that Robert Hokins (sic) did confesse he brake open the Doore of the Shew howse and saith that Robt Hopkins vpon some words of p⟨ro⟩vocacon Robert Hopkins did assault and beate the Shewers.

there were p⟨re⟩sent George Goole Edw Harper Andrew Plott & himselfe

29 August 1670

(*Record of Lord Chamberlain's warrant to arrest unlicensed showmen*)

R84 A Warr[t] to apprehend John perin John Nash John Russell Thomas Cosby Stephen Scudamore and George Harman for setting forth dumb shewes, dancing vpon the Ropes and for keeping Lotteryes and exercising the part of Montebankes without leaue of the Master of His Ma[ts] Revells dated Aug 29. 1670 To Th Widdowe

7 December 1670

(*Norwich*)

R85 M[r] Jo: Almond produced a Lycence from the M[r] of the Reuells to shew a Daunceinge Mare & he hath till [y[s] da] saterday fortnight giuen him to make shew of the sd Mare

R84. PRO LC5/188/37 (Milhous–Hume, 573)
R85. MCB 5, f. 159[v]. On 17 Dec. (f. 161) Almond had leave to show his dancing mare 'till wednesday next'.

25 February 1670/1

(*Record of Lord Chamberlain's warrant to arrest unlicensed showmen*)

R86 A Warr^r. to App Robert Parker & Samuell Tanton for acting Interludes & Stage playes without lycence from ye Master of his Ma^{ts} Revells And &c Dated Feb: 25 1670/

To Tho: Dixon

31 March 1671

(*Record of Lord Chamberlain's warrant to arrest unlicensed showmen*)

R87 A Warr^r. to App Will: Cavile for setting forth a dumbe shew called Paradise without leaue from ye Master of his Ma^{ts} Revells. And &c Dated March 31 1671   To Mr Potts./

2 September 1671

(*Norwich*)

R88 John Symons hath liberty to shew strang ffeates p⟨er⟩formed by his mouth according to Sr Henry Harberts Comission this his licence to continue for one weeke from this day

2 October 1671

(*Norwich*)

R89 Mr Thomas Cosby wth his servants are licenced to make shew of daunceing on a low rope vaulting on a high Rope & agility of body on the ground vntill this day fortnight he having a licence to doe ye same by virtue of a Comission from his Matie as also from Sr Charles (*sic*) Herbert Master of the Revells

4 October 1671

(*Norwich*)

R90 That if one Peter Dollman comes to this City to make shew of a Motion p⟨er⟩formed by Puppets vnles he show authority from

---

R86. PRO LC5/188/97^v (Milhous–Hume, 608). There are numerous later references to Parker in Milhous–Hume.

R87. PRO LC5/188/111 (Milhous–Hume, 614). Probably not the same as the show seen by Evelyn at Hatton Garden (*Diary*, 23 Sept. 1673).

R88. MCB 5, f. 184^v.

R89. MCB 5, f. 186. See R84 above. On 22 Oct. 'ffurther time is given to Mr Tho: Cosby wth his servants to make shew of daunceing on a low rope vntill Satterday come seaven night \at night/ he paying xx^s to be put into the Hamper' (f. 187^v).

R90. MCB 5, f. 186^v. The previous year, 18 June 1670, Dolman was allowed to show at Norwich 'one Motion shew consisting of three dancing monkeyes a peice of water

his Maties office of Revelles he shall not be p⟨er⟩mitted to shew yᵉ same

15 November 1671
(*Norwich*)

R91 John Parker vpon his Produceinge a Patent vnder the Seale of the office of yᵉ Reuells to make shew of a motion of puppetts had tyme giuen him till this day senight.

23 December 1671
(*Norwich*)

R92 Mʳˢ Peters Widdow produced a Patent from yᵉ Master of the Reuells to make shew of a Worke Called the Wisdome of Solomon for 14 daies.

15 January 1671/2
(*Licence for a revival of Cartwright's* The Ordinary)

R93   This Comedy, called th Ordinary
       [the Reformations obserued]
          nay (*sic*) bee acted, not other wise
            January 15. 1671
              Henry Herbert
               M R.

9 March 1671/2
(*Licence for a revival of Cartwright's* The Lady Errant)

R94   March: 9: 1671. This Play Called The Lady
       Errant may bee Acted by the Dukes Company
       of Actors as Lycenced by
Millb: Westmʳ   Henry Herbert
               M.R.

worke & pollishanella for one weeke from this time' (f. 140); on 25 June he was allowed an extension for two more weeks (f. 141).

R91. MCB 5, f. 189ᵛ.

R92. MCB 5, f. 192. On 10 Jan. 1671/2 she was given further permission (f. 192ᵛ), but on 17 Jan. she was ordered to leave the city (f. 193ᵛ). These later entries make it clear that she ran a puppet-show.

R93. Written in Sir Henry's hand on p. 89 of a copy of the 1651 edn. used as a prompt-copy for a revival, now in the University of Illinois Library. Reproduced in Evans, facing 260, and in Langhans, 337. The second line is cancelled with a single long pen-stroke.

R94. Written on p. 80 of a copy of the 1651 edn. used as a prompt-copy for a revival, now in the University of Illinois Library. Only the signature is in Herbert's hand. Facs. in Langhans, 380.

12 September 1672

(*Sturbridge Fair*)

R95 Quibus &ᶜ co⟨m⟩p⟨ar⟩vit Powell, and shewed a Patent vnder the Seale of Sʳ. Hen: Harbert to act Comedies [in the] and by the said Patent had acted in this faire contrary to the Statutes of the University.

1–5 May 1673

(*Announcement by Thomas Killigrew that he is now Master of the Revels*)

R96   *Advertisements.*

The Office of the Master of the Revels, void by the death of Sir *Henry Herbert*, who deceased the 27 of *April* last, is now enjoyed by *Thomas Killegrew* Esquire, one of the Grooms of His Majesties Bed Chamber, at whose Lodgings in *White-hall* any Person or Persons may be informed, whither those who had any Licenses from the said Sir *Henry*, or are otherwise concerned in the said Office of Master of the Revels, may make their applications for renewing of former, or taking out of new Licenses, or what else relates unto the said Office.

15–19 May 1673

(*Second announcement*)

R97   *Advertisement.*

THat all Justices of the Peace and others His Majesties Officers, whom it may concern, do take care that all Persons that present publickly any Playes, Showes, or Operations upon any Stage, &c. may produce their Licence, under the Hand and Seal of *Thomas Killegrew Esquire*, now Master of the Revels, and in case they want such Licenses, that they be layd hold on, and the said Mr *Killegrew* Certified of the same.

R95. *CCB*, f. 195ᵛ (Milhous–Hume, 723). A marginal note indicates that Martin Powell was fined 3*s.* 8*d.* Powell was a player in the King's company from 1669 onwards; there are numerous entries for him in Milhous–Hume.

R96. *London Gazette*, no. 778 (1–5 May 1673), repeated in no. 780 (8–12 May 1673). Thomas Killigrew was sworn in as new Master of the Revels on 1 May (Milhous–Hume, 774).

R97. *London Gazette*, no. 782 (15–19 May 1673); repeated in no. 785 (26–29 May 1673) (Milhous–Hume, 777).

Documents not Precisely Datable

?1661–2

(Sir Henry Herbert's losses)

R98 Sir H⟨enry Her⟩bert \K^t/ Master of his Maiesties office of the Revells by Grant under the great Seale 5 Caro^{li} pri. Hath time out of minde whereof the memory of man is not to the Contrary, As soly belonging and properly apertaininge to the said office of the Revells, the Allowance of all playes in England and the ordering and reforming of all players and the ffees and profitts arysing thereby and hath receiued seuerall ffees and profitts from the said players that doe now Act for a Certaine time but of Late the said players doe refuse to pay the said ffees and profitts formerly payd and due to the said office and haue totally withdrawne the payment of them to S^{ir}. Henry Herberts damage of fiue thousand pounds.

?Possibly July 1663

(Financial arrangements of the Revels Office)

R99   The Office of M^r of the Revells.

The Accomptants Leidgerbookes to bee Signed by the Comptroller Clerke and Yeoman of the Revells aswell as the Master according to the Course of the office.

A dorm⟨an⟩^{t} warr^t of the Ld Threasurer or Chancello^r of the Excheq^r for 50^{li}. p⟨er⟩ ann' Rent of the Masters howse & office wanting.

The like for 15^{li} p⟨er⟩ ann' for Rent of a howse for ye Clerke of the Revells.

The like for 15^{li} p⟨er⟩ ann' for Rent of a howse for the Yeoman of the Revells.

Order of the Ld Chamberlaine for Extraord^y Allowances to ye Officers of the Revells at xxiii^{li}, xiii^s iiii^d p⟨er⟩ ann' wanting.

R98. A72 (Milhous–Hume, 133). Scribal copy, damaged at the top. Milhous and Hume tentatively suggest 'ca. May 1662?', but there is nothing in the document to indicate a definite date.

R99. A99 (Milhous–Hume, 228). Milhous and Hume suggest that it was drawn up in connection with Hayward's appointment as Sir Henry's deputy, but it could have been earlier. There is a gap of about three inches between the sixth and last items. Mostly a scribal copy, but 'From Auditor Beale' appears to be in Herbert's hand.

q⟨uery⟩ what shalbee allowed for the ffees of the Clerks of the Signett & privy Seale & Offic^rs of the Receipt ye Accomptant demands x^li p⟨er⟩ ann'.

The M^r and the rest of the Officers of the Revells theire patents not yet p⟨ro⟩duced.
(*in left margin beginning opposite* q⟨uery⟩:)
There hath bin 20^li formerly allowed for 3 years: Now there is 10^li demanded yearely.
(*in left margin at right angle*:)
Revells. From Auditor Beale.

?1670

(*Licence for Elizabeth Polwhele's* The Faithful Virgins)
R100   This Tragedy apoynted to be acted
              by the dukes Company of Actors only
              leauing out what was Cross'd by
                        Henry Herbertt
                        M: R.

After May 1671

(*Application for a licence for a mechanical horse*)
R101   A Mylord St. Alban grand chamberlan.
     Supplient humblement François Durdon et André pellerin fran-
çois de Nation disant que depuis quelque temps jl a esté establi vne
machine en France et particulierement a Versailles par laquelle on
court la bague artiffreictement sur des chevaux de bois, Et comme
cet establissement ne regarde que la satisfaction du public, ce
consideré Mylord Il vous plaise permettre Aux suppliants de le faire

---

R100. Bodleian MS Rawlinson poet. 195, f. 49. This is placed at the beginning of the play, not the end, and is in the same hand as the text of the play. For discussion of the date and authorship of the play see Elizabeth Polwhele, *The Frolicks or the Lawyer Cheated*, ed. Judith Milhous and Robert D. Hume (Ithaca, NY, 1977), 39–44.
R101. A107^{r–v}. This must date from after 13 May 1671, when Henry Jermyn, Earl of St Albans, succeeded Manchester as Lord Chamberlain (Milhous–Hume, 623).

en ceste ville de Londres, Et attendu quil ne se peut qu'a grands frais, et pour leur donner moyen de se rembourser des dep⟨en⟩^ces quil leur conuiendra faire Il vous plaise aussy My lord faire deffences a toutes autres personnes de faire, ou jmiter ladite machine durant le temps de trois années a peyne de cinq cent liures sterlins damande et de tous despens dommages & jnteretz.

Monsieur Durdin for a lycence to shew a wooden horse
French Ambassado^rs Secretary

APPENDIX A.

Miscellaneous Revels Documents, 1622–31

1622

Undated, but early 1622. (*Petition from Robert Wright and other revels workmen to Cranfield*)

A1   *To the right honorable the Lo: Cranfeild Lord-high Threasurer of England:*

The humble Peticon of Robert Wright, and of the poore workmen belonging to the Office of y^f Reuells.

Humblie shewing, That whereas S^r. George Bucke & the rest of ye Officers of the Revells obtained a privie seale of 700^{li}. for 2. yeres service wch was performed six yeres past, and now the greatest part of the 7th yere performed by the said Wright, vppon the humble suite vnto yor Hono^r before Christmas last did obtaine 200^{li} wch it pleased yor Hono^r to order, that 100^{li}. should be paid vnto yor peticoners, wch was not performed by Sr George Bucke according to yor Hono^{rs} pleasure, but he hath deteyned 22^{li}. of the said 100^{li}. And also further humblie shewing that yor said peticoners having performed this last service wth soe much Charges that the said Wright is rather worse in his estate then he was, especiallie inregard he is out for his Ma^{ts}. service in the Office of the Revells and the Ordinance & other places to the vallewe of 1300^{li}. and vpwards, The long forbearance wth interest paid for parte of the same hath soe overthrowen his Estate, that he can neither pay for Stuff nor workmens wages for the performing of this last service, vnlesse yor Hono^r bee pleased in yor accustomed Clemencie to further him therein.

Wherefore their humble request vnto yor Hono^r is, that you would be pleased to give present order for payment of the rest of the privie Seale wch is 300^{li}. whereof there is due vnto poore workmen & poore Orphants the some of 104 16^s. 8^d. That soe Stuffe & poore mens wages for this last Service may be satisfied. And as in dutie bound they will eu⟨er⟩ pray for yor Hono^{rs} continuall happines.

A1 Kent Archive Office, U269/1 OE 817. This item and **A7, 9**, and **14**, are not mentioned in Eccles, 479–81.

29 Mar. 1622. (*Warrant for Sir John Astley*)

A2 29° Marcii. A warrant to sweare Sr John Ashley M^r of his Ma^ts Revells

2–3 May 1622. (*Warrant setting out the powers of Sir John Astley as Master*)

A3 . . . And further also wee have, and doe by these presents authorize and comaund o^r said servant Sr John Ashley Master of o^r Revells, by himself, or his sufficient deputie, or deputies, to warne, comaund, and appoint in all places wth in this o^r Realme of England, aswell wth in Franchises and liberties as wth out, all and every player and players, wth the playmak-ers⟨,⟩ either belonging to any Noblemen, or otherwise bearing the name or names of using the facultie of playmakers, or players of Comedies, tragedies, Interludes, or what other showes soever from time to time and at all times to appeare before him wth all such plaies, tragedies, Comedies, or showes, as they shall have in readines or meane to sett foorth, and them to present, and recite before o^r said servant, or his sufficient deputy, whome wee ordaine, appoint, and authorise by these presents of all such showes, plaies, players, and playmakers, together wth their playing places, to order and reforme, authorise and put downe, as shalbe thought meete, or vnmeete vnto himself, or his said deputie in the behalf.

16 May 1622. (*Letter from the Lord Chamberlain's office to 'Mr Buck'*)

A4 16° May. A lre on the behalf of Sr John Ashley to Mr Buck for deliverie vp of the books and other things of the Office of Revells vnto him, being now M^r of the same office

20–2 May 1622. (*Warrant for payment of revels arrears of £301 to Sir John Astley*)

A5 . . . forasmuch as the said S^r. George Buck by reason of sicknes and indisposition of body wherw^th it hath pleased god latelie to visite him is

---

A2 Inner Temple MS 515, no. 7, f. 31^v. This seems to be a copy of a warrant and letter record-book from the Lord Chamberlain's office for 1621–2, the original of which does not survive. Printed in Murray, 193.

A3 Extracted from Astley's warrant, PRO PSO2/50 no. 19, printed in full in Collier, i. 419–22, and W. C. Hazlitt, *English Drama and Stage* (1869), 52–6, who seem to have assumed that it was specially prepared for Astley. It is, however, a reissue of the 'Commission Touching the Powers of the Master' issued to Tyllney in 1581, printed in Feuillerat, 51–2, and to Buc in 1603 (see Eccles, 444).

A4 Inner Temple MS 515, no. 7, f. 59^v. 'Mr Buck' was presumably a male relative of the insane Sir George. Clearly each new Master of the Revels expected to take over the records of his predecessors.

A5 Extract from PRO E403/2562/61. Buc's warrant of 1621 is declared void, and the residue of £301 assigned to Astley. For other copies see PSO2/50 no. 17 and SO3/7, May 1622 (summary only).

become disabled and insufficient to vndergoe and performe o^r. service in the said Office of M^r of the Revells wch office we have conferred vppon Sr John Ashley knight . . .

29 July 1622. (*Reversionary grant of Master's place to William Painter*)
A6 This bill conteyneth yor ma^{tes} graunte vnto Willm Payneter esq^r, during his life of the office of Maister of yor ma^{tes} revells in revertion after Sr John Ashley knight, and Beniamin Jonson gent and is agreable in substance wth the former patentes.

Signified to be yor ma^{tes} pleasure by Sr Edward Powell.

Thomas Coventrye

31 July 1622. (*Petition from William Honninge to Cranfield*)
A7 *To the right ho^{ble} the Lord Cranfeild Lord high Threasurer of England*
The humble peticon of William Honninge Clarke of his Maties Revells and Tents
Shewinge y^t whereas he havinge served fforty yeares the late Queene Elizabeth of famous memory, as also our now most gratious Soveraigne, havinge consumed in followinge the Court to p⟨er⟩forme his s^{r}vice most p⟨ar⟩te of his portion wch was left him, hopinge y^t his Office would haue mayntayned him the remaynder of his life/
But now in theis latter yeares in regard the best parte of ye said Office, and ye officers lodgings in St Johns house, by his Maties graunt hath byn taken away from vs: Besides ye longe tarryeing wthout paym^t of our Allowances & disbursm^{ts} due, of wch wee are behind ffower yeares in both ye Offices, wch makes him hazard both his Credit & bonds/
Hee therefore humblie beseecheth yor Lo^{pp} y^t in yor Ho^{ble} Comisseracon & pittie yor Lo^{pp} wilbe pleased to vouchsafe to releive him wth some p⟨ar⟩te wch is due, whereby he may make paym^t to his deare friend to whome he standeth indebted for 2 yeares bord, and to preserve his Credit in other places where he likewyse standeth indebted, so y^t thereby he shalbe the better inabled to discharge his s^{r}vice to his Highnes, And he will daylie pray for yor Honno^{rs} long health & p⟨ro⟩speritie/
(*Endorsed*:) Rd 31. July. 1622 Wm Honing Clark of the Revelles

A6 PRO SP39/14/42. The bulk of the document is in Latin, and much of it is taken up with a rehearsal of earlier grants. This note in English occurs at the end. The brief summary in SO3/7, July 1622, has the word 'stayed' in the margin.
A7 Kent Archive Office, U269/1 OE367. Honninge died at the end of 1622 without receiving his money, which was paid to his executors several years later (*MSC* xiii. 85–6, 139, 146).

20 Nov. 1622. (*Warrant by Pembroke as Lord Chamberlain supporting Sir John Astley*)

A8   The Copy of a warrant signed by the right Honorable the Earle of Penbrooke Lo: Chamberlaine to his Matie

To all Maiors Sheriffs Iustices of peace Baliffs Constables & other his Maties officers true leigemen & Subiects whome yt may concerne & eu⟨er⟩y of them, whereas I am credibly informed that there are many & very great disorders & abuses daily comitted by diu⟨er⟩se & sundry Companyes of Stage players Tumblers vaulters Dauncers on the Ropes And also by such as goe about wth motions & Shewes & other the like kinde of p⟨er⟩sons by reason of certaine grants Comissions & lycences wch they haue by secret meanes p⟨ro⟩cured both from the kings Matie & also from diu⟨er⟩se noblemen by vertue whereof they do abusiuely Clayme vnto themselues a kinde of licentious fredome to travell aswell to shew play & exercise in eminent Cities & Corporacions w^{th}in this kingdome as also from place to place w^{th}out the knowledge & approbacon of his Ma^{tes} office of the Revels & by that meanes doe take vpon them at their owne pleasure to act & sett forth in many places of this kingdome diu⟨er⟩se & sundry playes & shewes wch for the most p⟨ar⟩t are full of scandall & offence both against the Church & State & doe lykewise greatly abuse their authority in lendinge lettinge & sellynge their said Comissions & lycences to others by reason whereof diu⟨er⟩se lawles & wandringe p⟨er⟩sons are suffered to haue free passage vnto whome such grants & lycences were neu⟨er⟩ intended contrary to his ma^{tes} pleasure & the lawes of this land his ma^{tes} grant & Comission to the master of the Revells & the first institucon of the said office Theise are therefore in his ma^{tes} name straightly to chardge & comand yo^u & eu⟨er⟩y of yo^u that whosoeu⟨er⟩ shall repaire to any of yor Cityes Borowes Townes Corporate viliges hamlets or p⟨ar⟩ishes & shall shewe or p⟨re⟩sent any play shew motion feats of actiuity & sights whatsoeu⟨er⟩ not hauinge a lycence nowe in force vnder the hand & seale of office of Sr Iohn Ashly knight now m^r of his ma^{tes} office of the Revells or vnder the hand of his Deputy & sealed likewise wth the seale of office that yo^u & eu⟨er⟩y of yo^u at all tymes foreu⟨er⟩ hereafter doe sease & take away eu⟨er⟩y such grant patent Comission or lycence whatsoeu⟨er⟩ from the bringer or bearer thereof & that yo^u forthw^{th} cause the said grant or lycence to be conveyed & sent to his ma^{tes} office of the Revells there to remayne at the disposicon of the m^r of the said office And that to the vtmost of yor power yo^u doe forbid & suppresse all such playes shewes motions feates of actiuity sights & eu⟨er⟩y of them vntill

A8 MCB 2, f. 31^{r−v}; also *Norwich*, 188–9. It is described as a 'printed warrant' which was shown to the court by the player Gilbert Reason, but no copy of it is recorded in *STC*. Sir Henry arranged for the document to be reissued in his own name on 31 July 1661 (see **R28**).

they shalbe approved lycenced & authorised by the said Sr Iohn Ashely
or his said Deputy in mann⟨er⟩ aforesaid who are appointed by his ma^tie
vnder the greate seale of England to that end & purpose Herein fayle
not as yo^u will answer the contrary at yor p⟨er⟩ills / And for yor more
Certayntety I advise yo^u to take an exact Copy of this my mandate, Gyven
vnder my hand at whitehall the 20th day of November Anno Dni 1622
(*In left margin:*) The copy of a warrant signed by the Lord Chamberlyn
touchinge Players

1623

24/5 Feb. 1622/3. (*Petition of William Painter to Cranfield*)

A9   Right honor:^ble
The true affection of my hart to yor Lord:^p & ye iustnes of my cause
encourageth me to this boldnes, thus occasioned, Since his Ma^ty was
graciously pleased to discharge my lands of an vniust burthen vnder w^ch
my ancesters & my selfe long suffered, I petitioned that in his royall
Justice & charitye for ye 800^li vnduely leuied & of my great charge of
many yeares suite in redress therof his Matie would be pleased to bestowe
on me the next Reuersion of the M^r of the Reuels place, after Sr John
Ashley & Ben Johnson, wch his Matie very graciously assented vnto, And
bycause the place had relation to my Lord Chamberlaine I desiered S^r
Edward Powell ye m^r of Requests to goe with me to my Lord & to
acquaint his Lo:^p wth his Ma^ts pleasure & my duetifull respect, before I
carried ye warr^t to m^r Attourney, wch his Lo^p tooke very well & fairly
gaue way to, when I proceeded with my Bill & obteyned his Ma^ts royall
signature thervnto, & had the same filed at ye Signet office, & presented
to m^r Secretary Caluert, who refused to seale it bycause his Matie had
giuen especiall order to stay all Reuersions, wch restraint was conceiued
to endure but a while, & I confident of my fair proceding thought my
self secure, till lately I vnderstood that my Lo: Chamblaine disclaimed
any notice therof, and in the interim whilst I addressed my self to giue
his ho:^r satisfaction, one of his Servants hath preuailed with him to
comend a newe graunt in his behalf to his Ma:^tie that should pass ye seales
before myne, & thus whilst I should waite his ho:^rs pleasure to surprise
me, and since his Lop:^s cominge to towne (keepeing his chamber) I was
forced to press vnto him and to require right at his hands, whom I finde
much enclyning to his Servant, yet like him self very noble & hath
retayned this busines into his consideration, his S^rvant haveing no coullor
to confirme himself, but that ye place is meerly in his Lords guift, & that
I should therby offer his Lo: such an affront as neuer Lord Chamberlyn
suffered, and therfore confident to be my competitor though the thing be
little worth it. Now my humble request to yor ho^r is that you would

A9 Kent Archive Office, U269/1 OE560.

spedily moue my Lo: for me, & to acquaint his Lo:ᴾ how equitable yoʳ honoʳ knowes my case to be, In wᶜʰ fauour you will raise my credit to yᵉ life, & saue me from such disgrace as I would not for tenne tymes the valewe vndergoe, So wᵗʰ my due prayers for yoʳ hoʳˢ life & happines, I remayne

ffaithfully at yo.ʳ ho:ʳˢ dispose.

Will: Payneter.

Sᵗ Johns streate
25ᵗʰ of febr. 1622:
(*Endorsed in a different hand*:) Rd 24. (*sic*) Febr: 1622 Mʳ Paynter to my Lo; for speaking with my Lo: Chamberlaine, touching his Patent of Mʳ of the Revells in Reversion.

28 Feb. 1622/3. (*Letter from Sir Edward Conway to Pembroke*)
A10 Newmarkett   February 1622
28 *Lo: Chamberlen* Concerninge the Bill sent by his Lp. to haue signed contayninge a Graunt in reversion of the place of Mʳ. of the Revells, to Mʳ. *Thorrowgoode*

2 Mar. 1622/3. (*Letter from Pembroke to Sir Edward Conway*)
A11 Good Mʳ Secretary,
I would not haue used an other hand vnto you, if then I could haue used mine owne, neither would I originally haue presented a reuersion to be signed by his Maᵗⁱᵉ howeuer belonging to my place; but that his Maᵗⁱᵉ hath bene pleased vppon a motion of a Master of the requests to pass this very thing to one painter; but that I getting notice of it, stopt it at the Seales as belonging to my place. Now I beseech you represent it barely to his Maᵗⁱᵉˢ iudgment, what the world may think, when they shall find his Maᵗⁱᵉ hath denyed me, for a place in mine owne guift, which he hath allready past vnder his hand to one whose face he neuer saw, nor euer receaud one houres seruice from him; the man I haue recomended I will answer for wᵗʰ my reputation; for the rest I wholy leaue it to his Maᵗⁱᵉ acknowledging my self Infinitely beholding to you for yoʳ respect, wᶜʰ I will euer striue to deserve by vnfaynedly remaining

yoʳ most affectionate
frend to Comaunde

Whitehall this 2. of March   Pembroke

3 Mar. 1622/3. (*Letter from Pembroke to the Stationers' Company*)
A12 This Daie a letter from my lord Chamberlayne was openly read to all the Master Printers concerning the lycensing of Playes &c by Sʳ. John Ashley, The Copie whereof is in the booke of letters.

A10 PRO SP14/214/6 (Conway's letter-book); *CSPD 1619–23*, 503.
A11 PRO SP14/139/18; inaccurate summary in *CSPD 1619–23*, 508.
A12 Stationers' Company Archives, Court Book C, f. 76; printed in W. A. Jackson, *Records of the Court of the Stationers' Company 1602 to 1640* (1947), 155. The full text of the letter has not been traced.

21 Mar. 1622/3. (*Letter from Sir Edward Conway to Pembroke*)

A13 Newmarkett   March 1622/3
21 *Lo: Chamberlein* A Bill sent by his *Lp*. to bee signed for a reversion
of the *M*.^{r} of Revells place and refused by the Kinge.

30 Mar. 1623. (*Petition from Robert Wright to Cranfield*)

A14 *To the right hon.*^{ble} *Lionell Earle of Middlesex*
Lord high Treasurer of England
The humble peticon of Robert wright
Sheweth, That yor pet.^{r} having often solicited yor lo^{pp} by his peticons
and otherwise for the some of 19.^{li} 16.^{s} appearing due vnto him,
wherevnto yor lo^p was pleased to giue ord (*sic*) answere, That such order
should bee taken therein as was fitting
fforasmuch as yor petr hath long attended and noe course taken with
him Humblie craveth that it would please yor Lo^{pp} to giue order for his
satisfaccon without further troubling yor Honor, And hee shall dailie
pray &c
(*Endorsed:*) Rd 30 March 1623 Robert Wright for 19–16–0 due to him

9 May 1623. (*Petition from workmen of the revels to Cranfield*)

A15 To the righte hon:^{ble} the Earle of Midd: Lo: high Tresorer of England.
The humble peticon of his Maties Servaunts and many others, poore
Artificers & Workmen in the office of the Revells.
Humblie sheweth vnto yor Lo.^{p} that Whereas there was due vnto yor
peticoners from his ma.^{tie} for wagis, Stuffe, and workmanshippe in the
office of the Revells on the accompte taken by the Auditors for 2 yeares
ended ye last of October 1617 the sume of 701.^{li} as appeares by privie
Seale remayninge in the hands of Sr Rob: Pye, Whereof there remaynes
201.^{li} yet vnpayde; and alsoe that they are for 5 succeedinge yeares more
behinde not yet accompted for.
    Theire moste humble peticon vnto Yo^r good Lo.^{p} is, that out of yor noble
and Charitable disposicon you will be pleased to Commaunde paym^t. of y^e
sayd sume of 201.^{li} to releive yor poore peticoners theire wives and Children
wch in this deare and miserable time are readie to sterve for wante of foode.
And they as in duty most bounde shall ever pray for yor Lo.^{p}
(*In a different hand, possibly Cranfield's:*)
        Chelsey   May: 1623:
Sr Robert Pye.   Let an order be made for paym^t
of the some of   in parte of
the CCj^{li}. arere vpon the Privy seale abouemencond.
(*Endorsed:*) Rd. 9. May. 1623. Artificers of the office of Revells for 201.^{li}.
arere.   Mr Hunt.

A13 PRO SP14/214/17 (Conway's letter-book); *CSPD 1619–23*, 534.
A14 Kent Archive Office, U269/1 OE817.
A15 Kent Archive Office, U269/1 OE602. See Eccles, 481.

1628

9 July 1628. (*Agreement between Sir Henry and other officers of the revels*)
A16 Whereas S[r] Henry Harbert knight M[r]. of his Ma[ties] Reuells, for the
obtaynem[t] of two hundred pounds, hath disbursed in fees and Gratuities
the some of Twent⟨y⟩ five pound sixteene shillings & eightpence and
likewise formerly for the getting of five hundred pounds hath disbursed
seueral⟨l⟩ somes of mony in ffees & gratuities \ouer & aboue what is
allowed him vppon the seu[r]all accounts/ w[ch] we the Rest of the Officers
do promise to beare every man his part proportionally according to the
moneys [they] \we/ haue and are seuerally to Receaue in wittnes we
haue here vnto sett our hands this 9[th] of July 1628./

> A Stafford
> Jo: Wytton
> Wllm Hunt

(*Endorsed*:) The offisers of y[e] Reuells noate for the payment of such
monies vnto mee as haue byn disbursed for their benefit

1631

Dec. 1631. (*Reservation of the Master's powers in a company licence*)
A17 *Prouided alwaies* and our will & pleasure is that all authority, power,
priviledge and profitt whatsoever belonging or properly apperteyning to
the Master of the Revells in respect of his office, And every Article and
graunt conteyned within the lres Patents or Comission w[ch] hath been
heretofore graunted or directed by our late deere father or our selfe to
our welbeloved servant S[r] Henry Harbert knight Master of the said
Revells, shall remaine and abide in full force effect and virtue and in as
ample sort as if theis our letters had never been made.

A16 Document inserted in Burn, 177. Burn does not say how he obtained it, but it
shows every sign of being authentic. The endorsement is in Herbert's hand; Stafford
was the Clerk-Comptroller of the Revells, Wytton the Clerk, and Hunt the Yeoman.
A17 Extract from a draft of a licence for Andrew Cane and his company, BL Add.
Charter 9291. This is not dated, but the summary in PRO SO3/10 is entered under
Dec. 1631. For similar reservations to earlier Masters see *MSC* i. 269, 271, 273–4, 275,
276–7, and 280.

APPENDIX B.

Licences Issued by Herbert or his Deputies

April–May 1624 (*William Perry and Company*)

B1 To all Mayo^rs Sheriffs Iust⟨ic⟩es of peace Bayleiffs Constables Head
Bouroughes and all other his Mattes officers true legmen (*sic*) and Subiectes
and to every of them greetinge Knowe yee that where as the kingis most
Excellent Matie hath graunted to the M^r of the Revells a Commission
vnder the great Seale of England giuing there by Charg Wth full power
and Authoretye to the said M^r of the Revells and his deputie for the
orderinge Reforminge Authorisinge and Puttinge downe of all and everye
Playes Players and Playemakers as of all other shewes whatsoever in all
places wthin his maties Realme of England as well wthin ffranchises and
liberties as wthout And where as it hath pleased the kinges most Excellent
Matie by his Hignes Grant Vnder his hand and Signett Bearing date of
the last day of October in the ffiftenth yeare of his Raigne of England
ffrance and Ireland and of Scotland the one and ffifteth Subscribed by the
Right Honorable the Earle of Pembrocke Lord Chamberlayne of his Ma^{tes}
Houshold to giue and Graunt Licence and Authoretye Vnto William
Perry and the Rest of his associattes to prouide and keepe and bring vp a
Convenient Number of youthes and Children and them to practize and
Exc⟨er⟩size in the Qualetye of Playinge by the Name of Children of the
Revells To the Late Queene Anna as p⟨e⟩r the said grant doth more at
large appeare. I haue alowed and confirmed and by these p^rsentes doe
allow and confirme thaforsaid grant Vnder his Matie Royall hand and
Signett to bee and continew Vnto the said William Perrie and his
associates (Viz^{tt}.) George Bosegraue Ric^d. Backster Thomas Band Iames
Iones Walter Barrett Iames Kneller and E\d/ward Tobye and the Rest
of there companie not Exceeding the nu⟨m⟩ber of Twentye from the daye
of the date of these p^rsentes for and during the Terme and space of one
whole yeare in and by all thinges accordinge to the Tenor effect and True
meaning of his ma^{tie}. graunt and what Companie soever shall Repai\r/e
Vnto any of yor Townes Corporatt Cittyes or Bouroughes not havinge

B1 Exeter City Archives, Letter-Book 60D, letter 267. Transcript also in *Devon*,
192–3. Sir Henry's confirmation of William Perry's royal warrant of 31 Oct. 1617 was
entered into the Exeter city records by the town clerk, Samuel Izack, as a permanent
record of what Sir Henry expected them to do.

there Authoreties Confirmed by me and Sealed wth the Seale of the office
of the Revalls that forth wth yo^u seize any such graunt or Comission and
send it to mee accordinge to those Warrants directed to yo^u heretofor by
The Right Honorable The Lord Chamberlaine. Given att his ma^{ttes}. office
of The Revells Vnder my hand and The Seale of the Said office the Nynth
daie of Aprill in the yeare of the Raigne of o^r Sou⟨er⟩ainge Lord Iames by
the grace of god Kinge of England ffrance and Ireland king defender of
the ffaith &c. the Two and Twenteth and of Scotland The Seuen and
ffifteth Ann°. Domin. 1624

ex^a & concord. 31°. Maij. 1624.   Iames Tucker
p⟨er⟩ me Sam: Izacke, cler.   HHerbert   Tristram Michell
Wm Winkle

1630 (*John Jones and company*)

B2 To all Mayors Sheriffes Iustices of the peace Bayliffes Co⟨ . . . ⟩and all other
his ma^{ties} officers true Leigemen and subiectes and to eu⟨er⟩y of them
greeting know yee that whereas the kinges most excellent ma^{tie} hath
graunted vnto the ⟨master⟩ ⟨. . .⟩ Commission vnder the greate Seale of
England Giveing thereby charge wth full power and authoritie to the
Master of the Revells and his deputy for the order⟨ing⟩ ⟨. . .⟩ and
putteing downe of all & eu⟨er⟩y Playes Players & Playmakers As of all
other shewes whatsoever in all places wthin his ma^{ties} Realme of England
aswell w⟨. . .⟩ as wthout I have by these p⟨rese⟩ntes lycenced and
authorised Iohn Iones Anne his wief Richard Payne Richard Iones and
their assistance To sett forth and shewe⟨. . .⟩ Motion wth dyvers storyes
in ytt As alsoe tumbleing vaulteing sleight of hand and other such like
feates of Activety Requyreing you and eu⟨er⟩y of you ⟨in⟩ ⟨. . .⟩ suffer
and p⟨er⟩mytt the said Iohn Iones Anne his wief Richard Payne Richard
Iones and their assistantes quietly to passe and to try their said shewes wth
⟨. . .⟩ Trumpettes as they or any of them shall thinke fitteing for the
same from tyme to tyme and att all tyme & tymes wthout any of yor letts

B2 Worcestershire Quarter Sessions archives, 110: 55/31 BA 1, printed in *Worcestershire County Records: Calendar of the Quarter Sessions Papers*, vol. i, *1591–1643*, ed.
J. W. Willis Bund (Worcester, 1900), 470. John Jones of the parish of St Michael in
Bedwardine, Worcestershire, labourer, was indicted at Worcester in 1630 for having
given a performance at Upton on Severn on 24 June 1629 using a spurious licence in
the name of Sir Henry Herbert; the indictment, in Latin, includes a copy of the licence.
The document is very severely damaged, and the right-hand side and much of the
centre have vanished. The second half of the licence is so fragmentary that it has not
been reproduced, but the surviving portions closely follow the wording of the next
licence, **B3**. The language of the licence is authentic, and possibly Jones borrowed a
genuine licence and copied it. For John Jones and Richard Jones see Bentley, ii. 485–7.
Full transcripts of both Latin and English are given in *Herefordshire, Worcestershire*,
394–5, with a translation of the Latin, 567–8.

having their authority imediately from me or confirmed by me and Sealed with the Seale of the Office of the Revells that forthwith you take from them any Grant or comission whatsoeuer they beare and send it to mee according to the Warrants of former Lord Chamberlaynes and the present warrant of the R^t Honble Edwarde Earle of Manchester Lo: Chamberlayne of his Maj^s Household.

Provided that they or any of them do not acte any thing offensiue against the Laws of God or of the land And that they make shew on lawful times with Exception of the Lord's Day or any other Day in the Tyme of Divine Service or any Day prohibited by proclamation or other lawful authority And this Lycence to continue for the Space of Twelve Months and not longer from the Day of the date hereof And to serve throughout his Ma^s Realme of Englande upon the conditions aforesaid Given at his Ma^s office of the Revells under my hand and the Seale of the said office the first Day of August in the Fourteenthe yeare of the Reigne of our Sovereign Lorde Charles the Second, by the Grace of God of England Scotland France and Ireland King, Defender of the Faith etc. And in the yeare of our Lorde God one thousand six hundred sixty and two.

January 1662/3 (*George Jolly and company*)

To all Mayors Sherifs Iustices of ye peace Baylifs Constables headborroughs and all other his Maties Officers true Liege men louing Subjects and to euery of them greeting know ye that wheras George Jolly hath desired an Authority from me to raise a Company of Stage playo^rs to act Comedies Tragedies Trage-Comedies pastoralls and enterludes throughout Eng: These are therefore (by uertue of a Grant made unto me under the Seale of England) to authorize and license ye sd G. Jolly to raise a company of Stage players or less to act Comedies &c throughout England with exception onely to ye Cities of London and Westm: and the suburbs of each respectiue city requiring you ye sd Sheriffs Iustices of ye peace, Bayliffes, Constables, Headboroughs and all other his Maties officers in his Maties name to permitt and suffer ye sd company quietly to pass without any of your letts and molestacons and to bee aiding and assisting them or any of them if any wrong or iniury bee offered them or any of them you affording them some conuenient place as aforesaid and to continue in any one place during ye space of 40 days, and what company soeuer either Stage playo^rs musicians, mountebanks, or such as go about with monsters and strange Sights shall repaire unto any of y^r cities towns corporate hamlets or villages, not hauing their authority immediately from me or confirmed by mee and sealed with ye seale of ye office of ye reuells, that forthwith you take from ym any grant or Commission whatsoeuer

B7 PRO SP44/48/6a–7; Hotson, 405; Milhous–Hume, 183.

or molesta⟨cons⟩ w^th⟨. . .⟩ places of Iurisdiccon Townes Corporate Citties or Buroughes whatsoever w^thin the Realme of England They behaveing themselves ho⟨. . .⟩

29 August 1631 (*Sisley* [*?Cicely*] *Peadle and company*)

B3 To all Maiors, Sheriffes, Iustices of the Peace, Bayliffes, Constables, Headborroughes and all other his Ma:^ties Officers, true Leigemen and Subiects and to euery of them *Greeting* **Knowe yee** that whereas the Kings most Excellent Ma:^tie hath graunted vnto the Master of the Revells a Comission vnder the great Seale of England, Giveing thereby charge wth full power and authoritie to the said Master of the Revells and his Deputie for the ordering Reformeing authorizing and putting downe of all and euery playes, Players and Playmakers as of all other Shewes whatsoeuer in all places w^thin his Ma:^ties Realme of England aswell w^thin ffranchises and Liberties as w^thout **I haue** by these p⟨rese⟩ntes Licensed and authorized Sisley Peadle; Thomas Peadle her sonne Elias Grundling and three more in theire Company to vse and exercise Daunceing on the Roapes, Tumbling, Vaulting and other such like ffeates which they or any of them are practized in or can performe **Requireing** you and euery of you in his Ma:^ties name to suffer and p⟨er⟩mitt them the said Sisley Peadle; Thomas Peadle, Elias Grundling and theire said assotiats quietly to passe and to sett forth and shewe those things before menconed wth such musicke Drume or Trumpetts as they shall thinke fitting for the same ffrom time to time and att all time and times w^thout any of your Letts or molestacions w^thin any of your Liberties and places of Iurisdiccon Townes Corporate Citties or Borroughes wheresoeuer w^thin the Realme of England, and alsoe to be aydeing and assisting vnto them if any wrong or Iniury shall be offered vnto them or any of them They behaueing themselues honestly and according to the Lawes of this Realme and forbearing to make shewe on the Saboth day Or in the time of Devine service *you* affording them your Townehalls, Mootehalls, Guildhalls or some convenient place to shewe in **And** what Company soeuer eyther Stage Players or such as make shewe of mocons and strange Sights shall repaire vnto any of your Townes Corporate, Citties Boroughes or Villages not haueing theire authoritie ymediatlie from me or confirmed by me and Sealed wth the Seale of the Office of the Revells That forthw^th you seize and take from them any Graunt or Comission whatsoeuer they beare and send yt to me According to those Warrants directed to you the Mayors, Sheriffes, Iustices of the Peace, Bayliffes Constables of all Townes Corporate, Citties, Boroughes or Villages heretofore by the right Hono:^ble the Lord *Chamberlaine* of the *Kings Ma:^ties* most Hono:^ble household **And**

B3 In the possession of E. J. Winnington-Ingram, Esq. For the Peadle family of tumblers and rope-dancers see above, 80 n. 15.

if you find any traveyling w^{th}out License That forthwith you apprehend and imprison them or give them such condigne punishment as in yor discretions they shall deserue **prouided** that this License continue in force but for and dureing the terme and space of one whole yeare and noe longer next ensueing the date hereof **Giuen** att his Ma:^{ties} Office of the Revells vnder my hand and the Seale of the said Office the nyne and twentieth daie of August In the Seaventh yeare of the Raigne of our most gracious Sou⟨er⟩aigne Lord *Charles* by the grace of God King of England Scotland ffraunce and Ireland defender of the faith etc Annoq^e Dni One thousand sixe hundred thirtie one.

Henry Herbert.

August 1636 (*Francisco [no Surname] and Thomas Finochello*)

B4 ⟨?I⟩t Hath pleased his Gratious Matie: to grante liberty to Francisco ⟨. . .⟩ ⟨?pra⟩ctice the Game called 1 Occa di Catalonia. Thes are to ⟨. . .⟩ whom It may concerne not to moleste or disturbe the said ⟨. . .⟩ [wth the] or Thomas Finochello wth two servants [to] ⟨. . .⟩ ⟨?the⟩ire Game called 1 Occa di Catalonia. And this shall ⟨. . .⟩ ent warrant In that behalfe. given at ye Office of the ⟨. . .⟩ August In ye twelue yeare of his Ma^{tes}. Reigne
HH

14 April 1662 (*George Bayley and company*)

B5 To all Mayo^{rs} Sherriffs Justices of the Peace Bayliffs Constables Headborroughs and all other his Maties. Officers true Leigmen & loueing Subiects & to euery of them Greeting. Know yee that wheras George Bayley of London Musitioner desires of me a Placard to make Shew of a Play called Noahs fflood wth other Seuerall Scenes These are therfore by Vertue of his Maties. Lett^{rs} Patents made ouer vnto me vnder the great seale of England to license & allow the said George Bayley wth. eight seruants wch are of his Company to make shew of the said Play called Noahs flood wth. other Scenes requireing you and euery of you in his Maties. Name to p⟨er⟩mitt and suffer the said Persons to shew the said Play called Noahs flood & to be aiding & assisting them & euery of them if any wrong or iniury be offered vnto him or any of them Provided that he & they doe not act any thing offensiue against ye lawes of God or of the Land and that he & they doe make Shew of the said Noahs flood at lawfull times wth Exception of the Lords Day or any other Day in the time of Devine

---

B4 Inserted into Burn, 185, with no indication of its origin. A triangular portion on the left-hand side has vanished. The name of the game appears to mean 'the Catalonian goose'; how it is played is not known.

B5 Guildhall MS 2833. Milhous–Hume, 129. On 26 Apr. and 18 June 1662 the Lord Chamberlain issued warrants for the arrest of Poyntz for issuing commissions without authority, **R**32 and **36**.

Service or one any other day prohibited by Procla[m] Authority And this Licence to continue for a year day of the date hearof and to serve throughout the Scotland & Ireland & all other his Maties. Territo[ry] said Geo: Bayly haueing giuen me security for h hee doe not intrench vpon the lawes of the land G of the Revells vnder my hand & seale of the said day of Aprill one thousand six hundred sixty & tw year of the raigne of o^r Soueraigne Lord Charles of god of England Scotland ffrance & Ireland king

(*In left-hand margin, at right angle to main text:*)
You are to allow him either Town hall Guild hall other convenient place for his vse & to continue space of fforty Daies.

1 August 1662 (*William Lyde and company*)

B6 To all Mayors Sherriffes Justices of the Pea[ce] Headboroughs and all others his Ma^{ys} officers Subjects and to every of them Greeting—Know Lyde hath desired an Authority from me to make containing Twelve Blanks to a Prize These are Grant made unto me under the Great Seale of Lycense the said William Lyde to make sh containin^g twelve Blanks to a Prize with Music are of his company Requiring you the said Ma the Peace Bayliffes Constables & Headboroug[hs] Officers in his Ma^{es} name to Permitt and suffe to pass w^{th}out any of your letts and Molestatio[n] assisting unto them and any of them if any w them or any of them You affording them y Guild halls Schoolhouses or some other conve[nient] to continue in any one Place during the Spac[e] company soeuer—Eyther Stage-players Musiti as goe about with Motions and Strange Sight your Cityes Universities Townes Corporate,

---

B6 From a copy made by the Revd Joseph Hunter, B According to Hunter 'it is from a parchment cover of a[...] Sir H. Herbert'; this book has not been located. On 9 allowed 'to make shew of his Blank booke according to but the next year, 11 Sept. 1663, he was fined £2 for h an vnlawfull game, and contrary to the Statutes in tha 82^v and 105).

they beare and send it to mee according to ye warrts of former Ld Chamberlains and ye present warr[ts] of the Right honoble Edw: E of Manchester: Ld Chamberlaine of his Ma[ties] houshold prouided that they or any of ym do not act any thing offensiue against ye laws of god or ye land and y[t] they act as aforesaid at lawfull times with ye exception of ye Lds day or any other day in ye time of publique diuine Services or on any day prohibited by proclamation: or other lawfull authority and this license to continue in force during the terme of my life. Given at his Maties office of ye reuells under my hand and the seale of ye sd office ye 1st day of Jan: in ye 14th year of ye raigne of Our Soueraigne Ld K Ch 2 by ye Grace of God K &c in ye year of Our Ld 1662.

(*In left margin opposite first line*: 'Players license'; *opposite seventh line*: 'M[r] of Reuels')

APPENDIX C.

Printing Licences Issued by Astley, Herbert, and Herbert's Deputies

The material in this appendix is taken mostly from Arber, Eyre, and Greg's *Bibliography*. Licences recorded in the office-book (abbreviated OB) are also included. The full entry is given only where there is something unusual about it, and play-titles have been modernized. In some cases the licences were printed in the book itself, and these have been quoted in full here.

SIR JOHN ASTLEY

20 January 1622/3
C1 Philip Massinger, *The Duke of Milan* (SR)

3 March 1622/3
See A12

3 September 1623
C2 'A Booke of Iiggs conteyning three books or partes' (not identified) (SR)

SIR HENRY HERBERT

12 March 1623/4
C3 Philip Massinger, *The Bondman* (OB, SR)

15 May 1624
C4 Anon., *Nero* (published in 1624, but not entered in SR until 24 Oct. 1633; previously licensed by Sir George Buc, 10 Apr. 1607) (OB)

2 July 1624
C5 Thomas Drue, *The Duchess of Suffolk* (not in SR until 13 Nov. 1629; published 1631) (OB)

29 December 1624
C6 'The Masque book' (= Ben Jonson, *The Fortunate Isles*. Not in SR) (OB)

7 November 1627
C7 Henry Reynolds, *Torquato Tasso's Aminta Englished* (SR)

27 February 1627/8
C8 Robert Gomersall, *The Tragedy of Lodovick Sforza, Duke of Milan* (SR)

2 June 1629
C9 John Ford, *The Lover's Melancholy* (SR)

13 November 1629
See 2 July 1624

1 January 1629/30
C10 Sir William Davenant, *The Colonel* (probably the play published as *The Siege* in 1673, Bentley, iii. 215–16) (SR)

10 January 1629/30
C11 Sir William Davenant, *The Cruel Brother* (SR)
C12 Sir William Davenant, *The Just Italian* (SR)

26 February 1629/30
C13 Henry Chettle, *Hoffman* (SR)
C14 James Shirley, *The Grateful Servant* (SR)

27 February 1629/30
C15 *The Spanish Bawd* (= James Mabbe's trans. of Fernando de Rojas, *Celestina*) (SR)

22 March 1629/30
C16 Philip Massinger, *The Renegado* (SR)

26 March 1630
C17 Thomas Randolph, *Aristippus* (SR)
C18 Thomas Randolph, *The Conceited Pedlar* (SR)

8 April 1630
C19 Thomas Middleton, *A Chaste Maid in Cheapside* (SR)
C20 Robert Davenport, *The Pedlar* (SR)

16 April 1630
C21 *The Battle of the Affections, or Love's Loadstone* (published anon. as *Pathomachia, or the Battle of the Affections*) (SR)

29 June 1630
C22 Thomas Dekker, *The Honest Whore, Part II* (previously licensed by Sir George Buc on 29 Apr. 1608) (SR)

20 July 1630
C23 George Ruggle, *Ignoramus* (previously entered on 18 Apr. 1615) (SR)

13 September 1630
C24 John Hacket, *Loyola* (SR)

8 November 1630
C25 Thomas Dekker, *Match Me in London* (SR)

16 November 1630
C26 'an abstract of the histories of . . . Queene Elizabeth by M. Parker and a short chronicle of the kinges' (= Martin Parker, *An Abstract of the History of . . . Queen Elizabeth*, STC 19217.5) (SR)

25 February 1630/1
C27 James Shirley, *The School of Compliment* (SR)

17 April 1631
C28 Ben Jonson, *The New Inn* (SR)

25 April 1631
C29 Phineas Fletcher, *Sicelides* (SR)

16 May 1631
C30 Thomas Dekker, *The Wonder of a Kingdom* (re-entered SR, 24 Feb. 1635/6 and published 1636) (SR)
C31 Thomas Dekker, *The Noble Spanish Soldier* (re-entered SR, 9 Dec. 1633 and published in 1634) (SR)

18 May 1631
C32 George Chapman, *Caesar and Pompey* (SR)

16 June 1631
C33 Thomas Heywood, *The Fair Maid of the West, Parts I and II* (SR)

7 September 1631
C34 Thomas Goffe, *The Courageous Turk, or Amurath the First* (SR)
C35 Thomas Goffe, *The Raging Turk, or Bajazet the Second* (SR)

28 September 1631
C36 Edmund Stubbe, *Fraus Honesta* (SR)

12 November 1631
C37 'a Booke called a fflora show at Norwich' (= Ralph Knevet, *Rhodon and Iris. A Pastorall, As it was Presented at the Florists Feast in Norwich, May 3. 1631.*) (SR)

19 November 1631
C38 Philip Massinger, *The Emperor of the East* (SR)

24 November 1631
C39 William Rowley, *A New Wonder, A Woman Never Vexed* (SR)

16 January 1631/2
C40 Philip Massinger, *The Maid of Honour* (SR)

26 January 1631/2

C41 **John Groue** Entred for his Copy vnder the hands of S^r. Henry Herbert & Mr Smethwicke warden a [Playbrooke *sic*] \Comedy/ called the Leaguer (the reformacons [cros not being] \to be/ strictly obserued may be printed not otherwise) expressed by thaforesaid wordes by Sr Hen: Herbert (= Shakerly Marmion, *Holland's Leaguer*) (SR)

9 February 1631/2

C42 James Shirley, *The Changes, or Love in a Maze* (SR)

24 March 1631/2

C43 Richard Brome, *The Northern Lass* (SR)

30 March 1632

C44 Philip Massinger and Nathan Field, *The Fatal Dowry* (SR)

9 May 1632

C45 William Alabaster, *Roxana* (licence printed on E5 of 1632 edn.: 'Imprimatur; primo die Martii Anno Salutis Nostrae Millesimo Sexentesimo (*sic*) Trigesimo secundo. Per me Henricum Herbert') (SR)

13 June 1632

C46 Peter Hausted, *The Rival Friends* (SR)

20 June 1632

C47 Ovid's *Epistles* (?= 20 Oct. 1632) (OB)

23 June 1632
See 10 Nov. 1632

13 September 1632

C48 '*a booke of verses and Poems* (the five *satires*, the first, second, Tenth, Eleauenth and Thirteenth *Elegies* being excepted) and these before excepted to be his, when he bringe lawfull authority written by Doctor John Dunn' (= Donne, *Poems* (1633), *STC* 7045) (SR)

27 September 1632

C49 William Rowley, *All's Lost by Lust* (SR)

17 October 1632

C50 Fulke Greville, *Poems* (see 10 Nov.) (OB)
C51 Abraham Cowley, *Poems* (see 24 Oct.) (OB)

20 October 1632

C52 Wye Saltonstall, *Ovid's Tristia* (*STC* 18979) (SR)

24 October 1632

C53 Abraham Cowley, *Poetical Blossoms* (*STC* 5906) (SR)

C54 John Donne, *Paradoxes and Problems* (*STC* 7043; licences printed on F1ᵛ, '*These eleuen Paradoxes, may bee printed: this fiue and twentieth of* October, Anno Domini, *one thousand six hundred thirty and two.* Henry Herbert.' and H4ᵛ, '*These ten Problemes, may bee printed: this fiue and twentieth of* October, Anno Domini, *one thousand six hundred thirty and two.* Henry Herbert.' Licences omitted in 2nd edn. of 1633, *STC* 7044) (SR)

31 October 1632
C55 '*The five Satires* written by Doctor Dun these being excepted in his last entrance' (SR)

2 November 1632
C56 Anon., *The Costly Whore* (SR)

9 November 1632
C57 I. S. *A Dialogue of Riches and Honour* (= James Shirley, *A Contention for Honour and Riches*, *STC* 22439) (SR)

10 November 1632
C58 Fulke Greville, *Certain Learned and Elegant Works* (STC 12361; play-licences printed in 1633 edn., '*This Tragedy, called* Alaham, *may bee printed, this* 23. *of Iune* 1632. Henry Herbert', N4, p. 79; and 'This *Tragedie* called Mustapha, may bee printed: Dated the three and twentieth Day of Ivne, in the yeare of our Lord God, one thousand, six hundred, thirty and two. *HENRY HERBERT*', Z4ᵛ, p. 160) (SR)
C59 Philip Massinger, *A New Way to Pay Old Debts*

20 November 1632
C60 Christopher Marlowe, *The Jew of Malta* (SR)

15 January 1632/3
C61 William Rowley, *A Match at Midnight* (SR)
C62 James Shirley, *The Witty Fair One* (licence printed on K4 of 1633 edn., 'This Play, called The Witty Faire One, as it was Acted on the Stage, may be Printed, this 14. of *Ianuary*. 1632. Henry Herbert.') (SR)

17 January 1632/3
C63 Edward May, *Epigrams Divine and Moral* (*STC* 17708) (SR)

21 January 1632/3
C64 John Ford, *Love's Sacrifice* (SR)

19 March 1632/3
C65 James Shirley, *The Bird in a Cage* (SR)

28 March 1633
C66 John Ford, *The Broken Heart* (SR)

15 June 1633
C67 Shakerly Marmion, *A Fine Companion* (SR)

15 July 1633
C68 Thomas Heywood, *The English Traveller* (SR)

1 August 1633
C69 Jasper Fisher, *Fuimus Troes* (SR)

24 October 1633
See 15 May 1624 (this second entry does not mention Herbert)

9 December 1633
See 16 May 1631

24 February 1633/4
C70 **Hugh Beeston**. Entred for his Copy vnder the hands of S^r. Henry Herbert & Mr Aspley warden (observing the Caution in the License) a Tragedy called Perkin Warbecke by Io: fford (SR)

8 April 1634
C71 John Fletcher and William Shakespeare, *The Two Noble Kinsmen* (SR)

17 April 1634
C72 'a book called Bellum gramaticale &c by M^r. Spense' (= Leonard Hutton, *Bellum Grammaticale*) (SR)

28 October 1634
C73 Richard Brome and Thomas Heywood, *The Late Lancashire Witches* (SR)

3 November 1634
C74 James Shirley, *The Traitor* (SR)

19 January 1634/5
C75 Joseph Rutter, *The Shepherd's Holiday* (SR)

7 December 1635
C76 Philip Massinger, *The Great Duke of Florence* (SR)

14 December 1635
C77 The Pastoral of Florimene (= *The Argument of the Pastoral of Florimene, STC* 11095) (OB)

4 February 1635/6
C78 Sir William Davenant, *The Platonic Lovers* (licence printed on A2^v of 1636 edn., 'This Play of The Platonick Lovers, may be Printed this 19. Ianuary, 1635. Henry Herbert') (SR)

C79 Sir William Davenant, *The Wits* (licence printed opposite title-page of some copies of 1636 edn.: '*This Play, called The Witts, as it was Acted without offence, may bee Printed, not otherwise.* 19 Ianuary 1635. Henry Herbert.') (SR)

24 February 1635/6
See 16 May 1631

17 June 1636
C80 Thomas Heywood, *A Challenge for Beauty* (SR)

8 January 1637/8
C81 Sir William Davenant, *Britannia Triumphans* (not entered in SR until 1658, without mention of Sir Henry) (OB)

29 January 1637/8
C82 Joseph Rutter, translation of Corneille's *Le Cid* (licences printed on D4^v: 'This Tragicomedy, called, *The Valiant Cid*, translated out of the French, as it was acted before the King and Queene at Court, may be printed. Henry Herbert. *Janu.* 12. 1637.', and D5, '*Imprimatur.* Tho. Wykes. *Jan.* 26. 1637.') (SR)

24 November 1640 (SR)
25 November 1640 (OB)
C83 John Sadler, *Masquerade du Ciel* (licence printed opposite title-page of 1640 edn.: 'This *Masquarade Du Ciel* may be printed. Henry Herbert. *Novemb.* 24. 1640.')

1 October 1660
C84 Mr of the Revells to license Printing of Playes
In pursuance of a Warrant vnder the hand of Sr Henry Herbert Master of the Revells dat 17 Septemb^r last prohibiting the printing any Playes Tragedies Comedies Trage-Comedies or Pastoralls without his allowance being read. It was Ordered that the Wardens be desired to forbeare to giving their hands & the Clerke is not to Enter any Plaies &c w^thout authority from ye Mr of ye Revells.
(Printed by Williams, 'Licensing', 255, from Court Book D of the Stationers' Company, f. 60^v; Milhous–Hume, 28)

15 June 1663
C85 Thomas Porter, *The Villain* (SR)

4 February 1663/4
(Entered by Herbert in conjunction with his deputy Edward Hayward)
C86 John Dryden, *The Indian Queen* (SR)
C87 Robert Howard, *The Surprisal* (SR)

C88 Edward Howard, *The Usurper* (SR)
C89 Richard Rhodes, *Flora's Vagaries* (SR)

WILLIAM BLAGRAVE

25 June 1634
C90 **Nich: Oakes** Entred for his Copy vnder the hands of [Sr Hen:] M^r. Blagrave deputy to S^r. Henry Herbert & Mr Aspley warden a play called A Maidenhead well lost.   (By Thomas Heywood) (SR)

30 September 1635
C91 Thomas Heywood, *Love's Mistress, or The Queen's Masque* (SR)

6 August 1636
C92 Thomas Nabbes, *Hannibal and Scipio* (SR)
C93 Thomas Nabbes, *Microcosmus* (SR)

THOMAS HERBERT

24 March 1636/7
C94 John Fletcher, *The Elder Brother* (SR)

25 March 1637
C95 Thomas Heywood, *The Royal King and the Loyal Subject* (SR)

13 April 1637
C96 James Shirley, *Hyde Park* (SR)
C97 James Shirley, *The Lady of Pleasure* (SR)
C98 James Shirley, *The Young Admiral* (SR)

22 April 1637
C99 Mary Fage, *Fame's Roll* (*STC* 10667) (SR)

26 April 1637
C100 'J. W.', *The Valiant Scot* (SR)

INDEX

References are given first to page-numbers in the introduction, in ordinary type, and then to document numbers in bold type, in the order in which the documents are printed in this book. Place-names are indexed only if they are associated with players or showmen; acting companies and theatres are included only if they are explicitly named in the documents. The main entries for players and other theatrical personnel follow the form of the name used in vol. ii of Bentley.

Shirley, James (*Contd*)
  Maid's Revenge, The 160
  Opportunity, The 307; R40
  Politique Father, The 423
  Rosania 414
  Royal Master, The 383
  School of Compliment, The 149 n.; C27
  Sisters, The 432
  Traitor, The 214; R3, R40; C74
  Triumph of Peace, The 288
  Wedding, The R3, R40
  Witty Fair One, The 47; 180; C62
  Young Admiral, The 44, 73, 75; 259, 272; C98
Shore, Richard R78
Shovelboard, licence for *see* Travelling Shows: Miscellaneous
Shurlock, William *see* Sherlock, William
Shutterell, Robert *see* Shatterell, Robert
Siamese twins *see* Travelling Shows: Monsters
Sicelides see Fletcher, Phineas
Sidney, Sir Philip, *The Arcadia* 148a
Siege, The see Davenant, Sir William
Silent Woman, The see Jonson, Ben, *Epicoene, or the Silent Woman*
Silver Age, The see Heywood, Thomas
Sir John Falstaff see Shakespeare, William, *Henry IV*
Sir William Longsword see Drayton, Michael
Sisters, The see Shirley, James
Skynner, Robert 124
Smedley, Robert 122, 129
Smethwicke, Mr — C41
Smith, —, *The Fair Foul One, or the Baiting of the Jealous Knight* 43; 69
Smith, Francis 162b
Smith, Jane 116
Smith, William 116
Snelling, Mr — 156–7
Sodom and Gomorrah see Travelling Shows: Motions
Soldier's March, The (dance) 30
Sophy, The see Denham, Sir John
Sotherton, Young 401
South, Mrs Ada 15
South, Andrew 15, 113 n. 7
South, C. A. 113 n. 8
Southampton, third Earl of 20
Sow *see* Travelling Shows: Animals, etc.
Spalding, John, *Memorials of the Troubles in England and in Scotland* 121 n. 28

Spain, King of *see* Philip II; Philip IV
Spanish Ambassador 68, 72; 114
Spanish Bawd, The see Mabbe, James
Spanish Contract, The see Anonymous Plays
Spanish Curate, The see Fletcher, John
Spanish Gypsy, The see Middleton, Thomas, and Rowley, William
Spanish Lovers, The see Davenant, William
Spanish Purchase see Anonymous Plays
Spanish Viceroy, The see Anonymous Plays
Spartan Ladies, The see Carlell, Lodowick
Spencer, Nicholas R30
Spense, Mr — C72
Stafford, Alexander 96; A16
Staple of News, The see Jonson, Ben
Starr (starling) *see* Travelling Shows: Animals, etc
Stationers' Company, The 34, 47, 95; A12; C84
Stepney, George 14–15
Stokes, W. R. 14
Stone, John 278
Strafford, Earl of *see* Wentworth, Thomas
Strangers, A Company of *see* Acting Companies
Strode, William, *The Floating Island* 41
Stubbe, Edmund, *Fraus Honesta* C36
Sturbridge Fair 51 n.; R65–7, R72 n., R95; B6 n.
Stuteville, Sir Martin 31
Stutville, George 412
Suckling, Sir John,
  Aglaura 41; 380; R40
  Brennoralt, or the Discontented Colonel R40
Sumner, John 367
Sunn, —, *The Protector* 106
Sun's Darling, The see Dekker, Thomas, and Ford, John
Surprisal, The see Howard, Sir Robert
Swan theatre *see* Theatres
Swanston, Eyllaerdt 46; 5, 265d, f, 324
Swinnerton, Thomas 161
Symons, John R88

Tailor, Robert, *The Hog Hath Lost His Pearl* R29, R33
Tale of a Tub, A see Jonson, Ben
Tamer Tamed, The see Fletcher, John, *The Woman's Prize*
Taming of the Shrew, The see Shakespeare, William
Tandy, John 304